# On Core
# Mathematics

## Geometry

 HOUGHTON MIFFLIN HARCOURT

Cover photo: water droplet/leaf    Dimitri Vervitsiotis/Getty Images

Printed in the U.S.A.

ISBN 978-0-547-57530-8

4 5 6 7 8 9 10  1409  20 19 18 17 16 15 14 13 12

4500367325      B C D E F G

# Contents

© Houghton Mifflin Harcourt Publishing Company

# Unit 3   Congruence and Triangles

# Unit 4   Quadrilaterals and Polygons

# Unit 5   Transformations and Similarity

# Unit 6    Trigonometry

# Unit 7    Circles

# Unit 8   Geometry Using Coordinates and Equations

# Unit 9   Linear and Area Measurement

# Unit 10    Three-Dimensional Figures and Volume

# Unit 11    Probability

# Learning the Common Core State Standards

Has your state adopted the Common Core standards? If so, then you'll be learning both mathematical content standards and the mathematical practice standards that underlie them. The supplementary material found in *On Core Mathematics Geometry* will help you succeed with both.

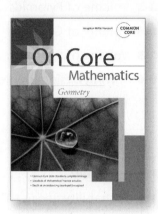

▶ Here are some of the special features you'll find in *On Core Mathematics Geometry.*

## INTERACTIVE LESSONS

You actively participate in every aspect of a lesson. You read the mathematical concepts in an Engage, carry out an activity in an Explore, complete the solution of an Example, and demonstrate reasoning in a Proof. This interactivity promotes a deeper understanding of the mathematics.

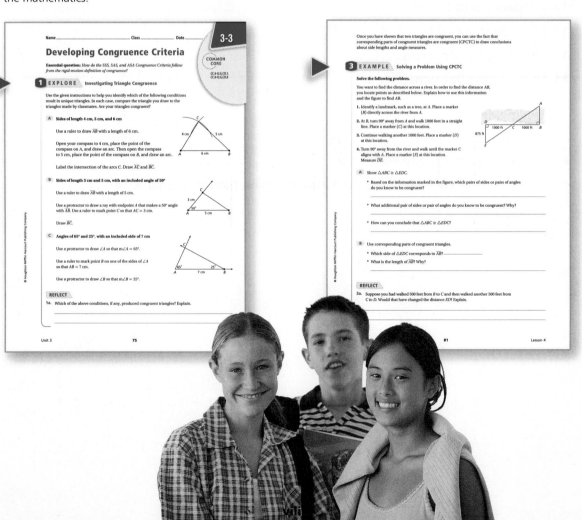

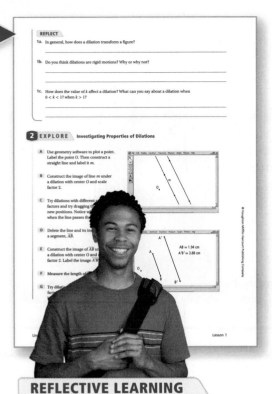

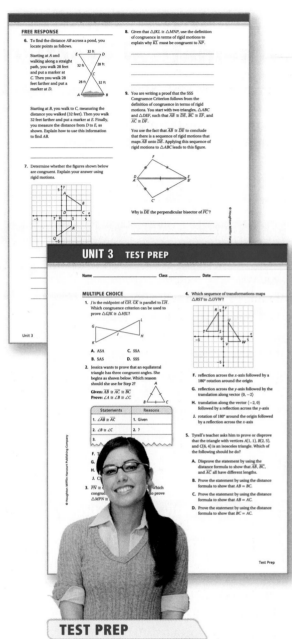

## REFLECTIVE LEARNING

You learn to be a reflective thinker through the follow-up questions after each Engage, Explore, Example, and Proof in a lesson. The Reflect questions challenge you to really think about the mathematics you have just encountered and to share your understanding with the class.

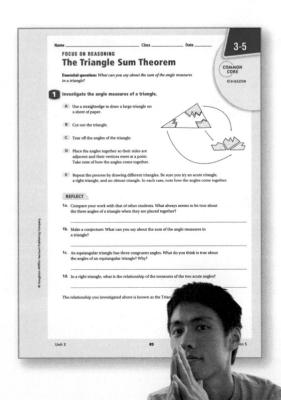

## TEST PREP

At the end of a unit, you have an opportunity to practice the material in multiple choice and free response formats used on standardized tests.

## FOCUS ON REASONING

Special lessons focus on reasoning. They provide opportunities for you to explore concepts using inductive reasoning, to make conjectures, and to prove your conjectures using deductive reasoning.

# Learning the Standards for Mathematical Practice

The Common Core State Standards include eight Standards for Mathematical Practice. Here's how *On Core Mathematics Geometry* helps you learn those standards as you master the Standards for Mathematical Content.

## ① Make sense of problems and persevere in solving them.

In *On Core Mathematics Geometry*, you will work through Explores and Examples that present a solution pathway for you to follow. You will be asked questions along the way so that you gain an understanding of the solution process, and then you will apply what you've learned in the Practice for the lesson.

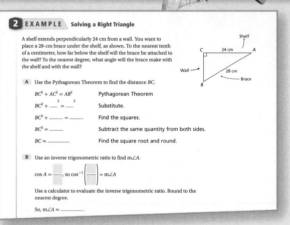

**2  EXAMPLE**  Solving a Right Triangle

A shelf extends perpendicularly 24 cm from a wall. You want to place a 28-cm brace under the shelf, as shown. To the nearest tenth of a centimeter, how far below the shelf will the brace be attached to the wall? To the nearest degree, what angle will the brace make with the shelf and with the wall?

**A**  Use the Pythagorean Theorem to find the distance $BC$.

$BC^2 + AC^2 = AB^2$    Pythagorean Theorem

$BC^2 + \underline{\phantom{xx}}^2 = \underline{\phantom{xx}}^2$    Substitute.

$BC^2 + \underline{\phantom{xx}} = \underline{\phantom{xx}}$    Find the squares.

$BC^2 = \underline{\phantom{xx}}$    Subtract the same quantity from both sides.

$BC \approx \underline{\phantom{xx}}$    Find the square root and round.

**B**  Use an inverse trigonometric ratio to find $m\angle A$.

$\cos A = \dfrac{\phantom{xx}}{\phantom{xx}}$, so $\cos^{-1}\left(\dfrac{\phantom{xx}}{\phantom{xx}}\right) = m\angle A$

Use a calculator to evaluate the inverse trigonometric ratio. Round to the nearest degree.

So, $m\angle A \approx \underline{\phantom{xx}}$.

## ② Reason abstractly and quantitatively.

When you solve a real-world problem in *On Core Mathematics Geometry*, you will learn to represent the situation symbolically by translating the problem into a mathematical expression or equation. You will use these mathematical models to solve the problem and then state your answer in terms of the problem context. You will reflect on the solution process in order to check your answer for reasonableness and to draw conclusions.

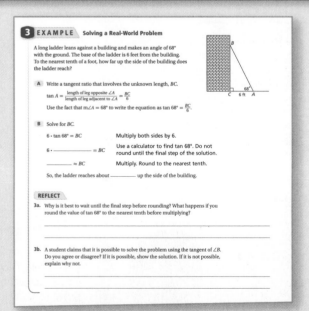

**3  EXAMPLE**  Solving a Real-World Problem

A long ladder leans against a building and makes an angle of 68° with the ground. The base of the ladder is 6 feet from the building. To the nearest tenth of a foot, how far up the side of the building does the ladder reach?

**A**  Write a tangent ratio that involves the unknown length, $BC$.

$\tan A = \dfrac{\text{length of leg opposite } \angle A}{\text{length of leg adjacent to } \angle A} = \dfrac{BC}{6}$

Use the fact that $m\angle A = 68°$ to write the equation as $\tan 68° = \dfrac{BC}{6}$.

**B**  Solve for $BC$.

$6 \cdot \tan 68° = BC$    Multiply both sides by 6.

$6 \cdot \underline{\phantom{xx}} = BC$    Use a calculator to find tan 68°. Do not round until the final step of the solution.

$\underline{\phantom{xx}} \approx BC$    Multiply. Round to the nearest tenth.

So, the ladder reaches about $\underline{\phantom{xx}}$ up the side of the building.

**REFLECT**

**3a.**  Why is it best to wait until the final step before rounding? What happens if you round the value of tan 68° to the nearest tenth before multiplying?

_____

_____

**3b.**  A student claims that it is possible to solve the problem using the tangent of $\angle B$. Do you agree or disagree? If it is possible, show the solution. If it is not possible, explain why not.

_____

_____

## ③ Construct viable arguments and critique the reasoning of others.

Throughout *On Core Mathematics Geometry*, you will be asked to make conjectures, construct a mathematical argument, explain your reasoning, and justify your conclusions. Reflect questions offer opportunities for cooperative learning and class discussion. You will have additional opportunities to critique reasoning in Error Analysis problems.

**REFLECT**

2a. Given that $\triangle PQR \cong \triangle STU$, $PQ = 2.7$ ft, and $PR = 3.4$ ft, is it possible to determine the length of $\overline{TU}$? If so, find the length. If not, explain why not.

2b. A student claims that any two congruent triangles must have the same perimeter. Do you agree or disagree? Why?

3. **Error Analysis** A student who is 72 inches tall wants to find the height of a flagpole. He measures the length of the flagpole's shadow and the length of his own shadow at the same time of day, as shown in his sketch below. Explain the error in the student's work.

The triangles are similar by the AA Similarity Criterion, so corresponding sides are proportional.
$\frac{x}{72} = \frac{48}{128}$
$x = 72 \cdot \frac{48}{128}$, so $x = 27$ in.

72 in.    48 in.

x    128 in.

## ④ Model with mathematics.

*On Core Mathematics Geometry* presents problems in a variety of contexts such as science, business, and everyday life. You will use models such as equations, tables, diagrams, and graphs to represent the information in the problem and to solve the problem. Then you will interpret your results in context.

**④ EXAMPLE**   Solving a Real-World Problem

Police want to set up a camera to identify drivers who run the red light at point *C* on Mason Street. The camera must be mounted on a fence that intersects Mason Street at a 40° angle, as shown, and the camera should ideally be 120 feet from point *C*. What points along the fence, if any, are suitable locations for the camera?

**A** Because the side opposite $\angle A$ is shorter than $\overline{AC}$, it may be possible to form two triangles. Use the Law of Sines to find possible values for m$\angle B$.

$\frac{\sin A}{a} = \frac{\sin B}{b}$     Law of Sines

$\frac{\sin 40°}{120} = \frac{\sin B}{170}$     Substitute.

$\frac{170 \sin 40°}{120} = \sin B$     Solve for sin *B*.

_____ $\approx \sin B$     Use a calculator. Round to 4 decimal places.

There is an acute angle and an obtuse angle that have this value as their sine. To find the acute angle, use a calculator and round to the nearest tenth.

$\sin^{-1}(\underline{\phantom{xxx}}) \approx \underline{\phantom{xxx}}$

To find the obtuse angle, note that $\angle 1$ and $\angle 2$ have the same sine, $\frac{y}{\sqrt{x^2+y^2}}$, and notice that these angles are supplementary. Thus, the obtuse angle is supplementary to the acute angle you found above.

So, m$\angle B \approx$ _____ or _____.

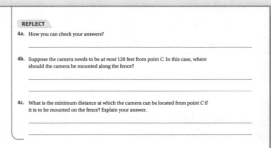

**REFLECT**

4a. How you can check your answers?

4b. Suppose the camera needs to be *at most* 120 feet from point *C*. In this case, where should the camera be mounted along the fence?

4c. What is the minimum distance at which the camera can be located from point *C* if it is to be mounted on the fence? Explain your answer.

## ⑤ Use appropriate tools strategically.

You will use a variety of tools in *On Core Mathematics Geometry*, including manipulatives, paper and pencil, and technology. You might use manipulatives to develop concepts, paper and pencil to practice skills, and technology (such as graphing calculators, spreadsheets, or geometry software) to investigate more complicated mathematical ideas.

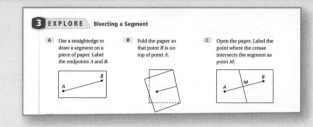

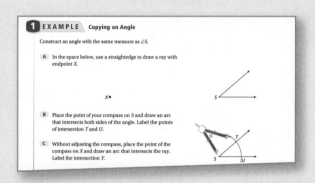

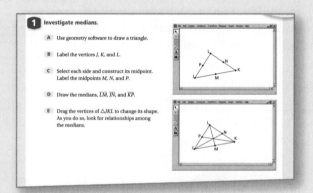

## ⑥ Attend to precision.

Precision refers not only to the correctness of arithmetic calculations, algebraic manipulations, and geometric reasoning but also to the proper use of mathematical language, symbols, and units to communicate mathematical ideas. Throughout *On Core Mathematics Geometry* you will demonstrate your skills in these areas when you are asked to calculate, describe, show, explain, prove, and predict.

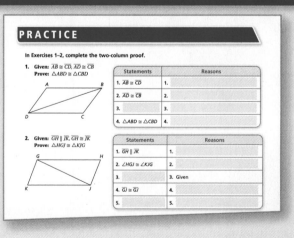

## ⑦ Look for and make use of structure.

In *On Core Mathematics Geometry*, you will look for patterns or regularity in mathematical structures such as expressions, equations, geometric figures, and graphs. Becoming familiar with underlying structures will help you build your understanding of more complicated mathematical ideas.

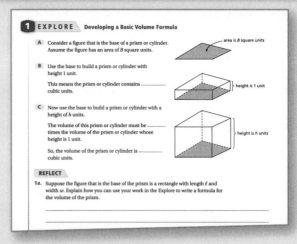

**1 EXPLORE** Developing a Basic Volume Formula

A Consider a figure that is the base of a prism or cylinder. Assume the figure has an area of *B* square units.

B Use the base to build a prism or cylinder with height 1 unit.

This means the prism or cylinder contains _____ cubic units.

C Now use the base to build a prism or cylinder with a height of *h* units.

The volume of this prism or cylinder must be _____ times the volume of the prism or cylinder whose height is 1 unit.

So, the volume of the prism or cylinder is _____ cubic units.

**REFLECT**

1a. Suppose the figure that is the base of the prism is a rectangle with length ℓ and width *w*. Explain how you can use your work in the Explore to write a formula for the volume of the prism.

_____

_____

## ⑧ Look for and express regularity in repeated reasoning.

In *On Core Mathematics Geometry*, you will have the opportunity to explore and reflect on mathematical processes in order to come up with general methods for performing calculations and solving problems.

**2 EXPLORE** Developing a Formula for Conditional Probability

You can generalize your work from the previous example to develop a formula for finding conditional probabilities.

A Recall how you calculated $P(B \mid A)$, the probability that a participant who took the medicine did not get a headache.

You found that $P(B \mid A) = \frac{48}{60}$.

Use the table shown here to help you write this quotient in terms of events *A* and *B*.

|  |  | Event A | | |
|---|---|---|---|---|
|  |  | Took Medicine | No Medicine | TOTAL |
| Event B | Headache | 12 | 15 | 27 |
|  | No Headache | $48 = n(A \cap B)$ | 25 | $73 = n(B)$ |
|  | TOTAL | $60 = n(A)$ | 40 | 100 |

$P(B \mid A) = $ _____

B Now divide the numerator and denominator of the quotient by $n(S)$, the number of outcomes in the sample space. This converts the counts to probabilities.

$P(B \mid A) = \dfrac{\phantom{xx} / n(S)}{\phantom{xx} / n(S)} = $ _____

**REFLECT**

2a. Write a formula for $P(A \mid B)$ in terms of $n(A \cap B)$ and $n(B)$.

_____

2b. Write a formula for $P(A \mid B)$ in terms of $P(A \cap B)$ and $P(B)$.

_____

# Lines and Angles

## Unit Focus

This unit introduces the building blocks of geometry. You will learn how definitions of essential geometric terms, such as *line segment* and *angle*, are built from more basic terms. You will also learn to use a variety of tools and techniques to construct geometric figures. Finally, you will begin to write proofs that justify key relationships among lines and angles.

## Unit at a Glance

COMMON CORE

UNIT 1

# Unpacking the Common Core State Standards

Use the table to help you understand the Standards for Mathematical Content that are taught in this unit. Refer to the lessons listed after each standard for exploration and practice.

| COMMON CORE Standards for Mathematical Content | What It Means For You |
|---|---|
| **CC.9-12.G.CO.1 Know precise definitions of angle, circle, perpendicular line, parallel line, and line segment, based on the undefined notions of point, line, distance along a line, and distance around a circular arc.** Lessons 1-1, 1-4, 1-5 | In geometry, it is important to understand the exact meaning of the terms you use. You will see how definitions of geometric terms are built upon the definitions of more basic terms and upon several terms that are understood without being formally defined. |
| **CC.9-12.G.CO.9 Prove theorems about lines and angles.** Lessons 1-6, 1-7 | A proof is a logical argument that uses definitions, properties, and previously proven facts to demonstrate that a mathematical statement is true. You will learn to write proofs about relationships among angles formed by intersecting lines and among angles formed by a line that crosses parallel lines. |
| **CC.9-12.G.CO.12 Make formal geometric constructions with a variety of tools and methods (compass and straightedge, string, reflective devices, paper folding, dynamic geometric software, etc.).** Lessons 1-1, 1-4, 1-5 | A construction is a method of drawing a geometric figure while adhering to certain rules. For example, using only a compass and an unmarked straightedge, you can copy and bisect segments and angles, and you can construct perpendicular and parallel lines. |
| **CC.9-12.G.GPE.4 Use coordinates to prove simple geometric theorems algebraically.** Lessons 1-2, 1-3 | You will be introduced to two useful formulas in this unit: the distance formula and the midpoint formula. You will use these formulas here and in later units to write proofs about figures on a coordinate plane. |

# Basic Terms and Constructions

COMMON CORE

CC.9-12.G.CO.1,
CC.9-12.G.CO.12

**Essential question:** *What tools and methods can you use to copy a segment, bisect a segment, and construct a circle?*

In geometry, the terms *point* and *line* are undefined terms. Although these terms do not have formal definitions, the table shows how mathematicians use these words.

| Term | Geometric Figure | Ways to Reference the Figure |
|---|---|---|
| A **point** is a specific location. It has no dimension and is represented by a dot. | • P | Point P |
| A **line** is a connected straight path. It has no thickness and it continues forever in both directions. | A B ℓ | Line ℓ , line AB, line BA, $\overleftrightarrow{AB}$, or $\overleftrightarrow{BA}$ |

As shown in the following table, other terms can be defined using the above terms as building blocks.

| Term | Geometric Figure | Ways to Reference the Figure |
|---|---|---|
| A **line segment** (or *segment*) is a portion of a line consisting of two points and all points between them. | C D | Line segment CD, line segment DC, $\overline{CD}$, or $\overline{DC}$ |
| A **ray** is a portion of a line that starts at a point and continues forever in one direction. | G H | Ray GH or $\overrightarrow{GH}$ |

An **endpoint** is a point at either end of a line segment or the starting point of a ray. In the above examples, C and D are the endpoints of $\overline{CD}$, and point G is the endpoint of $\overrightarrow{GH}$.

**1 EXAMPLE** Naming Geometric Figures

**Use the figure below in Parts A and B.**

**A** One name for the line shown in the figure is $\overleftrightarrow{PQ}$ .

Other names for $\overleftrightarrow{PQ}$ are _____

**B** $\overline{PQ}$ is a line segment because it is a portion of a line consisting of two points and all the points between them.

Other names for $\overline{PQ}$ are _____

© Houghton Mifflin Harcourt Publishing Company

The **distance along a line** is undefined until a unit distance, such as 1 inch or 1 centimeter, is chosen. By placing a ruler alongside the line, you can associate a number from the ruler with each of two points on the line and then take the absolute value of the difference of the numbers to find the distance between the points. This distance is the **length** of the segment determined by the points.

In the figure, the length of $\overline{RS}$, written $RS$, is the distance between $R$ and $S$. $RS = |4 - 1| = |3| = 3$ cm.

A *construction* is a geometric drawing that uses only a compass and a straightedge. You can construct a line segment whose length is equal to that of a given segment by using only these tools.

**2 EXAMPLE**   **Copying a Segment**

Construct a segment with the same length as $\overline{AB}$ .

**A**   In the space below, draw a line segment that is longer than $\overline{AB}$. Choose an endpoint of the segment and label it $C$.

**B**   Set the opening of your compass to the distance $AB$, as shown.

**C**   Place the point of the compass on $C$. Make a small arc that intersects your line segment. Label the point $D$ where the arc intersects the segment. $\overline{CD}$ is the required line segment.

**REFLECT**

**2a.**  Why does this construction result in a line segment with the same length as $\overline{AB}$?

_____

_____

**2b.**  What must you assume about the compass for this construction to work?

_____

_____

The **midpoint** of a line segment is the point that divides the segment into two segments that have the same length. The midpoint is said to **bisect** the segment. In the figure, the tick marks show that $PM = MQ$. Therefore, $M$ is the midpoint of $\overline{PQ}$ and $M$ bisects $\overline{PQ}$.

## 3 EXPLORE   Bisecting a Segment

**A** Use a straightedge to draw a segment on a piece of paper. Label the endpoints *A* and *B*.

**B** Fold the paper so that point *B* is on top of point *A*.

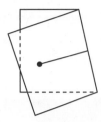

**C** Open the paper. Label the point where the crease intersects the segment as point *M*.

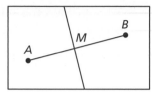

### REFLECT

**3a.** How can you use a ruler to check the construction?

_____

**3b.** Explain how you could use paper folding to divide a line segment into four segments of equal length.

_____

_____

The final undefined term you will work with in this lesson is *plane*. A **plane** is understood to be a flat surface with no thickness that extends forever in all directions. Notice how this term is used as an element in the following definition.

A **circle** is the set of all points in a plane that are a fixed distance from a point called the **center** of the circle. A **radius** is a line segment whose endpoints are the center of the circle and any point on the circle. The length of such a segment is also called the radius.

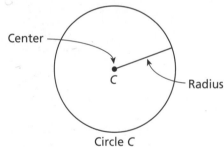

## 4 EXAMPLE   Constructing a Circle

Construct a circle with radius *AB*.

**A** In the space at right, draw a point and label it *C*. This will be the center of the circle.

**B** Set the opening of your compass to the distance *AB*.

**C** Place the point of the compass on *C* and draw a circle.

© Houghton Mifflin Harcourt Publishing Company

**4a.** How could you use a piece of string, a thumbtack, and a pencil to construct a circle with radius *AB*?

_____

_____

_____

# PRACTICE

**Use the figure to name each of the following.**

**1.** a line          _____

**2.** two line segments _____

**3.** three rays        _____

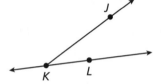

**Use the figure from Exercises 1–3 to construct each figure in the space provided.**

**4.** a segment with the same length as $\overline{KJ}$          **5.** a circle with radius *KL*

**6.** Is it possible to construct the midpoint of a ray? Why or why not?

_____

_____

**In Exercises 7 and 8, use the segments shown.**

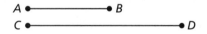

**7.** In the space below, use a compass and straightedge to construct a segment whose length is $AB + CD$.

**8.** In the space below, use a compass and straightedge to construct a segment whose length is $CD - AB$.

# The Distance Formula

**Essential question:** *How do you use the distance formula to find distances and lengths in the coordinate plane?*

COMMON CORE

CC.9-12.G.GPE.4

**1 EXPLORE**    **Finding a Distance in the Coordinate Plane**

You can use the Pythagorean Theorem to help you find the distance between the points $A(2, 5)$ and $B(-4, -3)$.

**A**   Plot the points $A$ and $B$ in the coordinate plane at right.

**B**   Draw $\overline{AB}$.

**C**   Draw a vertical line through point $A$ and a horizontal line through point $B$ to create a right triangle. Label the intersection of the vertical line and the horizontal line as point $C$.

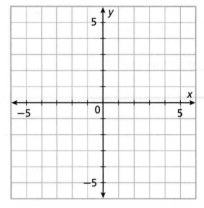

**D**   Each small grid square is 1 unit by 1 unit. Use this fact to find the lengths $AC$ and $BC$.

$AC =$ _____        $BC =$ _____

**E**   By the Pythagorean Theorem, $AB^2 = AC^2 + BC^2$. Complete the following using the lengths from Step D.

$$AB^2 = \boxed{\phantom{xx}}^2 + \boxed{\phantom{xx}}^2$$

**F**   Simplify the right side of the equation. Then solve for $AB$.

$AB^2 =$ _____, $AB =$ _____

**REFLECT**

**1a.** Explain how you solved for $AB$ in Step F.

_____

**1b.** Can you use the above method to find the distance between any two points in the coordinate plane? Explain.

_____

_____

The process of using the Pythagorean Theorem can be generalized to give a formula for finding the distance between two points in the coordinate plane.

### The Distance Formula

The distance between two points $(x_1, y_1)$ and $(x_2, y_2)$ in the coordinate plane is

$$\sqrt{(x_2 - x_1)^2 + (y_2 - y_1)^2}.$$

## 2 EXAMPLE  Using the Distance Formula

Prove that $\overline{CD}$ is longer than $\overline{AB}$.

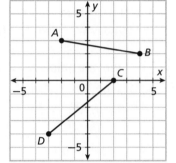

**A**  Write the coordinates of A, B, C, and D.

$A(-2, 3)$, $B$ _____, $C$ _____, $D$ _____

**B**  Use the distance formula to find $AB$ and $CD$.

$$AB = \sqrt{[4 - (-2)]^2 + (2 - 3)^2} = \sqrt{6^2 + (-1)^2} = \sqrt{36 + 1} = \sqrt{37}$$

$$CD = \sqrt{(\boxed{\phantom{x}} - \boxed{\phantom{x}})^2 + (\boxed{\phantom{x}} - \boxed{\phantom{x}})^2} = \sqrt{(\boxed{\phantom{x}})^2 + (\boxed{\phantom{x}})^2} = \sqrt{\boxed{\phantom{xx}}}$$

So, $\overline{CD}$ is longer than $\overline{AB}$ because _____.

### REFLECT

**2a.** When you use the distance formula, does the order in which you subtract the x-coordinates and the y-coordinates matter? Explain.

_____

# PRACTICE

**Use the figure for Exercises 1–3.**

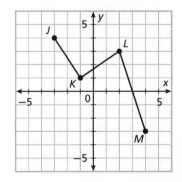

**1.** Find the distance between J and L.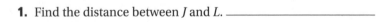

**2.** Find the length of $\overline{LM}$. _____

**3.** Prove that $JK = KL$.

© Houghton Mifflin Harcourt Publishing Company

**1-3**

# The Midpoint Formula

**Essential question:** *How do you use the midpoint formula to find the midpoint of a line segment in a coordinate plane?*

COMMON
CORE

CC.9-12.G.GPE.4

## 1  EXPLORE  Finding Midpoints of Line Segments

**Follow the steps below for each of the given line segments.**

**A**  Use a ruler to measure the length of the line segment to the nearest millimeter.

**B**  Find half the length of the segment. Measure this distance from one endpoint to locate the midpoint of the segment. Plot a point at the midpoint.

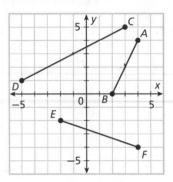

**C**  Record the coordinates of the segment's endpoints and the coordinates of the segment's midpoint in the table below.

**D**  In each row of the table, compare the *x*-coordinates of the endpoints to the *x*-coordinate of the midpoint. Then compare the *y*-coordinates of the endpoints to the *y*-coordinate of the midpoint. Look for patterns.

| Endpoint | Endpoint Coordinates | Endpoint | Endpoint Coordinates | Midpoint Coordinates |
|---|---|---|---|---|
| A | | B | | |
| C | | D | | |
| E | | F | | |

### REFLECT

**1a.** Make a conjecture: If you know the coordinates of the endpoints of a line segment, how can you find the coordinates of the midpoint?

_____

_____

**1b.** What are the coordinates of the midpoint of a line segment with endpoints at the origin and at the point $(a, b)$?

_____

The patterns you observed can be generalized to give a formula for the coordinates of the midpoint of any line segment in the coordinate plane.

## The Midpoint Formula

The midpoint $M$ of $\overline{AB}$ with endpoints $A(x_1, y_1)$ and $B(x_2, y_2)$ is given by

$$M\left(\frac{x_1 + x_2}{2}, \frac{y_1 + y_2}{2}\right).$$

## 2 EXAMPLE    Using the Midpoint Formula

$\overline{PQ}$ has endpoints $P(-4, 1)$ and $Q(2, -3)$. Prove that the midpoint $M$ of $\overline{PQ}$ lies in Quadrant III.

**A**  Use the given endpoints to identify $x_1$, $x_2$, $y_1$, and $y_2$.

$x_1 = -4$, $x_2 = 2$, $y_1 =$ _____, $y_2 =$ _____

**B**  By the midpoint formula, the $x$-coordinate of $M$ is $\dfrac{x_1 + x_2}{2} = \dfrac{-4 + 2}{2} = \dfrac{-2}{2} = -1$.

The $y$-coordinate of $M$ is $\dfrac{y_1 + y_2}{2} = \dfrac{\boxed{\phantom{x}} + \boxed{\phantom{x}}}{2} = \dfrac{\boxed{\phantom{x}}}{2} = \boxed{\phantom{x}}$.

$M$ lies in Quadrant III because _____

## REFLECT

**2a.** What must be true about $PM$ and $QM$? Show that this is the case.

_____

_____

# PRACTICE

**1.** Find the coordinates of the midpoint of
$\overline{AB}$ with endpoints $A(-10, 3)$ and $B(2, -2)$. _____

**2.** $\overline{RS}$ has endpoints $R(3, 5)$ and $S(-3, -1)$. Prove that the midpoint $M$ of $\overline{RS}$ lies on the $y$-axis.

_____

_____

**3.** $\overline{CD}$ has endpoints $C(1, 4)$ and $D(5, 0)$. $\overline{EF}$ has endpoints $E(4, 5)$ and $F(2, -1)$. Prove that the segments have the same midpoint.

_____

_____

© Houghton Mifflin Harcourt Publishing Company

# Angles

**Essential question:** *What tools and methods can you use to copy an angle and bisect an angle?*

COMMON
CORE

CC.9-12.G.CO.1,
CC.9-12.G.CO.12

An **angle** is a figure formed by two rays with the same endpoint. The common endpoint is the **vertex** of the angle. The rays are the **sides** of the angle.

Angles may be measured in degrees (°). There are 360° in a circle, so an angle that measures 1° is $\frac{1}{360}$ of a circle. You write m∠A for the measure of ∠A.

Angles may be classified by their measures.

| Acute Angle | Right Angle | Obtuse Angle | Straight Angle |
|---|---|---|---|
| | | | |
| $0° < m\angle A < 90°$ | $m\angle A = 90°$ | $90° < m\angle A < 180°$ | $m\angle A = 180°$ |

## 1 EXAMPLE  Copying an Angle

Construct an angle with the same measure as ∠S.

**A**  In the space below, use a straightedge to draw a ray with endpoint X.

X•

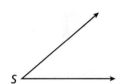

S

**B**  Place the point of your compass on S and draw an arc that intersects both sides of the angle. Label the points of intersection T and U.

**C**  Without adjusting the compass, place the point of the compass on X and draw an arc that intersects the ray. Label the intersection Y.

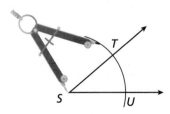

**D**  Place the point of the compass on U and open it to the distance TU.

**E**  Without adjusting the compass, place the point of the compass on Y and draw an arc. Label the intersection with the first arc Z.

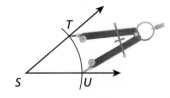

**F**  Use a straightedge to draw $\overrightarrow{XZ}$.

**1a.** How can you use a protractor to check your construction?

_____

**1b.** If you draw ∠X so that its sides appear to be longer than the sides shown for ∠S, can the two angles have the same measure? Explain.

_____

_____

An **angle bisector** is a ray that divides an angle into two angles that both have the same measure. In the figure, $\overrightarrow{BD}$ bisects ∠ABC, so m∠ABD = m∠DBC. The arcs in the figure show equal angle measures.

The following example shows how you can use a compass and straightedge to bisect an angle.

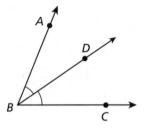

**2  EXAMPLE  Constructing the Bisector of an Angle**

Construct the bisector of ∠M. Work directly on the angle at right.

**A**  Place the point of your compass on point M. Draw an arc that intersects both sides of the angle. Label the points of intersection P and Q.

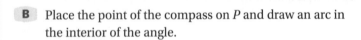

**B**  Place the point of the compass on P and draw an arc in the interior of the angle.

**C**  Without adjusting the compass, place the point of the compass on Q and draw an arc that intersects the arc from Step B. Label the intersection of the arcs R.

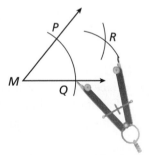

**D**  Use a straightedge to draw $\overrightarrow{MR}$.

**2a.** Explain how you could use paper folding to construct the bisector of an angle.

_____

_____

**Construct an angle with the same measure as the given angle.**

**1.**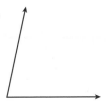

**2.**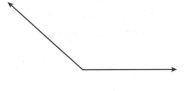

**3.**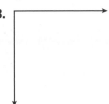

**Construct the bisector of the angle.**

**4.**

**5.**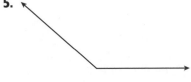

**6.**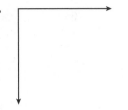

**7.** Explain how you can use a compass and straightedge to construct an angle that has twice the measure of $\angle A$. Then do the construction in the space provided.

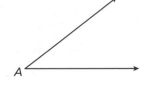

_____

_____

_____

**8.** Explain how you can use a compass and straightedge to construct an angle that has $\frac{1}{4}$ the measure of $\angle B$. Then do the construction in the space provided.

_____

_____

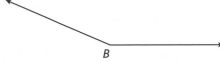

_____

_____

# Parallel and Perpendicular Lines

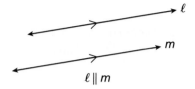

COMMON
CORE

CC.9-12.G.CO.1,
CC.9-12.G.CO.12

**Essential question:** *What tools and methods can you use to construct parallel lines and perpendicular lines?*

**Parallel lines** lie in the same plane and do not intersect. In the figure, line $\ell$ is parallel to line $m$ and you write $\ell \parallel m$. The arrows on the lines also indicate that the lines are parallel.

$\ell \parallel m$

**1** **EXAMPLE** **Constructing Parallel Lines**

Construct a line parallel to line $m$ that passes through point $P$. Work directly on the figure below.

**A** Choose points $Q$ and $R$ on line $m$.

**B** Use a straightedge to draw $\overleftrightarrow{PQ}$.

**C** Copy $\angle PQR$ at point $P$, as shown. Label line $\ell$. Line $\ell$ is the required line.

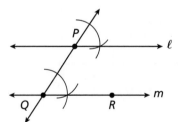

**REFLECT**

**1a.** Why does it make sense to copy $\angle PQR$ to get a line parallel to line $m$?

_____

_____

**1b.** Is it possible to construct a line parallel to a given line $m$ that passes through a point $P$ that is *on* line $m$? Why or why not?

_____

_____

**Perpendicular lines** are lines that intersect at right angles. In the figure, line $\ell$ is perpendicular to line $m$ and you write $\ell \perp m$. The right angle mark in the figure indicates that the lines are perpendicular.

The **perpendicular bisector** of a line segment is a line perpendicular to the segment at the segment's midpoint.

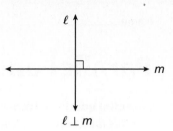

$\ell \perp m$

**2 EXAMPLE** **Constructing a Perpendicular Bisector**

Construct the perpendicular bisector of $\overline{AB}$. Work directly on the figure below.

**A** Place the point of your compass at $A$. Using a compass setting that is greater than half the length of $\overline{AB}$, draw an arc.

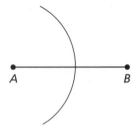

**B** Without adjusting the compass, place the point of the compass at $B$ and draw an arc intersecting the first arc at $C$ and $D$.

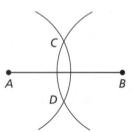

**C** Use a straightedge to draw $\overleftrightarrow{CD}$. $\overleftrightarrow{CD}$ is the perpendicular bisector of $\overline{AB}$.

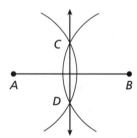

**REFLECT**

**2a.** How can you use a ruler and protractor to check the construction?

_____

_____

**2b.** Would the results be different if a different compass setting were used to draw the arcs?

_____

_____

Construct a line perpendicular to line *m* that passes
through point *P*. Work directly on the figure at right.

P •

**A**   Place the point of your compass at *P*.
Draw an arc that intersects line *m* at
two points, *A* and *B*.

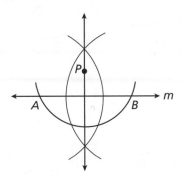

**B**   Construct the perpendicular bisector of $\overline{AB}$.
This line will pass through *P* and be perpendicular
to line *m*.

**REFLECT**

**3a.**   Does the construction still work if point *P* is on line *m*? Why or why not?

_____

_____

# P R A C T I C E

Construct a line parallel to line *m* that passes through point *P*.

**1.**

P
•

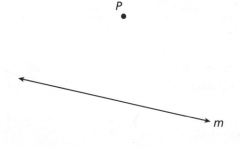

**2.**

•
P

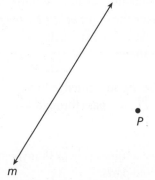

**Construct the perpendicular bisector of $\overline{AB}$.**

**3.**

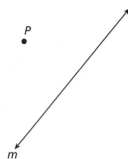

**4.**

**Construct a line perpendicular to line $m$ that passes through point $P$.**

**5.**

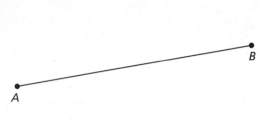

**6.**

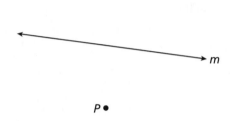

**7.** You can use what you know about constructing parallel lines to divide a given line segment into three equal parts. Follow the directions and work directly on $\overline{AB}$ in the space below.

**a.** Use a straightedge to draw a ray $\overrightarrow{AC}$ as shown.

**b.** Place the point of your compass on $A$ and make an arc that intersects $\overrightarrow{AC}$. Without adjusting the compass, place the point on the intersection of the arc with $\overrightarrow{AC}$ and make another arc. Place the point on the intersection of the new arc with $\overrightarrow{AC}$ and make a third arc. Label the points of intersection with $\overrightarrow{AC}$ as shown.

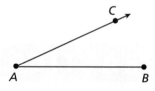

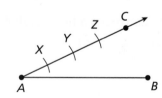

**c.** Use the straightedge to draw $\overleftrightarrow{ZB}$. Then construct lines parallel to $\overline{ZB}$ that pass through $X$ and $Y$. These lines divide $\overline{AB}$ into three equal parts.

**d.** Use a ruler to check that you have divided $\overline{AB}$ into three equal parts.

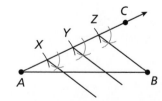

# Proofs About Line Segments and Angles

**Essential question:** *How do you prove basic theorems about line segments and angles?*

## 1 ENGAGE   Introducing Proofs

In mathematics, a **proof** is a logical argument that uses a sequence of statements to prove a conjecture. Once the conjecture is proved, it is called a **theorem**.

Each statement in a proof must follow logically from what has come before and must have a reason to support it. The reason may be a piece of given information, a definition, a previously proven theorem, or a mathematical property.

The table states some properties of equality that you have seen in earlier courses. You have used these properties to solve algebraic equations and you will often use these properties as reasons in a proof.

| Properties of Equality | |
|---|---|
| Addition Property of Equality | If $a = b$, then $a + c = b + c$. |
| Subtraction Property of Equality | If $a = b$, then $a - c = b - c$. |
| Multiplication Property of Equality | If $a = b$, then $ac = bc$. |
| Division Property of Equality | If $a = b$ and $c \neq 0$, then $\frac{a}{c} = \frac{b}{c}$. |
| Reflexive Property of Equality | $a = a$ |
| Symmetric Property of Equality | If $a = b$, then $b = a$. |
| Transitive Property of Equality | If $a = b$ and $b = c$, then $a = c$. |
| Substitution Property of Equality | If $a = b$, then $b$ can be substituted for $a$ in any expression. |

### REFLECT

**1a.** Given the equation $3 = x - 2$, you quickly write the solution as $x = 5$. Which property or properties of equality are you using? Explain.

_____

_____

**1b.** Give an example of an equation that you can solve using the Division Property of Equality. Explain how you would use this property to solve the equation.

_____

_____

A **postulate** (or *axiom*) is a statement that is accepted as true without proof. Like undefined terms, postulates are basic building blocks of geometry. The following postulate states that the lengths of segments "add up" in a natural way.

## Segment Addition Postulate

If $B$ is between $A$ and $C$, then $AB + BC = AC$.

$$A \quad\quad\quad B \quad\quad C$$

Notice how the Segment Addition Postulate and some properties of equality are used in the following proof. Also, note how the proof is arranged in a two-column format so that it is easy to see the logical sequence of the statements and their corresponding reasons.

## 2 PROOF   Common Segments Theorem

If $A$, $B$, $C$, and $D$ are collinear, as shown in the figure, with $AB = CD$, then $AC = BD$.

$$A \quad B \quad\quad\quad C \quad D$$

**Given:** $AB = CD$
**Prove:** $AC = BD$

**A**   Develop a plan for the proof.

Since it is given that $AB = CD$, you can add the length of the "common segment" $BC$ to each side of the equation to get $AB + BC = BC + CD$. Explain how this lets you conclude that $AC = BD$.

_____

**B**   Write the proof in two-column format. Write a logical sequence of statements, starting with the given information and ending with the statement to be proved. Give a reason for each statement. Complete the proof by writing the missing reasons. Choose from the following reasons.

| Additional Property of Equality | | Given | | Substitution Property of Equality |

| Segment Addition Postulate | | Reflexive Property of Equality |

| Statements | Reasons |
|---|---|
| **1.** $AB = CD$ | **1.** |
| **2.** $BC = BC$ | **2.** |
| **3.** $AB + BC = BC + CD$ | **3.** |
| **4.** $AB + BC = AC$; $BC + CD = BD$ | **4.** |
| **5.** $AC = BD$ | **5.** |

**2a.** A student writes the equation in Step 3 of the proof as $AB + BC = CD + BC$. Explain why the right side of this equation is equivalent to the right side of the equation in the proof.

_____

_____

**2b.** A student claims that $PR = QS$ by the Common Segments Theorem. Do you agree or disagree? Why?

_____

_____

_____

The Angle Addition Postulate is similar to the Segment Addition Postulate.

### Angle Addition Postulate

If $D$ is in the interior of $\angle ABC$, then
$m\angle ABD + m\angle DBC = m\angle ABC$.

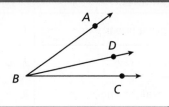

You will use the Angle Addition Postulate and the following definitions to prove an important theorem about angles.

**Opposite rays** are two rays that have a common endpoint and form a straight line. A **linear pair** of angles is a pair of adjacent angles whose noncommon sides are opposite rays.

In the figure, $\overrightarrow{JK}$ and $\overrightarrow{JL}$ are opposite rays; $\angle MJK$ and $\angle MJL$ are a linear pair of angles.

Recall that two angles are *complementary* if the sum of their measures is 90°. Two angles are *supplementary* if the sum of their measures is 180°. The following theorem ties together some of the preceding ideas.

### Linear Pair Theorem

If two angles form a linear pair, then they are supplementary.
$m\angle MJK + m\angle MJL = 180°$

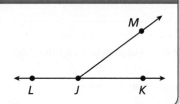

**PROOF**       **Linear Pair Theorem**

If two angles form a linear pair, then they are supplementary.

**Given:** ∠MJK and ∠MJL are a linear pair of angles.

**Prove:** ∠MJK and ∠MJL are supplementary.

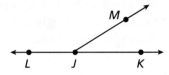

**A**   Develop a plan for the proof.

Since it is given that ∠MJK and ∠MJL are a linear pair of angles, $\overrightarrow{JL}$ and $\overrightarrow{JK}$ are opposite rays. They form a straight angle. Explain why m∠MJK + m∠MJL must equal 180°.

_____

**B**   Complete the proof by writing the missing reasons. Choose from the following reasons.

| Angle Addition Postulate | Definition of opposite rays |
|---|---|

| Substitution Property of Equality | Given |
|---|---|

| Statements | Reasons |
|---|---|
| **1.** ∠MJK and ∠MJL are a linear pair. | **1.** |
| **2.** $\overrightarrow{JL}$ and $\overrightarrow{JK}$ are opposite rays. | **2.** Definition of linear pair |
| **3.** $\overrightarrow{JL}$ and $\overrightarrow{JK}$ form a straight line. | **3.** |
| **4.** m∠LJK = 180° | **4.** Definition of straight angle |
| **5.** m∠MJK + m∠MJL = m∠LJK | **5.** |
| **6.** m∠MJK + m∠MJL = 180° | **6.** |
| **7.** ∠MJK and ∠MJL are supplementary. | **7.** Definition of supplementary angles |

**REFLECT**

**3a.**  Is it possible to prove the theorem by measuring ∠MJK and ∠MJL in the figure and showing that the sum of the angle measures is 180°? Explain.

_____

_____

**3b.**  The proof shows that if two angles form a linear pair, then they are supplementary. Is this statement true in the other direction? That is, if two angles are supplementary, must they be a linear pair? Why or why not?

_____

_____

Recall that two angles are *vertical angles* if their sides form two pairs of opposite rays. In the figure below, ∠1 and ∠3 are vertical angles, as are ∠2 and ∠4.

**4** **PROOF**    **Vertical Angles Theorem**

If two angles are vertical angles, then they have equal measures.

**Given:** ∠1 and ∠3 are vertical angles.
**Prove:** m∠1 = m∠3

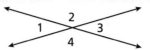

**A** Develop a plan for the proof.

Since ∠1 and ∠2 are a linear pair, and ∠2 and ∠3 are a linear pair, these pairs of angles are supplementary. This means m∠1 + m∠2 = 180° and m∠2 + m∠3 = 180°. By substitution, m∠1 + m∠2 = m∠2 + m∠3. What is the final step in the plan?

_____

**B** Complete the proof by writing the missing reasons. Choose from the following reasons.

| Definition of supplementary angles | Subtraction Property of Equality |
| Substitution Property of Equality | Linear Pair Theorem | Given |

| Statements | Reasons |
|---|---|
| **1.** ∠1 and ∠3 are vertical angles. | **1.** |
| **2.** ∠1 and ∠2 are a linear pair;<br>∠2 and ∠3 are a linear pair. | **2.** Definition of linear pair |
| **3.** ∠1 and ∠2 are supplementary;<br>∠2 and ∠3 are supplementary. | **3.** |
| **4.** m∠1 + m∠2 = 180°;<br>m∠2 + m∠3 = 180° | **4.** |
| **5.** m∠1 + m∠2 = m∠2 + m∠3 | **5.** |
| **6.** m∠1 = m∠3 | **6.** |

**REFLECT**

**4a.** Explain how to find m∠1, m∠2, and m∠3 in the figure.

_____

_____

_____

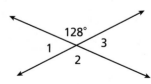

# PRACTICE

In Exercises 1–2, complete each proof by writing the missing statements or reasons.

**1.** If $A$, $B$, $C$, and $D$ are collinear, as shown in the figure, with $AC = BD$, then $AB = CD$.

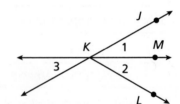

**Given:** $AC = BD$
**Prove:** $AB = CD$

| Statements | Reasons |
|---|---|
| 1. $AC = BD$ | 1. |
| 2. $AC = AB + BC;\ BD = BC + CD$ | 2. |
| 3. | 3. Substitution Property of Equality |
| 4. $AB = CD$ | 4. |

**2. Given:** $\overrightarrow{KM}$ bisects $\angle JKL$.
   **Prove:** $m\angle 2 = m\angle 3$

| Statements | Reasons |
|---|---|
| 1. $\overrightarrow{KM}$ bisects $\angle JKL$. | 1. |
| 2. $m\angle 1 = m\angle 2$ | 2. |
| 3. $\angle 1$ and $\angle 3$ form two pairs of opposite rays. | 3. Given |
| 4. $\angle 1$ and $\angle 3$ are vertical angles. | 4. |
| 5. $m\angle 1 = m\angle 3$ | 5. Vertical Angles Theorem |
| 6. $m\angle 2 = m\angle 3$ | 6. Substitution Property of Equality |

**3.** In the figure, $X$ is the midpoint of $\overline{WY}$, and $Y$ is the midpoint of $\overline{XZ}$. Explain how to prove $WX = YZ$.

_____

_____

# Proofs About Parallel and Perpendicular Lines

COMMON CORE

CC.9-12.G.CO.9

**Essential question:** *How do you prove theorems about parallel and perpendicular lines?*

## 1 ENGAGE — Introducing Transversals

Recall that a *transversal* is a line that intersects two coplanar lines at two different points. In the figure, line *t* is a transversal. The table summarizes the names of angle pairs formed by a transversal.

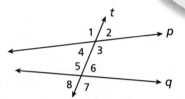

| Angle Pair | Example |
|---|---|
| *Corresponding angles* lie on the same side of the transversal and on the same sides of the intersected lines. | ∠1 and ∠5 |
| *Same-side interior angles* lie on the same side of the transversal and between the intersected lines. | ∠3 and ∠6 |
| *Alternate interior angles* are nonadjacent angles that lie on opposite sides of the transversal between the intersected lines. | ∠3 and ∠5 |
| *Alternate exterior angles* are angles that lie on opposite sides of the transversal outside the intersected lines. | ∠2 and ∠8 |

The following postulate is the starting point for proving theorems about parallel lines that are intersected by a transversal.

### Same-Side Interior Angles Postulate

If two parallel lines are cut by a transversal, then the pairs of same-side interior angles are supplementary.

Given $p \parallel q$, ∠4 and ∠5 are supplementary.
Given $p \parallel q$, ∠3 and ∠6 are supplementary.

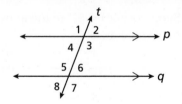

### REFLECT

**1a.** Explain how you can find m∠3 in the postulate diagram if $p \parallel q$ and m∠6 = 61°.

_____

_____

**1b.** In the postulate diagram, suppose $p \parallel q$ and line *t* is perpendicular to line *p*. Can you conclude that line *t* is perpendicular to line *q*? Explain.

_____

_____

## 2 PROOF   Alternate Interior Angles Theorem

If two parallel lines are cut by a transversal, then the
pairs of alternate interior angles have the same measure.

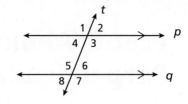

**Given:** $p \parallel q$
**Prove:** $m\angle 3 = m\angle 5$

Complete the proof by writing the missing reasons. Choose from the following reasons.
You may use a reason more than once.

| Same-Side Interior Angles Postulate | Given | Definition of supplementary angles |
|---|---|---|

| Subtraction Property of Equality | Substitution Property of Equality | Linear Pair Theorem |
|---|---|---|

| Statements | Reasons |
|---|---|
| **1.** $p \parallel q$ | **1.** |
| **2.** $\angle 3$ and $\angle 6$ are supplementary. | **2.** |
| **3.** $m\angle 3 + m\angle 6 = 180°$ | **3.** |
| **4.** $\angle 5$ and $\angle 6$ are a linear pair. | **4.** |
| **5.** $\angle 5$ and $\angle 6$ are supplementary. | **5.** |
| **6.** $m\angle 5 + m\angle 6 = 180°$ | **6.** |
| **7.** $m\angle 3 + m\angle 6 = m\angle 5 + m\angle 6$ | **7.** |
| **8.** $m\angle 3 = m\angle 5$ | **8.** |

### REFLECT

**2a.** Suppose $m\angle 4 = 57°$ in the above figure. Describe two different ways to
determine $m\angle 6$.

_____

_____

**2b.** In the above figure, explain why $\angle 1$, $\angle 3$, $\angle 5$, and $\angle 7$ all have the same measure.

_____

_____

_____

**2c.** In the above figure, is it possible for all eight angles to have the same measure?
If so, what is that measure?

_____

_____

## 3 PROOF   Corresponding Angles Theorem

If two parallel lines are cut by a transversal, then the
pairs of corresponding angles have the same measure.

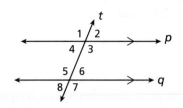

**Given:** $p \parallel q$
**Prove:** $m\angle 1 = m\angle 5$

Complete the proof by writing the missing reasons.

| Statements | Reasons |
|---|---|
| 1. $p \parallel q$ | 1. |
| 2. $m\angle 3 = m\angle 5$ | 2. |
| 3. $m\angle 1 = m\angle 3$ | 3. |
| 4. $m\angle 1 = m\angle 5$ | 4. |

### REFLECT

**3a.** Explain how you can you prove the Corresponding Angles Theorem using the
Same-Side Interior Angles Postulate and a linear pair of angles.

_____

_____

_____

Many postulates and theorems are written in the form "If $p$, then $q$." The **converse** of
such a statement has the form "If $q$, then $p$." The converse of a postulate or theorem may
or may not be true. The converse of the Same-Side Interior Angles Postulate is accepted
as true, and this makes it possible to prove that the converses of the previous theorems
are true.

> **Converse of the Same-Side Interior Angles Postulate**
>
> If two lines are cut by a transversal so that a pair of same-side interior
> angles are supplementary, then the lines are parallel.
>
> **Converse of the Alternate Interior Angles Theorem**
>
> If two lines are cut by a transversal so that a pair of alternate interior
> angles have the same measure, then the lines are parallel.
>
> **Converse of the Corresponding Angles Theorem**
>
> If two lines are cut by a transversal so that a pair of corresponding
> angles have the same measure, then the lines are parallel.

© Houghton Mifflin Harcourt Publishing Company

A *paragraph proof* is another way of presenting a mathematical argument. As in a two-column proof, the argument must flow logically and every statement should have a reason. The following example shows a paragraph proof.

## 4 PROOF   Equal-Measure Linear Pair Theorem

If two intersecting lines form a linear pair of angles with equal measures, then the lines are perpendicular.

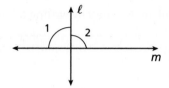

**Given:** $m\angle 1 = m\angle 2$
**Prove:** $\ell \perp m$

Complete the following paragraph proof.

It is given that $\angle 1$ and $\angle 2$ form a linear pair. Therefore, $\angle 1$ and $\angle 2$ are supplementary

by the _____ . By the definition of supplementary angles,

$m\angle 1 + m\angle 2 = 180°$. It is also given that $m\angle 1 = m\angle 2$. So, $m\angle 1 + m\angle 1 = 180°$ by the

_____ . Simplifying gives $2m\angle 1 = 180°$ and $m\angle 1 = 90°$

by the Division Property of Equality. Therefore, $\angle 1$ is a right angle and $\ell \perp m$ by the

_____ .

### REFLECT

**4a.** State the converse of the Equal-Measure Linear Pair Theorem shown above. Is the converse true?

_____

_____

# PRACTICE

**In Exercises 1–2, complete each proof by writing the missing statements or reasons.**

**1.** If two parallel lines are cut by a transversal, then the pairs of alternate exterior angles have the same measure.

**Given:** $p \parallel q$
**Prove:** $m\angle 1 = m\angle 7$

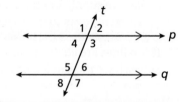

| Statements | Reasons |
|---|---|
| **1.** $p \parallel q$ | **1.** |
| **2.** $m\angle 1 = m\angle 5$ | **2.** |
| **3.** $m\angle 5 = m\angle 7$ | **3.** |
| **4.** $m\angle 1 = m\angle 7$ | **4.** |

**2.** Prove the Converse of the Alternate Interior Angles Theorem.

**Given:** $m\angle3 = m\angle5$
**Prove:** $p \parallel q$

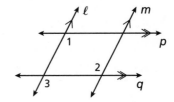

| Statements | Reasons |
|---|---|
| **1.** $m\angle3 = m\angle5$ | **1.** |
| **2.** $\angle5$ and $\angle6$ are a linear pair. | **2.** Definition of linear pair |
| **3.** | **3.** Linear Pair Theorem |
| **4.** $m\angle5 + m\angle6 = 180°$ | **4.** |
| **5.** $m\angle3 + m\angle6 = 180°$ | **5.** |
| **6.** $\angle3$ and $\angle6$ are supplementary. | **6.** |
| **7.** $p \parallel q$ | **7.** |

**3.** Complete the paragraph proof.

**Given:** $\ell \parallel m$ and $p \parallel q$
**Prove:** $m\angle1 = m\angle2$

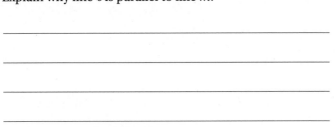

It is given that $p \parallel q$, so $m\angle1 = m\angle3$ by the _____.

It is also given that $\ell \parallel m$, so $m\angle3 = m\angle2$ by the _____.

Therefore, $m\angle1 = m\angle2$ by the _____.

**4.** The figure shows a given line $m$, a given point $P$, and the construction of a line $\ell$ that is parallel to line $m$. Explain why line $\ell$ is parallel to line $m$.

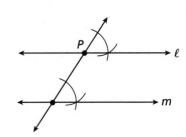

_____

_____

_____

_____

**5.** Can you use the information in the figure to conclude that $p \parallel q$? Why or why not?

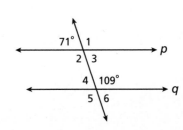

_____

_____

_____

_____

**Name** _____ **Class** _____ **Date** _____

## MULTIPLE CHOICE

**1.** Which term has the following definition?

*It is a portion of a line consisting of two points and all points between them.*

   **A.** angle       **C.** line segment

   **B.** endpoint     **D.** ray

**2.** Alberto is proving that vertical angles have the same measure. He begins as shown below. Which reason should he use for Step 3?

**Given:** ∠1 and ∠2 are vertical angles.
**Prove:** m∠1 = m∠2

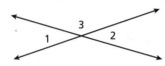

| Statements | Reasons |
|---|---|
| **1.** ∠1 and ∠2 are vertical angles. | **1.** Given |
| **2.** ∠1 and ∠3 are a linear pair. | **2.** Definition of linear pair |
| **3.** ∠1 and ∠3 are supplementary. | **3.** ? |

   **F.** Definition of supplementary angles

   **G.** Definition of vertical angles

   **H.** Vertical Angles Theorem

   **J.** Linear Pair Theorem

**3.** Lisa wants to use a compass and straightedge to copy $\overline{XY}$. She uses the straightedge to draw a line segment, and she labels one endpoint $Q$. What should she do next?

   **A.** Open the compass to distance $XY$.

   **B.** Open the compass to distance $XQ$.

   **C.** Use a ruler to measure $\overline{XY}$.

   **D.** Use the straightedge to draw $\overline{XQ}$.

**4.** You want to prove that $\overline{AB}$ is longer than $\overline{CD}$. To do so, you use the distance formula to find the lengths of the segments. Which of the following are the correct lengths?

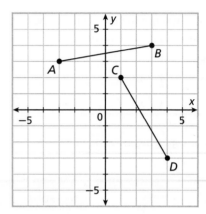

   **F.** $AB = 7$, $CD = 8$

   **G.** $AB = \sqrt{37}$, $CD = \sqrt{34}$

   **H.** $AB = \sqrt{49}$, $CD = \sqrt{64}$

   **J.** $AB = 37$, $CD = 34$

**5.** Kendrick is using a compass and straightedge to copy ∠Q. The figure shows the portion of the construction that he has already completed. Where should Kendrick place the point of the compass to do the next step of the construction?

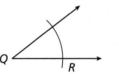

   **A.** point $Q$

   **B.** point $R$

   **C.** point $X$

   **D.** point $Y$

**6.** Which of the following is the correct phrase to complete the definition of an angle?

*An angle is a figure formed by two rays* _____.

   **F.** that intersect

   **G.** with one point in common

   **H.** that do not overlap

   **J.** with the same endpoint

**7.** Keiko is writing the proof shown below. Which reason should she use for Step 2?

**Given:** $\ell \parallel m$
**Prove:** $m\angle 4 = m\angle 6$

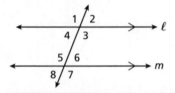

| Statements | Reasons |
|---|---|
| **1.** $\ell \parallel m$ | **1.** Given |
| **2.** $\angle 4$ and $\angle 5$ are supplementary. | **2.** ? |

   **A.** Definition of supplementary angles

   **B.** Same-Side Interior Angles Postulate

   **C.** Linear Pair Theorem

   **D.** Vertical Angles Theorem

**8.** Which compass-and-straightedge construction do you use when you construct a line parallel to a given line through a point not on the line?

   **F.** copying an angle

   **G.** copying a segment

   **H.** bisecting an angle

   **J.** bisecting a segment

**FREE RESPONSE**

**9.** Work directly on the figure below to construct the perpendicular bisector of $\overline{JK}$.

**10.** $\overline{GH}$ has endpoints $G(1, 3)$ and $H(-5, -1)$. Prove that the midpoint of $\overline{GH}$ lies in Quadrant II.

_____

_____

_____

_____

_____

_____

_____

_____

# Transformations

## Unit Focus

A transformation is a function that changes the position, shape, and/or size of a figure. In this unit, you will work with a variety of transformations, but you will focus on transformations that are rigid motions. Rigid motions preserve the size and shape of a figure. As you will see, reflections (flips), translations (slides), and rotations (turns) are all rigid motions. As you work with these transformations, you will learn to draw transformed figures and apply the transformations to help you write proofs.

## Unit at a Glance

COMMON CORE

UNIT 2

# Unpacking the Common Core State Standards

Use the table to help you understand the Standards for Mathematical Content that are taught in this unit. Refer to the lessons listed after each standard for exploration and practice.

© Houghton Mifflin Harcourt Publishing Company

| COMMON CORE Standards for Mathematical Content | What It Means For You |
|---|---|
| **CC.9-12.G.CO.2 Represent transformations in the plane using, e.g., transparencies and geometry software; describe transformations as functions that take points in the plane as inputs and give other points as outputs. Compare transformations that preserve distance and angle to those that do not (e.g., translation versus horizontal stretch).** Lessons 2-1, 2-2, 2-3, 2-4, 2-5, 2-6 | You will explore several different transformations and compare their properties. You will also learn to use function notation to describe transformations. |
| **CC.9-12.G.CO.4 Develop definitions of rotations, reflections, and translations in terms of angles, circles, perpendicular lines, parallel lines, and line segments.** Lessons 2-2, 2-5, 2-6 | You are already familiar with reflections, translations, and rotations as flips, slides, and turns, respectively. Now you will develop more rigorous mathematical definitions for these transformations. |
| **CC.9-12.G.CO.5 Given a geometric figure and a rotation, reflection, or translation, draw the transformed figure using, e.g., graph paper, tracing paper, or geometry software. Specify a sequence of transformations that will carry a given figure onto another.** Lessons 2-2, 2-5, 2-6 | In this unit, you will use a variety of tools to show the effect of a transformation upon a figure. |
| **CC.9-12.G.CO.6 Use geometric descriptions of rigid motions to transform figures and to predict the effect of a given rigid motion on a given figure; given two figures, use the definition of congruence in terms of rigid motions to decide if they are congruent.** Lessons 2-2, 2-5, 2-6 | The result of a transformation can sometimes be surprising. With experience, you will learn to predict the effect of a transformation upon a given figure. |
| **CC.9-12.G.CO.9 Prove theorems about lines and angles.** Lessons 2-3, 2-4 | You can use what you know about transformations to help you prove theorems about basic geometric figures, such as bisectors of angles and perpendicular bisectors of segments. |

# Transformations and Rigid Motions

COMMON CORE

CC.9-12.G.CO.2

**Essential question:** *How do you identify transformations that are rigid motions?*

## 1 ENGAGE    Introducing Transformations

A **transformation** is a function that changes the position, shape, and/or size of a figure. The inputs for the function are points in the plane; the outputs are other points in the plane. A figure that is used as the input of a transformation is the **pre-image**. The output is the **image**.

For example, the transformation $T$ moves point $A$ to point $A'$. Point $A$ is the pre-image, and $A'$ is the image. You can use function notation to write $T(A) = A'$. Note that a transformation is sometimes called a *mapping*. Transformation $T$ maps point $A$ to point $A'$.

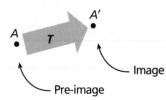

Coordinate notation is one way to write a rule for a transformation on a coordinate plane. The notation uses an arrow to show how the transformation changes the coordinates of a general point, $(x, y)$.

For example, the notation $(x, y) \rightarrow (x + 2, y - 3)$ means that the transformation adds 2 to the $x$-coordinate of a point and subtracts 3 from its $y$-coordinate. Thus, this transformation maps the point $(6, 5)$ to the point $(8, 2)$.

### REFLECT

**1a.** Explain how to identify the pre-image and image in $T(E) = F$.

_____

**1b.** Consider the transformation given by the rule $(x, y) \rightarrow (x + 1, y + 1)$. What is the domain of this function? What is the range? Describe the transformation.

_____

_____

_____

**1c.** Transformation $T$ maps points in the coordinate plane by moving them vertically up or down onto the $x$-axis. (Points on the $x$-axis are unchanged by the transformation.) Explain how to use coordinate notation to write a rule for transformation $T$.

_____

_____

Investigate the effects of various transformations on the given right triangle.

- Use coordinate notation to help you find the image of each vertex of the triangle.
- Plot the images of the vertices.
- Connect the images of the vertices to draw the image of the triangle.

**A**   $(x, y) \rightarrow (x - 4, y + 3)$

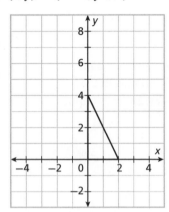

**B**   $(x, y) \rightarrow (-x, y)$

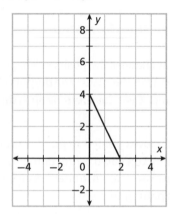

**C**   $(x, y) \rightarrow (-y, x)$

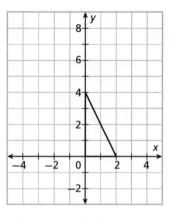

**D**   $(x, y) \rightarrow (2x, 2y)$

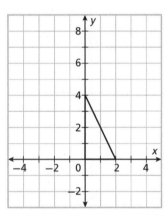

**E**   $(x, y) \rightarrow (2x, y)$

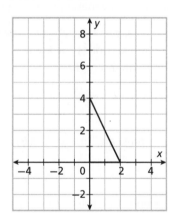

**F**   $(x, y) \rightarrow (x, \frac{1}{2}y)$

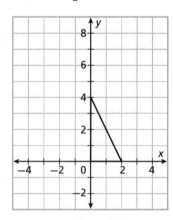

**REFLECT**

**2a.** A transformation *preserves distance* if the distance between any two points of the pre-image equals the distance between the corresponding points of the image. Which of the above transformations preserve distance?

_____

**2b.** A transformation *preserves angle measure* if the measure of any angle of the pre-image equals the measure of the corresponding angle of the image. Which of the above transformations preserve angle measure?

_____

A **rigid motion** (or *isometry*) is a transformation that changes the position of a figure without changing the size or shape of the figure.

**3 EXAMPLE** Identifying Rigid Motions

The figures show the pre-image (△ABC) and image (△A'B'C') under a transformation. Determine whether the transformation appears to be a rigid motion. Explain.

**A**

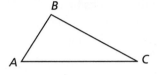 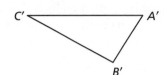

The transformation does not change the size or shape of the figure

Therefore, _____

**B**

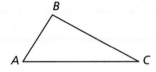 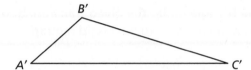

The transformation changes the shape of the figure.

Therefore, _____

**C**

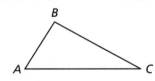 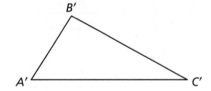

_____

_____

**REFLECT**

**3a.** How could you use tracing paper or a transparency to help you identify rigid motions?

_____

_____

_____

_____

**3b.** Which of the transformations on the previous page appear to be rigid motions?

_____

© Houghton Mifflin Harcourt Publishing Company

Rigid motions have some important properties. These are summarized below.

## Properties of Rigid Motions (Isometries)

- Rigid motions preserve distance.
- Rigid motions preserve angle measure.
- Rigid motions preserve betweenness.
- Rigid motions preserve collinearity.

The above properties ensure that if a figure is determined by certain points, then its image after a rigid motion is also determined by those points. For example, $\triangle ABC$ is determined by its vertices, points $A$, $B$, and $C$. The image of $\triangle ABC$ after a rigid motion is the triangle determined by $A'$, $B'$, and $C'$.

## PRACTICE

**Draw the image of the triangle under the given transformation. Then tell whether the transformation appears to be a rigid motion.**

**1.** $(x, y) \to (x + 3, y)$

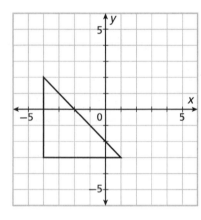

_____

**2.** $(x, y) \to (3x, 3y)$

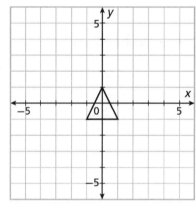

_____

**3.** $(x, y) \to (x, -y)$

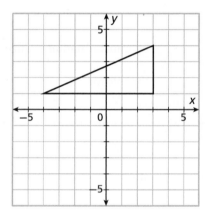

_____

**4.** $(x, y) \to (-x, -y)$

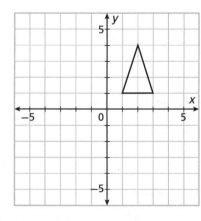

_____

**5.** $(x, y) \to (x, 3y)$

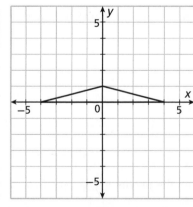

_____

**6.** $(x, y) \to (x - 4, y - 4)$

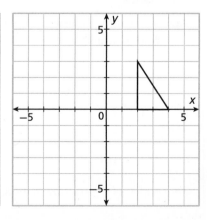

_____

The figures show the pre-image (*ABCD*) and image (*A'B'C'D'*) under a transformation. Determine whether the transformation appears to be a rigid motion. Explain.

**7.**

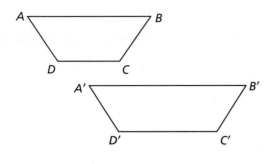

_____

_____

**8.**

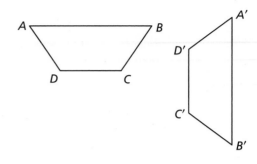

_____

_____

**9.**

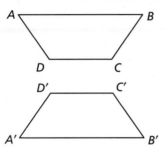

_____

_____

**10.**

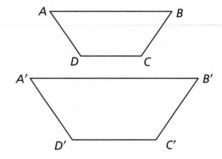

_____

_____

In Exercises 11–14, consider a transformation *T* that maps △*XYZ* to △*X'Y'Z'*.

**11.** What is the image of $\overline{XY}$?  _____

**12.** What is $T(Z)$?  _____

**13.** What is the pre-image of $\angle Y'$?  _____

**14.** Can you conclude that $XY = X'Y'$? Why or why not?

_____

**15.** Point *M* is the midpoint of $\overline{AB}$. After a rigid motion, can you conclude that *M'* is the midpoint of $\overline{A'B'}$? Why or why not?

_____

_____

_____

# Reflections

COMMON
CORE

CC.9-12.G.CO.2,
CC.9-12.G.CO.4,
CC.9-12.G.CO.5,
CC.9-12.G.CO.6

**Essential question:** *How do you draw the image of a figure under a reflection?*

One type of rigid motion is a reflection. A *reflection* is a transformation that moves points by flipping them over a line called the *line of reflection*. The figure shows the reflection of quadrilateral *ABCD* across line ℓ. Notice that the pre-image and image are mirror images of each other.

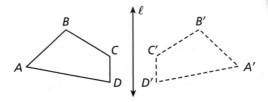

## 1 EXPLORE  Drawing a Reflection Image

Follow the steps below to draw the reflection image of each figure.

**A**

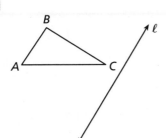

**B**

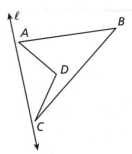

- Place a sheet of tracing paper over the figure. Use a straightedge to help you trace the figure and the line of reflection with its arrowheads.

- Flip the tracing paper over and move it so that line ℓ lies on top of itself.

- Trace the image of the figure on the tracing paper. Press firmly to make an impression on the page below.

- Lift the tracing paper and draw the image of the figure. Label the vertices.

### REFLECT

**1a.** Make a conjecture about the relationship of the line of reflection to any segment drawn between a pre-image point and its image point.

_____

_____

**1b.** Make a conjecture about the reflection image of a point that lies on the line of reflection.

_____

_____

Your work may help you understand the formal definition of a reflection.

A **reflection** across line $\ell$ maps a point $P$ to its image $P'$ as follows.

- If $P$ is not on line $\ell$, then $\ell$ is the perpendicular bisector of $\overline{PP'}$.

- If $P$ is on line $\ell$, then $P = P'$.

The notation $r_\ell(P) = P'$ says that the image of point $P$ after a reflection across line $\ell$ is $P'$.

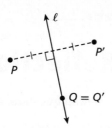

## 2 EXAMPLE Constructing a Reflection Image

Work directly on the figure below and follow the given steps to construct the image of $\triangle ABC$ after a reflection across line $m$.

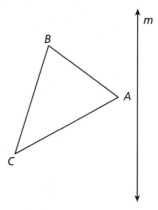

**A** Start with point $A$. Construct a perpendicular to line $m$ that passes through point $A$.

**B** Label the intersection of the perpendicular and line $m$ as point $X$.

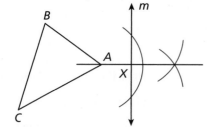

**C** Place the point of your compass on point $X$ and open the compass to the distance $XA$. Make an arc to mark this distance on the perpendicular on the other side of line $m$.

**D** Label the point where the arc intersects the perpendicular as point $A'$.

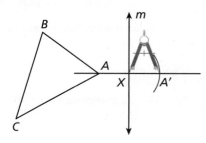

**E** Repeat the steps for the other vertices of $\triangle ABC$. (*Hint:* It may be helpful to extend line $m$ in order to construct perpendiculars from points $B$ and $C$.)

### REFLECT

**2a.** Reflections have all the properties of rigid motions. For example, reflections preserve distance and angle measure. Explain how you could use a ruler and protractor to check this in your construction.

_____

_____

The table provides coordinate notation for reflections in a coordinate plane.

| Rules for Reflections in a Coordinate Plane | |
| --- | --- |
| Reflection across the x-axis | $(x, y) \rightarrow (x, -y)$ |
| Reflection across the y-axis | $(x, y) \rightarrow (-x, y)$ |
| Reflection across the line $y = x$ | $(x, y) \rightarrow (y, x)$ |

**3 EXAMPLE** **Drawing a Reflection in a Coordinate Plane**

You are designing a logo for a bank. The left half of the logo is shown. You will complete the logo by reflecting this figure across the y-axis.

**A** In the space below, sketch your prediction of what the completed logo will look like.

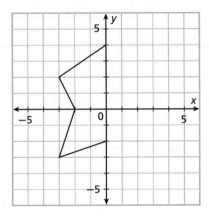

**B** In the table at right, list the vertices of the left half of the logo. Then use the rule for a reflection across the y-axis to write the vertices of the right half of the logo.

**C** Plot the vertices of the right half of the logo. Then connect the vertices to complete the logo. Compare the completed logo to your prediction.

| Left Half (x, y) | Right Half (−x, y) |
| --- | --- |
| (0, 4) | (0, 4) |
| (−3, 2) | (3, 2) |
| (−2, 0) | |
| | |
| | |

**REFLECT**

**3a.** Explain how your prediction compares to the completed logo.

_____

_____

**3b.** How can you use paper folding to check that you completed the logo correctly?

_____

_____

Use tracing paper to help you draw the reflection image of each figure across line *m*. Label the vertices of the image using prime notation.

**1.**

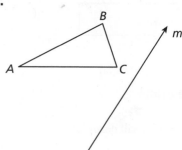

**2.**

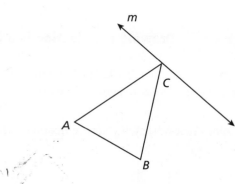

**3.**

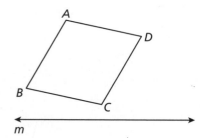

**4.**

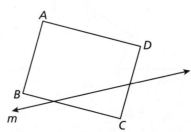

**5.**

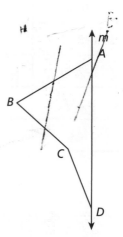

**6.**

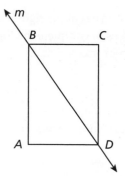

**Use a compass and straightedge to construct the reflection image of each figure across line _m_. Label the vertices of the image using prime notation.**

**7.**

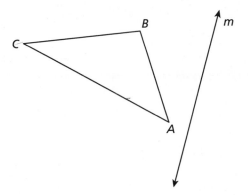

**8.**

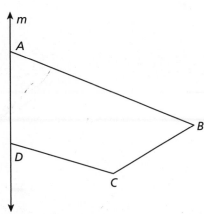

**Give the image of each point after a reflection across the given line.**

**9.** (3, 1); _x_-axis

_____

**10.** (−6, −3); _y_-axis

_____

**11.** (0, −2); $y = x$

_____

**12.** (−4, 3); _y_-axis

_____

**13.** (5, 5); $y = x$

_____

**14.** (−7, 0); _x_-axis

_____

**15.** As the first step in designing a logo, you draw the figure shown in the first quadrant of the coordinate plane. Then you reflect the figure across the _x_-axis. You complete the design by reflecting the original figure and its image across the _y_-axis. Draw the completed design.

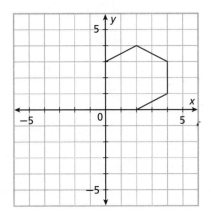

**16.** When point _P_ is reflected across the _y_-axis, its image lies in Quadrant IV. When point _P_ is reflected across the line $y = x$, its position does not change. What can you say about the coordinates of point _P_?

_____

## FOCUS ON REASONING
# Angle Bisectors

**Essential question:** *What are the key theorems about angle bisectors?*

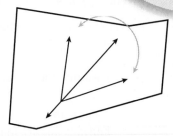

COMMON CORE

CC.9-12.G.CO.2,
CC.9-12.G.CO.9

**1** **Investigate angle bisectors.**

**A** Follow these steps to explore reflections across an angle bisector.

- Use a straightedge to draw a large angle on a sheet of paper.
- Use a protractor to help you draw the bisector of the angle.
- Fold the paper along the angle bisector and note the result.
- Compare your observations with those of other students.

Make a conjecture about the sides of an angle under a reflection across a line that bisects the angle.

_____

_____

**B** Follow these steps to explore reflections for which each side of an angle is the image of the other.

- Use a straightedge to draw a large angle on a sheet of paper.
- Fold the paper so that the sides of the angle match up.
- Unfold the paper and use a protractor to measure the two angles formed by the fold line. Note the result.
- Compare your observations with those of other students.

Make a conjecture about the line of reflection when each side of an angle is the image of the other under a reflection.

_____

_____

**REFLECT**

**1a.** How are your two conjectures related to each other?

_____

**1b.** Line $m$ bisects $\angle PQR$. What do you think is the image of $\overrightarrow{PQ}$ under a reflection across line $m$? Why?

_____

_____

You can use reflections and their properties to prove theorems about angle bisectors. These theorems will be very useful in proofs later on.

The first proof is an **indirect proof** (or a *proof by contradiction*). To write such a proof, you assume that what you are trying to prove is false and you show that this assumption leads to a contradiction.

## 2 Prove the Angle Bisection Theorem.

If a line bisects an angle, then each side of the angle is the image of the other under a reflection across the line.

**Given:** Line $m$ is the bisector of $\angle ABC$.

**Prove:** The image of $\overrightarrow{BA}$ under a reflection across line $m$ is $\overrightarrow{BC}$.

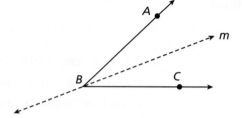

**A** Assume what you are trying to prove is false.

Assume that the image of $\overrightarrow{BA}$ under a reflection across line $m$ is *not* $\overrightarrow{BC}$. In that case, let the reflection image of $\overrightarrow{BA}$ be $\overrightarrow{BA'}$, which is not the same ray as $\overrightarrow{BC}$.

**B** Complete the following to show that this assumption leads to a contradiction.

Let $D$ be a point on line $m$ in the interior of $\angle ABC$. Then $\angle DBC$ and $\angle DBA'$ must have different measures.

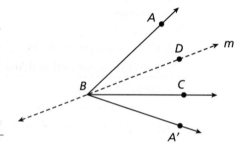

However, m$\angle DBA$ = m$\angle DBC$ since line $m$ is

_____

That means $\angle DBA$ and $\angle DBA'$ must have different measures.

This is a contradiction because reflections preserve _____

Therefore, the initial assumption must be incorrect, and the image of $\overrightarrow{BA}$ under a reflection across line $m$ is $\overrightarrow{BC}$.

---

### REFLECT

**2a.** Explain how you can use paper folding to explain why the Angle Bisection Theorem makes sense.

_____

_____

© Houghton Mifflin Harcourt Publishing Company

**3** **Prove the Converse of the Angle Bisection Theorem.**

If each side of an angle is the image of the other under a reflection across a line, then the line bisects the angle.

**Given:** ∠ABC and line *m* such that the image of $\overrightarrow{BA}$ under a reflection across line *m* is $\overrightarrow{BC}$.

**Prove:** Line *m* bisects ∠ABC.

Complete the following proof.

It is given that the image of $\overrightarrow{BA}$ under a reflection across line *m* is $\overrightarrow{BC}$. This means the image of point *B* is point *B*.

Therefore, *B* is fixed under the reflection, so *B* lies on _____

Let point *D* be any other point on line *m* in the interior of ∠ABC. Then *D* is also fixed under the reflection across line *m* since it lies on line *m*.

Since ∠ABD is determined by the rays $\overrightarrow{BA}$ and $\overrightarrow{BD}$, its image under the reflection must be determined by the images of the rays, which are $\overrightarrow{BC}$ and $\overrightarrow{BD}$.

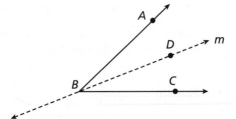

Thus, the image of ∠ABD is _____

Since reflections preserve angle measure, m∠ABD = m∠CBD.

Therefore, _____

---

**REFLECT**

**3a.** What can you conclude about ∠ABC if you know that $\overrightarrow{BC}$ is the image of $\overrightarrow{BA}$ under a reflection across line *m* and m∠ABD = 45°? Explain.

_____

**3b.** If ∠ABC is a straight angle and line *m* bisects the angle and contains points *B* and *D*, what can you conclude about the measures of ∠ABD and ∠CBD?

_____

_____

## 4 Prove the Reflected Points on an Angle Theorem.

If two points of an angle are located the same distance from the vertex but on different sides of the angle, then the points are images of each other under a reflection across the line that bisects the angle.

**Given:** Line $m$ is the bisector of $\angle ABC$ and $BA = BC$.

**Prove:** $r_m(A) = C$ and $r_m(C) = A$.

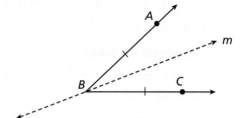

Complete the following proof.

It is given that line $m$ is the bisector of $\angle ABC$. Therefore, when $\overrightarrow{BA}$ is reflected across line $m$, its image is $\overrightarrow{BC}$.

This is justified by _____

This means that $r_m(A)$ lies on $\overrightarrow{BC}$. Let $r_m(A) = A'$.

Since point $B$ is on the line of reflection, $r_m(B) = B$, and since reflections preserve distance, $BA = BA'$.

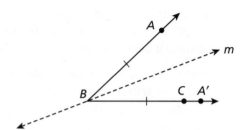

However, it is given that $BA = BC$. By the Substitution Property of Equality, you can conclude that

_____

Thus, $A'$ and $C$ are two points on $\overrightarrow{BC}$ that are the same distance from point $B$. This means $A' = C$, so $r_m(A) = C$.

A similar argument shows that $r_m(C) = A$.

---

**REFLECT**

**4a.** Using the above argument as a model, write out a similar argument that shows that $r_m(C) = A$.

_____

_____

_____

_____

_____

_____

**4b.** In the above figure, suppose you reflect point $A$ across line $m$. Then you reflect the image of point $A$ across line $m$. What is the final location of the point? Why?

_____

_____

_____

# Perpendicular Bisectors

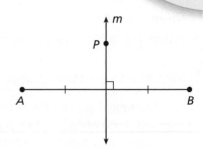

COMMON CORE

CC.9-12.G.CO.2,
CC.9-12.G.CO.9

**Essential question:** *What are the key theorems about perpendicular bisectors?*

You can use reflections and their properties to prove theorems about perpendicular bisectors. These theorems will be very useful in proofs later on.

## 1 PROOF   Perpendicular Bisector Theorem

If a point is on the perpendicular bisector of a segment, then it is equidistant from the endpoints of the segment.

**Given:** $P$ is on the perpendicular bisector $m$ of $\overline{AB}$.

**Prove:** $PA = PB$

Complete the following proof.

Consider the reflection across line $m$. Then $r_m(P) = P$ because

_____

Also, $r_m(A) = B$ by the definition of reflection.

Therefore, $PA = PB$ because _____

### REFLECT

**1a.** Suppose you use a compass and straightedge to construct the perpendicular bisector of a segment, $\overline{AB}$. If you choose a point $P$ on the perpendicular bisector, how can you use your compass to check that $P$ is equidistant from $A$ and $B$?

_____

_____

_____

**1b.** What conclusion can you make about $\triangle KLJ$ in the figure? Explain.

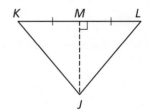

_____

_____

**1c.** Describe the point on the perpendicular bisector of a segment that is closest to the endpoints of the segment.

_____

_____

The converse of the Perpendicular Bisector Theorem is also true. In order to prove the converse, you will use an indirect proof and the Pythagorean Theorem.

Recall that the Pythagorean Theorem states that in a right triangle with legs of length $a$ and $b$ and hypotenuse of length $c$, $a^2 + b^2 = c^2$.

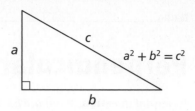

## 2 PROOF   Converse of the Perpendicular Bisector Theorem

If a point is equidistant from the endpoints of a segment, then it lies on the perpendicular bisector of the segment.

**Given:** $PA = PB$

**Prove:** $P$ is on the perpendicular bisector $m$ of $\overline{AB}$.

**A** Assume what you are trying to prove is false.

Assume that point $P$ is *not* on the perpendicular bisector $m$ of $\overline{AB}$. Then when you draw a perpendicular from $P$ to the line containing $A$ and $B$, the perpendicular intersects this line at a point $Q$, which is not the midpoint of $\overline{AB}$.

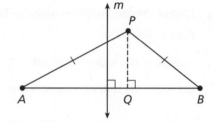

**B** Complete the following to show that this assumption leads to a contradiction.

$\overline{PQ}$ forms two right triangles, $\triangle AQP$ and $\triangle BQP$.

$AQ^2 + QP^2 = PA^2$ and $BQ^2 + QP^2 = PB^2$ by _____

Subtract these equations:

$$\begin{array}{c} AQ^2 + QP^2 = PA^2 \\ BQ^2 + QP^2 = PB^2 \\ \hline AQ^2 - BQ^2 = PA^2 - PB^2 \end{array}$$

However, $PA^2 - PB^2 = 0$ because _____

Therefore, $AQ^2 - BQ^2 = 0$. This means $AQ^2 = BQ^2$ and $AQ = BQ$. This contradicts the fact that $Q$ is not the midpoint of $\overline{AB}$. Thus, the initial assumption must be incorrect, and $P$ must lie on the perpendicular bisector of $\overline{AB}$.

### REFLECT

**2a.** In the proof, once you know $AQ^2 = BQ^2$, why can you conclude $AQ = BQ$?

_____

**2b.** Explain how the converse of the Perpendicular Bisector Theorem justifies the compass-and-straightedge construction of the perpendicular bisector of a segment.

_____

_____

_____

_____

# Translations

2-5

COMMON
CORE

CC.9-12.G.CO.2,
CC.9-12.G.CO.4,
CC.9-12.G.CO.5,
CC.9-12.G.CO.6

**Essential question:** *How do you draw the image of a figure under a translation?*

You have seen that a reflection is one
type of rigid motion. A *translation*
is another type of rigid motion.
A translation slides all points of
a figure the same distance in the
same direction. The figure shows a
translation of a triangle.

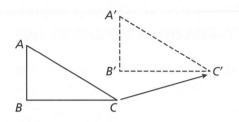

It is convenient to describe translations using the language
of vectors. A **vector** is a quantity that has both direction and
magnitude. The **initial point** of a vector is the starting point.
The **terminal point** of a vector is the ending point. The vector
at right may be named $\overrightarrow{EF}$ or $\vec{v}$.

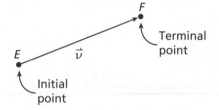

A vector can also be named using **component form**, $\langle a, b \rangle$, which
specifies the horizontal change $a$ and the vertical change $b$ from the
initial point to the terminal point. The component form for $\overrightarrow{PQ}$ is $\langle 5, 3 \rangle$.

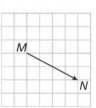

## 1 EXAMPLE  Naming a Vector

Name the vector and write it in component form.

**A**  To name the vector, identify the initial point and the terminal point.

The initial point is _____. The terminal point is _____.

The name of the vector is _____.

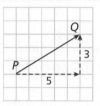

**B**  To write the vector in component form, identify the horizontal change
and vertical change from the initial point to the terminal point.

The horizontal change is _____. The vertical change is _____.

The component form for the vector is _____.

### REFLECT

**1a.** Is $\overrightarrow{XY}$ the same as $\overrightarrow{YX}$? Why or why not?

_____

**1b.** How is $\overrightarrow{AB}$ different from $\overline{AB}$?

_____

You can use vectors to give a formal definition of *translation*.

A **translation** is a transformation along a vector such that the segment joining a point and its image has the same length as the vector and is parallel to the vector.

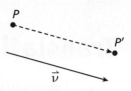

The notation $T_{\vec{v}}(P) = P'$ says that the image of point $P$ after a translation along vector $\vec{v}$ is $P'$.

## 2 EXAMPLE   Constructing a Translation Image

Work directly on the figure below and follow the given steps to construct the image of $\triangle ABC$ after a translation along $\vec{v}$.

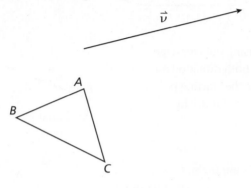

**A**   Start with point $A$. Construct a line parallel to $\vec{v}$ that passes through point $A$.

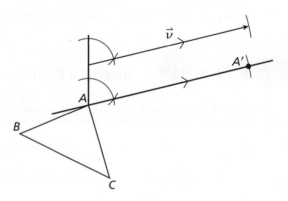

**B**   Place the point of your compass on the initial point of $\vec{v}$ and open the compass to the length of $\vec{v}$. Then move the point of the compass to point $A$ and make an arc on the line parallel to $\vec{v}$. Label the intersection of the arc and the line $A'$.

**C**   Repeat the process for points $B$ and $C$ to locate points $B'$ and $C'$.

### REFLECT

**2a.** Why do you begin by constructing a line parallel to $\vec{v}$?

_____

_____

A translation in a coordinate plane can be specified by the component form of a vector. For example, the translation along $\langle 3, -4 \rangle$ moves each point of the coordinate plane 3 units to the right and 4 units down.

More generally, a translation along vector $\langle a, b \rangle$ in the coordinate plane can be written in coordinate notation as $(x, y) \rightarrow (x + a, y + b)$.

## 3 EXAMPLE  Drawing a Translation in a Coordinate Plane

Draw the image of the triangle under a translation along $\langle -3, 2 \rangle$.

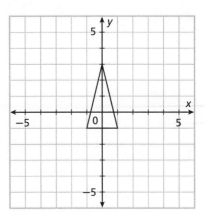

**A**  Before drawing the image, predict the quadrant in which the image will lie.

_____

**B**  In the table below, list the vertices of the triangle. Then use the rule for the translation to write the vertices of the image.

| Pre-Image (x, y) | Image (x − 3, y + 2) |
|:---:|:---:|
| (0, 3) | |
| (1, −1) | |
| (−1, −1) | |

**C**  Plot the vertices of the image. Then connect the vertices to complete the image. Compare the completed image to your prediction.

### REFLECT

**3a.**  Give an example of a translation that would move the original triangle into Quadrant IV.

_____

**3b.**  Suppose you translate the original triangle along $\langle -10, -10 \rangle$ and then reflect the image across the y-axis. In which quadrant would the final image lie? Explain.

_____

_____

# PRACTICE

**Name the vector and write it in component form.**

**1.**
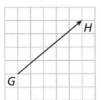

_____

**2.**
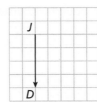

_____

**3.**

_____

**Draw and label a vector with the given name and component form.**

**4.** $\overrightarrow{MP}$; $\langle 3, -1 \rangle$

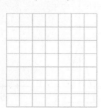

**5.** $\overrightarrow{CB}$; $\langle -3, 0 \rangle$

**6.** $\overrightarrow{HK}$; $\langle -5, 4 \rangle$

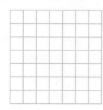

**7.** A vector has initial point $(-2, 2)$ and terminal point $(2, -1)$. Write the vector in component form. Then find the magnitude of the vector by using the distance formula.

_____

**Use a compass and straightedge to construct the image of each triangle after a translation along $\vec{v}$. Label the vertices of the image.**

**8.**

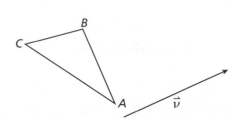

**9.**

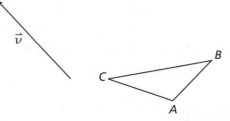

**Draw the image of the figure under the given translation.**

**10.** $\langle 3, -2 \rangle$

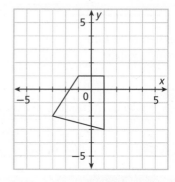

**11.** $\langle -4, 4 \rangle$

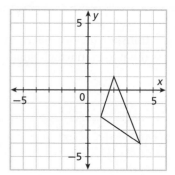

**12. a.** Use coordinate notation to name the translation that maps $\triangle ABC$ to $\triangle A'B'C'$.

_____

**b.** What distance does each point move under this translation?

_____

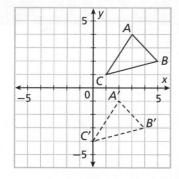

# Rotations

COMMON
CORE

CC.9-12.G.CO.2,
CC.9-12.G.CO.4,
CC.9-12.G.CO.5,
CC.9-12.G.CO.6

**Essential question:** *How do you draw the image of a figure under a rotation?*

You have seen that reflections and translations are two types of rigid motions. The final rigid motion you will consider is a *rotation*. A rotation turns all points of the plane around a point called the **center of rotation**. The **angle of rotation** tells you the number of degrees through which points rotate around the center of rotation.

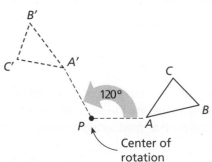

The figure shows a 120° counterclockwise rotation around point *P*. When no direction is specified, you can assume the rotation is in the counterclockwise direction.

## 1 EXPLORE  Investigating Rotations

Use geometry software to investigate properties of rotations.

**A**  Plot a point and label it *P*.

**B**  Plot three new points. Then use the segment tool to connect the points to make a triangle. Label the vertices *A*, *B*, and *C*.

**C**  Select point *P*. Go to the Transform menu and choose Mark Center. (This marks *P* as the center of rotation.)

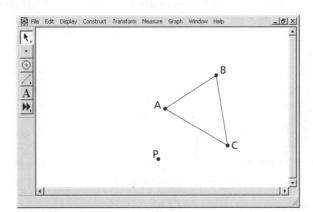

**D**  Select the triangle. Go to the Transform menu and choose Rotate. In the pop-up window, use the default setting of a 90° rotation around point *P*.

**E**  Label the vertices of the image *A′*, *B′*, and *C′*.

**F**  Select points *P* and *A*. Go to the Measure menu and choose Distance. Do the same for points *P* and *A′*.

**G**  Modify the shape or location of △*ABC* and notice what changes and what remains the same.

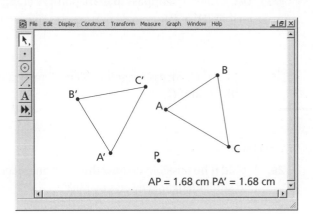

**1a.** Make a conjecture about the distance of a point and its image from the center of rotation.

_____

**1b.** What are the advantages of using geometry software rather than tracing paper or a compass and straightedge to investigate rotations?

_____

_____

A **rotation** is a transformation about a point $P$ such that (1) every point and its image are the same distance from $P$ and (2) all angles with vertex $P$ formed by a point and its image have the same measure.

The notation $R_{P,\,m°}(A) = A'$ says that the image of point $A$ after a rotation of $m°$ about point $P$ is $A'$.

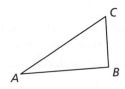

## 2 EXAMPLE   Drawing a Rotation Image

Work directly on the figure below and follow the given steps to draw the image of $\triangle ABC$ after a 150° rotation about point $P$.

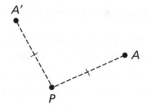

**A**  Draw $\overline{PA}$. Then use a protractor to draw a ray that forms a 150° angle with $\overline{PA}$.

**B**  Use a ruler or compass to mark point $A'$ along the ray so that $PA' = PA$.

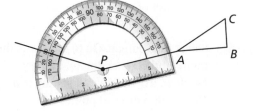

**C**  Repeat the process for points $B$ and $C$ to locate points $B'$ and $C'$.

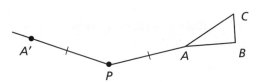

REFLECT

**2a.** Would it be possible to draw the rotation image of $\triangle ABC$ using only a compass and straightedge? Why or why not?

_____

_____

The table provides coordinate notation for rotations in a coordinate plane. You can assume that all rotations in a coordinate plane are rotations about the origin. Also, note that a 270° rotation is equivalent to turning $\frac{3}{4}$ of a complete circle.

| Rules for Rotations in a Coordinate Plane | |
|---|---|
| Rotation of 90° | $(x, y) \rightarrow (-y, x)$ |
| Rotation of 180° | $(x, y) \rightarrow (-x, -y)$ |
| Rotation of 270° | $(x, y) \rightarrow (y, -x)$ |

**3  EXAMPLE**    **Drawing a Rotation in a Coordinate Plane**

Draw the image of the quadrilateral under a 270° rotation.

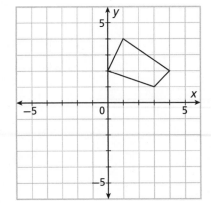

**A**    Before drawing the image, predict the quadrant in which the image will lie.

_____

**B**    In the table below, list the vertices of the quadrilateral. Then use the rule for the rotation to write the vertices of the image.

| Pre-Image (x, y) | Image (y, −x) |
|---|---|
| (3, 1) | (1, −3) |
| (4, 2) |  |
| (1, 4) |  |
| (0, 2) |  |

**C**    Plot the vertices of the image. Then connect the vertices to complete the image. Compare the completed image to your prediction.

**REFLECT**

**3a.**  What would happen if you rotated the image of the quadrilateral an additional 90° about the origin? Why does this make sense?

_____

_____

**3b.**  Suppose you rotate the original quadrilateral by 810°. In which quadrant will the image lie? Explain.

_____

_____

# PRACTICE

Use a ruler and protractor to draw the image of each figure after a rotation about point *P* by the given number of degrees. Label the vertices of the image.

**1.** 50°

**2.** 80°

*P* •

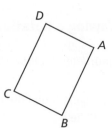

**3.** 160°

•
*P*

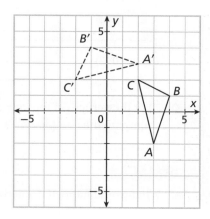

**4. a.** Use coordinate notation to write a rule for the rotation that maps △*ABC* to △*A'B'C'*.

_____

**b.** What is the angle of rotation?

_____

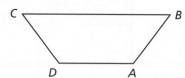

**Draw the image of the figure after the given rotation.**

**5.** 180°

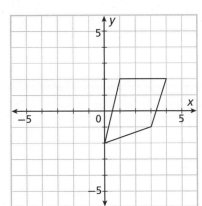

**6.** 90°

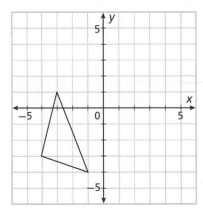

**7.** 270°

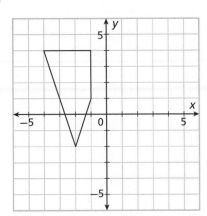

**8.** 180°

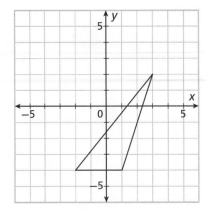

**9. a.** Reflect △JKL across the x-axis. Then reflect the image across the y-axis. Draw the final image of the triangle and label it △J'K'L'.

**b.** Describe a single rotation that maps △JKL to △J'K'L'.

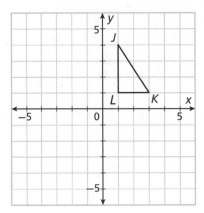

_____

**c.** Use coordinate notation to show that your answer to part **b** is correct.

_____

_____

_____

**10. Error Analysis** A student was asked to use coordinate notation to describe the result of a 180° rotation followed by a translation 3 units to the right and 5 units up. The student wrote this notation: $(x, y) \rightarrow (-[x + 3], -[y + 5])$. Describe and correct the student's error.

_____

_____

_____

Name _____ Class _____ Date _____

## MULTIPLE CHOICE

**1.** The function notation $R_{P,60°}(G) = G'$ describes the effect of a rotation. Which point is the image under this rotation?

**A.** point $R$   **C.** point $G$

**B.** point $P$   **D.** point $G'$

**2.** What is the image of the point $(4, -1)$ after a reflection across the line $y = x$?

**F.** $(-4, 1)$   **H.** $(-1, 4)$

**G.** $(4, 1)$   **J.** $(1, -4)$

**3.** Each figure shows the pre-image ($\triangle JKL$) and image ($\triangle J'K'L'$) under a transformation. Which transformation appears to be a rigid motion?

**A.**

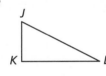

**B.**

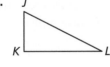

**C.**

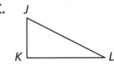

**D.**

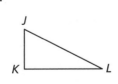

**4.** Which transformation is defined as a transformation along a vector such that the segment joining a point and its image has the same length as the vector and is parallel to the vector?

**F.** reflection

**G.** rigid motion

**H.** rotation

**J.** translation

**5.** Keisha wants to use a compass and straightedge to draw the image of $\triangle XYZ$ after a reflection across line $m$. What should she do first?

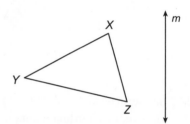

**A.** Construct a perpendicular to line $m$ that passes through point $X$.

**B.** Construct a line parallel to line $m$ that passes through point $X$.

**C.** Copy $\angle X$ on the opposite side of line $m$.

**D.** Copy $\overline{XZ}$ on the opposite side of line $m$.

**6.** You transform a figure on the coordinate plane using the rigid motion $(x, y) \rightarrow (-y, x)$. What effect does this transformation have on the figure?

**F.** 90° rotation about the origin

**G.** 180° rotation about the origin

**H.** reflection across the $x$-axis

**J.** reflection across the $y$-axis

© Houghton Mifflin Harcourt Publishing Company

**7.** Which transformation has a definition that is based on perpendicular bisectors?

**A.** reflection

**B.** rigid motion

**C.** rotation

**D.** translation

## FREE RESPONSE

**8.** Work directly on the figure below to construct the image of $\triangle ABC$ after a translation along $\vec{v}$. Label the image $\triangle A'B'C'$.

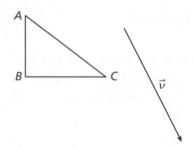

**9.** $\triangle RST$ has vertices $R(1, -3)$, $S(3, -1)$, and $T(4, -3)$. Give the coordinate notation for a transformation that rotates $\triangle RST$ 180° about the origin. Then give the coordinates of the vertices of the image of $\triangle RST$ under this transformation.

_____

_____

_____

**10.** The Reflected Points on an Angle Theorem states that if two points of an angle are located the same distance from the vertex but on different sides of the angle, then the points are images of each other under a reflection across the line that bisects the angle.

To prove the theorem, you set up the figure shown below, in which line $m$ is the bisector of $\angle ABC$ and $BA = BC$. You want to prove that $r_m(A) = C$.

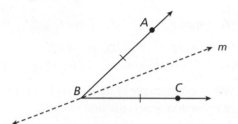

**a.** You first state that when $\overrightarrow{BA}$ is reflected across line $m$, its image is $\overrightarrow{BC}$. What postulate or theorem justifies this?

_____

**b.** You conclude that $r_m(A)$ must lie on $\overrightarrow{BC}$, and you let $r_m(A) = A'$. You also state that $r_m(B) = B$ since $B$ is on the line of reflection. Then you conclude that $BA = BA'$. What reason do you give?

_____

**c.** It is given that $BA = BC$, so you use the Substitution Property of Equality to conclude that $BA' = BC$. How do you complete the proof?

_____

_____

_____

# Congruence and Triangles

## Unit Focus

You have already learned that rigid motions preserve the size and shape of a figure. In this unit, you will learn that two figures are congruent (have the same size and shape) if and only if one figure can be mapped to the other by a sequence of rigid motions. You will also learn that there are some shortcuts for showing that triangles are congruent. Once you know these shortcuts, which are called congruence criteria, you will use them to prove facts about triangles. Along the way, you will also learn to write coordinate proofs.

## Unit at a Glance

**COMMON CORE**

# Unpacking the Common Core State Standards

Use the table to help you understand the Standards for Mathematical Content that are taught in this unit. Refer to the lessons listed after each standard for exploration and practice.

| COMMON CORE Standards for Mathematical Content | What It Means For You |
|---|---|
| **CC.9-12.G.CO.5** Given a geometric figure and a rotation, reflection, or translation, draw the transformed figure using, e.g., graph paper, tracing paper, or geometry software. **Specify a sequence of transformations that will carry a given figure onto another.** Lesson 3-1 | Given two figures with the same size and shape, you will find a sequence of reflections, translations, and/or rotations that moves one figure onto the other. |
| **CC.9-12.G.CO.6** Use geometric descriptions of rigid motions to transform figures and to predict the effect of a given rigid motion on a given figure; **given two figures, use the definition of congruence in terms of rigid motions to decide if they are congruent.** Lesson 3-1 | You will learn that two figures are congruent if and only if there is a sequence of reflections, translations, and/or rotations that maps one figure onto the other. You will use this definition to decide if figures are congruent. |
| **CC.9-12.G.CO.7** Use the definition of congruence in terms of rigid motions to show that two triangles are congruent if and only if corresponding pairs of sides and corresponding pairs of angles are congruent. Lessons 3-2, 3-3 | You will use the definition of congruence to develop a method of determining whether two triangles are congruent. The method is based on comparing corresponding parts of the triangles. |
| **CC.9-12.G.CO.8 Explain how the criteria for triangle congruence (ASA, SAS, and SSS) follow from the definition of congruence in terms of rigid motions.** Lesson 3-3 | You will use the definition of congruence to develop several shortcuts for proving that two triangles are congruent. |
| **CC.9-12.G.CO.10 Prove theorems about triangles.** Lessons 3-5, 3-6, 3-7, 3-8, 3-9 | You will explore and prove theorems about the interior and exterior angles of triangles, base angles of isosceles triangles, properties of midsegments of triangles, and the concurrency of medians of a triangle. |
| **CC.9-12.G.SRT.5 Use congruence** and similarity **criteria for triangles to solve problems and to prove relationships in geometric figures.** Lesson 3-4 | Once you know how to prove that two triangles are congruent, you will use triangle congruence to solve real-world and mathematical problems. |
| **CC.9-12.G.GPE.4 Use coordinates to prove simple geometric theorems algebraically.** Lessons 3-7, 3-8, 3-9 | You have already seen a wide range of purely geometric proofs. These proofs used postulates and theorems to build logical arguments. Now you will learn how to write coordinate proofs. These proofs also use logic, but they apply ideas from algebra to help demonstrate geometric relationships. |

UNIT 3

# Congruence

3-1

COMMON
CORE

CC.9-12.G.CO.5,
CC.9-12.G.CO.6

**Essential question:** *What does it mean for two figures to be congruent?*

Two figures are *congruent* if they have the same size and shape.
A more formal mathematical definition of congruence depends
on the notion of rigid motions.

Two plane figures are **congruent** if and only if one can be obtained
from the other by rigid motions (that is, by a sequence of reflections,
translations, and/or rotations.)

## 1 EXAMPLE   Determining If Figures are Congruent

Use the definition of congruence in terms of rigid motions to determine whether the
two figures are congruent and explain your answer.

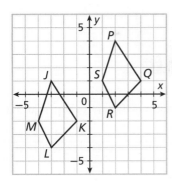

**A**   △*ABC* and △*DEF* have different sizes.

Since rigid motions preserve distance, there is no
sequence of rigid motions that will map △*ABC* to
△*DEF*.

Therefore, _____

**B**   You can map *JKLM* to *PQRS* by the translation
that has the following coordinate notation:

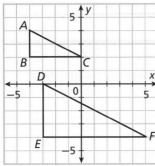

_____

A translation is a rigid motion.

Therefore, _____

## REFLECT

**1a.**   Why does the fact that △*ABC* and △*DEF* have different sizes lead to the conclusion
that there is no sequence of rigid motions that maps △*ABC* to △*DEF*?

_____

_____

_____

The definition of congruence tells you that when two figures are known to be congruent, there must be some sequence of rigid motions that maps one to the other. You will investigate this idea in the next example.

## 2 EXAMPLE  Finding a Sequence of Rigid Motions

For each pair of congruent figures, find a sequence of rigid motions that maps one figure to the other.

**A** You can map △ABC to △RST by a reflection followed by a translation. Provide the coordinate notation for each.

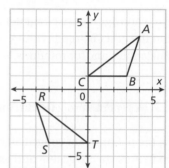

Reflection: _____

Followed by...

Translation: _____

**B** You can map △DFG to △HJK by a rotation followed by a translation. Provide the coordinate notation for each.

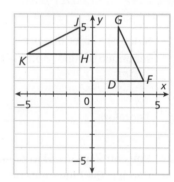

Rotation: _____

Followed by...

Translation: _____

### REFLECT

**2a.** Explain how you could use tracing paper to help you find a sequence of rigid motions that maps one figure to another congruent figure.

_____

_____

_____

**2b.** Given two congruent figures, is there a *unique* sequence of rigid motions that maps one figure to the other? Use one or more of the above examples to explain your answer.

_____

_____

© Houghton Mifflin Harcourt Publishing Company

**A**  Use a straightedge to trace $\overline{AB}$ on a piece of tracing paper. Then slide, flip, and/or turn the tracing paper to determine if there is a sequence of rigid motions that maps $\overline{AB}$ to one of the other line segments.

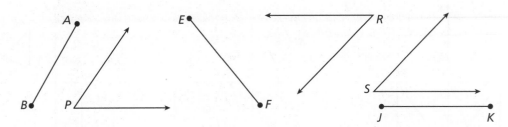

**B**  Repeat the process with the other line segments and the angles in order to determine which pairs of line segments and which pairs of angles, if any, are congruent.

Congruent line segments: _____

Congruent angles: _____

**C**  Use a ruler to measure the congruent line segments. Use a protractor to measure the congruent angles.

**REFLECT**

**3a.** Make a conjecture about congruent line segments.

_____

**3b.** Make a conjecture about congruent angles.

_____

The symbol of congruence is ≅. You read the statement $\overline{UV} \cong \overline{XY}$ as "Line segment $UV$ is congruent to line segment $XY$."

Congruent line segments have the same length, so $\overline{UV} \cong \overline{XY}$ implies $UV = XY$ and vice versa. Congruent angles have the same measure, so $\angle C \cong \angle D$ implies $m\angle C = m\angle D$ and vice versa. Because of this, there are properties of congruence that resemble the properties of equality, and you can use these properties as reasons in proofs.

| Properties of Congruence | |
|---|---|
| Reflexive Property of Congruence | $\overline{AB} \cong \overline{AB}$ |
| Symmetric Property of Congruence | If $\overline{AB} \cong \overline{CD}$, then $\overline{CD} \cong \overline{AB}$. |
| Transitive Property of Congruence | If $\overline{AB} \cong \overline{CD}$ and $\overline{CD} \cong \overline{EF}$, then $\overline{AB} \cong \overline{EF}$. |

# PRACTICE

**Use the definition of congruence in terms of rigid motions to determine whether the two figures are congruent and explain your answer.**

**1.**

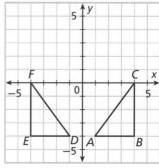

**2.**

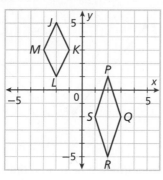

**3.**

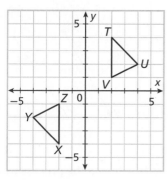

_____     _____     _____

_____     _____     _____

_____     _____     _____

**For each pair of congruent figures, find a sequence of rigid motions that maps one figure to the other. Give coordinate notation for the transformations you use.**

**4.**

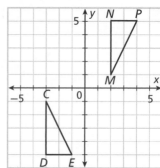

**5.**

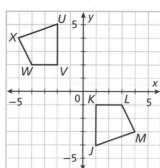

**6.**

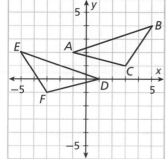

_____     _____     _____

_____     _____     _____

_____     _____     _____

_____     _____     _____

**7.** $\triangle ABC \cong \triangle DEF$ and $\triangle DEF \cong \triangle GHJ$. Can you conclude $\triangle ABC \cong \triangle GHJ$? Explain.

_____

_____

# Congruence and Triangles

**Essential question:** *What can you conclude about two triangles that are congruent?*

When you know that two triangles are congruent, you can make conclusions about the sides and angles of the triangles.

COMMON
CORE

CC.9-12.G.CO.7

**1. EXAMPLE** Finding an Unknown Dimension

$\triangle ABC \cong \triangle DEF$. Find $DE$ and m$\angle B$. Explain your reasoning.

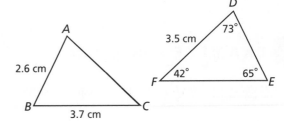

**A** Complete the following to find $DE$.

Because $\triangle ABC \cong \triangle DEF$, there is a sequence of rigid motions that maps $\triangle ABC$ to $\triangle DEF$.

This same sequence of rigid motions

maps $\overline{AB}$ to _____.

This means $\overline{AB} \cong$ _____.

Congruent segments have the same length, so $AB =$ _____.

$AB =$ _____, so $DE =$ _____.

**B** To find m$\angle B$, use similar reasoning to show that $\angle B \cong$ _____.

So, m$\angle B =$ _____.

**REFLECT**

**1a.** If you know $\triangle ABC \cong \triangle DEF$, what six congruence statements about segments and angles can you write? Why?

_____

_____

_____

When two triangles are congruent, the **corresponding parts** are the sides and angles that are images of each other. You write a congruence statement for two figures by matching the corresponding parts. In other words, the statement $\triangle ABC \cong \triangle DEF$ contains the information that $\overline{AB}$ corresponds to $\overline{DE}$ (and $\overline{AB} \cong \overline{DE}$), $\angle A$ corresponds to $\angle D$ (and $\angle A \cong \angle D$), and so on.

The following theorem is often abbreviated CPCTC. The proof of the theorem is similar to the argument presented in the previous example.

> ### Corresponding Parts of Congruent Triangles are Congruent Theorem (CPCTC)
>
> If two triangles are congruent, then corresponding sides are congruent and corresponding angles are congruent.

The converse of CPCTC is also true. That is, if you are given two triangles and you know that the six pairs of corresponding sides and corresponding angles are congruent, then you can conclude that the triangles are congruent. In the next lesson, you will see that you need only three pairs of congruent corresponding parts in order to conclude that the triangles are congruent, provided they are chosen in the right way.

## 2 EXAMPLE   Using CPCTC

$\triangle RGK \cong \triangle MQB$. Write six congruence statements about corresponding parts.

**A**   Identify corresponding sides.

Corresponding sides are pairs of letters in the same position on either side of the congruence statement.

$\overline{RG} \cong \overline{MQ}$; $\overline{GK} \cong$ _____; _____ $\cong$ _____

$\triangle RGK \cong \triangle MQB$

Corresponding sides

**B**   Identify corresponding angles.

Corresponding angles are letters in the same position on either side of the congruence statement.

$\angle R \cong \angle M$; $\angle G \cong$ _____; _____ $\cong$ _____

$\triangle RGK \cong \triangle MQB$

Corresponding angles

### REFLECT

**2a.** Given that $\triangle PQR \cong \triangle STU$, $PQ = 2.7$ ft, and $PR = 3.4$ ft, is it possible to determine the length of $\overline{TU}$? If so, find the length. If not, explain why not.

_____

_____

**2b.** A student claims that any two congruent triangles must have the same perimeter. Do you agree or disagree? Why?

_____

_____

**1.** △ABC ≅ △DEF. Find AB and m∠E.

**2.** △MNP ≅ △QRS. Find NP and m∠P.

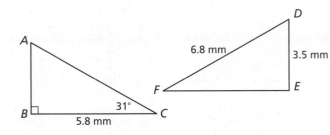

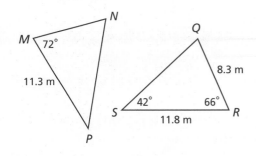

_____

_____

**3.** △JKL ≅ △LMJ. Find JK and m∠JLM.

**4.** △ABC ≅ △DEF. Find DF and m∠EDC.

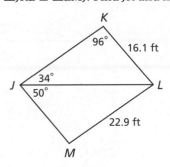

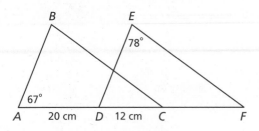

_____

_____

**For each given congruence statement, write six congruence statements about corresponding parts.**

**5.** △JWT ≅ △GKH

**6.** △PQL ≅ △KYU

**7.** △HTJ ≅ △NRZ

_____  _____  _____

_____  _____  _____

_____  _____  _____

**8.** The figure shows a portion of the truss of a bridge. △ABG ≅ △BCH ≅ △HGB.

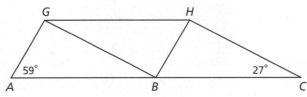

**a.** Is it possible to determine m∠GBH? If so, how? If not, why not?

_____

_____

**b.** A student claims that B is the midpoint of $\overline{AC}$. Do you agree? Explain.

_____

_____

# Developing Congruence Criteria

**Essential question:** *How do the SSS, SAS, and ASA Congruence Criteria follow from the rigid-motion definition of congruence?*

COMMON CORE

CC.9-12.G.CO.7,
CC.9-12.G.CO.8

## 1  EXPLORE   Investigating Triangle Congruence

Use the given instructions to help you identify which of the following conditions result in unique triangles. In each case, compare the triangle you draw to the triangles made by classmates. Are your triangles congruent?

**A  Sides of length 4 cm, 5 cm, and 6 cm**

Use a ruler to draw $\overline{AB}$ with a length of 6 cm.

Open your compass to 4 cm, place the point of the compass on *A*, and draw an arc. Then open the compass to 5 cm, place the point of the compass on *B*, and draw an arc.

Label the intersection of the arcs *C*. Draw $\overline{AC}$ and $\overline{BC}$.

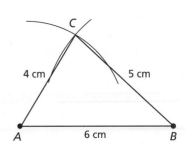

**B  Sides of length 3 cm and 5 cm, with an included angle of 50°**

Use a ruler to draw $\overline{AB}$ with a length of 5 cm.

Use a protractor to draw a ray with endpoint *A* that makes a 50° angle with $\overline{AB}$. Use a ruler to mark point *C* so that *AC* = 3 cm.

Draw $\overline{BC}$.

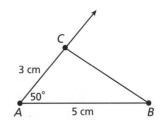

**C  Angles of 65° and 25°, with an included side of 7 cm**

Use a protractor to draw ∠*A* so that m∠*A* = 65°.

Use a ruler to mark point *B* on one of the sides of ∠*A* so that *AB* = 7 cm.

Use a protractor to draw ∠*B* so that m∠*B* = 25°.

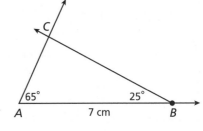

### REFLECT

**1a.** Which of the above conditions, if any, produced congruent triangles? Explain.

_____

_____

You have seen that when two triangles are congruent, the corresponding sides and corresponding angles are congruent. Conversely, if all six pairs of corresponding sides and corresponding angles of two triangles are congruent, then the triangles are congruent.

Each of the following proofs serves as a proof of this converse. In each case, the proof demonstrates a "shortcut," in which only three pairs of congruent corresponding parts are needed in order to conclude that the triangles are congruent.

## 2 PROOF — SSS Congruence Criterion

If three sides of one triangle are congruent to three sides of another triangle, then the triangles are congruent.

**Given:** $\overline{AB} \cong \overline{DE}$, $\overline{BC} \cong \overline{EF}$, and $\overline{AC} \cong \overline{DF}$.

**Prove:** $\triangle ABC \cong \triangle DEF$

To prove the triangles are congruent, you will find a sequence of rigid motions that maps $\triangle ABC$ to $\triangle DEF$. Complete the following steps of the proof.

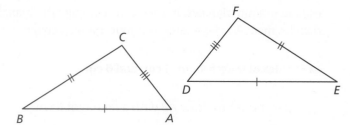

**A** Since $\overline{AB} \cong \overline{DE}$, there is a sequence of rigid motions that maps $\overline{AB}$ to _____.

Apply this sequence of rigid motions to $\triangle ABC$ to get $\triangle A'B'C'$, which shares a side with $\triangle DEF$.

If $C'$ lies on the same side of $\overline{DE}$ as $F$, reflect $\triangle A'B'C'$ across $\overline{DE}$. This results in the figure at right.

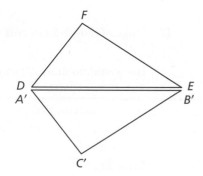

**B** $\overline{A'C'} \cong \overline{AC}$ because _____.

It is also given that $\overline{AC} \cong \overline{DF}$.

Therefore, $\overline{A'C'} \cong \overline{DF}$ because of the _____ Property of Congruence.

By a similar argument, $\overline{B'C'} \cong$ _____.

**C** Because $\overline{A'C'} \cong \overline{DF}$, $D$ lies on the perpendicular bisector of $\overline{FC'}$, by the Perpendicular Bisector Theorem. Similarly, because $\overline{B'C'} \cong \overline{EF}$, $E$ lies on the perpendicular bisector of $\overline{FC'}$. So, $\overline{DE}$ is the perpendicular bisector of $\overline{FC'}$.

By the definition of reflection, the reflection across $\overline{DE}$ maps $C'$ to _____.

The proof shows that there is a sequence of rigid motions that maps $\triangle ABC$ to $\triangle DEF$. Therefore, $\triangle ABC \cong \triangle DEF$.

© Houghton Mifflin Harcourt Publishing Company

**2a.** The proof uses the fact that congruence is transitive. That is, if you know figure $A \cong$ figure $B$, and figure $B \cong$ figure $C$, you can conclude that figure $A \cong$ figure $C$. Why is this true?

_____

_____

_____

**3 PROOF**     **SAS Congruence Criterion**

If two sides and the included angle of one triangle are congruent to two sides and the included angle of another triangle, then the triangles are congruent.

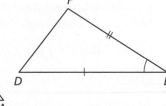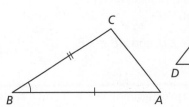

**Given:** $\overline{AB} \cong \overline{DE}$, $\angle B \cong \angle E$, and $\overline{BC} \cong \overline{EF}$.

**Prove:** $\triangle ABC \cong \triangle DEF$

To prove the triangles are congruent, you will find a sequence of rigid motions that maps $\triangle ABC$ to $\triangle DEF$. Complete the following steps of the proof.

**A** The first step is the same as the first step in the proof of the SSS Congruence Criterion. In particular, the fact that $\overline{AB} \cong \overline{DE}$ means there is a sequence of rigid motions that results in the figure at right.

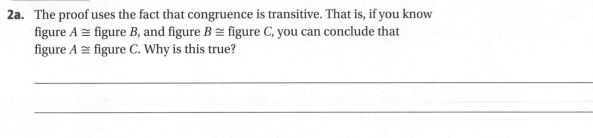

**B** Rigid motions preserve distance, so $\overline{B'C'} \cong \overline{BC}$. Also, it is given that $\overline{BC} \cong \overline{EF}$.

So, _____ because congruence is transitive.

It is given that $\angle DEF \cong \angle B$. Also, $\angle B \cong$ _____ because rigid motions preserve angle measure.

Therefore, $\angle DEF \cong$ _____ because congruence is transitive. You can use this to conclude that $\overline{DE}$ is the bisector of $\angle FEC'$.

**C** Now consider the reflection across $\overline{DE}$.

Under this reflection, the image of $C'$ is _____ by the Reflected Points on an Angle Theorem.

The proof shows that there is a sequence of rigid motions that maps $\triangle ABC$ to $\triangle DEF$. Therefore, $\triangle ABC \cong \triangle DEF$.

**3a.** Explain how the Reflected Points on an Angle Theorem lets you conclude that the image of $C'$ under a reflection across $\overline{DE}$ is $F$.

_____

_____

## 4  PROOF     ASA Congruence Criterion

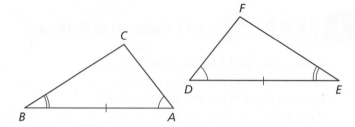

If two angles and the included side of one triangle are congruent to two angles and the included side of another triangle, then the triangles are congruent.

**Given:** $\overline{AB} \cong \overline{DE}$, $\angle A \cong \angle D$, and $\angle B \cong \angle E$.

**Prove:** $\triangle ABC \cong \triangle DEF$

To prove the triangles are congruent, you will find a sequence of rigid motions that maps $\triangle ABC$ to $\triangle DEF$. Complete the following steps of the proof.

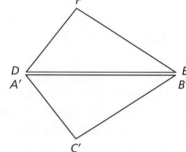

**A**  The first step is the same as the first step in the proof of the SSS Congruence Criterion. In particular the fact that $\overline{AB} \cong \overline{DE}$, means there is a sequence of rigid motions that results in the figure at right.

**B**  As in the previous proofs, you can use the fact that rigid motions preserve angle measure and transitivity of congruence to show the following:

$\angle C'A'B' \cong$ _____ and $\angle C'B'A' \cong$ _____.

This means $\overline{DE}$ bisects both $\angle FDC'$ and _____.

By the Angle Bisection Theorem, under a reflection across $\overline{DE}$, $\overrightarrow{A'C'}$ maps to $\overrightarrow{DF}$, and $\overrightarrow{B'C'}$ maps to $\overrightarrow{EF}$. Since the image of $C'$ lies on both $\overrightarrow{DF}$ and $\overrightarrow{EF}$, the image of $C'$ must be $F$.

The proof shows that there is a sequence of rigid motions that maps $\triangle ABC$ to $\triangle DEF$. Therefore, $\triangle ABC \cong \triangle DEF$.

REFLECT

**4a.** Explain how knowing that the image of $C'$ lies on both $\overrightarrow{DF}$ and $\overrightarrow{EF}$ allows you to conclude that the image of $C'$ is $F$.

_____

© Houghton Mifflin Harcourt Publishing Company

# Using Congruence Criteria

**COMMON CORE**

CC.9-12.G.SRT.5

**Essential question:** *How do you use congruence criteria in proofs and to solve problems?*

You have seen that it is possible to prove that two triangles are congruent without using the definition of congruence. Instead, you can use the theorems known as the SSS, SAS, and ASA Congruence Criteria.

## 1 EXAMPLE   Using the SAS Congruence Criterion

Complete the proof.

**Given:** $\overrightarrow{BD}$ bisects $\angle ABC$ and $\overline{AB} \cong \overline{BC}$.

**Prove:** $\triangle ABD \cong \triangle CBD$

**A**  Use a colored pen or pencil to mark the figure using the given information.

**B**  For each statement in the two-column proof below, write one of the reasons from the set of reasons given below. You may use each reason more than once or not at all.

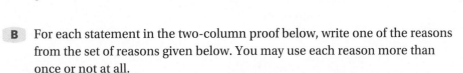

| Reflexive Property of Congruence | | SAS Congruence Criterion |
| Definition of midpoint | Given | Definition of angle bisector |

| Statements | Reasons |
|---|---|
| 1. $\overline{AB} \cong \overline{BC}$ | 1. |
| 2. $\overrightarrow{BD}$ bisects $\angle ABC$. | 2. |
| 3. $\angle ABD \cong \angle CBD$ | 3. |
| 4. $\overline{BD} \cong \overline{BD}$ | 4. |
| 5. $\triangle ABD \cong \triangle CBD$ | 5. |

### REFLECT

**1a.** Suppose the length of $\overline{AD}$ is 3 centimeters. What other length in the figure can you determine? Explain.

_____

**1b.** Suppose the given information had been $\overline{AB} \cong \overline{BC}$ and $\overline{AD} \cong \overline{CD}$. Which congruence criterion could you have used to prove the triangles congruent? Explain.

_____

A **flow proof** makes it possible to see how the steps of the proof are logically connected to each other. The next example shows how to develop a flow proof.

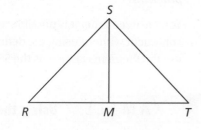

## 2 EXAMPLE   Using the SSS Congruence Criterion

Complete the flow proof.

**Given:** $M$ is the midpoint of $\overline{RT}$; $\overline{SR} \cong \overline{ST}$

**Prove:** $\triangle RSM \cong \triangle TSM$

**A**   Use a colored pen or pencil to mark the figure using the given information.

**B**   Write a statement in each cell to complete the flow proof. The reason for each statement is provided.

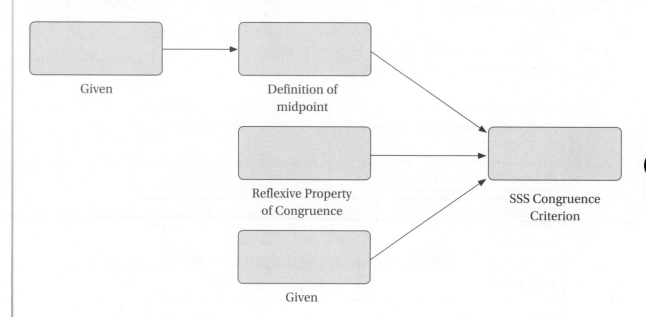

Given

Definition of midpoint

Reflexive Property of Congruence

SSS Congruence Criterion

Given

**REFLECT**

**2a.**   What piece of additional given information in the above example would allow you to use the SAS Congruence Criterion to prove that $\triangle RSM \cong \triangle TSM$?

_____

_____

**2b.**   Suppose the given information had been that $M$ is the midpoint of $\overline{RT}$ and $\angle R \cong \angle T$. Would it have been possible to prove $\triangle RSM \cong \triangle TSM$? Explain.

_____

_____

Once you have shown that two triangles are congruent, you can use the fact that corresponding parts of congruent triangles are congruent (CPCTC) to draw conclusions about side lengths and angle measures.

**3 EXAMPLE** Solving a Problem Using CPCTC

**Solve the following problem.**

You want to find the distance across a river. In order to find the distance *AB*, you locate points as described below. Explain how to use this information and the figure to find *AB*.

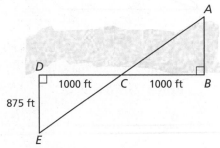

1. Identify a landmark, such as a tree, at *A*. Place a marker (*B*) directly across the river from *A*.

2. At *B*, turn 90° away from *A* and walk 1000 feet in a straight line. Place a marker (*C*) at this location.

3. Continue walking another 1000 feet. Place a marker (*D*) at this location.

4. Turn 90° away from the river and walk until the marker *C* aligns with *A*. Place a marker (*E*) at this location. Measure $\overline{DE}$.

**A** Show △*ABC* ≅ △*EDC*.

• Based on the information marked in the figure, which pairs of sides or pairs of angles do you know to be congruent?

_____

• What additional pair of sides or pair of angles do you know to be congruent? Why?

_____

• How can you conclude that △*ABC* ≅ △*EDC*?

_____

**B** Use corresponding parts of congruent triangles.

• Which side of △*EDC* corresponds to $\overline{AB}$? _____

• What is the length of $\overline{AB}$? Why?

_____

**REFLECT**

**3a.** Suppose you had walked 500 feet from *B* to *C* and then walked another 500 feet from *C* to *D*. Would that have changed the distance *ED*? Explain.

_____

_____

# PRACTICE

**In Exercises 1–2, complete the two-column proof.**

**1.** **Given:** $\overline{AB} \cong \overline{CD}$, $\overline{AD} \cong \overline{CB}$
   **Prove:** $\triangle ABD \cong \triangle CBD$

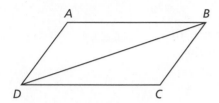

| Statements | Reasons |
|---|---|
| 1. $\overline{AB} \cong \overline{CD}$ | 1. |
| 2. $\overline{AD} \cong \overline{CB}$ | 2. |
| 3. | 3. |
| 4. $\triangle ABD \cong \triangle CBD$ | 4. |

**2.** **Given:** $\overline{GH} \parallel \overline{JK}$, $\overline{GH} \cong \overline{JK}$
   **Prove:** $\triangle HGJ \cong \triangle KJG$

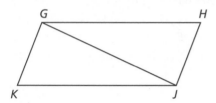

| Statements | Reasons |
|---|---|
| 1. $\overline{GH} \parallel \overline{JK}$ | 1. |
| 2. $\angle HGJ \cong \angle KJG$ | 2. |
| 3. | 3. Given |
| 4. $\overline{GJ} \cong \overline{GJ}$ | 4. |
| 5. | 5. |

**3. a.** Write a two-column proof in the table provided at right. You may not need to use all the rows of the table for your proof.
   **Given:** $\angle MQP \cong \angle NPQ$,
   $\angle MPQ \cong \angle NQP$
   **Prove:** $\triangle MQP \cong \triangle NPQ$

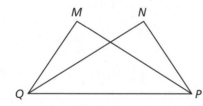

| Statements | Reasons |
|---|---|
| 1. | 1. |
| 2. | 2. |
| 3. | 3. |
| 4. | 4. |
| 5. | 5. |
| 6. | 6. |

**b.** What additional congruence statements can you write using CPCTC?

_____

**4.** Complete the flow proof.

**Given:** $\overline{GE}$ bisects ∠*DGF* and ∠*DEF*.

**Prove:** △*GDE* ≅ △*GFE*

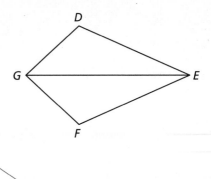

| Given | Definition of bisector |

| Given | Definition of bisector |

_____

_____

_____

_____

**5.** To find the distance *JK* across a large rock formation, you locate points as shown in the figure. Explain how to use this information to find *JK*.

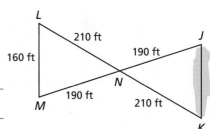

_____

_____

**6.** To find the distance *RS* across a lake, you locate points as shown in the figure. Can you use this information to find *RS*? Explain.

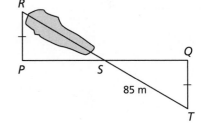

_____

_____

**7.** △*DEF* ≅ △*GHJ*, *DF* = 3*x* + 2, *GJ* = 6*x* − 13, and *HJ* = 5*x*. Find *HJ*.

_____

**8.** In the figure, $\overleftrightarrow{MC}$ is the perpendicular bisector of $\overline{AB}$. Is it possible to prove that △*AMC* ≅ △*BMC*? Why or why not?

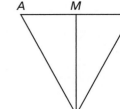

_____

_____

_____

FOCUS ON REASONING
# The Triangle Sum Theorem

**Essential question:** *What can you say about the sum of the angle measures in a triangle?*

**1** Investigate the angle measures of a triangle.

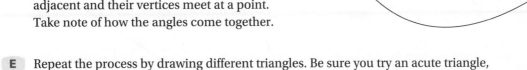

**A** Use a straightedge to draw a large triangle on a sheet of paper.

**B** Cut out the triangle.

**C** Tear off the angles of the triangle.

**D** Place the angles together so their sides are adjacent and their vertices meet at a point. Take note of how the angles come together.

**E** Repeat the process by drawing different triangles. Be sure you try an acute triangle, a right triangle, and an obtuse triangle. In each case, note how the angles come together.

 **REFLECT**

**1a.** Compare your work with that of other students. What always seems to be true about the three angles of a triangle when they are placed together?

_____

**1b.** Make a conjecture: What can you say about the sum of the angle measures in a triangle?

_____

**1c.** An equiangular triangle has three congruent angles. What do you think is true about the angles of an equiangular triangle? Why?

_____

**1d.** In a right triangle, what is the relationship of the measures of the two acute angles?

_____

The relationship you investigated above is known as the Triangle Sum Theorem.

### The Triangle Sum Theorem

The sum of the angle measures in a triangle is 180°.

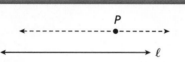

$$m\angle A + m\angle B + m\angle C = 180°$$

The proof of the Triangle Sum Theorem depends upon a postulate known as the Parallel Postulate.

### The Parallel Postulate

Through a point $P$ not on a line $\ell$, there is exactly one line parallel to $\ell$.

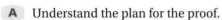

**2** **Prove the Triangle Sum Theorem.**

The sum of the angle measures in a triangle is 180°.

**Given:** $\triangle ABC$
**Prove:** $m\angle 1 + m\angle 2 + m\angle 3 = 180°$

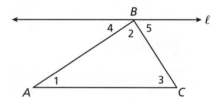

**A** Understand the plan for the proof.

Draw a line through $B$ that is parallel to $\overline{AC}$. This creates three angles that form a straight angle, so the sum of their measures is 180°. Use the fact that alternate interior angles have the same measure to conclude that the sum of the measures of the angles in a triangle is 180°.

**B** Complete the proof.

| Statements | Reasons |
|---|---|
| **1.** Draw $\ell$ through point $B$ parallel to $\overline{AC}$. | **1.** |
| **2.** $m\angle 4 = m\angle 1$ and $m\angle 5 = m\angle 3$ | **2.** |
| **3.** $m\angle 4 + m\angle 2 + m\angle 5 = 180°$ | **3.** Angle Addition Postulate and definition of straight angle |
| **4.** | **4.** |

REFLECT

**2a.** Give an indirect proof to show why it is not possible for a triangle to have two right angles.

_____

_____

_____

A **corollary** to a theorem is a statement that can be proved easily by using the theorem. A useful corollary to the Triangle Sum Theorem involves exterior angles of a triangle.

When you extend the sides of a polygon, the original angles may be called **interior angles** and the angles that form linear pairs with the interior angles are the **exterior angles**.

Each exterior angle of a triangle has two remote interior angles. A **remote interior angle** is an interior angle that is not adjacent to the exterior angle.

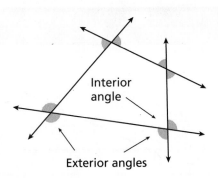

Interior angle

Exterior angles

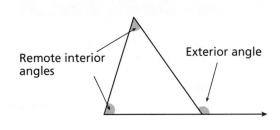

Remote interior angles

Exterior angle

**3** **Prove the Exterior Angle Theorem.**

The measure of an exterior angle of a triangle is equal to the sum of the measures of its remote interior angles.

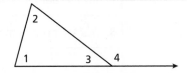

**Given:** $\triangle ABC$
**Prove:** $m\angle 4 = m\angle 1 + m\angle 2$

Complete the proof.

| Statements | Reasons |
|---|---|
| **1.** $\angle 3$ and $\angle 4$ are supplementary. | **1.** |
| **2.** $m\angle 3 + m\angle 4 = 180°$ | **2.** |
| **3.** | **3.** Triangle Sum Theorem |
| **4.** $m\angle 3 + m\angle 4 = m\angle 1 + m\angle 2 + m\angle 3$ | **4.** |
| **5.** $m\angle 4 = m\angle 1 + m\angle 2$ | **5.** |

**REFLECT**

**3a.** Explain how you could verify the Exterior Angle Theorem using a method similar to that of the Explore.

_____

_____

Another important corollary of the Triangle Sum Theorem is the Quadrilateral Sum Theorem. You will prove the theorem as an exercise.

**Quadrilateral Sum Theorem**

The sum of the angle measures in a quadrilateral is 360°.

# PRACTICE

1. Complete the proof that the acute angles of a right triangle are complementary.

   **Given:** △*ABC* with ∠*C* a right angle
   **Prove:** ∠*A* and ∠*B* are complementary.

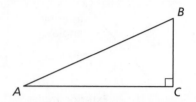

| Statements | Reasons |
|---|---|
| **1.** ∠C is a right angle. | **1.** |
| **2.** m∠C = 90° | **2.** |
| **3.** m∠A + m∠B + m∠C = 180° | **3.** |
| **4.** | **4.** Substitution Property of Equality |
| **5.** | **5.** Subtraction Property of Equality |
| **6.** ∠A and ∠B are complementary. | **6.** |

2. Write a paragraph proof of the Quadrilateral Sum Theorem.

   **Given:** Quadrilateral *ABCD*
   **Prove:** m∠*A* + m∠*B* + m∠*C* + m∠*D* = 360°
   (*Hint:* Draw diagonal $\overline{AC}$ and number the angles formed.)

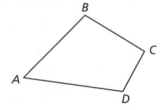

_____

_____

_____

_____

3. If two angles of one triangle are congruent to two angles of another triangle, must the third angles of the triangles also be congruent? Why or why not?

_____

_____

_____

_____

**FOCUS ON REASONING**
# The Isosceles Triangle Theorem

COMMON
CORE

CC.9-12.G.CO.10

**Essential question:** *What can you say about the base angles of an isosceles triangle?*

Recall that an *isosceles* triangle is a triangle with at least two congruent sides. The congruent sides are called the **legs** of the triangle. The angle formed by the legs is the **vertex angle**. The side of the triangle opposite the vertex angle is the **base**. The angles that have the base as a side are the **base angles**.

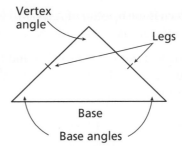

**1** **Investigate isosceles triangles.**

**A** Work on a separate sheet of paper. Use a straightedge to draw an angle. Label it ∠*A*.

**B** Place the point of your compass on the vertex of the angle and draw an arc that intersects the sides of the angle at *B* and *C*.

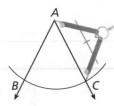

**C** Use the straightedge to draw $\overline{BC}$.

**D** Use a protractor to measure ∠*B* and ∠*C*. Record the measures in the table under the column for Triangle 1.

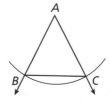

**E** Repeat the process two more times, drawing different angles and using different compass settings. In each case, note m∠*B* and m∠*C* in the table.

|  | Triangle 1 | Triangle 2 | Triangle 3 |
|---|---|---|---|
| m∠B |  |  |  |
| m∠C |  |  |  |

**REFLECT**

**1a.** How do you know the triangles you constructed were isosceles triangles?

_____

_____

**1b.** Compare your work with that of other students. Then make a conjecture about isosceles triangles.

_____

## 2 Prove the Isosceles Triangle Theorem.

The base angles of an isosceles triangle are congruent.

**Given:** $\overline{AB} \cong \overline{AC}$
**Prove:** $\angle B \cong \angle C$

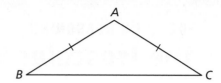

Complete the proof.

Draw line *m*, which is the bisector of $\angle A$. Consider the reflection across line *m*.

Because $AB = AC$, you can conclude that *B* and *C* are images of each other under the reflection across line *m*. This is justified by

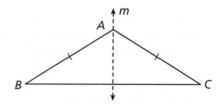

_____

So, $\angle B$ and $\angle C$ are images of each other and therefore $\angle B \cong \angle C$, because

_____

---

REFLECT

**2a.** A different proof of the Isosceles Triangle Theorem is based on letting point *M* be the midpoint of $\overline{BC}$ and drawing $\overline{AM}$. Explain the steps of this proof.

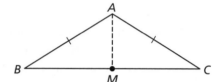

_____

_____

_____

You have already used three triangle congruence criteria: SSS, SAS, and ASA. There is another criterion that is useful in proofs, the AAS Congruence Criterion.

### AAS Congruence Criterion

If two angles and a non-included side of one triangle are congruent to two angles and the corresponding non-included side of another triangle, then the triangles are congruent.

To justify this congruence criterion, note that the Triangle Sum Theorem guarantees that $\angle A \cong \angle D$. Therefore $\triangle ABC \cong \triangle DEF$ by the ASA Congruence Criterion.

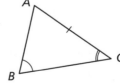
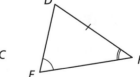

**3** **Prove the Converse of the Isosceles Triangle Theorem.**

If two angles of a triangle are congruent, then the sides opposite them are congruent.

**Given:** $\angle B \cong \angle C$
**Prove:** $\overline{AB} \cong \overline{AC}$

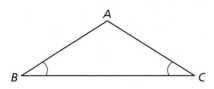

Complete the proof.

Draw line $m$, which is the bisector of $\angle A$. Let point $X$ be the point where line $m$ intersects $\overline{BC}$.

Then, by the definition of angle bisector,

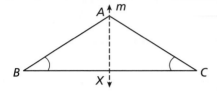

_____

Also, $\overline{AX} \cong \overline{AX}$ by the Reflexive Property of Congruence. Therefore, $\triangle BAX \cong \triangle CAX$ by the AAS Congruence Criterion.

So, $\overline{AB} \cong \overline{AC}$ by _____

---

**REFLECT**

**3a.** An equiangular triangle has three congruent angles. An equilateral triangle has three congruent sides. Use the figure to help you explain why an equiangular triangle must also be an equilateral triangle.

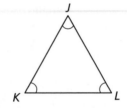

_____

_____

_____

# PRACTICE

**Find the measure of the indicated angle.**

**1.** m$\angle B$

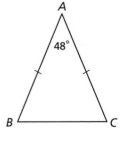

_____

**2.** m$\angle J$

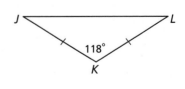

_____

**3.** m$\angle R$

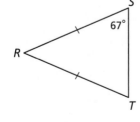

_____

**Find the length of the indicated side.**

**4.** $\overline{DF}$

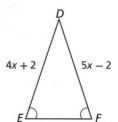

**5.** $\overline{LM}$

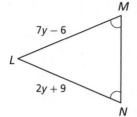

**6.** $\overline{RS}$

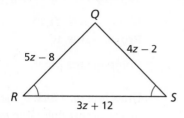

_____  _____  _____

**7. Error Analysis** Two students are asked to find the angle measures of $\triangle XYZ$, given that $\triangle XYZ$ is isosceles. Their work is shown below. Is either answer incorrect? Explain.

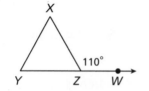

| Lee's Answer | Skyler's Answer |
|---|---|
| $m\angle Z = 70°$. Since an isosceles triangle has two congruent angles, $m\angle X = m\angle Y = 55°$. | $m\angle Z = 70°$. Since base angles are congruent, $m\angle Y = 70°$ also. This leaves 40° for $m\angle X$. |

_____

_____

**8.** A boat travels at a constant speed parallel to a coastline that is approximately a straight line. An observer on the coast at point $P$ uses radar to find the distance to the boat when the boat makes an angle of 35° with the coastline. Then, 5 seconds later, the observer finds the distance to the boat when it makes an angle of 70° with the coastline. The observer wants to know if it is possible to calculate the speed of the boat.

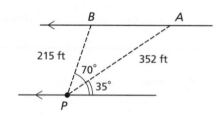

**a.** Is it possible to determine the distance the boat traveled, $AB$? If so, find the distance and explain your method. If not, explain why not.

_____

_____

_____

**b.** Is it possible to determine the speed of the boat? If so, find the speed and explain your method. If not, explain why not.

_____

_____

# Coordinate Proofs

**3-7**

**Essential question:** *How do you write a coordinate proof?*

You have already seen a wide range of purely geometric proofs. These proofs used postulates and theorems to build logical arguments. Now you will learn how to write coordinate proofs. These proofs also use logic, but they apply ideas from algebra to help demonstrate geometric relationships.

**COMMON CORE**

CC.9-12.G.CO.10,
CC.9-12.G.GPE.4

**1 EXAMPLE** Proving or Disproving a Statement

Prove or disprove that the triangle with vertices $A(4, 2)$, $B(-1, 4)$, and $C(2, -3)$ is an isosceles triangle.

**A** Plot the vertices and draw the triangle.

**B** Use the distance formula to find the length of each side of $\triangle ABC$.

$$AB = \sqrt{(-1-4)^2 + (4-2)^2} = \sqrt{(-5)^2 + 2^2} = \sqrt{29}$$

$BC = $ _____

$AC = $ _____

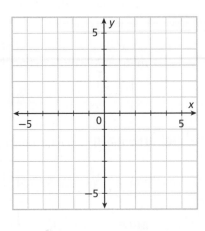

**C** Draw a conclusion based on your results. State whether or not the triangle is isosceles and why.

_____

**REFLECT**

**1a.** What other conclusion(s) can you make about the sides or angles of $\triangle ABC$? Explain.

_____

_____

**1b.** Suppose you map $\triangle ABC$ to $\triangle A'B'C'$ by the translation $(x, y) \rightarrow (x - 3, y - 2)$. Is $\triangle A'B'C'$ an isosceles triangle? Why or why not?

_____

_____

You can write a coordinate proof to prove general facts about geometric figures. The first step in such a proof is using variables to assign general coordinates to a figure using only what is known about the figure.

## 2 EXAMPLE Writing a Coordinate Proof

Prove that in a right triangle, the midpoint of the hypotenuse is equidistant from all three vertices.

**A** Assign coordinates to the figure.

Let the triangle be $\triangle ABC$. Since the triangle is a right triangle, assume $\angle B$ is a right angle. Place $\angle B$ at the origin and place the legs along the positive $x$- and $y$-axes.

Since the proof involves a midpoint, use multiples of 2 in assigning coordinates to $A$ and $C$, as shown.

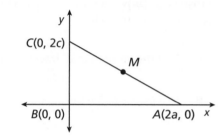

**B** Let $M$ be the midpoint of the hypotenuse, $\overline{AC}$. Use the midpoint formula to find the coordinates of $M$.

$$M\left(\frac{\boxed{\phantom{x}}+\boxed{\phantom{x}}}{2}, \frac{\boxed{\phantom{x}}+\boxed{\phantom{x}}}{2}\right) = M\left(\boxed{\phantom{x}}, \boxed{\phantom{x}}\right)$$

**C** Use the distance formula to find $MA$, $MB$, and $MC$.

$$MA = \sqrt{\left(\boxed{\phantom{x}}-\boxed{\phantom{x}}\right)^2 + \left(\boxed{\phantom{x}}-\boxed{\phantom{x}}\right)^2} = \sqrt{\boxed{\phantom{x}}^2 + \boxed{\phantom{x}}^2}$$

$$MB = \sqrt{\left(\boxed{\phantom{x}}-\boxed{\phantom{x}}\right)^2 + \left(\boxed{\phantom{x}}-\boxed{\phantom{x}}\right)^2} = \sqrt{\boxed{\phantom{x}}^2 + \boxed{\phantom{x}}^2}$$

$$MB = \sqrt{\left(\boxed{\phantom{x}}-\boxed{\phantom{x}}\right)^2 + \left(\boxed{\phantom{x}}-\boxed{\phantom{x}}\right)^2} = \sqrt{\boxed{\phantom{x}}^2 + \boxed{\phantom{x}}^2}$$

So, the midpoint of the hypotenuse is equidistant from all three vertices because

_____

### REFLECT

**2a.** Explain why it is more convenient to assign the coordinates as $A(2a, 0)$ and $C(0, 2c)$ rather than $A(a, 0)$ and $C(0, c)$.

_____

**2b.** Can you write the proof by assigning the coordinates as $A(2n, 0)$ and $C(0, 2n)$?

_____

_____

© Houghton Mifflin Harcourt Publishing Company

1. Prove or disprove that the triangle with vertices $R(-2, -2)$, $S(1, 4)$, and $T(4, -5)$ is an equilateral triangle.

_____

_____

_____

_____

_____

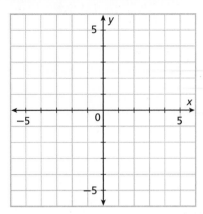

2. $\triangle ABC$ has vertices $A(-4, 1)$, $B(-3, 4)$, and $C(-1, 1)$. $\triangle DEF$ has vertices $D(2, -3)$, $E(5, -2)$, and $F(2, 0)$. Prove or disprove that the triangles are congruent.

_____

_____

_____

_____

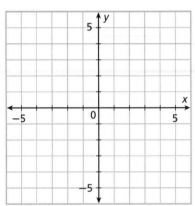

3. Write a coordinate proof to prove that the diagonals of a rectangle are congruent. Use the space at right to show how to assign coordinates. Then write the proof below.

_____

_____

_____

_____

4. **Error Analysis** A student proves that every right triangle is isosceles by assigning coordinates as shown at right and by using the distance formula to show that $PQ = a$ and $RQ = a$. Explain the error in the student's proof.

_____

_____

_____

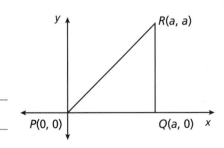

**FOCUS ON REASONING**

# Midsegments of a Triangle

**Essential question:** *What must be true about the segment that connects the midpoints of two sides of a triangle?*

A **midsegment** of a triangle is a line segment that connects the midpoints of two sides of the triangle.

**1** **Investigate midsegments.**

**A** Use geometry software to draw a triangle.

**B** Label the vertices *A, B,* and *C*.

**C** Select $\overline{AB}$ and construct its midpoint. Select $\overline{AC}$ and construct its midpoint. Label the midpoints *D* and *E*.

**D** Draw the midsegment, $\overline{DE}$.

**E** Measure the lengths of $\overline{DE}$ and $\overline{BC}$.

**F** Measure ∠*ADE* and ∠*ABC*.

**G** Drag the vertices of △*ABC* to change its shape. As you do so, look for relationships in the measurements.

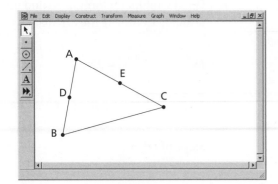

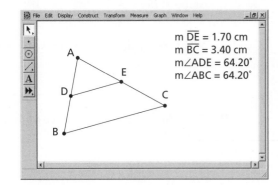

**REFLECT**

**1a.** How is the length of $\overline{DE}$ related to the length of $\overline{BC}$?

_____

**1b.** How is m∠*ADE* related to m∠*ABC*? What does this tell you about $\overline{DE}$ and $\overline{BC}$? Explain.

_____

**1c.** Compare your results with those of other students. Then state a conjecture about a midsegment of a triangle.

_____

_____

## 2 Prove the Midsegment Theorem.

A midsegment of a triangle is parallel to the third side of the triangle and is half as long as the third side.

**Given:** $\overline{DE}$ is a midsegment of $\triangle ABC$.
**Prove:** $\overline{DE} \parallel \overline{BC}$ and $DE = \frac{1}{2}BC$.

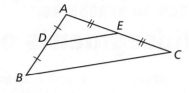

**A** Use a coordinate proof. Place $\triangle ABC$ on a coordinate plane so that one vertex is at the origin and one side lies on the *x*-axis, as shown. For convenience, assign vertex *C* the coordinates $(2p, 0)$ and assign vertex *A* the coordinates $(2q, 2r)$.

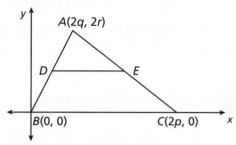

**B** Use the midpoint formula to find the coordinates of *D* and *E*. Complete the calculations.

$$D\left(\frac{2q + 0}{2}, \frac{2r + 0}{2}\right) = D(q, r) \qquad E\left(\frac{\boxed{\phantom{x}} + \boxed{\phantom{x}}}{2}, \frac{\boxed{\phantom{x}} + \boxed{\phantom{x}}}{2}\right) = E\left(\boxed{\phantom{xx}}, \boxed{\phantom{xx}}\right)$$

**C** To prove that $\overline{DE} \parallel \overline{BC}$, first find the slopes of $\overline{DE}$ and $\overline{BC}$.

Slope of $\overline{DE} = \dfrac{\boxed{\phantom{x}} - \boxed{\phantom{x}}}{\boxed{\phantom{x}} - \boxed{\phantom{x}}} = \boxed{\phantom{x}}$

Slope of $\overline{BC} = \dfrac{\boxed{\phantom{x}} - \boxed{\phantom{x}}}{\boxed{\phantom{x}} - \boxed{\phantom{x}}} = \boxed{\phantom{x}}$

What conclusion can you make based on the slopes? Why?

_____

**D** Show how to use the distance formula to prove that $DE = \frac{1}{2}BC$.

_____

_____

### REFLECT

**2a.** Explain why it is more convenient to assign the coordinates as $C(2p, 0)$ and $A(2q, 2r)$ rather than $C(p, 0)$ and $A(q, r)$.

_____

**2b.** Explain how the perimeter of $\triangle JKL$ compares to that of $\triangle MNP$.

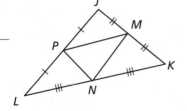

_____

**FOCUS ON REASONING**

# Medians of a Triangle

**COMMON CORE**

CC.9-12.G.CO.10,
CC.9-12.G.GPE.4

**Essential question:** *What can you conclude about the medians of a triangle?*

A **median** of a triangle is a line segment whose endpoints are a vertex of the triangle and the midpoint of the opposite side. Every triangle has three medians. In the figure, $\overline{LM}$ is a median of $\triangle JKL$.

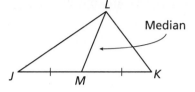

Median

**1** **Investigate medians.**

  **A**  Use geometry software to draw a triangle.

  **B**  Label the vertices *J*, *K*, and *L*.

  **C**  Select each side and construct its midpoint. Label the midpoints *M*, *N*, and *P*.

  **D**  Draw the medians, $\overline{LM}$, $\overline{JN}$, and $\overline{KP}$.

  **E**  Drag the vertices of $\triangle JKL$ to change its shape. As you do so, look for relationships among the medians.

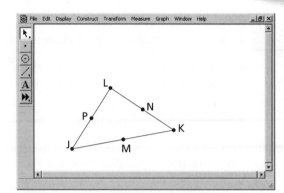

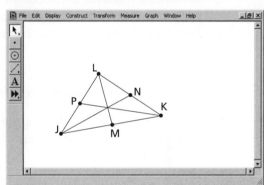

**REFLECT**

**1a.** Compare your observations with those of other students. Then make a conjecture. What can you say about the medians of a triangle?

_____

_____

**1b.** Paul draws $\triangle ABC$ and the medians from vertices *A* and *B*. He finds that the medians intersect at a point and he labels this point *X*. Paul claims that point *X* lies outside $\triangle ABC$. Do you think this is possible? Explain.

_____

_____

Three or more lines are said to be **concurrent** when they intersect at a point. The point is called the **point of concurrency**. You have seen that the medians of a triangle are concurrent. The point of concurrency of the medians of a triangle is called the **centroid** of the triangle.

**Concurrency of Medians Theorem**

The medians of a triangle are concurrent.

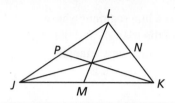

2 **Prove the Concurrency of Medians Theorem.**

**Given:** $\triangle JKL$ with medians $\overline{LM}$, $\overline{JN}$, and $\overline{KP}$.
**Prove:** The medians intersect at a point.

Complete the coordinate proof.

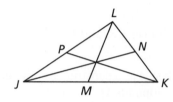

**A** Understand the plan for the proof.

Assign coordinates to the vertices of the triangle and find the coordinates of the midpoint of each side. Write an equation for the line containing each median. Determine the point of intersection of two of the lines. Show that this point lies on the third line.

**B** Assign coordinates to the vertices of the triangle.

Place $J$ at the origin and $\overline{JK}$ along the $x$-axis. Assign coordinates to $K$ and $L$ as shown.

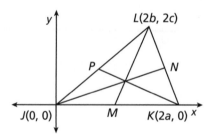

**C** Find the coordinates of the midpoint of each side. Use the midpoint formula.

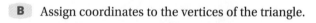

$$M\left(\frac{\boxed{\phantom{x}} + \boxed{\phantom{x}}}{2}, \frac{\boxed{\phantom{x}} + \boxed{\phantom{x}}}{2}\right) = M\left(\boxed{\phantom{xx}}, \boxed{\phantom{xx}}\right)$$

$$N\left(\frac{\boxed{\phantom{x}} + \boxed{\phantom{x}}}{2}, \frac{\boxed{\phantom{x}} + \boxed{\phantom{x}}}{2}\right) = N\left(\boxed{\phantom{xx}}, \boxed{\phantom{xx}}\right)$$

$$P\left(\frac{\boxed{\phantom{x}} + \boxed{\phantom{x}}}{2}, \frac{\boxed{\phantom{x}} + \boxed{\phantom{x}}}{2}\right) = P\left(\boxed{\phantom{xx}}, \boxed{\phantom{xx}}\right)$$

© Houghton Mifflin Harcourt Publishing Company

**D** Write the equation for the line containing $\overline{JN}$. To do so, use the *point-slope form* of the equation of a line: If a line has slope $m$ and passes through $(x_0, y_0)$, then the line's equation is $y - y_0 = m(x - x_0)$.

Slope of $\overline{JN} = \dfrac{c - 0}{a + b - 0} = \dfrac{c}{a + b}$

To write the equation of $\overleftrightarrow{JN}$, use the fact that the line passes through $(0, 0)$.

Equation of $\overleftrightarrow{JN}$: $y - 0 = \dfrac{c}{a + b}(x - 0)$ or $y = \dfrac{c}{a + b}x$

**E** Write the equations for the lines containing $\overline{LM}$ and $\overline{PK}$.

Slope of $\overline{LM} = \dfrac{\boxed{\phantom{x}} - \boxed{\phantom{x}}}{\boxed{\phantom{x}} - \boxed{\phantom{x}}} = \dfrac{\boxed{\phantom{x}}}{\phantom{xx}}$

Equation of $\overleftrightarrow{LM}$: $y - \boxed{\phantom{x}} = \dfrac{\boxed{\phantom{x}}}{\phantom{x}}(x - \boxed{\phantom{x}})$ or $y = \dfrac{\boxed{\phantom{x}}}{\phantom{x}}(x - \boxed{\phantom{x}})$

Slope of $\overline{PK} = \dfrac{\boxed{\phantom{x}} - \boxed{\phantom{x}}}{\boxed{\phantom{x}} - \boxed{\phantom{x}}} = \dfrac{\boxed{\phantom{x}}}{\phantom{xx}}$

Equation of $\overleftrightarrow{PK}$: $y - \boxed{\phantom{x}} = \dfrac{\boxed{\phantom{x}}}{\phantom{x}}(x - \boxed{\phantom{x}})$ or $y = \dfrac{\boxed{\phantom{x}}}{\phantom{x}}(x - \boxed{\phantom{x}})$

**F** Find the point of intersection of $\overleftrightarrow{JN}$ and $\overleftrightarrow{LM}$. To do so, set the right side of the equation for $\overleftrightarrow{JN}$ equal to the right side of the equation for $\overleftrightarrow{LM}$. Then solve for $x$, to find the $x$-coordinate of the point of intersection.

| | |
|---|---|
| $\dfrac{c}{a + b}x = \dfrac{2c}{2b - a}(x - a)$ | Write the equation for $x$. |
| $cx(2b - a) = 2c(x - a)(a + b)$ | Multiply both sides by $(a + b)(2b - a)$. |
| $2bcx - acx = (2cx - 2ac)(a + b)$ | Multiply. |
| _____ | Multiply on right side of equation. |
| _____ | Subtract $2bcx$ from both sides. |
| _____ | Subtract $2acx$ from both sides. |
| _____ | Factor out $ac$; divide both sides by $ac$. |
| _____ | Divide both sides by $-3$. |

To find the $y$-coordinate of the point of intersection, substitute this value of $x$ into the equation for $\overleftrightarrow{JN}$ and solve for $y$.

$y = \dfrac{c}{a + b}x = \dfrac{c}{a + b} \cdot \dfrac{\boxed{\phantom{x}}}{\boxed{\phantom{x}}} = \dfrac{\boxed{\phantom{x}}}{\boxed{\phantom{x}}}$

The coordinates of the point of intersection of $\overleftrightarrow{JN}$ and $\overleftrightarrow{LM}$ are _____.

**G** Now show that the point you found in Step F lies on $\overleftrightarrow{PK}$. To do so, substitute the x-coordinate of the point into the equation for $\overleftrightarrow{PK}$. Then simplify to show that the corresponding y-value is the same as the y-coordinate you calculated in Step F.

$y = \dfrac{c}{b - 2a}(x - 2a)$    Write the equation for $\overleftrightarrow{PK}$.

_____    Substitute the x-coordinate of the point.

_____    Subtract inside the parentheses.

_____    Factor the numerator inside the parentheses.

_____    Divide to remove common factors.

_____    Simplify.

Because this y-value is the same as the y-coordinate of the point of intersection from Step F, the point also lies on $\overleftrightarrow{PK}$. This shows that the medians are concurrent.

**REFLECT**

**2a.** Explain how you can find the coordinates of the centroid of a triangle with vertices $R(0, 0)$, $S(6, 0)$, and $T(3, 9)$.

_____

_____

_____

**2b.** A student proves the Concurrency of Medians Theorem by first assigning coordinates to the vertices of $\triangle JKL$ as $J(0, 0)$, $K(2a, 0)$, and $L(2a, 2c)$. The students says that this choice of coordinates makes the algebra in the proof a bit easier. Do you agree with the student's choice of coordinates? Explain.

_____

_____

**2c.** A student claims that the averages of the x-coordinates and of the y-coordinates of the vertices of a triangle are the x- and y-coordinates of the centroid. Does the coordinate proof of the Concurrency of Medians Theorem support the claim? Explain.

_____

_____

_____

© Houghton Mifflin Harcourt Publishing Company

Name _____ Class _____ Date _____

## MULTIPLE CHOICE

**1.** *J* is the midpoint of $\overline{GH}$. $\overline{GK}$ is parallel to $\overline{LH}$. Which congruence criterion can be used to prove △*GJK* ≅ △*HJL*?

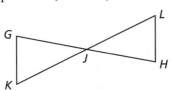

   **A.** ASA         **C.** SSA

   **B.** SAS         **D.** SSS

**2.** Jessica wants to prove that an equilateral triangle has three congruent angles. She begins as shown below. Which reason should she use for Step 2?

**Given:** $\overline{AB} \cong \overline{AC} \cong \overline{BC}$
**Prove:** ∠*A* ≅ ∠*B* ≅ ∠*C*

| Statements | Reasons |
|---|---|
| 1. $\overline{AB} \cong \overline{AC}$ | 1. Given |
| 2. ∠*B* ≅ ∠*C* | 2. ? |
| 3. | 3. |

   **F.** Triangle Sum Theorem

   **G.** ASA Congruence Criterion

   **H.** Isosceles Triangle Theorem

   **J.** CPCTC

**3.** $\overline{PN} \cong \overline{QN}$, and $\overline{MN}$ bisects ∠*PNQ*. Which congruence criterion can be used to prove △*MPN* ≅ △*MQN*?

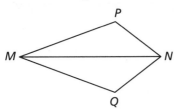

   **A.** ASA         **C.** SSA

   **B.** SAS         **D.** SSS

**4.** Which sequence of transformations maps △*RST* to △*UVW*?

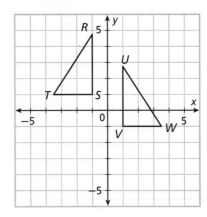

   **F.** reflection across the *x*-axis followed by a 180° rotation around the origin

   **G.** reflection across the *y*-axis followed by the translation along vector ⟨0, −2⟩

   **H.** translation along the vector ⟨−2, 0⟩ followed by a reflection across the *y*-axis

   **J.** rotation of 180° around the origin followed by a reflection across the *x*-axis

**5.** Tyrell's teacher asks him to prove or disprove that the triangle with vertices *A*(1, 1), *B*(2, 5), and *C*(6, 4) is an isosceles triangle. Which of the following should he do?

   **A.** Disprove the statement by using the distance formula to show that $\overline{AB}$, $\overline{BC}$, and $\overline{AC}$ all have different lengths.

   **B.** Prove the statement by using the distance formula to show that *AB* = *BC*.

   **C.** Prove the statement by using the distance formula to show that *AB* = *AC*.

   **D.** Prove the statement by using the distance formula to show that *BC* = *AC*.

**6.** To find the distance *AB* across a pond, you locate points as follows.

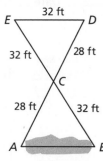

32 ft

E         D

32 ft      28 ft

C

28 ft      32 ft

A          B

Starting at *A* and walking along a straight path, you walk 28 feet and put a marker at *C*. Then you walk 28 feet farther and put a marker at *D*.

Starting at *B*, you walk to *C*, measuring the distance you walked (32 feet). Then you walk 32 feet farther and put a marker at *E*. Finally, you measure the distance from *D* to *E*, as shown. Explain how to use this information to find *AB*.

_____

_____

**7.** Determine whether the figures shown below are congruent. Explain your answer using rigid motions.

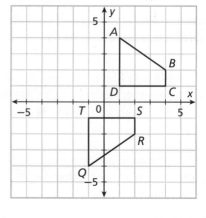

_____

_____

_____

_____

**8.** Given that $\triangle JKL \cong \triangle MNP$, use the definition of congruence in terms of rigid motions to explain why $\overline{KL}$ must be congruent to $\overline{NP}$.

_____

_____

_____

_____

**9.** You are writing a proof that the SSS Congruence Criterion follows from the definition of congruence in terms of rigid motions. You start with two triangles, $\triangle ABC$ and $\triangle DEF$, such that $\overline{AB} \cong \overline{DE}$, $\overline{BC} \cong \overline{EF}$, and $\overline{AC} \cong \overline{DF}$.

You use the fact that $\overline{AB} \cong \overline{DE}$ to conclude that there is a sequence of rigid motions that maps $\overline{AB}$ onto $\overline{DE}$. Applying this sequence of rigid motions to $\triangle ABC$ leads to this figure.

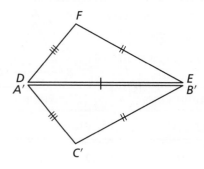

Why is $\overline{DE}$ the perpendicular bisector of $\overline{FC'}$?

_____

_____

_____

_____

_____

_____

_____

# Quadrilaterals and Polygons

## Unit Focus

At the beginning of this unit, you will apply what you know about reflections and rotations to investigate the concept of symmetry. You will also study parallelograms and explore the properties of these quadrilaterals. Your knowledge of triangle congruence criteria will be useful in proving properties of parallelograms. You will also develop criteria that can be used to show that a quadrilateral is a parallelogram and you will investigate special parallelograms, including rectangles and rhombuses.

## Unit at a Glance

COMMON CORE

UNIT 4

# Unpacking the Common Core State Standards

Use the table to help you understand the Standards for Mathematical Content that are taught in this unit. Refer to the lessons listed after each standard for exploration and practice.

| COMMON CORE Standards for Mathematical Content | What It Means For You |
|---|---|
| **CC.9-12.G.CO.3** Given a rectangle, **parallelogram, trapezoid, or regular polygon, describe the rotations and reflections that carry it onto itself.** Lesson 4-1 | You are already familiar with shapes that have symmetry. In this lesson, you will learn to discuss symmetry in terms of reflections and rotations. |
| **CC.9-12.G.CO.11 Prove theorems about parallelograms.** Lessons 4-2, 4-3, 4-4, 4-5 | A parallelogram is a quadrilateral with two pairs of parallel sides. You will investigate and prove properties involving the sides, angles, and diagonals of parallelograms, and you will develop criteria that can be used to show that a quadrilateral is a parallelogram. |
| **CC.9-12.G.SRT.5 Use congruence** and similarity **criteria for triangles to solve problems and to prove relationships in geometric figures.** Lessons 4-2, 4-3, 4-4, 4-5 | The congruence criteria for triangles that you studied in Unit 3 are useful elements in proofs about parallelograms and other quadrilaterals. You will learn how to use triangle congruence criteria in a wide range of proofs about quadrilaterals. |

UNIT 4

# Symmetry

**Essential question:** *How do you determine whether a figure has line symmetry or rotational symmetry?*

A figure has **symmetry** if there is a rigid motion such that the image of the figure coincides with the pre-image.

A figure has **line symmetry** (or *reflection symmetry*) if the figure can be reflected across a line so that the image coincides with the pre-image. In this case, the line of reflection is called the **line of symmetry**.

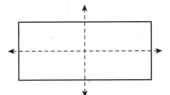

Line of symmetry

COMMON CORE

CC.9-12.G.CO.3

**1 EXAMPLE** Identifying Line Symmetry

Determine whether each figure has line symmetry. If so, draw all lines of symmetry. (Use the steps given for figure A to help you with the other figures.)

**A** Rectangle

- Trace the figure on a piece of tracing paper.

- Check to see if the figure can be folded along a straight line so that one half of the figure coincides with the other half. If so, the figure has line symmetry and the crease represents the line of symmetry.

- The rectangle has line symmetry. The two lines of symmetry are shown.

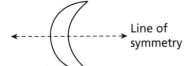

**B** Isosceles trapezoid

_____

**C** Parallelogram

**D** Regular hexagon

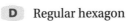

**REFLECT**

**1a.** What can you say about a triangle that has exactly one line of symmetry? Why?

_____

_____

**1b.** Does every non-straight angle have a line of symmetry? Explain.

_____

A figure has **rotational symmetry** if the figure can be rotated about a point by an angle greater than 0° and less than or equal to 180° so that the image coincides with the pre-image. The smallest angle that maps the figure onto itself is the **angle of rotational symmetry**.

Angle of rotational symmetry: 90°

**2** **EXAMPLE** **Identifying Rotational Symmetry**

Determine whether each figure has rotational symmetry. If so, give the angle of rotational symmetry. (Use the steps given for figure A to help you with the other figures.)

**A** Rectangle

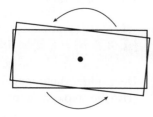

- Trace the figure on a piece of tracing paper.

- Without moving the tracing paper, firmly place the point of your pencil on the center point of the figure. Rotate the tracing paper. Check to see if the figure coincides with itself after a rotation by an angle less than or equal to 180°.

- The rectangle has rotational symmetry. The angle of rotational symmetry is 180°.

**B** Isosceles trapezoid **C** Parallelogram **D** Regular hexagon

  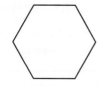

_____ _____ _____

**REFLECT**

**2a.** Is it possible for a figure to have rotational symmetry but not have line symmetry? Explain.

_____

_____

**2b.** **Error Analysis** A student claims that a figure has rotational symmetry and that the angle of rotational symmetry is 360°. Critique the student's statement.

_____

_____

© Houghton Mifflin Harcourt Publishing Company

# PRACTICE

Determine whether each figure has line symmetry. If so, draw all lines of symmetry.

**1.** Scalene triangle

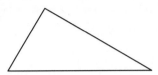

**2.** Regular pentagon

**3.** Kite

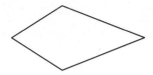

_____     _____     _____

Determine whether each figure has rotational symmetry. If so, give the angle of rotational symmetry.

**4.** Square

**5.** Isosceles triangle

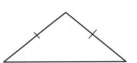

**6.** Equilateral triangle

_____     _____     _____

In the space provided, sketch a figure that has the given characteristics.

**7.** Exactly 3 lines of symmetry

**8.** No line symmetry; no rotational symmetry

**9.** Angle of rotational symmetry: 45°

**10.** A *regular n-gon* is a polygon with $n$ sides where all the sides are congruent and all the angles are congruent. For example, when $n = 4$, the regular $n$-gon is a square. When $n = 5$, the regular $n$-gon is a regular pentagon.

**a.** How many lines of symmetry does a regular $n$-gon have? _____

**b.** What is the angle of rotational symmetry for a regular $n$-gon? _____

**11.** A quadrilateral has vertices $A(4, 0)$, $B(0, 2)$, $C(-4, 0)$, and $D(0, -2)$. Describe all the reflections and rotations that map the quadrilateral onto itself.

_____

_____

© Houghton Mifflin Harcourt Publishing Company

**FOCUS ON REASONING**

# Sides and Angles of Parallelograms

**Essential question:** *What can you conclude about the sides and angles of a parallelogram?*

Recall that a *parallelogram* is a quadrilateral that has two pairs of parallel sides. You use the symbol □ to name a parallelogram. For example, the figure shows □*ABCD*.

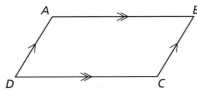

**1** **Investigate parallelograms.**

**A** Use the straightedge tool of your geometry software to draw a straight line. Then plot a point that is not on the line. Select the point and line, go to the Construct menu, and construct a line through the point that is parallel to the line. This will give you a pair of parallel lines, as shown.

**B** Repeat Step A to construct a second pair of parallel lines that intersect those from Step A.

**C** The intersections of the parallel lines create a parallelogram. Plot points at these intersections. Label the points *A, B, C,* and *D*.

**D** Use the Measure menu to measure each angle of the parallelogram.

**E** Use the Measure menu to measure the length of each side of the parallelogram. (You can do this by measuring the distance between consecutive vertices.)

**F** Drag the points and lines in your construction to change the shape of the parallelogram. As you do so, look for relationships in the measurements.

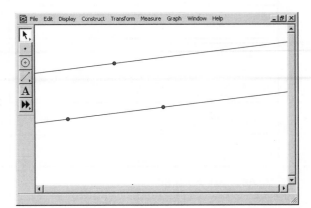

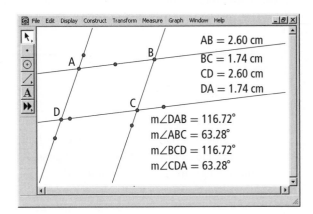

**REFLECT**

**1a.** Make a conjecture about the sides and angles of a parallelogram.

_____

_____

You may have discovered the following theorem about parallelograms.

**Theorem**

If a quadrilateral is a parallelogram, then opposite sides are congruent.

**2** **Prove that opposite sides of a parallelogram are congruent.**

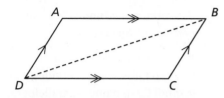

Complete the proof.

**Given:** *ABCD* is a parallelogram.

**Prove:** $\overline{AB} \cong \overline{CD}$ and $\overline{AD} \cong \overline{BC}$

| Statements | Reasons |
|---|---|
| 1. *ABCD* is a parallelogram. | 1. |
| 2. Draw $\overline{DB}$. | 2. Through any two points there exists exactly one line. |
| 3. $\overline{AB} \parallel \overline{DC}$; $\overline{AD} \parallel \overline{BC}$ | 3. |
| 4. $\angle ADB \cong \angle CBD$; $\angle ABD \cong \angle CDB$ | 4. |
| 5. $\overline{DB} \cong \overline{DB}$ | 5. |
| 6. | 6. ASA Congruence Criterion |
| 7. $AB \cong CD$; $AD \cong BC$ | 7. |

**REFLECT**

**2a.** Explain how you can use the rotational symmetry of a parallelogram to give an argument that supports the above theorem.

_____

_____

_____

**2b.** One side of a parallelogram is twice as long as another side. The perimeter of the parallelogram is 24 inches. Is it possible to find all the side lengths of the parallelogram? If so, find the lengths. If not, explain why not.

_____

_____

The angles of a parallelogram also have an important property. It is stated in the following theorem, which you will prove as an exercise.

**Theorem**

If a quadrilateral is a parallelogram, then opposite angles are congruent.

# PRACTICE

1. Prove the above theorem about opposite angles of a parallelogram.

   **Given:** *ABCD* is a parallelogram.
   **Prove:** ∠A ≅ ∠C and ∠B ≅ ∠D

   (*Hint:* You only need to prove that ∠A ≅ ∠C. A similar argument can be used to prove that ∠B ≅ ∠D. Also, you may or may not need to use all the rows of the table in your proof.)

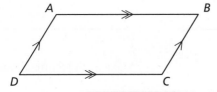

| Statements | Reasons |
|---|---|
| 1. | 1. |
| 2. | 2. |
| 3. | 3. |
| 4. | 4. |
| 5. | 5. |
| 6. | 6. |
| 7. | 7. |

2. Explain why consecutive angles of a parallelogram are supplementary.

   _____

   _____

   _____

3. In the figure, *JKLM* is a parallelogram. Find the measure of each of the numbered angles.

   _____

   _____

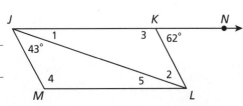

© Houghton Mifflin Harcourt Publishing Company

**4.** A city planner is designing a park in the shape of a parallelogram. As shown in the figure, there will be two straight paths through which visitors may enter the park. The paths are bisectors of consecutive angles of the parallelogram, and the paths intersect at point *P*.

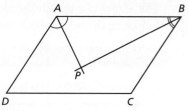

**a.** Work directly on the parallelograms below and use a compass and straightedge to construct the bisectors of ∠A and ∠B. Then use a protractor to measure ∠APB in each case.

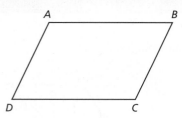 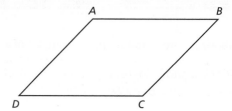

Make a conjecture about ∠APB.

_____

**b.** Write a paragraph proof to show that your conjecture is always true. (*Hint:* Suppose m∠BAP = x°, m∠ABP = y°, and m∠APB = z°. What do you know about x + y + z? What do you know about 2x + 2y?)

_____

_____

_____

_____

**c.** When the city planner takes into account the dimensions of the park, she finds that point *P* lies on $\overline{DC}$, as shown. Explain why it must be the case that DC = 2AD. (*Hint:* Use congruent base angles to show that △DAP and △CPB are isosceles.)

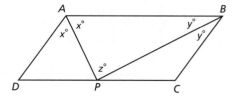

_____

_____

_____

_____

_____

## FOCUS ON REASONING
# Diagonals of Parallelograms

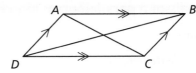

CC.9-12.G.CO.11, CC.9-12.G.SRT.5

**Essential question:** *What can you conclude about the diagonals of a parallelogram?*

A segment that connects any two nonconsecutive vertices of a polygon is a **diagonal**. A parallelogram has two diagonals. In the figure, $\overline{AC}$ and $\overline{BD}$ are diagonals of $\square ABCD$.

**1** **Investigate diagonals of parallelograms.**

**A** Use geometry software to construct a parallelogram. (See Lesson 4-2 for detailed instructions.) Label the vertices of the parallelogram *A*, *B*, *C*, and *D*.

**B** Use the segment tool to construct the diagonals, $\overline{AC}$ and $\overline{BD}$.

**C** Plot a point at the intersection of the diagonals. Label this point *E*.

**D** Use the Measure menu to measure the length of $\overline{AE}$, $\overline{BE}$, $\overline{CE}$, and $\overline{DE}$. (You can do this by measuring the distance between the relevant endpoints.)

**E** Drag the points and lines in your construction to change the shape of the parallelogram. As you do so, look for relationships in the measurements.

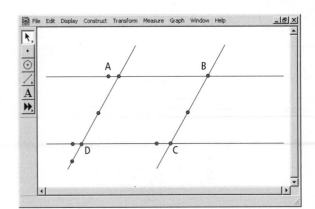

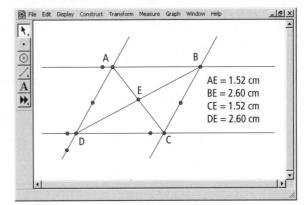

**REFLECT**

**1a.** Make a conjecture about the diagonals of a parallelogram.

_____

**1b.** A student claims that the perimeter of $\triangle AEB$ is always equal to the perimeter of $\triangle CED$. Without doing any further measurements in your construction, explain whether or not you agree with the student's statement.

_____

_____

You may have discovered the following theorem about parallelograms.

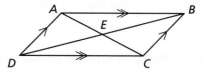

**Theorem**

If a quadrilateral is a parallelogram, then the diagonals bisect each other.

**2** **Prove diagonals of a parallelogram bisect each other.**

Complete the proof.

Given: ABCD is a parallelogram.

Prove: $\overline{AE} \cong \overline{CE}$ and $\overline{BE} \cong \overline{DE}$.

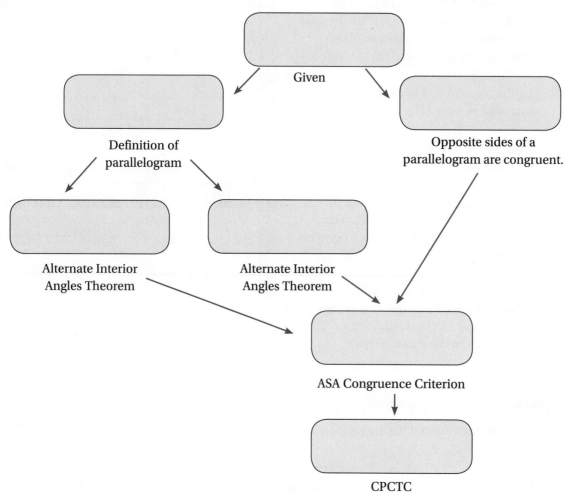

Given

Definition of
parallelogram

Opposite sides of a
parallelogram are congruent.

Alternate Interior
Angles Theorem

Alternate Interior
Angles Theorem

ASA Congruence Criterion

CPCTC

© Houghton Mifflin Harcourt Publishing Company

**REFLECT**

**2a.** Explain how you can prove the theorem using a different congruence criterion.

_____

_____

_____

# Criteria for Parallelograms

**Essential question:** *What criteria can you use to prove that a quadrilateral is a parallelogram?*

COMMON CORE

CC.9-12.G.CO.11,
CC.9-12.G.SRT.5

The converses of the theorems you developed in the last two lessons are all true. These provide several criteria that can be used to prove that a quadrilateral is a parallelogram.

**Opposite Sides Criterion for a Parallelogram**

If both pairs of opposite sides of a quadrilateral are congruent, then the quadrilateral is a parallelogram.

**1 PROOF**    **Opposite Sides Criterion for a Parallelogram**

Complete the proof.

**Given:** $\overline{AB} \cong \overline{DC}$ and $\overline{AD} \cong \overline{BC}$

**Prove:** *ABCD* is a parallelogram.

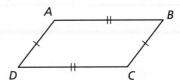

| Statements | Reasons |
|---|---|
| **1.** Draw $\overline{DB}$. | **1.** Through any two points there exists exactly one line. |
| **2.** $\overline{DB} \cong \overline{DB}$ | **2.** |
| **3.** $\overline{AB} \cong \overline{DC}$; $\overline{AD} \cong \overline{BC}$ | **3.** |
| **4.** | **4.** SSS Congruence Criterion |
| **5.** $\angle ABD \cong \angle CDB$; $\angle ADB \cong \angle CBD$ | **5.** |
| **6.** $\overline{AB} \parallel \overline{DC}$ ; $\overline{AD} \parallel \overline{BC}$ | **6.** |
| **7.** *ABCD* is a parallelogram. | **7.** |

**REFLECT**

**1a.** A quadrilateral has two sides that are 3 cm long and two sides that are 5 cm long. A student states that the quadrilateral must be a parallelogram. Do you agree? Why or why not?

_____

_____

## 2 PROOF    Opposite Angles Criterion for a Parallelogram

Complete the paragraph proof.

**Given:** $\angle A \cong \angle C$ and $\angle B \cong \angle D$.

**Prove:** $ABCD$ is a parallelogram.

$m\angle A + m\angle B + m\angle C + m\angle D = 360°$ by _____.

From the given information, $m\angle A = m\angle C$ and $m\angle B = m\angle D$. By substitution,

$m\angle A + m\angle D + m\angle A + m\angle D = 360°$ or $2m\angle A + 2m\angle D = 360°$. Dividing both

sides by 2 gives _____.

Therefore, $\angle A$ and $\angle D$ are supplementary and so $\overline{AB} \parallel \overline{DC}$ by

_____. A similar

argument shows that $\overline{AD} \parallel \overline{BC}$, so $ABCD$ is a parallelogram by definition.

> **REFLECT**

**2a.** What property or theorem justifies dividing both sides of the equation by 2 in the above proof?

_____

# PRACTICE

**1.** Write a paragraph proof for the following.

> **Bisecting Diagonals Criterion for a Parallelogram**

If the diagonals of a quadrilateral bisect each other, then the quadrilateral is a parallelogram.

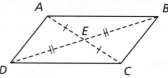

_____

_____

_____

_____

© Houghton Mifflin Harcourt Publishing Company

## FOCUS ON REASONING
# Special Parallelograms

**Essential question:** *What are the properties of rectangles and rhombuses?*

A **rectangle** is a quadrilateral with four right angles. The figure shows rectangle *ABCD*.

**1** **Investigate properties of rectangles.**

**A** Use a tile or pattern block and the following method to draw three different rectangles on a separate sheet of paper.

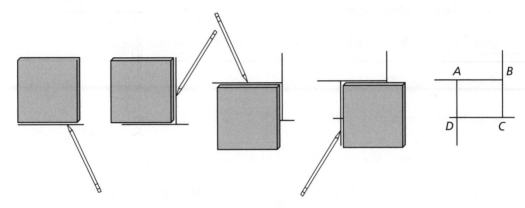

**B** Use a ruler to measure the sides and the diagonals of each rectangle. Keep track of the measurements and compare your results to those of other students.

**REFLECT**

**1a.** Why does the above method produce a rectangle? What must you assume about the tile?

_____

_____

_____

**1b.** Do you think every rectangle is a parallelogram? Make a conjecture based upon your measurements and explain your thinking.

_____

_____

**1c.** Make a conjecture about the diagonals of a rectangle.

_____

You may have discovered the following theorem about rectangles.

> ### Rectangle Theorem
>
> A rectangle is a parallelogram with congruent diagonals.

In order to prove the above theorem, it is convenient to use a theorem that states that all right angles are congruent. The proof of this theorem is straightforward: If $\angle X$ and $\angle Y$ are right angles, then $m\angle X = 90°$ and $m\angle Y = 90°$ so $m\angle X = m\angle Y$ and $\angle X \cong \angle Y$.

**2** **Prove the Rectangle Theorem.**

Complete the proof.

**Given:** $ABCD$ is a rectangle.
**Prove:** $ABCD$ is a parallelogram; $\overline{AC} \cong \overline{BD}$.

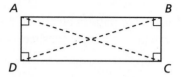

**A**   First prove that $ABCD$ is a parallelogram. Since $ABCD$ is a rectangle, $\angle A$ and

$\angle C$ are right angles. So, $\angle A \cong \angle C$ because _____.

By similar reasoning, $\angle B \cong \angle D$. Therefore, $ABCD$ is a parallelogram by

_____.

**B**   Now prove that the diagonals are congruent. Since $ABCD$ is a parallelogram,

$\overline{AD} \cong \overline{BC}$ because _____.

Also, $\overline{DC} \cong \overline{DC}$ by the reflexive property of congruence. By the definition

of a rectangle, $\angle D$ and $\angle C$ are right angles, and so $\angle D \cong \angle C$ because

all right angles are congruent.

Therefore, $\triangle ADC \cong \triangle BCD$ by _____

and $\overline{AC} \cong \overline{BD}$ by _____.

> **REFLECT**

**2a.** **Error Analysis** A student says you can also prove the diagonals are congruent by
using the SSS Congruence Criterion to show that $\triangle ADC \cong \triangle BCD$. Do you
agree? Explain.

_____

_____

© Houghton Mifflin Harcourt Publishing Company

A **rhombus** is a quadrilateral with four congruent sides. The figure shows rhombus *JKLM*.

The following is a summary of some properties of rhombuses. You will prove these properties below and in the exercises.

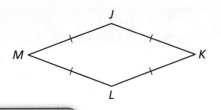

### Properties of Rhombuses

If a quadrilateral is a rhombus, then
• the quadrilateral is a parallelogram.
• the diagonals are perpendicular.
• each diagonal bisects a pair of opposite angles.

The proof of the first property is straightforward. If a quadrilateral is a rhombus, then opposite sides are congruent. Therefore, the quadrilateral is also a parallelogram by the Opposite Sides Criterion for a Parallelogram.

**3** **Prove diagonals of a rhombus are perpendicular.**

Complete the proof.

**Given:** *JKLM* is a rhombus.
**Prove:** $\overline{JL} \perp \overline{MK}$

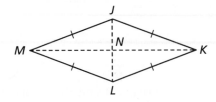

Since *JKLM* is a rhombus, $\overline{JM} \cong \overline{JK}$. Because *JKLM* is also a parallelogram,

$\overline{MN} \cong \overline{KN}$ because _____.

By the Reflexive Property of Congruence, $\overline{JN} \cong \overline{JN}$, so _____

by the SSS Congruence Criterion. So, $\angle JNM \cong \angle JNK$ by _____.

By the Linear Pair Theorem, $\angle JNM$ and $\angle JNK$ are _____.

This means m$\angle JNM$ + m$\angle JNK$ = 180°.

Since the angles are congruent, m$\angle JNM$ = _____

so m$\angle JNK$ + m$\angle JNK$ = 180° or 2m$\angle JNK$ = 180°. Therefore, m$\angle JNK$ = 90°

and $\overline{JL} \perp \overline{MK}$.

**REFLECT**

**3a.** What can you say about the image of *J* after a reflection across $\overline{MK}$? Why?

_____

1. Prove the converse of the Rectangle Theorem. That is, if a parallelogram has congruent diagonals, then the parallelogram is a rectangle.

   **Given:** *ABCD* is a parallelogram; $\overline{AC} \cong \overline{BD}$.
   **Prove:** *ABCD* is a rectangle.

   _____

   _____

   _____

   _____

   _____

   _____

   _____

2. Prove that if a quadrilateral is a rhombus, then each diagonal bisects a pair of opposite angles.

   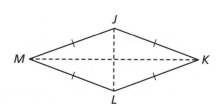

   **Given:** *JKLM* is a rhombus.
   **Prove:** $\overline{MK}$ bisects ∠*JML* and ∠*JKL*;
   $\overline{JL}$ bisects ∠*MJK* and ∠*MLK*.

   _____

   _____

   _____

   _____

   _____

3. A *square* is a quadrilateral with four right angles and four congruent sides. In the space at right, draw a Venn diagram to show how squares, rectangles, rhombuses, and parallelograms are related to each other.

Name _____ Class _____ Date _____

## MULTIPLE CHOICE

**1.** Which of the following figures has an angle of rotational symmetry of 90°?

**A.**

**B.**

**C.**

**D.**

**2.** Ming is proving that opposite sides of a parallelogram are congruent. He begins as shown. Which reason should he use for Step 3?

**Given:** *PQRS* is a parallelogram
**Prove:** $\overline{PQ} \cong \overline{RS}$; $\overline{PS} \cong \overline{QR}$

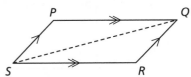

| Statements | Reasons |
|---|---|
| 1. *PQRS* is a parallelogram | 1. Given |
| 2. Draw $\overline{SQ}$. | 2. Through 2 pts. there is exactly one line. |
| 3. $\overline{PQ} \parallel \overline{RS}$; $\overline{PS} \parallel \overline{QR}$ | 3. ? |

**F.** Definition of parallelogram

**G.** Alternate Interior Angles Theorem

**H.** Reflexive Property of Congruence

**J.** CPCTC

**3.** *DEFG* is a rhombus. You want to prove the property that a diagonal of a rhombus bisects a pair of opposite angles. To prove that $\overrightarrow{DF}$ bisects $\angle GDE$, you first show that $\triangle GDF \cong \triangle EDF$ using the definition of rhombus, the Reflexive Property of Congruence, and the SSS Congruence Criterion. What other reasons are needed to complete the proof?

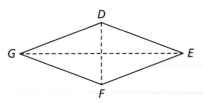

**A.** Isosceles Triangle Theorem; SAS Congruence Criterion

**B.** Definition of perpendicular; Triangle Sum Theorem

**C.** If a quadrilateral is a parallelogram, then opposite angles are congruent; definition of angle bisector

**D.** Congruent Parts of Congruent Triangles are Congruent; definition of angle bisector

**4.** Which is the best description of the symmetry of this regular pentagon?

**F.** has neither line symmetry nor rotational symmetry

**G.** has line symmetry but not rotational symmetry

**H.** has rotational symmetry but not line symmetry

**J.** has both line symmetry and rotational symmetry

## FREE RESPONSE

**5.** In the space below, draw an example of a trapezoid that does *not* have line symmetry.

**6.** In the space below, draw an example of a parallelogram that has exactly two lines of symmetry. Draw the lines of symmetry. Then give the most specific name for the parallelogram you drew.

**7.** Rosa is using the figure below to prove that the diagonals of a parallelogram bisect each other. She starts by stating that $\overline{LM} \cong \overline{PN}$ since opposite sides of a parallelogram are congruent. What should she do next in order to show that $\triangle LQM \cong \triangle NQP$? What congruence criterion will she use?

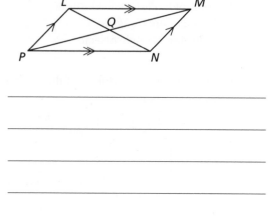

_____

_____

_____

_____

_____

_____

**8.** Prove the following. You may not need all the rows of the table in your proof.

**Given:** *ABCD* is a rectangle. $\overline{AE} \cong \overline{FB}$
**Prove:** $\triangle DAF \cong \triangle CBE$

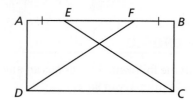

| Statements | Reasons |
|---|---|
| 1. | 1. |
| 2. | 2. |
| 3. | 3. |
| 4. | 4. |
| 5. | 5. |
| 6. | 6. |
| 7. | 7. |
| 8. | 8. |

# Transformations and Similarity

## Unit Focus

Informally speaking, two figures are similar if they have the same shape, but not necessarily the same size. In this unit, you will put this idea into mathematical terms. To do so, you will first study a new transformation, the dilation. Then you will see how to define similarity in terms of transformations. As you did with congruence, you will develop criteria that can be used to show that two triangles are similar. Then you will apply similarity to a wide range of real-world problems and mathematical theorems.

## Unit at a Glance

COMMON CORE

| Lesson | Standards for Mathematical Content |
|---|---|
| 5-1 Properties of Dilations | CC.9-12.G.SRT.1, CC.9-12.G.CO.2 |
| 5-2 Drawing Dilations | CC.9-12.G.CO.2 |
| 5-3 Similarity | CC.9-12.G.SRT.2, CC.9-12.G.C.1 |
| 5-4 Similarity and Triangles | CC.9-12.G.SRT.2, CC.9-12.G.SRT.3 |
| 5-5 Solving Problems Using Similarity | CC.9-12.G.SRT.5, CC.9-12.G.MG.3* |
| 5-6 The Triangle Proportionality Theorem | CC.9-12.G.SRT.4, CC.9-12.G.SRT.5 |
| 5-7 Proving the Pythagorean Theorem | CC.9-12.G.SRT.4, CC.9-12.G.SRT.5 |
| Test Prep | |

UNIT 5

# Unpacking the Common Core State Standards

Use the table to help you understand the Standards for Mathematical Content that are taught in this unit. Refer to the lessons listed after each standard for exploration and practice.

| COMMON CORE Standards for Mathematical Content | What It Means For You |
|---|---|
| **CC.9-12.G.CO.2** Represent transformations in the plane using, e.g., transparencies and geometry software; describe transformations as functions that take points in the plane as inputs and give other points as outputs. Compare transformations that preserve distance and angle to those that do not (e.g., translation versus horizontal stretch). Lessons 5-1, 5-2 | You have already worked with reflections, translations, and rotations. Now you will learn to draw and represent a new transformation, called a dilation. As you work with dilations, you will compare them to reflections, translations, and rotations. |
| **CC.9-12.G.SRT.1** Verify experimentally the properties of dilations given by a center and a scale factor: <br> a. A dilation takes a line not passing through the center of the dilation to a parallel line, and leaves a line passing through the center unchanged. <br> b. The dilation of a line segment is longer or shorter in the ratio given by the scale factor. Lesson 5-1 | You will use geometry software to explore properties of dilations. In particular, you will investigate how dilations affect lines and line segments. |
| **CC.9-12.G.SRT.2** Given two figures, use the definition of similarity in terms of similarity transformations to decide if they are similar; explain using similarity transformations the meaning of similarity for triangles as the equality of all corresponding pairs of angles and the proportionality of all corresponding pairs of sides. Lessons 5-3, 5-4 | As you will see, the definition of similar figures is based on transformations. You will use this definition to determine whether two given figures are similar. You will also use this definition to help you draw conclusions about similar triangles. |
| **CC.9-12.G.SRT.3** Use the properties of similarity transformations to establish the AA criterion for two triangles to be similar. Lesson 5-4 | Just as you did with congruence, you will develop "shortcuts" that you can use to prove that two triangles are similar. |
| **CC.9-12.G.SRT.4** Prove theorems about triangles. Lessons 5-6, 5-7 | Once you are familiar with similarity criteria for triangles, you will apply the criteria to prove theorems about proportions in triangles. |
| **CC.9-12.G.SRT.5** Use congruence and similarity criteria for triangles to solve problems and to prove relationships in geometric figures. Lessons 5-5, 5-6, 5-7 | You will see how similarity can be used to solve a variety of mathematics and real-world problems. |

| COMMON CORE Standards for Mathematical Content | What It Means For You |
|---|---|
| **CC.9-12.G.C.1 Prove that all circles are similar.** Lesson 5-3 | You will use what you learn about similarity to prove that all circles are similar. |
| **CC.9-12.G.MG.3 Apply geometric methods to solve design problems** (e.g., designing an object or structure to satisfy physical constraints or minimize cost; **working with typographic grid systems based on ratios).*** Lesson 5-5 | A typographic grid system is a tool that graphic designers use to prepare page layouts. You can apply similarity to help create a typographic grid system. |

UNIT 5

# Properties of Dilations

COMMON CORE

CC.9-12.G.SRT.1,
CC.9-12.G.CO.2

**Essential question:** *What are the key properties of dilations?*

You have already worked extensively with three transformations: reflections, translations, and rotations. Now you will focus on a fourth type of transformation: dilations. Dilations are defined as follows.

Let $O$ be a point and let $k$ be a positive real number. For any point $P$, let $D(P) = P'$, where $P'$ is the point on $\overrightarrow{OP}$ such that $OP' = k \cdot OP$. Then $D$ is the **dilation** with **center of dilation** $O$ and **scale factor** $k$. If necessary, the center of dilation and scale factor can be included in the function notation by writing $D_{O,k}(P) = P'$.

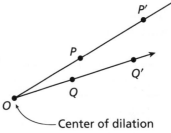

The figure shows a dilation with scale factor 2 because $OP' = 2OP$ and $OQ' = 2OQ$.

**1  EXPLORE**  Investigating Dilations

A  Use geometry software to plot a point. Label the point $O$. Then construct a triangle and label the vertices $P$, $Q$, and $R$.

B  Select point $O$. Go to the Transform menu and choose Mark Center. This makes point $O$ the center of a dilation.

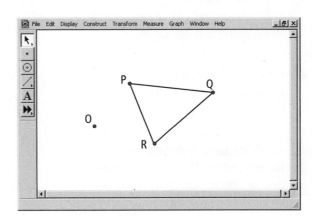

C  Select $\triangle PQR$. Go to the Transform menu and choose Dilate. In the pop-up window, the "fixed ratio" is the scale factor $k$. Enter a scale factor of 2 and click the Dilate button.

D  Label the image of $\triangle PQR$ as $\triangle P'Q'R'$. Compare the image to the pre-image. Change the shape of $\triangle PQR$ and observe the results.

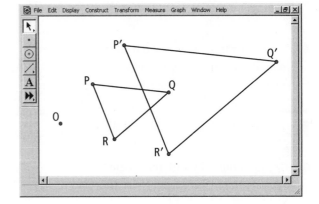

E  Experiment with dilations that have different scale factors. Be sure to try scale factors less than 1, equal to 1, and greater than 1.

**1a.** In general, how does a dilation transform a figure?

_____

**1b.** Do you think dilations are rigid motions? Why or why not?

_____

_____

**1c.** How does the value of $k$ affect a dilation? What can you say about a dilation when $0 < k < 1$? when $k > 1$?

_____

_____

## 2 EXPLORE  Investigating Properties of Dilations

**A** Use geometry software to plot a point. Label the point O. Then construct a straight line and label it $m$.

**B** Construct the image of line $m$ under a dilation with center O and scale factor 2.

**C** Try dilations with different scale factors and try dragging the line to new positions. Notice what happens when the line passes through O.

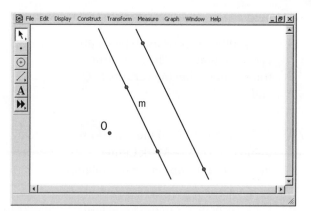

**D** Delete the line and its image. Construct a segment, $\overline{AB}$.

**E** Construct the image of $\overline{AB}$ under a dilation with center O and scale factor 2. Label the image $\overline{A'B'}$.

**F** Measure the length of $\overline{AB}$ and $\overline{A'B'}$.

**G** Try dilations with different scale factors. In each case, compare the lengths of $\overline{AB}$ and $\overline{A'B'}$.

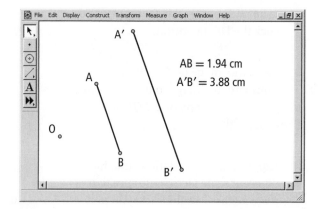

**2a.** What can you say about the image of a straight line under a dilation? Does your answer depend upon the location of the line? Explain.

_____

_____

_____

**2b.** How is the length of a line segment related to the length of its image under a dilation with scale factor $k$?

_____

_____

You may have discovered that dilations preserve the shape, but not the size, of figures. The following summary describes the key properties of dilations.

### Properties of Dilations

- Dilations preserve angle measure.

- Dilations preserve betweenness.

- Dilations preserve collinearity.

- A dilation maps a line not passing through the center of dilation to a parallel line and leaves a line passing through the center unchanged.

- The dilation of a line segment is longer or shorter in the ratio given by the scale factor.

# PRACTICE

**1.** The figure shows the image $A'$ of point $A$ under a dilation with center $O$. Explain how you can use a ruler to find the scale factor of the dilation. Then find the scale factor.

_____

_____

**2.** Compare dilations to rigid motions. How are they similar? How are they different?

_____

_____

**3.** Describe the effect of a dilation with scale factor 1.

_____

# Drawing Dilations

COMMON
CORE

CC.9-12.G.CO.2

**Essential question:** *How do you draw the image of a figure under a dilation?*

You have already used geometry software to draw the image
of a figure under a dilation. The following example shows how
to construct the image using a compass and straightedge.

**1** **EXAMPLE**  **Constructing a Dilation Image**

Work directly on the figure below and follow the given steps to construct the
image of $\triangle ABC$ after a dilation with center of dilation $O$ and scale factor 3.

**A**  Use a straightedge to draw $\overrightarrow{OA}$.

**B**  Place the point of your compass on
point $O$ and open the compass to the
distance $OA$.

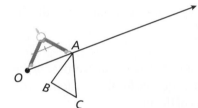

**C**  Without adjusting the compass, place
the point of the compass on point $A$
and make an arc that intersects $\overrightarrow{OA}$.

**D**  Move the compass to the point of
intersection of the arc and the ray.
Make another arc that intersects $\overrightarrow{OA}$.
Label this point of intersection $A'$.

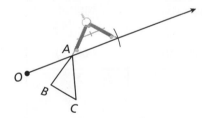

**E**  Repeat the steps for the other vertices
of $\triangle ABC$.

**F**  Once you have located $A'$, $B'$, and $C'$,
use a straightedge to draw $\triangle A'B'C'$.

**1a.** Explain how you can you use a ruler to check your construction.

_____

_____

**1b.** Without using a protractor, how does m∠OAB compare to m∠OA′B′? Why?

_____

**1c.** How can you change the construction to draw the image of △ABC after a dilation with center of dilation O and scale factor $\frac{1}{2}$?

_____

_____

When you work with dilations in the coordinate plane, you can assume the center of dilation is the origin. To find the image of a point after a dilation with scale factor $k$, multiply each coordinate of the point by $k$. Using coordinate notation, a dilation with scale factor $k$ is written as follows: $(x, y) \rightarrow (kx, ky)$.

## 2 EXAMPLE   Drawing a Dilation in a Coordinate Plane

Draw the image of the pentagon after a dilation with scale factor $\frac{3}{2}$.

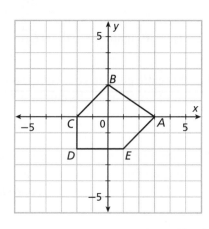

**A** In the table below, list the vertices of the pentagon. Then use the rule for the dilation to write the vertices of the image.

| Pre-Image (x, y) | Image $\left(\frac{3}{2}x, \frac{3}{2}y\right)$ |
|---|---|
| A(3, 0) | A′(4$\frac{1}{2}$, 0) |
| B(0, 2) |  |
|  |  |
|  |  |
|  |  |

**B** Plot the vertices of the image. Connect the vertices to complete the image.

**2a.** Explain how to use the distance formula to check that $\overline{B'C'}$ is the correct length.

_____

_____

**2b.** A student claims that under a dilation centered at the origin with scale factor $k$, a point and its image always lie in the same quadrant. Do you agree or disagree? Explain.

_____

_____

_____

# PRACTICE

**Use a compass and straightedge to construct the image of the figure after a dilation with center _O_ and the given scale factor. Label the vertices of the image.**

**1.** scale factor: 4

$O \bullet$

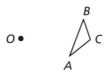

**2.** scale factor: $\frac{1}{2}$

$O \bullet$

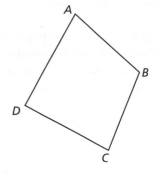

**Draw the image of the figure after a dilation with the given scale factor.**

**3.** scale factor: 2

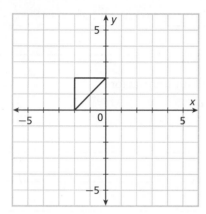

**4.** scale factor: $\frac{1}{4}$

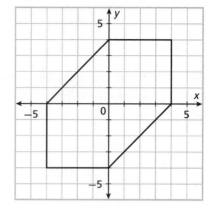

**5.** scale factor: $\frac{2}{3}$

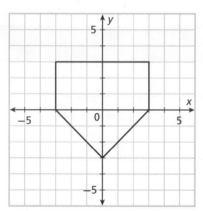

**6.** scale factor: 3

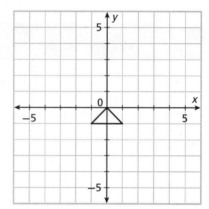

**7.** △A′B′C′ is the image of △ABC under a dilation. Explain how you can use a straightedge to find the center of dilation. Then use your method to draw a dot at the center of dilation.

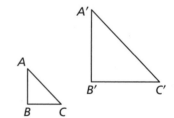

_____

_____

**8.** Each centimeter on scale drawing of a park represents three meters of actual distance. What is the scale factor of the dilation that maps the park to the scale drawing? _____

**9. Error Analysis** A student claims that a dilation with scale factor *m* and center of dilation *O* that is followed by a dilation with scale factor *n* and center of dilation *O* is equivalent to a single dilation with scale factor *m* + *n* and center of dilation *O*. Do you agree or disagree? Explain.

_____

_____

_____

# Similarity

COMMON
CORE

CC.9-12.G.SRT.2,
CC.9-12.G.C.1

**Essential question:** *What does it mean for two figures to be similar?*

## 1 ENGAGE   Introducing Similarity

A **similarity transformation** is a transformation in which the image has the same shape as the pre-image. Specifically, the similarity transformations are the rigid motions (reflections, translations, and rotations) as well as dilations.

Two plane figures are **similar** if and only if one can be obtained from the other by similarity transformations (that is, by a sequence of reflections, translations, rotations, and/or dilations).

The symbol for similar is ~. As with congruence, it is customary to write a similarity statement so that corresponding vertices of the figures are listed in the same order. In the figure below, $\triangle A'B'C'$ is the image of $\triangle ABC$ after a dilation with center $O$ and scale factor 2. Since a dilation is a similarity transformation, the two triangles are similar and you write $\triangle ABC \sim \triangle A'B'C'$.

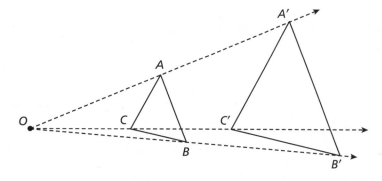

### REFLECT

**1a.** Explain why congruence can be considered a special case of similarity.

_____

_____

**1b.** If you know that two figures are similar, can you conclude that corresponding angles are congruent? Why or why not?

_____

_____

**1c.** Given that $\triangle RST \sim \triangle R'S'T'$, can you conclude that $\overline{RS} \cong \overline{R'S'}$? Explain.

_____

_____

Use the definition of similarity in terms of similarity transformations to determine whether the two figures are similar. Explain your answer.

**A**   △*JKL* and △*MNP* have different angle measures.

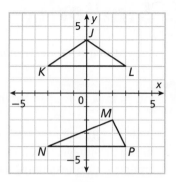

Since similarity transformations preserve angle measure, there is no sequence of similarity transformations that will map △*JKL* to △*MNP*.

Therefore, _____.

**B**   You can map △*RST* to △*XYZ* by the dilation that has the coordinate notation

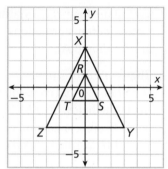

_____.

A dilation is a similarity transformation.

Therefore, _____.

**C**   You can map *ABCD* to *EFGH* by the dilation that has the coordinate notation

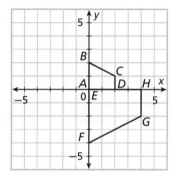

_____.

followed by the reflection that has the coordinate notation

_____.

Dilations and reflections are similarity transformations.

Therefore, _____.

**2a.** In Part B above, how can you show that the triangles are similar using a different similarity transformation?

_____

**2b.** In Part C above, does the order in which you perform the similarity transformations matter? Explain.

_____

_____

You can use the definition of similarity to prove theorems about figures.

> **Theorem**
>
> All circles are similar.

## 3 PROOF     All Circles Are Similar

Complete the proof.

**Given:** Circle $C$ with center $C$ and radius $r$;
circle $D$ with center $D$ and radius $s$.

**Prove:** Circle $C$ is similar to circle $D$.

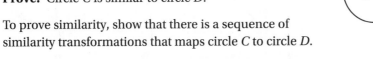

To prove similarity, show that there is a sequence of
similarity transformations that maps circle $C$ to circle $D$.

**A** First, transform circle $C$ with the translation
along the vector $\overrightarrow{CD}$.

Under this translation, the image
of point $C$ is _____.

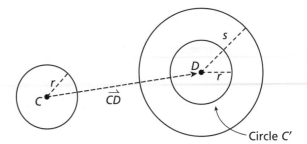

Circle $C'$

Let the image of circle $C$ be circle $C'$.
The center of circle $C'$ must lie at point
_____.

**B** Now, transform circle $C'$ with the dilation that has center of dilation $D$ and
scale factor $\frac{s}{r}$.

Circle $C'$ consists of all points at distance _____ from point $D$.

After the dilation, the image of circle $C'$ consists of all points at distance

_____ from point $D$. But these are exactly the points that form circle $D$.

Therefore, the translation followed by the dilation maps circle $C$ to circle $D$.

Since translations and dilations are _____,

you can conclude that _____.

> **REFLECT**

**3a.** Explain how to use a reflection and a dilation to prove that circle $C$ is similar to
circle $D$.

_____

_____

Use the definition of similarity in terms of similarity transformations to determine whether the two figures are similar. Explain your answer.

**1.**

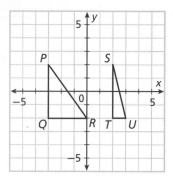

_____

_____

_____

_____

**2.**

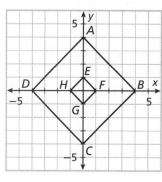

_____

_____

_____

_____

**3.**

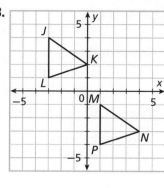

_____

_____

_____

_____

**4.**

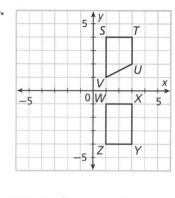

_____

_____

_____

_____

_____

_____

**5.**

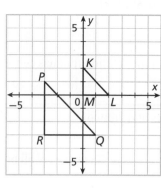

_____

_____

_____

_____

_____

_____

**6.**

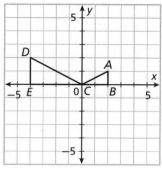

_____

_____

_____

_____

_____

_____

**7.** Given that △GMX ∼ △DPW, write as many congruence statements as possible about the sides and/or angles of the triangles.

_____

# Similarity and Triangles

COMMON
CORE

CC.9-12.G.SRT.2,
CC.9-12.G.SRT.3

**Essential question:** *What can you conclude about similar triangles and how can you prove triangles are similar?*

**1  ENGAGE**   **Applying Similarity to Triangles**

Recall that when two figures are similar, there is a sequence of similarity transformations that maps one figure to the other. In particular, given $\triangle ABC \sim \triangle DEF$, you can first apply a dilation to $\triangle ABC$ to make both triangles the same size. Then you can apply a sequence of rigid motions to the dilated image of $\triangle ABC$ to map it to $\triangle DEF$.

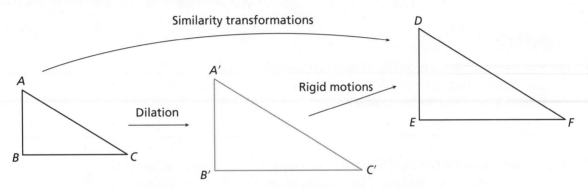

Because the similarity transformations that map $\triangle ABC$ to $\triangle DEF$ preserve angle measure, you can say that corresponding angles are congruent. Thus, $\triangle ABC \sim \triangle DEF$ implies $\angle A \cong \angle D$, $\angle B \cong \angle E$, and $\angle C \cong \angle F$.

Also, the initial dilation that makes the two triangles the same size shows that each side of $\triangle DEF$ is longer or shorter than the corresponding side of $\triangle ABC$ by the ratio given by the scale factor. Assuming the dilation has scale factor $k$, this means that $DE = k \cdot AB$, $EF = k \cdot BC$, and $DF = k \cdot AC$.

Solving for $k$ in these equations gives $k = \frac{DE}{AB}$, $k = \frac{EF}{BC}$, and $k = \frac{DF}{AC}$.

This shows that corresponding sides are proportional. That is, $\frac{DE}{AB} = \frac{EF}{BC} = \frac{DF}{AC}$.

**REFLECT**

**1a.** Is triangle similarity transitive? That is, if $\triangle ABC \sim \triangle DEF$ and $\triangle DEF \sim \triangle GHK$, can you conclude that $\triangle ABC \sim \triangle GHK$? Explain.

_____

_____

_____

Given that $\triangle RST \sim \triangle UVW$, write congruence statements for the corresponding angles and proportions for the corresponding sides.

**A**   Corresponding angles are listed in the same position in each triangle name.

$\angle R \cong \angle U,$ _____ , _____

**B**   Corresponding sides are pairs of letters in the same position in each triangle name.

$\dfrac{UV}{RS} =$ _____

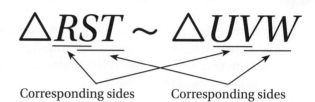

Corresponding sides      Corresponding sides

**REFLECT**

**2a.** Suppose the scale factor of the dilation in the sequence of similarity transformations that maps $\triangle RST$ to $\triangle UVW$ is 4 and suppose $RS = 8$ mm. Explain how to find the length of $\overline{UV}$.

_____

**2b.** A student identified $\overline{RS}$ and $\overline{UV}$ as a pair of corresponding sides and $\overline{ST}$ and $\overline{VW}$ as a pair of corresponding sides. The student wrote $\dfrac{RS}{UV} = \dfrac{VW}{ST}$. Is this a correct proportion? Why or why not? If the proportion is not correct, explain how to write correctly.

_____

_____

You have seen that when two triangles are similar, corresponding angles are congruent and corresponding sides are proportional. The converse is also true. That is, if you are given two triangles and you know that the corresponding angles are congruent and corresponding sides are proportional, you can conclude that the triangles are similar.

As with congruence, there are some "shortcuts" that make it a bit easier to prove that two triangles are congruent. The most important of these is known as the AA Similarity Criterion.

### AA Similarity Criterion

If two angles of one triangle are congruent to two angles of another triangle, then the triangles are similar.

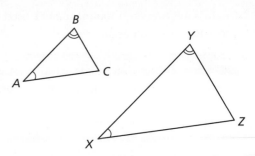

**Given:** $\angle A \cong \angle X$ and $\angle B \cong \angle Y$
**Prove:** $\triangle ABC \sim \triangle XYZ$

To prove the triangles are similar, you will find a sequence of similarity transformations that maps $\triangle ABC$ to $\triangle XYZ$. Complete the following steps of the proof.

**A** Apply a dilation to $\triangle ABC$ with scale factor $k = \frac{XY}{AB}$. Let the image of $\triangle ABC$ be $\triangle A'B'C'$.

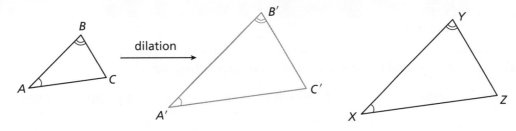

$\triangle A'B'C'$ is similar to $\triangle ABC$, and $\angle A' \cong$ _____ and $\angle B' \cong$ _____

because _____.

Also, $A'B' = k \cdot AB =$ _____.

**B** It is given that $\angle A \cong \angle X$ and $\angle B \cong \angle Y$.

By the Transitive Property of Congruence, $\angle A' \cong$ _____ and $\angle B' \cong$ _____.

So, $\triangle A'B'C' \cong \triangle XYZ$ by _____.

This means there is a sequence of rigid motions that maps $\triangle A'B'C'$ to $\triangle XYZ$.

The dilation followed by this sequence of rigid motions shows that there is a sequence of similarity transformations that maps $\triangle ABC$ to $\triangle XYZ$. Therefore, $\triangle ABC \sim \triangle XYZ$.

**REFLECT**

**3a.** In $\triangle JKL$, $m\angle J = 40°$ and $m\angle K = 60°$. In $\triangle MNP$, $m\angle M = 40°$ and $m\angle P = 80°$. A student concludes that the triangles are not similar. Do you agree or disagree? Why?

_____

_____

There is another criterion that can be used to show that two triangles are similar. You will prove this criterion as an exercise.

> ### SAS Similarity Criterion
>
> If two sides of one triangle are proportional to two sides of another triangle and their included angles are congruent, then the triangles are similar.

# PRACTICE

**For each similarity statement, write congruence statements for the corresponding angles and proportions for the corresponding sides.**

**1.** $\triangle GHJ \sim \triangle PQR$

**2.** $\triangle TWR \sim \triangle YSP$

**3.** $\triangle PJL \sim \triangle WDM$

_____

_____

_____

**4.** Prove the SAS Similarity Criterion.

**Given:** $\frac{XY}{AB} = \frac{XZ}{AC}$ and $\angle A \cong \angle X$

**Prove:** $\triangle ABC \sim \triangle XYZ$
(*Hint:* The main steps of the proof are similar to those of the proof of the AA Similarity Criterion.)

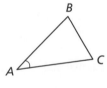 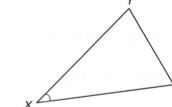

_____

_____

_____

_____

_____

_____

_____

_____

_____

# Solving Problems Using Similarity

**5-5**

COMMON
CORE

CC.9-12.G.SRT.5,
CC.9-12.G.MG.3*

**Essential question:** *How can you use similar triangles and similar rectangles to solve problems?*

When you know that two polygons are similar, you can often use the proportionality of corresponding sides to find unknown side lengths.

**1 EXAMPLE** Finding an Unknown Distance

You want to find the distance across a canyon. In order to find the distance *XY*, you locate points as described below. Explain how to use this information and the figure to find *XY*.

**1.** Identify a landmark, such as a tree, at *X*. Place a marker (*Y*) directly across the canyon from *X*.

**2.** At *Y*, turn 90° away from *X* and walk 400 feet in a straight line. Place a marker (*Z*) at this location.

**3.** Continue walking another 600 feet. Place a marker (*W*) at this location.

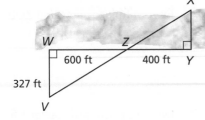

**4.** Turn 90° away from the canyon and walk until the marker *Z* aligns with *X*. Place a marker (*V*) at this location. Measure $\overline{WV}$.

**A** Show that $\triangle XYZ \sim \triangle VWZ$.

• How can you show that two pairs of angles in the triangles are congruent?

_____

_____

• What can you conclude? Why?

_____

**B** Use the fact that corresponding sides of similar triangles are proportional.

• Complete the proportion: $\frac{XY}{VW} =$ _____

• Substitute the known lengths in the proportion: _____

• Solve the proportion: $XY =$ _____

**REFLECT**

**1a.** Compare this problem to Example 3 in Lesson 3-4. How are the solution methods similar? How are they different?

_____

_____

_____

In order to find the height of a palm tree, you
measure the tree's shadow and, at the same time
of day, you measure the shadow cast by a meter
stick that you hold at a right angle to the ground.
The measurements are shown in the figure. Find
the height of the tree.

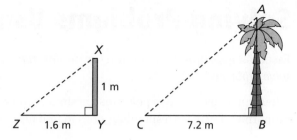

**A** Show that $\triangle ABC \sim \triangle XYZ$.

You can assume that the rays of the sun are parallel. This means that $\overline{ZX} \parallel \overline{CA}$.
What can you say about $\angle Z$ and $\angle C$? Why?

_____

Explain how to show that $\triangle ABC \sim \triangle XYZ$.

_____

_____

**B** Determine the scale factor $k$ for the dilation in the sequence of similarity
transformations that maps $\triangle XYZ$ to $\triangle ABC$.

Find the ratio of corresponding sides. The scale factor is $\frac{BC}{YZ} = \frac{7.2}{1.6} = 4.5$.

So, $AB = k \cdot XY =$ _____.

**REFLECT**

**2a.** How could you solve the problem by writing and solving a proportion?

_____

**2b.** How can you check that your answer is reasonable?

_____

_____

_____

**2c.** What must be true about the palm tree in order for this method to work?

_____

_____

A typographic grid system is a set of horizontal and vertical lines that determine the placement of type on a page. The lines create an array of identical rectangles.

A graphic designer wants to lay out a new grid system for a poster that is 54 cm wide by 72 cm tall. The grid must have margins of 2 cm along all edges and 2 cm between each horizontal row of rectangles. There must be 5 rows of rectangles and each rectangle must be similar to the poster itself.

What are the dimensions of the rectangles? How many rectangles should appear in each row? How much space should be between the columns of rectangles?

54 cm

72 cm

**Concert**
Monday 8

**A**   Determine the number of horizontal 2-centimeter bands that are needed, including the top and bottom margins.   _____

**B**   Find the remaining amount of vertical space and divide by 5 to find the height of each rectangle.   _____

**C**   To find the width of each rectangle, use the fact that the rectangles are similar to the overall poster. Show how to set up a proportion to find the width of each rectangle.

_____

**D**   Determine the maximum number of rectangles that can appear in a row.   _____

**E**   Find the total amount of horizontal space taken up by the rectangles and the left and right margins.   _____

**F**   Assuming the remaining space is distributed evenly, determine the amount of space that should appear between the columns of rectangles.   _____

**REFLECT**

**3a.**   Is there another solution to the problem? Explain.

_____

_____

_____

# PRACTICE

1. To find the distance *XY* across a lake, you locate points as shown in the figure. Explain how to use this information to find *XY*.

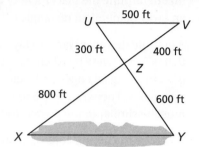

_____

_____

2. In order to find the height of a cliff, you stand at the bottom of the cliff, walk 60 ft from the base, and place a mirror on the ground. Then you face the cliff and step back 5 feet so that you can see the top of the cliff in the mirror. Assuming your eyes are 6 feet above ground, explain how to use this information to find the height of the cliff. (*Hint*: When light strikes a mirror, the angle of incidence is congruent to the angle of reflection, as marked in the figure.)

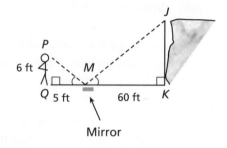

Mirror

_____

_____

3. **Error Analysis** A student who is 72 inches tall wants to find the height of a flagpole. He measures the length of the flagpole's shadow and the length of his own shadow at the same time of day, as shown in his sketch below. Explain the error in the student's work.

> The triangles are similar by the AA Similarity Criterion, so corresponding sides are proportional.
>
> $\frac{x}{72} = \frac{48}{128}$
>
> $x = 72 \cdot \frac{48}{128}$, so $x = 27$ in.

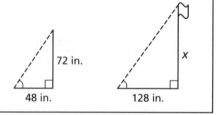

_____

_____

4. A graphic designer wants to lay out a grid system for a brochure that is 15 cm wide by 20 cm tall. The grid must have margins of 1 cm along all edges and 1 cm between each horizontal row of rectangles. There must be 4 rows of rectangles and each rectangle must be similar to the brochure itself. What are the dimensions of the rectangles? How many rectangles should appear in each row? How much space should be between the columns of rectangles? Give two different solutions.

_____

_____

# The Triangle Proportionality Theorem

COMMON
CORE

CC.9-12.G.SRT.4,
CC.9-12.G.SRT.5

**Essential question:** *How does a line that is parallel to one side of a triangle divide the two sides that it intersects?*

The following theorem is sometimes known as the Side-Splitting Theorem. It describes what happens when a line that is parallel to one side of a triangle "splits" the other two sides.

> ### Triangle Proportionality Theorem
> If a line parallel to one side of a triangle intersects the other two sides, then it divides those sides proportionally.

## 1 PROOF    Triangle Proportionality Theorem

**Given:** $\overleftrightarrow{EF} \parallel \overline{BC}$

**Prove:** $\dfrac{AE}{EB} = \dfrac{AF}{FC}$

Complete the proof.

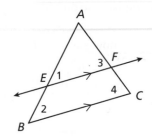

**A**  Show that $\triangle AEF \sim \triangle ABC$.

Since $\overleftrightarrow{EF} \parallel \overline{BC}$, you can conclude that $\angle 1 \cong \angle 2$ and $\angle 3 \cong \angle 4$ by

_____

So, $\triangle AEF \sim \triangle ABC$ by _____

**B**  Use the fact that corresponding sides of similar triangles are proportional.

$\dfrac{AB}{AE} =$ _____         Corresponding sides are proportional.

$\dfrac{AE + EB}{AE} =$ _____         Segment Addition Postulate

$1 + \dfrac{EB}{AE} =$ _____         Use the property that $\dfrac{a + b}{c} = \dfrac{a}{c} + \dfrac{b}{c}$.

$\dfrac{EB}{AE} =$ _____         Subtract 1 from both sides.

$\dfrac{AE}{EB} =$ _____         Take the reciprocal of both sides.

**1a.** Explain how you can conclude △AEF ~ △ABC without using ∠3 and ∠4.

_____

_____

**Converse of the Triangle Proportionality Theorem**

If a line divides two sides of a triangle proportionally,
then it is parallel to the third side.

**2 PROOF** **Converse of the Triangle Proportionality Theorem**

**Given:** $\frac{AE}{EB} = \frac{AF}{FC}$

**Prove:** $\overleftrightarrow{EF} \parallel \overline{BC}$

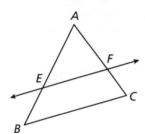

Complete the proof.

**A** Show that △AEF ~ △ABC.

It is given that $\frac{AE}{EB} = \frac{AF}{FC}$ and taking the reciprocal of both sides shows that

_____. Now add 1 to both sides by adding $\frac{AE}{AE}$ to the left

side and $\frac{AF}{AF}$ to the right side. This gives _____. Adding

and using the Segment Addition Postulate gives _____.

Since ∠A ≅ ∠A, △AEF ~ △ABC by _____.

**B** As corresponding angles of similar triangles, ∠AEF ≅ _____.

So, $\overleftrightarrow{EF} \parallel \overline{BC}$ by _____.

**2a.** A student states that $\overline{UV}$ must be parallel to $\overline{ST}$. Do you agree?
Why or why not?

_____

_____

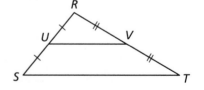

# Proving the Pythagorean Theorem

COMMON CORE

CC.9-12.G.SRT.4,
CC.9-12.G.SRT.5

**Essential question:** *How can you use triangle similarity to prove the Pythagorean Theorem?*

You have already used the Pythagorean Theorem in earlier courses and in earlier lessons of this book. There are many proofs of this familiar theorem. The proof in this lesson is based on using what you know about similar triangles.

> ### The Pythagorean Theorem
>
> In a right triangle, the sum of the squares of the lengths of the legs is equal to the square of the length of the hypotenuse.

**1 PROOF**    The Pythagorean Theorem

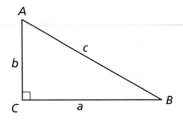

**Given:** $\triangle ABC$ is a right triangle with legs of length $a$ and $b$ and hypotenuse of length $c$.

**Prove:** $a^2 + b^2 = c^2$

Complete the proof.

**A**   Draw a perpendicular from $C$ to the hypotenuse. Label the point of intersection $X$.

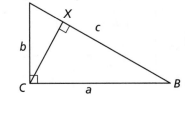

$\angle BXC \cong \angle BCA$ because _____

$\angle B \cong \angle B$ by _____

So, $\triangle BXC \sim \triangle BCA$ by _____

$\angle AXC \cong \angle ACB$ because _____

$\angle A \cong \angle A$ by _____

So, $\triangle AXC \sim \triangle ACB$ by _____

**B**   Let the lengths of the segments on the hypotenuse be $d$ and $e$, as shown in the figure.

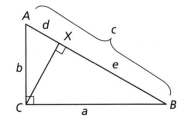

Use the fact that corresponding sides of similar triangles are proportional to write two proportions.

Proportion 1: Because $\triangle BXC \sim \triangle BCA$, $\dfrac{a}{c} = \dfrac{\phantom{XX}}{a}$.

Proportion 2: Because $\triangle AXC \sim \triangle ACB$, $\dfrac{b}{c} = \dfrac{\phantom{XX}}{b}$.

**C** Now perform some algebra to complete the proof as follows.

Multiply both sides of Proportion 1 by $ac$. Write the resulting equation.

_____

Multiply both sides of Proportion 2 by $bc$. Write the resulting equation.

_____

Adding the above equations gives this: _____

Factor the right side of the equation: _____

Finally, use the fact that $e + d =$ _____ by the Segment Addition

Postulate to rewrite the equation as _____.

**REFLECT**

**1a. Error Analysis** A student wrote a proof of the Pythagorean Theorem, as shown below.

$\triangle BXC \sim \triangle BCA$ and $\triangle BCA \sim \triangle CXA$, so $\triangle BXC \sim \triangle CXA$ by transitivity of similarity.

Since corresponding sides of similar triangles are proportional,
$\frac{e}{f} = \frac{f}{d}$ and $f^2 = ed$.

Because $\triangle BXC$ and $\triangle CXA$ are right triangles, $a^2 = e^2 + f^2$ and $b^2 = f^2 + d^2$.

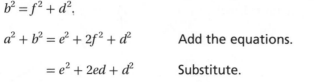

| | |
|---|---|
| $a^2 + b^2 = e^2 + 2f^2 + d^2$ | Add the equations. |
| $= e^2 + 2ed + d^2$ | Substitute. |
| $= (e + d)^2$ | Factor. |
| $= c^2$ | Segment Addition Postulate |

Critique the student's proof.

_____

_____

_____

Name _____ Class _____ Date _____

## MULTIPLE CHOICE

**1.** Which of the following transformations is a dilation?

    **A.** $(x, y) \rightarrow (2x, y)$

    **B.** $(x, y) \rightarrow (x + 2, y + 2)$

    **C.** $(x, y) \rightarrow (2x, 2y)$

    **D.** $(x, y) \rightarrow (x, y - 2)$

**2.** Juan is proving the Triangle Proportionality Theorem. Which reason should he use for Step 3?

**Given:** $\overleftrightarrow{XY} \parallel \overline{BC}$

**Prove:** $\dfrac{AX}{XB} = \dfrac{AY}{YC}$

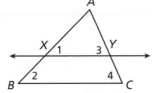

| Statements | Reasons |
|---|---|
| **1.** $\overleftrightarrow{XY} \parallel \overline{BC}$ | **1.** Given |
| **2.** $\angle 1 \cong \angle 2$; $\angle 3 \cong \angle 4$ | **2.** Corresponding Angles Theorem |
| **3.** $\triangle AXY \sim \triangle ABC$ | **3.** ? |

    **F.** ASA Congruence Criterion

    **G.** Definition of corresponding angles

    **H.** Definition of similarity

    **J.** AA Similarity Criterion

**3.** Katie uses geometry software to draw a line $\ell$ and a point $O$ that is not on line $\ell$. Then she constructs the image of line $\ell$ under a dilation with center $O$ and scale factor 4. Which of the following *best* describes the image of line $\ell$?

    **A.** a line parallel to line $\ell$

    **B.** a line perpendicular to line $\ell$

    **C.** a line passing through point $O$

    **D.** a line that coincides with line $\ell$

**4.** A graphic designer wants to lay out a grid system for a book cover that is 12 cm wide by 15 cm tall. The grid will have an array of identical rectangles, margins of 1 cm along all edges, and 1 cm between each horizontal row of rectangles. There must be 4 rows of rectangles and each rectangle must be similar to the cover itself. Which of the following are possible dimensions of the rectangles?

    **F.** 2.5 cm tall by 2 cm wide

    **G.** 2.75 cm tall by 2.2 cm wide

    **H.** 3 cm tall by 2.4 cm wide

    **J.** 3.25 cm tall by 2.6 cm wide

**5.** In order to find the height of a radio tower, you measure the tower's shadow and, at the same time of day, you measure the shadow cast by a mailbox that is 1.2 meters tall. The measurements are shown in the figure. What is the height of the tower?

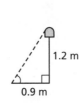

    **A.** 30.15 m      **C.** 44.67 m

    **B.** 40.5 m      **D.** 53.6 m

**6.** Which of the following is *not* preserved under a dilation?

    **F.** angle measure

    **G.** betweenness

    **H.** collinearity

    **J.** distance

7. Use the definition of similarity in terms of similarity transformations to determine whether the two figures are similar. Explain your answer.

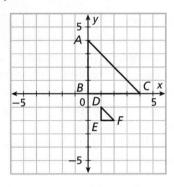

_____

_____

_____

8. You are proving that the AA Similarity Criterion follows from the definition of similarity in terms of similarity transformations.

   **Given:** $\angle R \cong \angle U$ and $\angle S \cong \angle V$
   **Prove:** $\triangle RST \sim \triangle UVW$

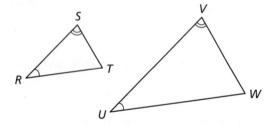

You begin by applying a dilation to $\triangle RST$. What is the scale factor $k$ of the dilation? Why do you choose this scale factor?

_____

_____

9. You are proving that all circles are similar. You start with the two circles shown below.

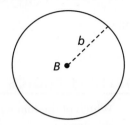

a. First you perform a transformation on circle $A$ so that the image of point $A$ is point $B$. Describe the transformation you use.

_____

b. The image of circle $A$ is circle $A'$, as shown.

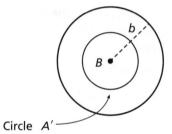

Circle $A'$

What transformation do you apply to circle $A'$ in order to complete the proof? Why?

_____

_____

_____

_____

_____

_____

_____

_____

# Trigonometry

## Unit Focus

In this unit, you will work with trigonometric ratios. Trigonometric ratios are based on right triangles and similarity. As you will see, these ratios are useful in solving a variety of mathematical and real-world problems. As you study trigonometry, you will learn about two special right triangles, and you will learn how to find unknown side lengths and unknown angle measures in right and non-right triangles.

## Unit at a Glance

COMMON
CORE

| Lesson | | Standards for Mathematical Content |
|---|---|---|
| 6-1 | The Tangent Ratio | CC.9-12.G.SRT.6 |
| 6-2 | The Sine and Cosine Ratios | CC.9-12.G.SRT.6, CC.9-12.G.SRT.7 |
| 6-3 | Special Right Triangles | CC.9-12.G.SRT.6, CC.9-12.G.SRT.7 |
| 6-4 | Solving Right Triangles | CC.9-12.G.SRT.8 |
| 6-5 | Trigonometric Ratios of Obtuse Angles | CC.9-12.G.SRT.9(+) |
| 6-6 | The Law of Sines | CC.9-12.G.SRT.10(+), CC.9-12.G.SRT.11(+) |
| 6-7 | The Law of Cosines | CC.9-12.G.SRT.10(+), CC.9-12.G.SRT.11(+) |
| | Test Prep | |

# Unpacking the Common Core State Standards

Use the table to help you understand the Standards for Mathematical Content that are taught in this unit. Refer to the lessons listed after each standard for exploration and practice.

| COMMON CORE Standards for Mathematical Content | What It Means For You |
|---|---|
| **CC.9-12.G.SRT.6 Understand that by similarity, side ratios in right triangles are properties of the angles in the triangle, leading to definitions of trigonometric ratios for acute angles.** Lessons 6-1, 6-2, 6-3 | Given an acute angle, all right triangles that contain this angle must be similar to each other. You will see how to use this idea to define the tangent, sine, and cosine ratios. |
| **CC.9-12.G.SRT.7 Explain and use the relationship between the sine and cosine of complementary angles.** Lessons 6-2, 6-3 | The acute angles in a right triangle are complementary. This leads to a useful relationship between the sine and cosine of complementary angles. |
| **CC.9-12.G.SRT.8 Use trigonometric ratios and the Pythagorean Theorem to solve right triangles in applied problems.** Lesson 6-4 | Trigonometric ratios are powerful tools for solving real-world problems. You will see how to use trigonometric ratios to find unknown heights, distances, and angle measures in a wide range of problems. |
| **CC.9-12.G.SRT.9(+) Derive the formula $A = \frac{1}{2}ab \sin(C)$ for the area of a triangle by drawing an auxiliary line from a vertex perpendicular to the opposite side.** Lesson 6-5 | You already know the formula $A = \frac{1}{2}bh$ for the area of a triangle. Now you will derive a new formula for the area of a triangle that does not depend upon knowing the altitude of the triangle. |
| **CC.9-12.G.SRT.10(+) Prove the Laws of Sines and Cosines and use them to solve problems.** Lessons 6-6, 6-7 | The Law of Sines and the Law of Cosines describe relationships among the sides and angles of a triangle. You will see how the definitions of trigonometric ratios can be used to prove these relationships. |
| **CC.9-12.G.SRT.11(+) Understand and apply the Law of Sines and the Law of Cosines to find unknown measurements in right and non-right triangles (e.g., surveying problems, resultant forces).** Lessons 6-6, 6-7 | You will use the Law of Sines and the Law of Cosines to find unknown distances and/or angle measures in real-world problems. |

# The Tangent Ratio

COMMON CORE

CC.9-12.G.SRT.6

**Essential question:** *How do you find the tangent ratio for an acute angle of a right triangle?*

In this unit, you will be working extensively with right triangles, so some new vocabulary will be helpful. Given a right triangle, $\triangle ABC$, with a right angle at vertex $C$, the leg **adjacent** to $\angle A$ is the leg that forms one side of $\angle A$. The leg **opposite** $\angle A$ is the leg that does not form a side of $\angle A$.

## 1 EXPLORE   Investigating a Ratio in a Right Triangle

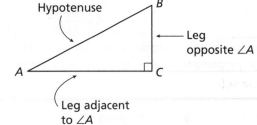

**A**   Use geometry software to draw a horizontal segment. Label one endpoint of the segment $A$.

**B**   Select point $A$, go to the Transform menu, and choose Mark Center.

**C**   Select the segment, go to the Transform menu, and choose Rotate. Enter 30° for the angle of rotation. Label the endpoint of the rotation image $B$.

**D**   Select point $B$ and the original line segment. Use the Construct menu to construct a perpendicular from $B$ to the segment. Plot a point at the point of intersection and label the point $C$.

**E**   Use the Measure menu to measure $\overline{BC}$ and $\overline{AC}$. Then use the Calculate tool to calculate the ratio $\frac{BC}{AC}$.

**F**   Drag the points and lines to change the size and location of the triangle. Notice what happens to the measurements.

**G**   Repeat the above steps using a different angle of rotation.

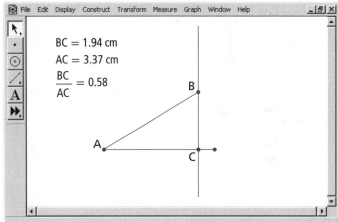

### REFLECT

**1a.**   Compare your findings with those of other students. For an acute angle in a right triangle, what can you say about the ratio of the length of the opposite leg to the length of the adjacent leg?

_____

_____

You may have discovered that in a right triangle the ratio of the length of the leg opposite an acute angle to the length of the leg adjacent to the angle is constant. You can use what you know about similarity to see why this is true.

Consider the right triangles $\triangle ABC$ and $\triangle DEF$, in which $\angle A \cong \angle D$, as shown. By the AA Similarity Criterion, $\triangle ABC \sim \triangle DEF$. This means the lengths of the sides of $\triangle DEF$ are each $k$ times the lengths of the corresponding sides of $\triangle ABC$.

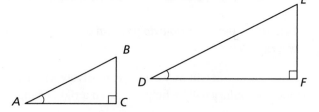

$$\frac{EF}{DF} = \frac{k \cdot BC}{k \cdot AC} = \frac{BC}{AC}$$

This shows that the ratio of the length of the leg opposite an acute angle to the length of the leg adjacent to the angle is constant. This ratio is called the *tangent* of the angle. Thus, the **tangent** of $\angle A$, written tan $A$, is defined as follows:

$$\tan A = \frac{\text{length of leg opposite } \angle A}{\text{length of leg adjacent to } \angle A} = \frac{BC}{AC}$$

You can find the tangent of an angle using a calculator or by using lengths that are given in a figure, as in the following example.

**2** **EXAMPLE**  **Finding the Tangent of an Angle**

Find the tangent of $\angle J$ and $\angle K$. Write each ratio as a fraction and as a decimal rounded to the nearest hundredth.

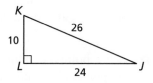

**A**  $\tan J = \dfrac{\text{length of leg opposite } \angle J}{\text{length of leg adjacent to } \angle J} = \dfrac{KL}{JL} = \dfrac{\phantom{0}}{24} = \dfrac{\phantom{0}}{12} \approx$ _____

**B**  $\tan K = \dfrac{\text{length of leg opposite } \angle K}{\text{length of leg adjacent to } \angle K} = \dfrac{JL}{KL} = \dfrac{\phantom{0}}{10} = \dfrac{\phantom{0}}{5} =$ _____

**REFLECT**

**2a.** What do you notice about the ratios you wrote for tan $J$ and tan $K$? Do you think this will always be true for the two acute angles in a right triangle?

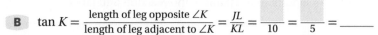

_____

_____

**2b.** Why does it not make sense to ask for the value of tan $L$?

_____

_____

When you know the length of a leg of a right triangle and the measure of one of the acute angles, you can use the tangent to find the length of the other leg. This is especially useful in real-world problems.

**3 EXAMPLE**    Solving a Real-World Problem

A long ladder leans against a building and makes an angle of 68° with the ground. The base of the ladder is 6 feet from the building. To the nearest tenth of a foot, how far up the side of the building does the ladder reach?

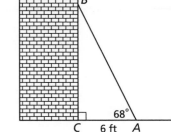

**A**   Write a tangent ratio that involves the unknown length, *BC*.

$$\tan A = \frac{\text{length of leg opposite } \angle A}{\text{length of leg adjacent to } \angle A} = \frac{BC}{6}$$

Use the fact that m$\angle A$ = 68° to write the equation as $\tan 68° = \frac{BC}{6}$.

**B**   Solve for *BC*.

$6 \cdot \tan 68° = BC$          Multiply both sides by 6.

$6 \cdot \underline{\hspace{2.5cm}} = BC$          Use a calculator to find tan 68°. Do not round until the final step of the solution.

$\underline{\hspace{2.5cm}} \approx BC$          Multiply. Round to the nearest tenth.

So, the ladder reaches about _____ up the side of the building.

**REFLECT**

**3a.**  Why is it best to wait until the final step before rounding? What happens if you round the value of tan 68° to the nearest tenth before multiplying?

_____

_____

**3b.**  A student claims that it is possible to solve the problem using the tangent of $\angle B$. Do you agree or disagree? If it is possible, show the solution. If it is not possible, explain why not.

_____

_____

**Find the tangent of ∠A and ∠B. Write each ratio as a fraction and as a decimal rounded to the nearest hundredth.**

**1.**

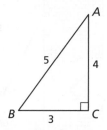

**2.**

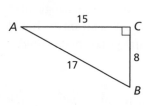

**3.**

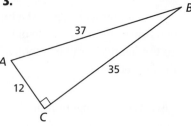

_____

_____

_____

_____

_____

_____

**Find the value of x to the nearest tenth.**

**4.**

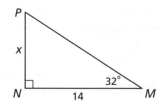

**5.**

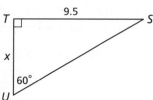

**6.**

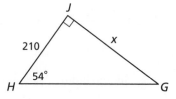

_____

_____

_____

**7.** A hiker whose eyes are 5.5 feet above ground stands 25 feet from the base of a redwood tree. She looks up at an angle of 71° to see the top of the tree. To the nearest tenth of a foot, what is the height of the tree?

_____

**8. Error Analysis** To find the distance *XY* across a large rock formation, a student stands facing one endpoint of the formation, backs away from it at a right angle for 20 meters, and then turns 55° to look at the other endpoint of the formation. The student's calculations are shown. Critique the student's work.

_____

_____

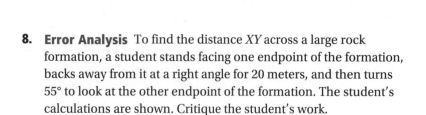

$$\tan 55° = \frac{20}{XY}$$

$$XY \cdot \tan 55° = 20$$

$$XY = \frac{20}{\tan 55°} \approx 14.0 \text{ m}$$

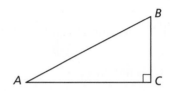

# The Sine and Cosine Ratios

**Essential question:** *How do you find the sine and cosine ratios for an acute angle of a right triangle?*

COMMON CORE

CC.9-12.G.SRT.6,
CC.9-12.G.SRT.7

A **trigonometric ratio** is a ratio of two sides of a right triangle. You have already seen one trigonometric ratio, the tangent. It is also possible to define two additional trigonometric ratios, the sine and the cosine, that involve the hypotenuse of a right triangle.

The **sine** of $\angle A$, written sin $A$, is defined as follows:

$$\sin A = \frac{\text{length of leg opposite } \angle A}{\text{length of hypotenuse}} = \frac{BC}{AB}$$

The **cosine** of $\angle A$, written cos $A$, is defined as follows:

$$\cos A = \frac{\text{length of leg adjacent to } \angle A}{\text{length of hypotenuse}} = \frac{AC}{AB}$$

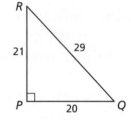

## 1 EXAMPLE Finding the Sine and Cosine of an Angle

Write each trigonometric ratio as a fraction and as a decimal rounded to the nearest hundredth.

**A** $\sin R = \frac{\text{length of leg opposite } \angle R}{\text{length of hypotenuse}} = \frac{PQ}{RQ} = \frac{20}{29} \approx 0.69$

**B** $\sin Q = \frac{\text{length of leg opposite } \angle Q}{\text{length of hypotenuse}} = \frac{RP}{RQ} = \frac{\phantom{xx}}{29} \approx$ _____

**C** $\cos R = \frac{\text{length of leg adjacent to } \angle R}{\text{length of hypotenuse}} = \frac{\phantom{xx}}{\phantom{xx}} \approx$ _____

**D** $\cos Q = \frac{\text{length of leg adjacent to } \angle Q}{\text{length of hypotenuse}} = \frac{\phantom{xx}}{\phantom{xx}} \approx$ _____

### REFLECT

**1a.** What do you notice about the sines and cosines you found? Do you think this relationship will be true for any pair of acute angles in a right triangle? Explain.

_____

_____

_____

© Houghton Mifflin Harcourt Publishing Company

You may have discovered a relationship between the sines and cosines of the acute angles in a right triangle. In particular, if $\angle A$ and $\angle B$ are the acute angles in a right triangle, then $\sin A = \cos B$ and $\sin B = \cos A$.

Note that the acute angles in a right triangle are complementary. The above observation leads to a more general fact: the sine of an angle is equal to the cosine of its complement, and the cosine of an angle is equal to the sine of its complement.

**2** **EXAMPLE**  **Using Complementary Angles**

Given that $\sin 57° \approx 0.839$, write the cosine of a complementary angle.

**A**  Find the measure $x$ of an angle that is complementary to a 57° angle.

$x + 57° = 90°$, so $x =$ _____

**B**  Use the fact that the cosine of an angle is equal to the sine of its complement.

$\cos$ _____ $\approx 0.839$

Given that $\cos 60° = 0.5$, write the sine of a complementary angle.

**C**  Find the measure $y$ of an angle that is complementary to a 60° angle.

$y + 60° = 90°$, so $y =$ _____

**D**  Use the fact that the sine of an angle is equal to the cosine of its complement.

$\sin$ _____ $= 0.5$

**REFLECT**

**2a.**  Is it possible to find m$\angle J$ in the figure? Explain.

_____

_____

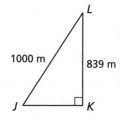

**2b.**  What can you conclude about the sine and cosine of 45° ? Explain.

_____

**2c.**  Is it possible for the sine of an angle to equal 1? Why or why not?

_____

_____

A loading dock at a factory has a 16-foot ramp in front of it, as shown in the figure. The ramp makes an angle of 8° with the ground. To the nearest tenth of a foot, what is the height of the loading dock? How far does the ramp extend in front of the loading dock? (The figure is not drawn to scale, so you cannot measure it to solve the problem.)

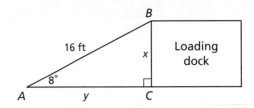

**A** Find the height $x$ of the loading dock.

$$\sin A = \frac{\text{length of leg opposite } \angle A}{\text{length of hypotenuse}} = \frac{x}{16}, \text{ so } \sin 8° = \frac{x}{16}.$$

Solve the equation for $x$.

_____

Use a calculator to evaluate the expression, then round.

$x \approx$ _____

So, the height of the loading dock is about _____.

**B** Find the distance $y$ that the ramp extends in front of the loading dock.

$$\cos A = \frac{\text{length of leg adjacent to } \angle A}{\text{length of hypotenuse}} = \frac{\phantom{xx}}{\phantom{xx}}, \text{ so } \cos \underline{\phantom{xxxx}} = \frac{\phantom{xx}}{\phantom{xx}}.$$

Solve the equation for $y$.

_____

Use a calculator to evaluate the expression, then round.

$y \approx$ _____

So, the distance the ramp extends in front of the loading dock is about _____.

**REFLECT**

**3a.** A student claimed that she found the height of the loading dock by using the cosine. Explain her thinking.

_____

_____

**3b.** Suppose the owner of the factory decides to build a new ramp for the loading dock so that the new ramp makes an angle of 5° with the ground. How far will this ramp extend from the loading dock? Explain.

_____

_____

# PRACTICE

Find the given trigonometric ratios. Write each ratio as a fraction and as a decimal rounded to the nearest hundredth.

**1.** sin R, cos R

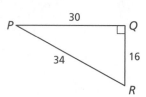

**2.** cos D, cos E

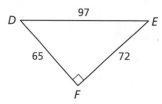

**3.** sin M, sin N

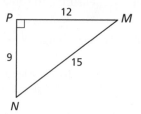

_____

_____

**4.** Given that sin 15° ≈ 0.259, write the cosine of a complementary angle. _____

**5.** Given that cos 62° ≈ 0.469, write the sine of a complementary angle. _____

Find the value of *x* to the nearest tenth.

**6.**

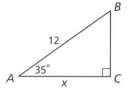

**7.**

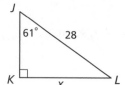

**8.**

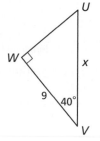

_____

**9.** You are building a skateboard ramp from a piece of wood that is 3.1 meters long. You want the ramp to make an angle of 25° with the ground. To the nearest tenth of a meter, what is the length of the ramp's base? What is its height?

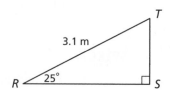

_____

**10. Error Analysis** Three students were asked to find the value of *x* in the figure. The equations they used are shown at right. Which students, if any, used a correct equation? Explain the other students' errors and then find the value of *x*.

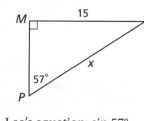

Lee's equation: $\sin 57° = \frac{x}{15}$

Jamila's equation: $\cos 33° = \frac{15}{x}$

Tyler's equation: $\sin 33° = \frac{x}{15}$

_____

_____

_____

_____

# Special Right Triangles

**Essential question:** *What can you say about the side lengths and the trigonometric ratios associated with special right triangles?*

COMMON CORE

CC.9-12.G.SRT.6,
CC.9-12.G.SRT.7

There are two special right triangles that arise frequently in problem-solving situations. It is useful to know the relationships among the sides, angles, and trigonometric ratios for these triangles.

**1  EXPLORE**   Investigating an Isosceles Right Triangle

**A**  The figure shows an isosceles right triangle. What is the measure of each base angle of the triangle? Why?

_____

_____

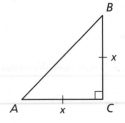

**B**  Let the legs of the right triangle have length $x$. You can use the Pythagorean Theorem to find the length of the hypotenuse in terms of $x$.

$AB^2 = x^2 + x^2$          Pythagorean Theorem

$AB^2 = $ _____          Combine like terms.

$AB = $ _____          Find the square root of both sides and simplify.

**REFLECT**

**1a.**  A student claims that if you know one side length of an isosceles right triangle, then you know all the side lengths. Do you agree or disagree? Explain.

_____

_____

**1b.**  Explain how to find $y$ in the right triangle at right.

_____

_____

_____

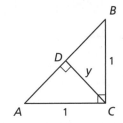

**A** In the figure, △*ABD* is an equilateral triangle and $\overline{BC}$ is a perpendicular from *B* to $\overline{AD}$. Explain how to find the angle measures in △*ABC*.

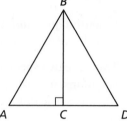

_____

_____

**B** Explain why △*ACB* ≅ △*DCB*.

_____

_____

_____

_____

**C** Let the length of $\overline{AC}$ be *x*. What is the length of $\overline{AB}$ ? Why?

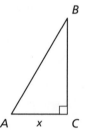

_____

**D** In the space below, show how to use the Pythagorean Theorem to find the length of $\overline{BC}$.

_____

_____

_____

_____

 **REFLECT**

**2a.** What is the ratio of the side lengths in a right triangle with acute angles that measure 30° and 60°?

_____

**2b.** **Error Analysis** A student drew a right triangle with a 60° angle and a hypotenuse of length 10. Then he labeled the other side lengths as shown. Explain how you can tell just by glancing at the side lengths that the student made an error. Then explain the error.

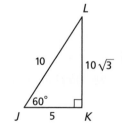

_____

_____

The right triangles you investigated are sometimes called 45°-45°-90° and 30°-60°-90° right triangles. The side-length relationships that you discovered are all you need to determine the exact values of the sine, cosine, and tangent of 30°, 45°, and 60°.

**3** **EXPLORE** Determining Trigonometric Ratios

**A** Use your previous work to fill in the missing side lengths.

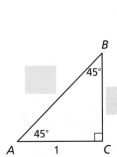
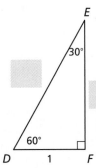

**B** Use the above triangles to help you complete the chart. Write each trigonometric ratio as a simplified fraction.

| Angle | Sine | Cosine | Tangent |
|-------|------|--------|---------|
| 30° |  |  |  |
| 45° |  |  |  |
| 60° |  |  |  |

**REFLECT**

**3a.** What patterns or relationships do you see in the sine and cosine columns? Why do these patterns or relationships make sense?

_____

_____

_____

**3b.** For which angles is the tangent ratio less than 1? equal to 1? greater than 1?

_____

_____

_____

**Find the value of *x*. Give your answer in simplest radical form.**

**1.**
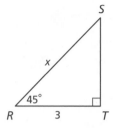

**2.**
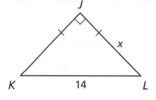

**3.**
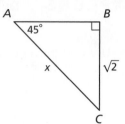

**4.**
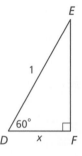

**5.**
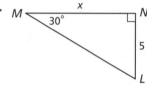

**6.**
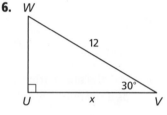

**7.**
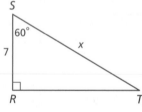

**8.**
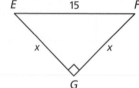

**9.**
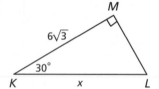

**10. Error Analysis** Two students were asked to find the value of *x* in the figure at right. Which student's work is correct? Explain the other student's error.

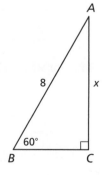

| Roberto's Work |
|---|
| $\sin 60° = \frac{\sqrt{3}}{2}$, but from the figure, $\sin 60° = \frac{x}{8}$, so $\frac{\sqrt{3}}{2} = \frac{x}{8}$. Multiplying both sides by 8 gives $8 \cdot \frac{\sqrt{3}}{2} = x$, so $x = 4\sqrt{3}$. |

| Aaron's Work |
|---|
| In a 30°-60°-90° triangle, the side lengths are in a ratio of $1:\sqrt{3}:2$, so *x* must be $\sqrt{3}$ times the length of $\overline{AB}$. Therefore, $x = 8\sqrt{3}$. |

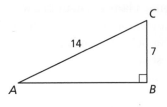

# Solving Right Triangles

**COMMON CORE**

CC.9-12.G.SRT.8

**Essential question:** *How do you find an unknown angle measure in a right triangle?*

In some cases, you may know the value of a
trigonometric ratio and want to know the measure
of the associated angle. For example, in the figure
at right, $\sin A = \frac{7}{14} = \frac{1}{2}$. Because you know that
$\sin 30° = \frac{1}{2}$, you can conclude that $m\angle A = 30°$ and
you can write $\sin^{-1}\left(\frac{1}{2}\right) = 30°$.

More generally, the **inverse trigonometric ratios** are defined as follows.

Given an acute angle, $\angle A$,

- if $\sin A = x$, then $\sin^{-1} x = m\angle A$.

- if $\cos A = x$, then $\cos^{-1} x = m\angle A$.

- if $\tan A = x$, then $\tan^{-1} x = m\angle A$.

You can use a calculator to evaluate inverse trigonometric ratios.

**1 EXAMPLE**  **Using an Inverse Trigonometric Ratio**

Find $m\angle J$. Round to the nearest degree.

**A**  Write a trigonometric ratio for $\angle J$.

Since you know the length of the side opposite $\angle J$ and the length
of the side adjacent to $\angle J$, use the tangent ratio.

$\tan J = \dfrac{\phantom{xx}}{\phantom{xx}}$

**B**  Write the inverse trigonometric ratio: $\tan^{-1}\left(\dfrac{\phantom{xx}}{\phantom{xx}}\right) = m\angle J$.

Use a calculator to evaluate the inverse trigonometric ratio. Round to the
nearest degree.

So, $m\angle J \approx$ _____.

**REFLECT**

**1a.**  What other angle measures or side lengths of $\triangle JKL$ can you determine? How?

_____

_____

*Solving a right triangle* means finding the lengths of all its sides and the measures of all its angles. To solve a right triangle you need to know two side lengths or one side length and an acute angle measure.

## 2 EXAMPLE  Solving a Right Triangle

A shelf extends perpendicularly 24 cm from a wall. You want to place a 28-cm brace under the shelf, as shown. To the nearest tenth of a centimeter, how far below the shelf will the brace be attached to the wall? To the nearest degree, what angle will the brace make with the shelf and with the wall?

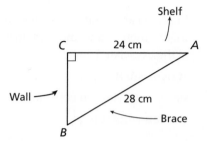

**A**  Use the Pythagorean Theorem to find the distance $BC$.

$BC^2 + AC^2 = AB^2$       Pythagorean Theorem

$BC^2 + \underline{\phantom{xx}}^2 = \underline{\phantom{xx}}^2$       Substitute.

$BC^2 + \underline{\phantom{xxxx}} = \underline{\phantom{xxxx}}$       Find the squares.

$BC^2 = \underline{\phantom{xxxx}}$       Subtract the same quantity from both sides.

$BC \approx \underline{\phantom{xxxxx}}$       Find the square root and round.

**B**  Use an inverse trigonometric ratio to find m$\angle A$.

$\cos A = \dfrac{\phantom{xx}}{\phantom{xx}}$, so $\cos^{-1}\left(\dfrac{\phantom{xx}}{\phantom{xx}}\right) = $ m$\angle A$

Use a calculator to evaluate the inverse trigonometric ratio. Round to the nearest degree.

So, m$\angle A \approx \underline{\phantom{xxxxx}}$.

**C**  Use the fact that the acute angles of a right triangle are complementary to find m$\angle B$.

So, m$\angle B \approx \underline{\phantom{xxxxx}}$.

## REFLECT

**2a.** Is it possible to find m$\angle B$ before you find m$\angle A$? If so, how?

_____

_____

You learned about vectors in Lesson 2-5. As you will see, vectors are useful for modeling real-world situations. To do so, it is helpful to know how to add vectors.

To add two vectors, $\vec{u}$ and $\vec{v}$, place the initial point of $\vec{v}$ on the terminal point of $\vec{u}$. The *resultant* is the vector that joins the initial point of $\vec{u}$ with the terminal point of $\vec{v}$.

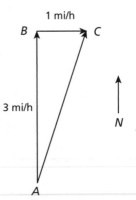

**3 EXAMPLE**  Modeling a Situation with Vectors

You paddle a canoe due north across a river at a rate of 3 mi/h. The river has a 1 mi/h current that flows due east. What is your canoe's actual speed and direction?

**A**  Model the situation with vectors. Use vectors to represent the motion of the canoe ($\overrightarrow{AB}$) and the current ($\overrightarrow{BC}$). The magnitude of vectors represents the speeds. The resultant ($\overrightarrow{AC}$) represents the actual speed and direction of the canoe.

**B**  Use the Pythagorean Theorem to find the magnitude of $\overrightarrow{AC}$.

$AC^2 = \underline{\quad}^2 + \underline{\quad}^2$        Pythagorean Theorem

$AC^2 = \underline{\quad\quad}$        Square the terms and add.

$AC \approx \underline{\quad\quad\quad}$        Take the square root of both sides. Round to the nearest tenth.

So, the actual speed of the canoe is about \underline{\quad\quad\quad\quad}.

**C**  Use an inverse trigonometric ratio to find m$\angle A$.

$\tan A = \dfrac{\phantom{xx}}{\phantom{xx}}$, so $\tan^{-1}\left(\dfrac{\phantom{xx}}{\phantom{xx}}\right) = $ m$\angle A$

Use a calculator to evaluate the inverse trigonometric ratio. Round to the nearest degree.

m$\angle A \approx$ \underline{\quad\quad\quad}

So, the canoe's actual direction is about \underline{\quad\quad} east of due north.

**REFLECT**

**3a.**  Why does it make sense that the canoe's actual speed is greater than both the speed at which you paddle and the speed of the current?

\underline{\hspace{100%}}

\underline{\hspace{100%}}

**Find m∠A. Round to the nearest degree.**

**1.**

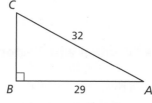

**2.**

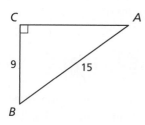

**3.**

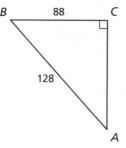

_____

_____

_____

**4.**

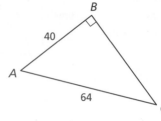

**5.**

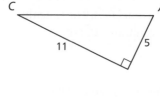

**6.**

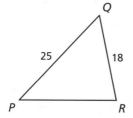

_____

_____

_____

**7.** A ladder leans against a wall and reaches a point 15 feet up the wall. The base of the ladder is 3.9 feet from the wall. To the nearest tenth of a foot, what is the length of the ladder? To the nearest degree, what angle does the ladder make with the wall and with the ground?

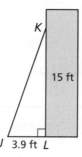

_____

**8.** A 7.2-meter guy wire goes from the top of a utility pole to a point on the ground that is 3 meters from the base of the pole. To the nearest tenth of a meter, how tall is the utility pole? To the nearest degree, what angle does the guy wire make with the pole and with the ground?

_____

**9.** A plane flies due north at 500 mi/h. There is a crosswind blowing due east at 60 mi/h. What is the plane's actual speed to the nearest tenth? What is the plane's actual direction to the nearest degree?

_____

**10. Error Analysis** A student found m∠P as shown. Critique the student's work.

_____

_____

_____

$\sin P = \frac{18}{25}$, so

$m\angle P = \sin^{-1}\left(\frac{18}{25}\right) \approx 46°$

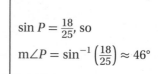

# Trigonometric Ratios of Obtuse Angles

COMMON CORE

CC.9-12.G.SRT.9(+)

**Essential question:** *How can you use the sine ratio to the find a formula for the area of a triangle?*

So far, you have used trigonometric ratios with acute angles in right triangles. You can also use trigonometric ratios with the angles in non-right triangles, but you will first need to extend the definitions of the trigonometric ratios as shown below.

## 1 EXPLORE  Extending the Trigonometric Ratios

**A**  First, extend the trigonometric ratios to right triangles on a coordinate plane.

Place right triangle $\triangle ABC$ with acute $\angle A$ on a coordinate plane as shown. Let the coordinates of $B$ be $B(x, y)$. Then the lengths of the legs are $x$ and $y$.

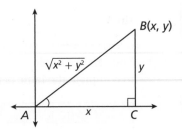

The length of the hypotenuse is $\sqrt{x^2 + y^2}$ by _____.

Now the trigonometric ratios for $\angle A$ can be expressed in terms of $x$ and $y$.

$$\sin A = \frac{y}{\sqrt{x^2 + y^2}} \qquad \cos A = \frac{\phantom{xx}}{\sqrt{x^2 + y^2}} \qquad \tan A = \frac{\phantom{xx}}{\phantom{xx}}$$

**B**  Next, extend the trigonometric ratios to acute angles in non-right triangles.

Place non-right triangle $\triangle ABC$ with acute $\angle A$ on a coordinate plane as shown. Let the coordinates of $B$ be $B(x, y)$.

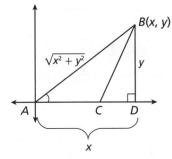

Draw a perpendicular from $B$ to the $x$-axis, and label the point of intersection $D$. Then the lengths of the legs in right triangle $\triangle ABD$ are $x$ and $y$.

The length of the hypotenuse is $\sqrt{x^2 + y^2}$ by _____.

Define the trigonometric ratios for $\angle A$ in terms of $x$ and $y$ by using the side lengths of $\triangle ABD$.

$$\sin A = \frac{y}{\sqrt{x^2 + y^2}} \qquad \cos A = \frac{\phantom{xx}}{\sqrt{x^2 + y^2}} \qquad \tan A = \frac{\phantom{xx}}{\phantom{xx}}$$

**C** Finally, extend the trigonometric ratios to obtuse angles in non-right triangles.

Place non-right triangle $\triangle ABC$ with obtuse $\angle A$ on a coordinate plane as shown. Let the coordinates of $B$ be $B(x, y)$.

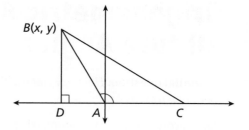

Draw a perpendicular from $B$ to the $x$-axis, and label the point of intersection $D$. Then let the "lengths" of the legs in right triangle $\triangle ABD$ be $x$ and $y$, where it is understood that $x < 0$.

The length of the hypotenuse, $\overline{AB}$, is _____ .

Define the trigonometric ratios for $\angle A$ in terms of $x$ and $y$ by using the sides of $\triangle ABD$.

$$\sin A = \frac{y}{\sqrt{x^2 + y^2}} \qquad \cos A = \frac{\phantom{xx}}{\sqrt{x^2 + y^2}} \qquad \tan A = \frac{\phantom{xx}}{\phantom{xx}}$$

**D** You can use a calculator to find trigonometric ratios for obtuse angles. Use a calculator to complete the table below. Round to the nearest hundredth.

| Angle | Sine | Cosine | Tangent |
|-------|------|--------|---------|
| 97° | | | |
| 122° | | | |
| 165° | | | |

**REFLECT**

**1a.** Look for patterns in your table. Make a conjecture about the trigonometric ratios of obtuse angles.

_____

_____

**1b.** Suppose $\angle A$ is obtuse. How do the definitions of the sine, cosine, and tangent for obtuse angles in Part C above explain why some of these trigonometric ratios are positive and some are negative?

_____

_____

_____

Now you can derive a formula for the area of a triangle that works for any triangle as long as you know two side lengths and the measure of the included angle.

**A** Let $\triangle ABC$ be a triangle with side lengths *a, b,* and *c,* as shown.

Draw an altitude from *A* to side $\overline{BC}$. Let *h* be the length of the altitude.

Then $\sin C = \frac{\phantom{xx}}{\phantom{xx}}$.

Solving for *h* shows that $h = $ _____.

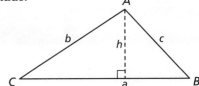

**B** The standard formula for the area of a triangle is Area $= \frac{1}{2}$(base)(height).

In $\triangle ABC$, the length of the base is _____ and the height is _____.

Area = _____

Now substitute the expression for *h* from Part A.

Area = _____

**REFLECT**

**2a.** How can you state in words the formula you derived above?

_____

_____

**2b.** Does the area formula work if angle *C* is a right angle? Explain.

_____

_____

Find the area of the triangle at right to the nearest tenth.

Let the known side lengths be *a* and *b*.

Then $a = $ _____ and $b = $ _____.

Let the known angle be *C*, so $m\angle C = $ _____.

Then Area $= \frac{1}{2} ab \sin C = \frac{1}{2}$ ⬜ • ⬜ • sin(_____).

Use a calculator to evaluate the expression. Then round.

So, the area of the triangle is _____.

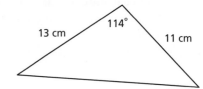

**3a.** Suppose you double each of the given side lengths in the triangle but keep the measure of the included angle the same. How does the area change? Explain.

_____

_____

# PRACTICE

**Find the area of each triangle to the nearest tenth.**

**1.**

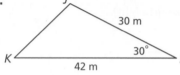

**2.**

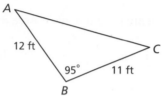

**3.**

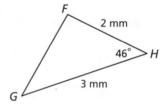

_____  _____  _____

**4.**

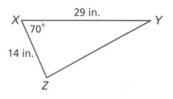

**5.**

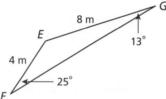

**6.**

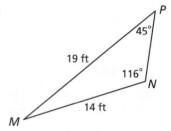

_____  _____  _____

**7.** Explain how you can derive a formula for the area of an equilateral triangle with side length *s*. (*Hint:* Use the area formula from this lesson and what you know about the angle measures of an equilateral triangle.)

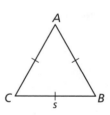

_____

_____

**8.** The isosceles triangle $\triangle RST$ has congruent sides that are 3 cm long, as shown. Write a function for the area *A* of the triangle in terms of m$\angle R$. Enter the function in your graphing calculator and use the calculator's table feature to make a conjecture about the measure of $\angle R$ that gives the greatest area. What is the maximum area?

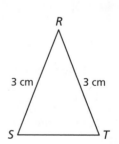

_____

_____

# The Law of Sines

**Essential question:** *What is the Law of Sines and how do you use it to solve problems?*

COMMON CORE

CC.9-12.G.SRT.10(+),
CC.9-12.G.SRT.11(+)

You can use sines and cosines to solve problems that involve non-right triangles. One example is the Law of Sines, which is a relationship that holds for any triangle.

**Law of Sines**

For $\triangle ABC$, $\dfrac{\sin A}{a} = \dfrac{\sin B}{b} = \dfrac{\sin C}{c}$.

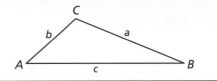

**1 PROOF**    The Law of Sines

Complete the proof.

**Given:** $\triangle ABC$
**Prove:** $\dfrac{\sin A}{a} = \dfrac{\sin B}{b} = \dfrac{\sin C}{c}$

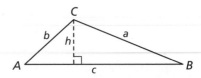

**A** Draw an altitude from $C$ to side $\overline{AB}$. Let $h$ be the length of the altitude.

Then $\sin A = \dfrac{\phantom{xx}}{\phantom{xx}}$ and $\sin B = \dfrac{\phantom{xx}}{\phantom{xx}}$.

Solve the two equations for $h$.

$h =$ _____ and $h =$ _____

**B** Write a new equation by setting the right sides of the above equations equal to each other.

_____ = _____    Substitute.

_____ = _____    Divide both sides by $ab$.

Similar reasoning shows that $\dfrac{\sin A}{a} = \dfrac{\sin C}{c}$ and $\dfrac{\sin B}{b} = \dfrac{\sin C}{c}$.

**REFLECT**

**1a.** Write an alternate form of the Law of Sines in which the side lengths are the numerators of the ratios. Explain why it is valid to rewrite the Law of Sines in this way.

_____

_____

You can use the Law of Sines to solve a triangle when you are given the following information.

- Two angle measures and any side length (AAS or ASA information).

- Two side lengths and the measure of a non-included angle (SSA information).

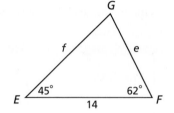

**2 EXAMPLE**    **Using the Law of Sines**

Solve the triangle. Round to the nearest tenth.

**A**   Find the unknown angle measure.

$m\angle E + m\angle F + m\angle G = 180°$      Triangle Sum Theorem

$45° + 62° + m\angle G = 180°$      Substitute.

$m\angle G = $ _____      Solve for $m\angle G$.

**B**   Use the Law of Sines to find the unknown side length $e$.

$\dfrac{\sin E}{e} = \dfrac{\sin G}{g}$      Law of Sines

$\dfrac{\sin 45°}{e} = \dfrac{\sin \boxed{\phantom{x}}}{\boxed{\phantom{x}}}$      Substitute.

$\underline{\phantom{xxxx}} \sin 45° = e \cdot \sin(\underline{\phantom{xx}})$      Multiply both sides by the product of the denominators.

$\dfrac{\boxed{\phantom{x}} \cdot \sin 45°}{\sin \boxed{\phantom{x}}} = e$      Solve for $e$.

$e \approx$ _____      Use a calculator to evaluate. Round.

**C**   Use the Law of Sines to find the unknown side length $f$.

$\dfrac{\sin F}{f} = \dfrac{\sin G}{g}$      Law of Sines

$\dfrac{\sin 62°}{f} = \dfrac{\sin \boxed{\phantom{x}}}{\boxed{\phantom{x}}}$      Substitute.

$\underline{\phantom{xxxx}} \sin 62° = f \cdot \sin(\underline{\phantom{xx}})$      Multiply both sides by the product of the denominators.

$\dfrac{\boxed{\phantom{x}} \cdot \sin 62°}{\sin \boxed{\phantom{x}}} = f$      Solve for $f$.

$f \approx$ _____      Use a calculator to evaluate. Round.

**2a.** In Part C, why is it better to write the Law of Sines as $\frac{\sin F}{f} = \frac{\sin G}{g}$ and use the known values of m∠G and g rather than write the Law of Sines as $\frac{\sin F}{f} = \frac{\sin E}{e}$ and use the known value of m∠E and the calculated value of e?

_____

_____

_____

The Law of Sines may be used to solve a triangle when you are given SSA information. However, you have seen that there is no SSA Congruence Criterion. Therefore, this type of given information may not lead to a unique triangle. This is known as the *ambiguous case* of the Law of Sines.

**3 EXPLORE**   Investigating the Ambiguous Case

You will investigate triangles for which you are given SSA information. In particular, you will be given m∠A and the side lengths a and b. You will then determine how many triangles, if any, may be formed.

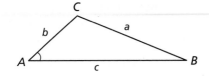

**A**   Use a straightedge and protractor to draw ∠A such that m∠A = 30°.

**B**   Use a ruler to mark a point C on one side of the angle so that b = 4 cm.

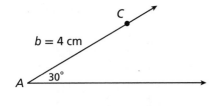

**C**   Now open your compass to a length a that is given in the table below. Place the point of the compass at point C and draw an arc that intersects the other side of ∠A. The point or points of intersection are possible locations for vertex B.

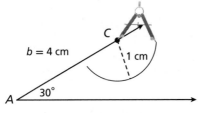

For example, when a = 1, there are no points of intersection, so no triangle is formed.

Repeat Step C for each given value of a and complete the table.

| Length a (cm) | 1 | 2 | 2.5 | 3 | 3.5 | 4 | 5 |
|---|---|---|---|---|---|---|---|
| Number of Triangles Formed | 0 | | | | | | |

**3a.** Compare your work with that of other students. Then make a conjecture: For what values of *a* are no triangles formed? For what values of *a* is exactly one triangle formed? For what values of *a* are two triangles formed?

_____

_____

When you are given SSA information and the side opposite the angle whose measure is known is shorter than the other known side, it may sometimes be possible to form two triangles. The following example illustrates this.

**4 EXAMPLE** **Solving a Real-World Problem**

Police want to set up a camera to identify drivers who run the red light at point *C* on Mason Street. The camera must be mounted on a fence that intersects Mason Street at a 40° angle, as shown, and the camera should ideally be 120 feet from point *C*. What points along the fence, if any, are suitable locations for the camera?

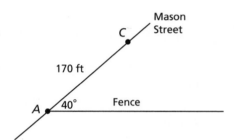

**A** Because the side opposite ∠*A* is shorter than $\overline{AC}$, it may be possible to form two triangles. Use the Law of Sines to find possible values for m∠*B*.

$$\frac{\sin A}{a} = \frac{\sin B}{b}$$ Law of Sines

$$\frac{\sin 40°}{120} = \frac{\sin B}{170}$$ Substitute.

$$\frac{170 \sin 40°}{120} = \sin B$$ Solve for sin *B*.

_____ ≈ sin *B* Use a calculator. Round to 4 decimal places.

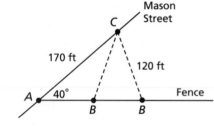

There is an acute angle and an obtuse angle that have this value as their sine. To find the acute angle, use a calculator and round to the nearest tenth.

$\sin^{-1}($ _____ $) \approx$ _____

To find the obtuse angle, note that ∠1 and ∠2 have the same sine, $\dfrac{y}{\sqrt{x^2+y^2}}$, and notice that these angles are supplementary. Thus, the obtuse angle is supplementary to the acute angle you found above.

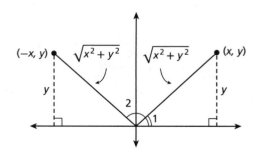

So, m∠*B* ≈ _____ or _____ .

© Houghton Mifflin Harcourt Publishing Company

**B**   For each possible measure of $\angle B$, find the corresponding measure of $\angle C$ and then find $c$.

**Case 1: $\angle B$ is acute.**

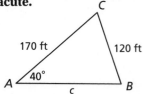

$$m\angle A + m\angle B + m\angle C = 180°$$

$$40° + \underline{\hspace{1cm}} + m\angle C = 180°$$

So, $m\angle C = \underline{\hspace{1cm}}$.

Use the Law of Sines to find $c$.

$$\frac{\sin A}{a} = \frac{\sin C}{c}$$

$$\frac{\sin 40°}{120} = \frac{\sin \boxed{\phantom{xx}}}{c}$$

$$c = \frac{120 \sin \boxed{\phantom{xx}}}{\sin 40°} \approx \underline{\hspace{2cm}}$$

**Case 2: $\angle B$ is obtuse.**

$$m\angle A + m\angle B + m\angle C = 180°$$

$$40° + \underline{\hspace{1cm}} + m\angle C = 180°$$

So, $m\angle C = \underline{\hspace{1cm}}$.

Use the Law of Sines to find $c$.

$$\frac{\sin A}{a} = \frac{\sin C}{c}$$

$$\frac{\sin 40°}{120} = \frac{\sin \boxed{\phantom{xx}}}{c}$$

$$c = \frac{120 \sin \boxed{\phantom{xx}}}{\sin 40°} \approx \underline{\hspace{2cm}}$$

So, the camera should be mounted on the fence about _____ ft or _____ ft from point $A$.

REFLECT

**4a.**  How you can check your answers?

_____

**4b.**  Suppose the camera needs to be *at most* 120 feet from point $C$. In this case, where should the camera be mounted along the fence?

_____

_____

**4c.**  What is the minimum distance at which the camera can be located from point $C$ if it is to be mounted on the fence? Explain your answer.

_____

_____

© Houghton Mifflin Harcourt Publishing Company

**Solve each triangle. Round to the nearest tenth.**

**1.**

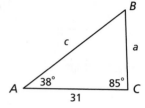

_____

_____

**2.**

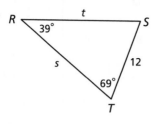

_____

_____

**3.**

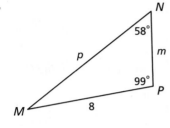

_____

_____

**4.**

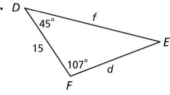

_____

_____

**5.**

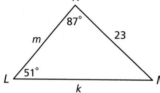

_____

_____

**6.**

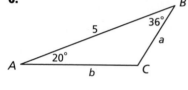

_____

_____

**7.** A stone wall makes an angle of 51° with the side of a barn that is 12 m long. You want to make a goat pen by using 10 m of fencing to enclose a triangular region, as shown. At what distance from point *C* should the fencing be attached to the stone wall? Is there more than one possibility?

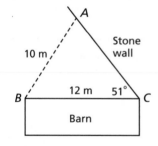

_____

_____

**8.** Two straight highways intersect in the town of Greenwood, as shown. City planners want to build a straight access road from Fernville to Highway 101, and they want the access road to be no more than 4 miles long. Describe the possible locations at which the new access road could meet Highway 101. Where should it meet Highway 101 for the shortest possible access road?

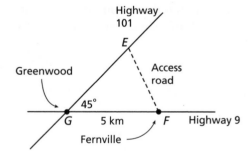

_____

_____

_____

_____

# The Law of Cosines

**Essential question:** *What is the Law of Cosines and how do you use it to solve problems?*

COMMON
CORE

CC.9-12.G.SRT.10(+),
CC.9-12.G.SRT.11(+)

When you are given SSS or SAS information about a triangle, you cannot use the Law of Sines to solve the triangle. However, this information determines a unique triangle, so there should be some way to find the unknown side lengths and angle measures. The Law of Cosines is useful in this case.

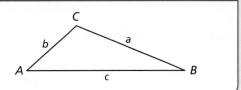

**Law of Cosines**

For $\triangle ABC$,

$a^2 = b^2 + c^2 - 2bc \cos A,$

$b^2 = a^2 + c^2 - 2ac \cos B,$

$c^2 = a^2 + b^2 - 2ab \cos C.$

---

**1** **PROOF**     **The Law of Cosines**

Complete the proof.

**Given:** $\triangle ABC$
**Prove:** $a^2 = b^2 + c^2 - 2bc \cos A$

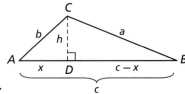

**A**   Draw an altitude $\overline{CD}$ to side $\overline{AB}$. Let $h$ be the length of the altitude.

Let $x$ be the length of $\overline{AD}$. Then $c - x$ is the length of $\overline{DB}$.

In $\triangle ADC$, $\cos A = \dfrac{\phantom{xx}}{\phantom{xx}}$ and so $x =$ _____.

Also, by the Pythagorean Theorem, $x^2 + h^2 =$ _____.

**B**   Now consider $\triangle CDB$.

$a^2 = (c - x)^2 + h^2$          Pythagorean Theorem

$a^2 = c^2 - 2cx + x^2 + h^2$        Expand $(c - x)^2$.

$a^2 = c^2 - 2cx +$ _____      Substitute _____ for $x^2 + h^2$.

$a^2 = b^2 + c^2 - 2cx$          Rearrange terms.

$a^2 = b^2 + c^2 - 2c(\underline{\phantom{xxxx}})$     Substitute _____ for $x$.

Similar reasoning shows that $b^2 = a^2 + c^2 - 2ac \cos B$ and $c^2 = a^2 + b^2 - 2ab \cos C$.

**1a.** Explain why the Law of Cosines may be considered a generalization of the Pythagorean Theorem. (*Hint:* When $\angle A$ is a right angle, what happens to the formula $a^2 = b^2 + c^2 - 2bc \cos A$?)

_____

_____

**2  E X A M P L E**    **Using the Law of Cosines**

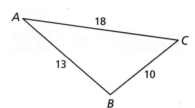

Solve the triangle. Round to the nearest tenth.

**A**  Find the measure of the obtuse angle first.

$b^2 = a^2 + c^2 - 2ac \cos B$          Law of Cosines

$18^2 = 10^2 + 13^2 - 2(10)(13)\cos B$          Substitute.

$\cos B = \dfrac{18^2 - 10^2 - 13^2}{-2(10)(13)}$          Solve for cos $B$.

$\cos B \approx$ _____          Simplify. Round to four decimal places.

$m\angle B \approx \cos^{-1}($_____$) \approx$ _____          Solve for m$\angle B$.

**B**  Use the Law of Sines to find m$\angle C$.

$\dfrac{\sin C}{c} = \dfrac{\sin B}{b}$          Law of Sines

$\dfrac{\sin C}{13} = \dfrac{\sin \boxed{\phantom{xx}}}{\boxed{\phantom{xx}}}$          Substitute.

$\sin C = \dfrac{13 \sin \boxed{\phantom{xx}}}{\boxed{\phantom{xx}}} \approx$ _____          Multiply both sides by 13, and then simplify.

$m\angle C \approx \sin^{-1}($_____$) \approx$ _____          Solve for m$\angle C$.

**C**  Use the Triangle Sum Theorem to find the remaining angle measure.

$m\angle A \approx 180° -$ _____ $-$ _____ $=$ _____

**REFLECT**

**2a.** Why is it best to find the measure of the obtuse angle first and then find another angle measure using the Law of Sines?

_____

_____

_____

**2b.** In Part B, is it possible to find m∠C without using the Law of Sines? Explain.

_____

_____

In the previous example, you were given SSS information about a triangle. In the following example about vectors, you will be given SAS information.

**3 EXAMPLE**   **Solving a Vector Problem**

A plane is flying at a rate of 600 mi/h in the direction 60° east of north. There is a 50 mi/h crosswind blowing due north. What is the final direction and speed of the plane?

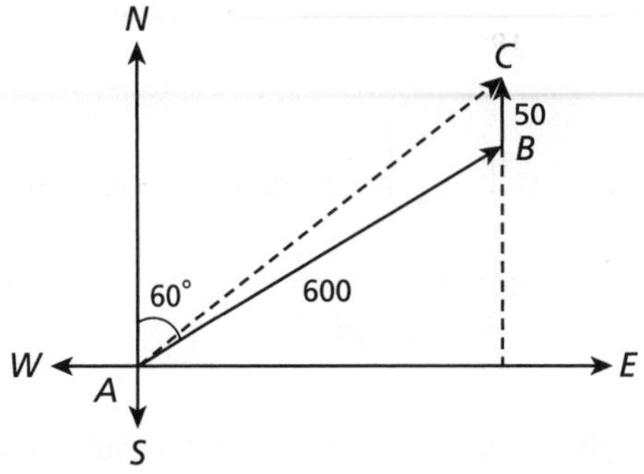

**A** Represent the situation with vectors. The plane's velocity is represented by $\overrightarrow{AB}$ and the wind's velocity is represented by $\overrightarrow{BC}$.

Explain how to find m∠ABC.

_____

_____

_____

**B** Use the Law of Cosines to find $b$, the magnitude of $\overrightarrow{AC}$.

$b^2 = a^2 + c^2 - 2ac \cos B$    Law of Cosines

$b^2 = 50^2 + 600^2 - 2(50)(600) \cos 120°$   Substitute.

$b^2 = $ _____    Simplify.

$b \approx $ _____    Take the square root. Round to the nearest tenth.

© Houghton Mifflin Harcourt Publishing Company

**C** Use the Law of Sines to find m∠A.

$$\frac{\sin A}{a} = \frac{\sin B}{b}$$   Law of Sines

$$\frac{\sin A}{50} = \frac{\sin \boxed{\phantom{xx}}}{\boxed{\phantom{xx}}}$$   Substitute.

$$\sin A = \frac{50 \sin \boxed{\phantom{xx}}}{\boxed{\phantom{xx}}} \approx \underline{\hspace{2cm}}$$   Multiply both sides by 50, and then simplify.

$$m\angle A \approx \sin^{-1}(\underline{\hspace{2cm}}) \approx \underline{\hspace{2cm}}$$   Solve for m∠A.

**D** Subtract m∠A from the original direction of the plane to find its final direction.

So, the final direction of the plane is about _____ east of north.

The plane's final speed is about _____.

## REFLECT

**3a.** Does your answer seem reasonable? Why?

_____

_____

**3b.** A student claimed that he solved the problem using only the Law of Sines. Explain his method or explain why he must have made an error.

_____

_____

# PRACTICE

**Solve each triangle. Round to the nearest tenth.**

**1.**

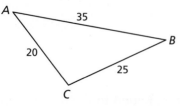

**2.**

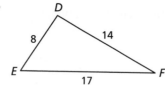

**3.**

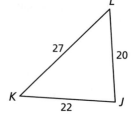

_____  _____  _____

_____  _____  _____

_____  _____  _____

**Solve each triangle. Round to the nearest tenth.**

**4.**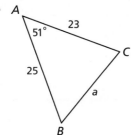

**5.**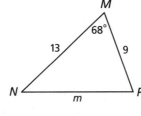

**6.**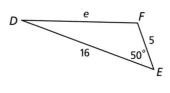

_____          _____          _____

_____          _____          _____

**7.** A sailboat sets out from shore, sailing due north at 10 mi/h. There is a crosswind blowing 5 mi/h in the direction 45° east of north. What is the final direct and speed of the sailboat?

_____

**8.** A plane is flying at a rate of 550 mi/h in the direction 40° east of north. There is a 30 mi/h crosswind blowing due south. What is the final direction and speed of the plane?

_____

**9.** A surveyor at point $S$ locates a rock formation 530 meters away at point $P$. The surveyor turns clockwise 102° and locates a rock formation 410 meters away at point $R$. To the nearest tenth of a meter, what is the distance between the rock formations?

_____

**10. Error Analysis** A student was asked to find m∠$A$ in the triangle shown below. The student's work is shown. Determine whether the student made an error and, if so, correct the error.

$$a^2 = b^2 + c^2 - 2bc \cos A$$
$$8^2 = 12^2 + 15^2 - 2(12)(15) \cos A$$
$$\cos A = \frac{8^2 - 12^2 - 15^2}{2(12)(15)} \approx -0.8472$$
$$m\angle A \approx \cos^{-1}(-0.8472) \approx 147.9°$$

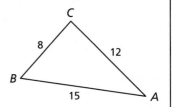

_____

_____

**Name** _____ **Class** _____ **Date** _____

## MULTIPLE CHOICE

**1.** Given that $x°$ is the measure of an acute angle, which of the following is equal to $\sin x°$?

  **A.** $\cos x°$

  **B.** $\cos(90 - x)°$

  **C.** $\sin(90 - x)°$

  **D.** $\tan x°$

**2.** Shauntay is proving the Law of Sines. She draws the figure below.

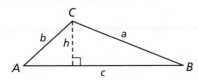

Then she writes $\sin A = \frac{h}{b}$ and $\sin B = \frac{h}{a}$. From this, she concludes that $h = b \sin A$ and $h = a \sin B$. What should she do next?

  **F.** Draw an altitude from $B$ to side $\overline{AC}$.

  **G.** Add the equations to get $2h = b \sin A + a \sin B.$

  **H.** Use the Pythagorean Theorem to write $c^2 + h^2 = a^2.$

  **J.** Write $b \sin A = a \sin B$ and then divide both sides by $ab$.

**3.** Which is closest to m$\angle S$?

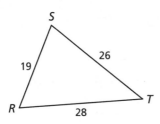

  **A.** $41°$

  **B.** $64°$

  **C.** $75°$

  **D.** $81°$

**4.** Connor is building a skateboard ramp with the dimensions shown. Which expression can he use to find the height $b$ of the ramp?

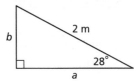

  **F.** $2 \sin 28°$

  **G.** $\dfrac{2}{\sin 28°}$

  **H.** $2 \cos 28°$

  **J.** $\dfrac{2}{\cos 28°}$

**5.** In the right triangles shown below, $\angle M \cong \angle Q$. This leads to the observation that $\triangle MNP \sim \triangle QRS$ by the AA Similarity Criterion. Therefore, corresponding sides are proportional, so $\frac{RS}{NP} = \frac{QR}{MN}$ and algebra shows that $\frac{RS}{QR} = \frac{NP}{MN}$. This last proportion is the basis for defining which of the following?

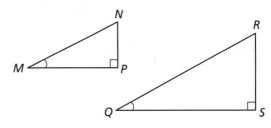

  **A.** the cosine of $\angle M$

  **B.** the cosine of $\angle P$

  **C.** the sine of $\angle M$

  **D.** the tangent of $\angle M$

## FREE RESPONSE

**6.** You are using the figure below to derive a formula for the area of a triangle that involves the sine ratio.

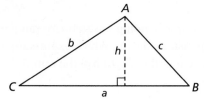

First you note that $\sin C = \frac{h}{b}$ and, therefore, $h = b \sin C$. How do you complete the derivation of the formula?

_____

_____

_____

**7.** You paddle a kayak due north at the rate of 2.5 mi/h. The river has a 2 mi/h current that flows due east. You want to find the kayak's actual speed and direction.

**a.** In the space below, sketch and label vectors that represent the situation.

**b.** Find the kayak's actual speed and direction.

_____

_____

_____

**8.** To prove the Law of Cosines, you first draw the following figure.

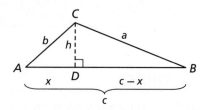

Then you note that $\cos A = \frac{x}{b}$ so $x = b \cos A$ and you note that $x^2 + h^2 = b^2$ by the Pythagorean Theorem. How do you complete the proof that $a^2 = b^2 + c^2 - 2bc \cos A$?

_____

_____

_____

_____

_____

_____

_____

**9.** A surveyor at point $P$ locates two landmarks, $A$ and $B$, as shown in the figure. Explain how the surveyor can find the distance between the landmarks to the nearest meter.

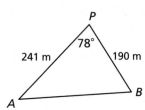

_____

_____

_____

_____

_____

_____

# Circles

## Unit Focus

In this unit, you will work with circles and explore their connection to other familiar geometric figures. First, you will learn some vocabulary associated with circles and investigate central and inscribed angles. You will also learn how to do constructions to inscribe polygons in circles and to inscribe circles in polygons. Along the way, you will study properties of tangent lines.

## Unit at a Glance

COMMON CORE

UNIT 7

# Unpacking the Common Core State Standards

Use the table to help you understand the Standards for Mathematical Content that are taught in this unit. Refer to the lessons listed after each standard for exploration and practice.

| COMMON CORE Standards for Mathematical Content | What It Means For You |
|---|---|
| **CC.9-12.G.CO.13** Construct an equilateral triangle, a square, and a regular hexagon inscribed in a circle. Lesson 7-3 | You will learn how to use a compass and straightedge to construct regular polygons in a given circle. |
| **CC.9-12.G.C.2** Identify and describe relationships among inscribed angles, radii, and chords. Lessons 7-1, 7-5 | After learning the key vocabulary associated with circles, you will explore relationships among the angles and arcs in a circle. |
| **CC.9-12.G.C.3** Construct the inscribed and circumscribed circles of a triangle, and prove properties of angles for a quadrilateral inscribed in a circle. Lessons 7-2, 7-4, 7-6 | Given a triangle, it is possible to construct a circle that passes through all three vertices. It is also possible to construct a circle such that each side of the triangle is tangent to the circle. You will see how to use a compass and straightedge to do both of these constructions. |
| **CC.9-12.G.C.4(+)** Construct a tangent line from a point outside a given circle to the circle. Lesson 7-5 | From a point outside a circle, there are two lines that are tangent to the circle. You will learn how to construct these lines. |

UNIT 7

# Central Angles and Inscribed Angles

COMMON CORE

CC.9-12.G.C.2

**Essential question:** *What is the relationship between central angles and inscribed angles in a circle?*

**1 ENGAGE**   **Introducing Angles and Arcs**

In order to begin working with circles, it is helpful to introduce some vocabulary.

A **chord** is a segment whose endpoints lie on a circle. A **central angle** is an angle whose vertex is the center of a circle. An **inscribed angle** is an angle whose vertex lies on a circle and whose sides contain chords of the circle.

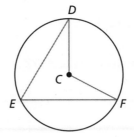

$\overline{DE}$ and $\overline{EF}$ are chords.
$\angle DCF$ is a central angle.
$\angle DEF$ is an inscribed angle.

An **arc** is a continuous portion of a circle consisting of two points on the circle, called the *endpoints* of the arc, and all the points of the circle between them. The table summarizes arc measurement and arc notation.

| Arc | Measure/Notation | Figure |
|---|---|---|
| A **minor arc** is an arc whose points are on or in the interior of a central angle. | The measure of a minor arc is the measure of its central angle.<br><br>$m\widehat{DF} = m\angle DCF$ | |
| A **major arc** is an arc whose points are on or in the exterior of a central angle. | The measure of a major arc is 360° minus the measure of its central angle.<br><br>$m\widehat{DEF} = 360° - m\angle DCF$ | |
| A **semicircle** is an arc whose endpoints are the endpoints of a diameter. | The measure of a semicircle is 180°.<br><br>$m\widehat{GHJ} = 180°$ | |

**REFLECT**

**1a.** Explain how $m\widehat{AB}$ compares to $m\widehat{CD}$.

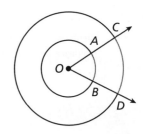

_____

**1b.** The minute hand of a clock sweeps out an arc as the time progresses from 12:05 to 12:20. What is the measure of the arc? Explain.

_____

Two arcs of a circle are *adjacent arcs* if they share an endpoint. The following postulate states that you can add the measures of adjacent arcs.

### Arc Addition Postulate

The measure of an arc formed by two adjacent arcs is the sum of the measures of the two arcs.

$m\widehat{ABC} = m\widehat{AB} + m\widehat{BC}$

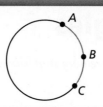

## 2 EXPLORE    Investigating Central Angles and Inscribed Angles

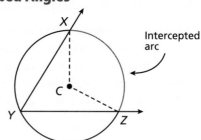

**A** Use a compass to draw a circle. Label the center *C*.

**B** Use a straightedge to draw an inscribed angle, $\angle XYZ$.

**C** Use the straightedge to draw the central angle, $\angle XCZ$.

**D** Use a protractor to measure the inscribed angle and the central angle. Use the measure of the central angle to determine the measure of the intercepted arc.

**E** Repeat the process four more times. Be sure to draw a variety of inscribed angles (acute, right, obtuse, passing through the center, etc.). Record your results in the table.

|  | Circle 1 | Circle 2 | Circle 3 | Circle 4 | Circle 5 |
|---|---|---|---|---|---|
| **Measure of Inscribed Angle** |  |  |  |  |  |
| **Measure of Intercepted Arc** |  |  |  |  |  |

### REFLECT

**2a.** Compare your work with that of other students. Then make a conjecture: What is the relationship between the measure of an inscribed angle and the measure of its intercepted arc?

_____

_____

**2b.** Suppose an inscribed angle, $\angle XYZ$, measures $x°$. If $\angle XYZ$ is acute, what is the measure of its associated central angle, $\angle XCZ$? What if $\angle XYZ$ is obtuse?

_____

You may have discovered the following relationship between an inscribed angle and its intercepted arc.

> ### Inscribed Angle Theorem
>
> The measure of an inscribed angle is half the measure of its intercepted arc.
>
> $m\angle ADB = \frac{1}{2}m\widehat{AB}$

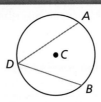

**3** **EXAMPLE**  **Finding Arc and Angle Measures**

Find $m\widehat{BC}$, $m\widehat{BD}$, $m\angle DAB$, and $m\angle ABC$.

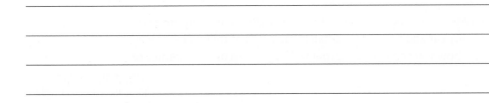

**A** Find $m\widehat{BC}$.

$m\angle BAC = \frac{1}{2}m\widehat{BC}$    Inscribed Angle Theorem

$2m\angle BAC = m\widehat{BC}$    Multiply both sides by 2.

$2 \cdot \underline{\hspace{1cm}} = m\widehat{BC}$    Substitute.

$\underline{\hspace{1cm}} = m\widehat{BC}$    Multiply.

**B** By the Arc Addition Postulate, $m\widehat{BD} = m\widehat{BC} + m\widehat{CD} = \underline{\hspace{1cm}} + 88° = \underline{\hspace{1cm}}$ .

**C** By the Inscribed Angle Theorem, $m\angle DAB = \frac{1}{2}m\widehat{BD} = \frac{1}{2} \cdot \underline{\hspace{1cm}} = \underline{\hspace{1cm}}$ .

**D** To find $m\angle ABC$, note that $\widehat{ADC}$ is a $\underline{\hspace{2cm}}$ .

Therefore, $m\widehat{ADC} = \underline{\hspace{1cm}}$ , and $m\angle ABC = \frac{1}{2}m\widehat{ADC} = \frac{1}{2} \cdot \underline{\hspace{1cm}} = \underline{\hspace{1cm}}$ .

**REFLECT**

**3a.** Is it possible to find $m\widehat{DAB}$? If so, how? If not, why not?

_____

**3b.** Show two different methods to find $m\widehat{AB}$.

_____

_____

_____

_____

_____

**3c.** Consider $\angle ABC$ and make a conjecture: What do you think must be true about any inscribed angle that contains endpoints of a diameter? Why?

_____

_____

The following theorem describes a key relationship between inscribed angles and diameters.

**Theorem**

The endpoints of a diameter lie on an inscribed angle if and only if the inscribed angle is a right angle.

# PRACTICE

**Use the figure to find each of the following.**

**1.** m$\widehat{BA}$ _____

**2.** m∠*BOA* _____

**3.** m$\widehat{AE}$ _____

**4.** m∠*AOE* _____

**5.** m$\widehat{BAE}$ _____

**6.** m∠*BDE* _____

**7.** m∠*DBE* _____

**8.** m$\widehat{DE}$ _____

**9.** m$\widehat{DB}$ _____

**10.** m$\widehat{ABD}$ _____

**11.** m∠*EDA* _____

**12.** m∠*OAD* _____

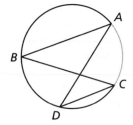

**13.** Prove that if two inscribed angles of a circle intercept the same arc, then the angles are congruent.

**Given:** ∠*ABC* and ∠*ADC* intercept $\widehat{AC}$ .

**Prove:** ∠*ABC* ≅ ∠*ADC*

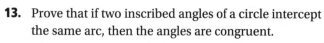

_____

_____

_____

**14.** A carpenter's square is a tool that is used to draw right angles. Suppose you are building a toy car and you have a small circle of wood that will serve as a wheel. Explain how you can use the carpenter's square to find the center of the circle.

_____

_____

_____

_____

_____

_____

Carpenter's square

© Houghton Mifflin Harcourt Publishing Company

# Constructing Circumscribed Circles

COMMON CORE

CC.9-12.G.C.3

**Essential question:** *How do you construct a circle that circumscribes a triangle?*

A circle is said to **circumscribe** a polygon if the circle passes through all of the polygon's vertices. In the figure, circle *C* circumscribes △*XYZ* and this circle is called the **circumcircle** of △*XYZ*.

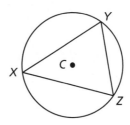

In order to construct the circumcircle of a triangle, you need to find the center of the circle. The following example will guide you through the reasoning process to do this.

## 1 EXAMPLE  Constructing a Circumscribed Circle

Work directly on the figure to construct the circumcircle of △*PQR*.

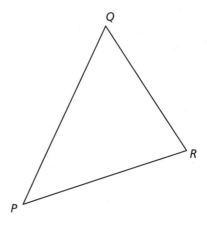

**A** The circumcircle will pass through *P*, *Q*, and *R*. So, the center of the circle must be equidistant from all three points. In particular, the center must be equidistant from *P* and *R*. What is the set of points equidistant from *P* and *R*?

_____

Use a compass and straightedge to construct this set of points.

**B** Similarly, the center must be equidistant from *Q* and *R*. What is the set of points equidistant from *Q* and *R*?

_____

Use a compass and straightedge to construct this set of points.

**C** The center must lie at the intersection of the two sets of points you constructed. Label this point *C*.

**D** Place the point of your compass at *C* and open it to the distance *CP*. Then draw the circumcircle.

### REFLECT

**1a.** Suppose you started by constructing the set of points equidistance from *P* and *Q*, and then you constructed the set of points equidistant from *Q* and *R*. Would you have found the same center point? Check by doing this construction.

_____

You may have discovered that the perpendicular bisectors of a triangle intersect at a common point. This point is called the **circumcenter** of the triangle. You will further investigate circumcenters in the exercises.

# PRACTICE

**Construct the circumcircle of each triangle.**

**1.**

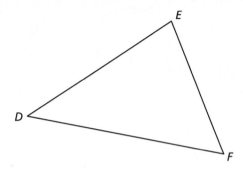

**2.**

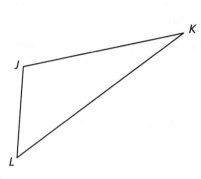

**3.**

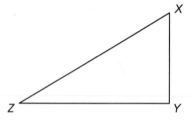

**4.**

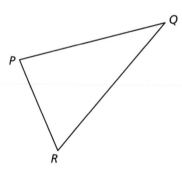

**5.** Explain how to use a compass and straightedge to locate the center of a circle. (*Hint:* Start by plotting three points on the circle.)

_____

_____

_____

**6.** Use a compass and straightedge to locate the circumcenter of an acute triangle, a right triangle, and an obtuse triangle. Considering these constructions and the other constructions from this lesson, what can you say about the location of a triangle's circumcenter?

_____

_____

_____

© Houghton Mifflin Harcourt Publishing Company

# Constructing Inscribed Polygons

COMMON CORE

CC.9-12.G.CO.13

**Essential question:** *How do you inscribe a regular polygon in a circle?*

A polygon is said to be **inscribed** in a circle if all of the polygon's vertices lie on the circle. In the figure, $\triangle XYZ$ is inscribed in circle $C$. You can also say that circle $C$ circumscribes $\triangle XYZ$.

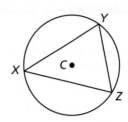

In this lesson, you will use a compass and straightedge to inscribe regular polygons in a circle.

**1  EXPLORE**    Inscribing a Regular Hexagon

Use the space at right to inscribe a regular hexagon in a circle.

**A**   Use your compass to draw a circle $O$. Label a point $A$ on the circle.

**B**   Without adjusting the compass, place the point of the compass at $A$ and draw an arc that intersects the circle. Label the point of intersection $B$.

**C**   Without adjusting the compass, place the point of the compass at $B$ and draw an arc that intersects the circle. Label the point of intersection $C$.

**D**   Continue in this way until you have located six points, $A$, $B$, $C$, $D$, $E$, and $F$. Then use your straightedge to draw $\overline{AB}$, $\overline{BC}$, $\overline{CD}$, $\overline{DE}$, $\overline{EF}$, and $\overline{FA}$.

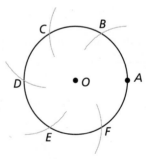

**REFLECT**

**1a.**  Explain why $ABCDEF$ must be a regular hexagon. (*Hint:* Consider the triangles that are formed when you draw the diameters $\overline{AD}$, $\overline{BE}$, and $\overline{CF}$.)

_____

_____

_____

**1b.**  How can you modify this construction to construct an inscribed equilateral triangle?

_____

Use the space at right to inscribe a square in a circle.

**A** Use your compass to draw a circle *O*.

**B** Use your straightedge to draw a diameter $\overline{AB}$.

**C** Use the compass and straightedge to construct the perpendicular bisector of $\overline{AB}$.

**D** Label the points where the perpendicular bisector intersects the circle as *C* and *D*.

**E** Use the straightedge to draw $\overline{AD}$, $\overline{DB}$, $\overline{BC}$, and $\overline{CA}$.

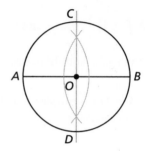

**REFLECT**

**2a.** Explain why *ADBC* must have four congruent sides.

_____

_____

_____

_____

**2b.** Explain why all of the angles of *ADBC* must be right angles.

_____

_____

_____

**2c.** How can you use the above construction as the starting point for inscribing a regular octagon in a circle?

_____

_____

_____

**FOCUS ON REASONING**
# Inscribed Quadrilaterals

**Essential question:** *What can you conclude about the angles of a quadrilateral inscribed in a circle?*

**1** **Investigate inscribed quadrilaterals.**

Use geometry software to inscribe a quadrilateral in a circle and explore its angle measures.

**A** Use geometry software to construct a circle.

**B** Plot points *A, B, C,* and *D* on the circle, as shown.

**C** Use the segment tool to draw $\overline{AB}$, $\overline{BC}$, $\overline{CD}$, and $\overline{DA}$.

**D** Use the Measure menu to measure ∠*DAB*, ∠*ABC*, ∠*BCD*, and ∠*CDA*.

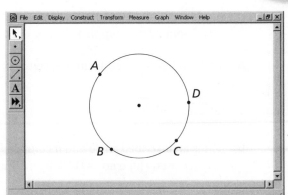

**E** Use the Calculate tool to calculate m∠*DAB* + m∠*BCD* and m∠*ABC* + m∠*CDA*.

**F** Drag the vertices of quadrilateral *ABCD* to change its shape. Change the size of the circle. Note any changes in the measurements.

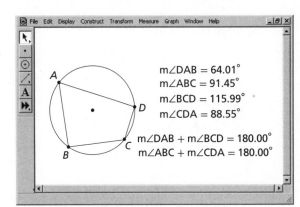

**REFLECT**

**1a.** Compare your findings with those of other students. Then make a conjecture: What can you say about the angles of a quadrilateral that is inscribed in a circle?

_____

_____

**1b.** Suppose you know both that quadrilateral *PQRS* is inscribed in a circle and that m∠*Q* = 43°. Is it possible to find the measure of some or all of the other angles? Explain.

_____

_____

_____

## Inscribed Quadrilateral Theorem

If a quadrilateral is inscribed in a circle, then its opposite angles are supplementary.

The converse of the Inscribed Quadrilateral Theorem is also true. Taken together, the theorem and its converse tell you that a quadrilateral can be inscribed in a circle *if and only if* its opposite angles are supplementary.

### 2 Prove the Inscribed Quadrilateral Theorem.

**Given:** Quadrilateral *ABCD* is inscribed in circle *O*.

**Prove:** ∠*A* and ∠*C* are supplementary;
∠*B* and ∠*D* are supplementary.

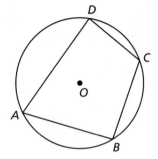

**A** $\widehat{BCD}$ and $\widehat{DAB}$ make a complete circle. Therefore,

$$m\widehat{BCD} + m\widehat{DAB} = \underline{\hspace{2cm}}.$$

**B** ∠*A* is an inscribed angle and its intercepted arc is $\widehat{BCD}$; ∠*C* is an inscribed angle and its intercepted arc is $\widehat{DAB}$. By the Inscribed Angle Theorem,

$$m\angle A = \underline{\hspace{2cm}} \text{ and } m\angle C = \underline{\hspace{2cm}}.$$

**C** So, m∠*A* + m∠*C* = \underline{\hspace{4cm}}     Substitution

= \underline{\hspace{3cm}}     Distributive Property

= \underline{\hspace{3cm}}     Substitution

= \underline{\hspace{3cm}}     Simplify.

This shows that ∠*A* and ∠*C* are supplementary. Similar reasoning shows that ∠*B* and ∠*D* are supplementary.

### REFLECT

**2a.** What must be true about a parallelogram that is inscribed in a circle? Explain.

_____

_____

**2b.** What must be true about a rhombus that is inscribed in a circle? Explain.

_____

_____

_____

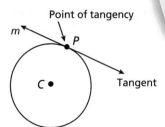

**7-5**

## FOCUS ON REASONING
# Tangent Lines

COMMON CORE

CC.9-12.G.C.2,
CC.9-12.G.C.4(+)

**Essential question:** *What are the key theorems about tangent lines to a circle?*

A **tangent** is a line in the same plane as a circle that intersects the circle in exactly one point. The point where a tangent and a circle intersect is the **point of tangency**. In the figure, line *m* is a tangent to circle *C*, and point *P* is the point of tangency.

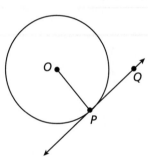

Point of tangency

Tangent

**1** **Investigate tangents and radii.**

**A** Use a compass to draw a circle *O*.

**B** Plot a point *P* on the circle.

**C** Using a straightedge, carefully draw a tangent to circle *O* through point *P*. Plot another point *Q* on the tangent line.

**D** Use the straightedge to draw the radius $\overline{OP}$.

**E** Use a protractor to measure ∠*OPQ*.

**F** Repeat the process, starting with a different circle.

**REFLECT**

**1a.** Compare your findings with those of other students. Then make a conjecture: What can you say about the relationship between a tangent line and a radius to the point of tangency?

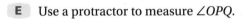

**1b.** Describe any inaccuracies related to the tools you used in the investigation.

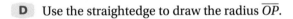

You may have discovered the following theorem.

---

🔑 **Tangent-Radius Theorem**

If a line is tangent to a circle, then it is perpendicular to the radius drawn to the point of tangency.

Line *m* is tangent to circle *C* at point *P*, so $\overline{CP} \perp m$.

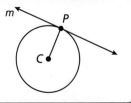

---

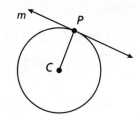

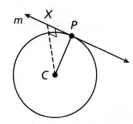

**2  Prove the Tangent-Radius Theorem.**

**Given:** Line $m$ is tangent to circle $C$ at point $P$.

**Prove:** $\overline{CP} \perp m$

Complete the proof.

Use an indirect proof. Assume that $\overline{CP}$ is *not* perpendicular to line $m$. Then it must be possible to draw $\overline{CX}$ so that $\overline{CX} \perp m$.

In this case, $\triangle CXP$ is a right triangle, so $CP > CX$ because

_____

Because line $m$ is a tangent line, it can intersect circle $C$ at only one point, $P$, and all other points of line $m$ are in the exterior of the circle. This means point $X$ is in the exterior of the circle. So, you can conclude that $CP < CX$ because

_____

This contradicts the fact that $CP > CX$. Therefore,

_____

_____

---

**REFLECT**

**2a.** In the figure, lines $m$ and $n$ are tangent lines to circle $A$. What can you say about quadrilateral $ABCD$? Explain.

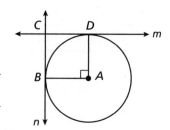

_____

_____

_____

_____

_____

_____

The converse of the Tangent-Radius Theorem is also true. You will be asked to prove the converse as an exercise.

**Converse of the Tangent-Radius Theorem**

If a line is perpendicular to a radius of a circle at a point on the circle, then the line is a tangent to the circle.

### 3 Construct a tangent to a circle.

Construct a tangent line from point $P$ to circle $C$.

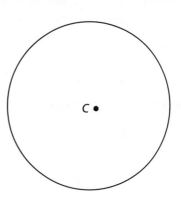

**A** Work directly on the figure at right. Use your straightedge to draw $\overline{CP}$.

**B** Construct the midpoint of $\overline{CP}$. Label the midpoint $M$.

**C** Place the point of your compass at $M$. Draw a circle with center $M$ and radius $CM$.

**D** Label the points of intersection of circle $M$ and circle $C$ as $X$ and $Y$.

**E** Use the straightedge to draw $\overleftrightarrow{PX}$ and $\overleftrightarrow{PY}$. Both lines are tangents to circle $C$.

---

**REFLECT**

**3a.** Give a justification for the construction. That is, explain how you know that $\overleftrightarrow{PX}$ is a tangent line. (*Hint:* In the figure at right, what can you conclude about $\angle CXP$? Why?)

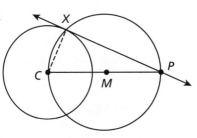

_____

_____

_____

_____

**3b.** Measure $\overline{PX}$ and $\overline{PY}$ in your construction. Then repeat the construction with a different circle and different point outside the circle. Measure $\overline{PX}$ and $\overline{PY}$. Compare your results with those of other students. Then make a conjecture based on your observations.

_____

_____

As you discovered in the above construction, given any point outside a circle, you can draw two tangent lines to the circle. The two tangent lines form a *circumscribed angle*.

A **circumscribed angle** is an angle formed by two tangents to a circle. In the figure, $\overrightarrow{QP}$ and $\overrightarrow{QR}$ are tangents to circle $C$, so $\angle PQR$ is a circumscribed angle.

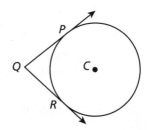

> ### Circumscribed Angle Theorem
>
> A circumscribed angle of a circle and its associated central angle are supplementary.

**4** **Prove the Circumscribed Angle Theorem.**

**Given:** ∠PQR is a circumscribed angle.

**Prove:** ∠PQR and ∠PCR are supplementary.

Complete the proof.

Since ∠PQR is a circumscribed angle, $\overrightarrow{QP}$ and $\overrightarrow{QR}$ are _____.

Therefore, ∠QPC and ∠QRC are _____

by _____.

So, m∠PQR + m∠QRC + m∠PCR + m∠QPC = 360°     Quadrilateral Sum Theorem

m∠PQR + _____ + m∠PCR + _____ = 360°     Substitution

m∠PQR + m∠PCR + _____ = 360°     Simplify.

m∠PQR + m∠PCR = 180°     Subtract 180° from both sides.

So, ∠PQR and ∠PCR are supplementary, by the definition of supplementary.

> **REFLECT**

**4a.** Is it possible for quadrilateral *PQRC* to be a parallelogram? If so, what type of parallelogram must it be? If not, why not?

_____

# PRACTICE

**In the figure, $\overrightarrow{KJ}$ and $\overrightarrow{KL}$ are tangents. Find the following.**

**1.** m∠CJK  _____     **2.** m∠JCL  _____

**3.** m$\widehat{JL}$  _____     **4.** m$\widehat{JML}$  _____

**5.** m∠JML  _____     **6.** m$\widehat{JM}$  _____

**7.** m$\widehat{MLJ}$  _____     **8.** m$\widehat{MJL}$  _____

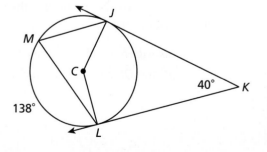

**9.** Prove the Converse of the Tangent-Radius Theorem.

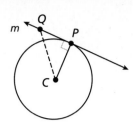

**Given:** $\overline{CP} \perp m$

**Prove:** Line $m$ is tangent to circle $C$.

(*Hint:* Let $Q$ be any point on $m$ other than $P$. Show that $CQ > CP$.)

_____

_____

_____

_____

_____

**10.** Construct two tangents from point $A$ to circle $O$.

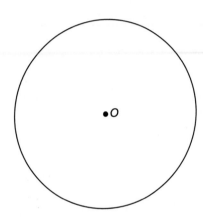

**11. Error Analysis** In the given figure, $\overrightarrow{QP}$ and $\overrightarrow{QR}$ are tangents. A student was asked to find m$\angle PSR$. Critique the student's work and correct any errors.

Since $\angle PQR$ is a circumscribed angle,
$\angle PQR$ and $\angle PCR$ are supplementary,
so m$\angle PCR = 110°$. Since $\angle PSR \cong \angle PCR$,
you can conclude that m$\angle PSR = 110°$.

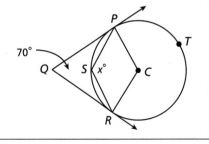

_____

_____

_____

© Houghton Mifflin Harcourt Publishing Company

# Constructing Inscribed Circles

**Essential question:** *How do you inscribe a circle in a triangle?*

A circle is **inscribed** in a polygon if each side of the polygon is tangent to the circle. In the figure, circle *C* is inscribed in quadrilateral *WXYZ*.

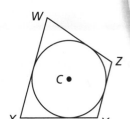

COMMON CORE

CC.9-12.G.C.3

The following example will guide you through the reasoning process for constructing an inscribed circle in a triangle.

1 **E X A M P L E**   **Constructing an Inscribed Circle**

Work directly on the figure to inscribe a circle in △*PQR*.

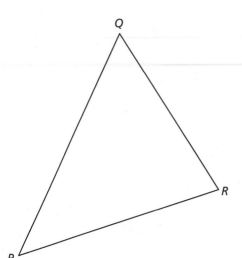

**A**  The center of the inscribed circle must be equidistant from the sides of △*PQR*. In particular, the center must be equidistant from $\overline{PQ}$ and $\overline{PR}$. What is the set of points equidistant from $\overline{PQ}$ and $\overline{PR}$?

_____

Use a compass and straightedge to construct this set of points.

**B**  Similarly, the center must be equidistant from $\overline{PR}$ and $\overline{QR}$. What is the set of points equidistant from $\overline{PR}$ and $\overline{QR}$?

_____

Use a compass and straightedge to construct this set of points.

**C**  The center must lie at the intersection of the two sets of points you constructed. Label this point *C*.

**D**  Place the point of your compass at *C* and open the compass until the pencil just touches a side of △*PQR*. Then draw the inscribed circle.

REFLECT

**1a.** Suppose you started by constructing the set of points equidistant from $\overline{PR}$ and $\overline{QR}$, and then constructed the set of points equidistant from $\overline{QR}$ and $\overline{QP}$. Would you have found the same center point? Check by doing this construction.

_____

You may have discovered that the angle bisectors of a triangle intersect at a common point. This point is called the **incenter** of the triangle. A circle that is inscribed in a triangle has its center at the incenter and is sometimes called the triangle's **incircle**.

# PRACTICE

**Construct the inscribed circle for each triangle.**

**1.**

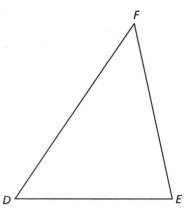

**2.**

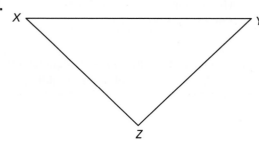

**3.**

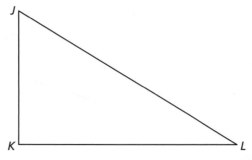

**4.**

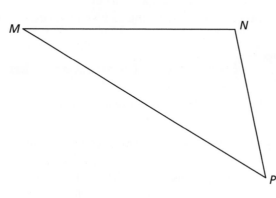

**5.** Explain how you can use paper folding to find the incenter of a triangle.

_____

_____

_____

**6.** The distance from a point to a line is the length of the perpendicular segment from the point to the line. Use this fact and the fact that $C$ is the incenter of $\triangle XYZ$ to find the length of $\overline{CN}$.

_____

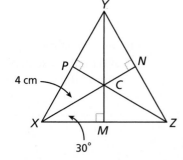

© Houghton Mifflin Harcourt Publishing Company

**Name** _____ **Class** _____ **Date** _____

## MULTIPLE CHOICE

**1.** Which statement describes the relationship between ∠XYZ and ∠XCZ?

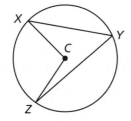

   **A.** ∠XYZ ≅ ∠XCZ

   **B.** m∠XYZ = 2m∠XCZ

   **C.** m∠XYZ = $\frac{1}{2}$m∠XCZ

   **D.** ∠XYZ and ∠XCZ are supplementary.

**2.** $\overline{PR}$ and $\overline{QR}$ are tangents to circle C. Which expression represents m∠C?

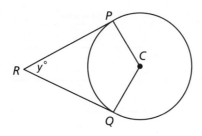

   **F.** (2y)°　　　　**H.** (90 − y)°

   **G.** (180 − y)°　　**J.** $\left(\frac{1}{2}y\right)°$

**3.** In circle O, ∠ABC is an inscribed angle and $\overline{AC}$ is a diameter. Which of the following must be true?

   **A.** ∠ABC is an acute angle.

   **B.** ∠ABC is a right angle.

   **C.** $\overline{AB}$ is a radius.

   **D.** $\overline{AC} \perp \overline{BC}$

**4.** Jessica is using a compass and straightedge to construct the inscribed circle for △PQR. Which of the following should be her first step?

   **F.** Construct the bisector of ∠Q

   **G.** Construct the perpendicular bisector of $\overline{QR}$

   **H.** Construct the perpendicular from P to $\overline{QR}$

   **J.** Construct the midpoint of $\overline{PR}$

**5.** $\overline{JK}$ is a tangent to circle C. What is m$\overset{\frown}{KL}$?

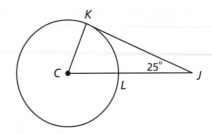

   **A.** 25°　　　　　**C.** 65°

   **B.** 50°　　　　　**D.** 130°

**6.** Noah is constructing a tangent from P to circle C. The figure shows what he has done so far. What should he do next?

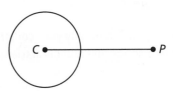

   **F.** Construct a perpendicular at point P.

   **G.** Construct a perpendicular at point C.

   **H.** Construct a circle whose center is at the intersection of $\overline{CP}$ and circle C.

   **J.** Construct the midpoint of $\overline{CP}$.

**7.** What is m∠GCJ?

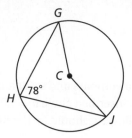

**A.** 39°     **C.** 102°

**B.** 78°     **D.** 156°

## FREE RESPONSE

**8.** Use a compass and straightedge to construct a regular hexagon that is inscribed in circle O.

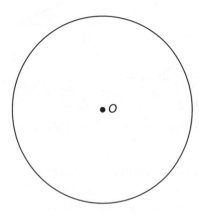

**9.** Explain how you can modify your construction in Item 8 to inscribe an equilateral triangle in circle O.

_____

_____

_____

_____

_____

**10.** Quadrilateral WXYZ is inscribed in circle O. Complete the following proof to show that opposite angles are supplementary.

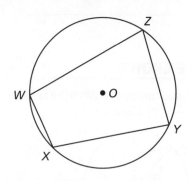

**a.** $\overparen{YZW}$ and $\overparen{WXY}$ make a complete circle.

Therefore, $m\overparen{YZW} + m\overparen{WXY} = $ _____.

**b.** By the Inscribed Angle Theorem,

m∠X = _____ and m∠Z = _____.

**c.** Complete the proof by showing that the sum of m∠X and m∠Z is 180°.

_____

_____

_____

_____

_____

_____

_____

_____

_____

# Geometry Using Coordinates and Equations

## Unit Focus

In this unit, you will explore analytic geometry, which is the study of geometry using a coordinate system. First you will learn how to use the distance formula to write the equation of a circle and the equation of a parabola. Then you will see how you can use slope to partition a segment into a given ratio and to determine when lines are parallel or perpendicular. You will also write coordinate proofs using slope and solve systems of equations.

## Unit at a Glance

**COMMON CORE**

**UNIT 8**

© Houghton Mifflin Harcourt Publishing Company

# Unpacking the Common Core State Standards

Use the table to help you understand the Standards for Mathematical Content that are taught in this unit. Refer to the lessons listed after each standard for exploration and practice.

| COMMON CORE Standards for Mathematical Content | What It Means For You |
|---|---|
| **CC.9-12.A.REI.7 Solve a simple system consisting of a linear equation and a quadratic equation in two variables algebraically and graphically.** Lesson 8-7 | You learned how to solve systems of linear equations in Algebra. Now you will extend what you know to solve systems that involve a line and a circle or a line and a parabola. |
| **CC.9-12.G.GPE.1 Derive the equation of a circle of given center and radius using the Pythagorean Theorem; complete the square to find the center and radius of a circle given by an equation.** Lesson 8-1 | Given the radius and center of a circle, you will write an equation for the circle. Conversely, given an equation of a circle, you will learn how to determine the radius and center. |
| **CC.9-12.G.GPE.2 Derive the equation of a parabola given a focus and directrix.** Lesson 8-2 | You will see that the points that form a parabola can be defined in terms of their distance from a fixed point and a given line. You will use this idea and the distance formula to derive the equation of a parabola. |
| **CC.9-12.G.GPE.4 Use coordinates to prove simple geometric theorems algebraically.** Lessons 8-1, 8-6 | As you will see, coordinates are useful for proving a wide range of geometry theorems. You will use what you learn about equations of circles and slopes of sides of quadrilaterals to help you write coordinate proofs. |
| **CC.9-12.G.GPE.5 Prove the slope criteria for parallel and perpendicular lines and use them to solve geometric problems (e.g., find the equation of a line parallel or perpendicular to a given line that passes through a given point).** Lessons 8-4, 8-5 | You can determine whether two lines are parallel or perpendicular if you know the slopes of the lines. You will see how to use this idea to write equations of lines and to write coordinate proofs. |
| **CC.9-12.G.GPE.6 Find the point on a directed line segment between two given points that partitions the segment in a given ratio.** Lesson 8-3 | You will learn how to find a point along a line segment that divides the segment in a particular way. |

UNIT 8

# The Equation of a Circle

**8-1**

COMMON CORE

CC.9-12.G.GPE.1,
CC.9-12.G.GPE.4

**Essential question:** *How do you write the equation of a circle if you know its radius and the coordinates of its center?*

Recall that a circle is the set of all points in a plane that are a fixed distance from a given point. You have already worked with circles in Unit 7. Now you will investigate circles in a coordinate plane.

## 1 EXPLORE  Deriving the Equation of a Circle

Consider the circle in a coordinate plane that has its center at $C(h, k)$ and that has radius $r$.

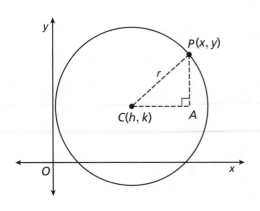

**A**  Let $P$ be any point on the circle and let the coordinates of $P$ be $(x, y)$.

Create a right triangle by drawing a horizontal line through $C$ and a vertical line through $P$, as shown.

What are the coordinates of point $A$? _____

Write expressions for the lengths of the legs of $\triangle CAP$.

$CA =$ _____ ; $PA =$ _____

**B**  Use the Pythagorean Theorem to write a relationship among the side lengths of $\triangle CAP$.

_____ + _____ = _____

### REFLECT

**1a.**  Compare your work with that of other students. Then write the equation of a circle with center $(h, k)$ and radius $r$.

_____

**1b.**  Why do you need absolute values when you write expressions for the lengths of the legs in Step A, but not when you write the relationship among the side lengths in Step B?

_____

_____

**1c.**  Suppose a circle has its center at the origin. What is the equation of the circle in this case?

_____

The equation of a circle with center $(h, k)$ and radius $r$ is $(x - h)^2 + (y - k)^2 = r^2$.

## 2 EXAMPLE  Finding the Center and Radius of a Circle

Find the center and radius of the circle whose equation is $x^2 - 4x + y^2 + 2y = 4$.
Then graph the circle.

**A**  Complete the square to write the equation in the form $(x - h)^2 + (y - k)^2 = r^2$.

$x^2 - 4x + \boxed{\phantom{0}} + y^2 + 2y + \boxed{\phantom{0}} = 4 + \boxed{\phantom{0}}$  Set up to complete the square.

$x^2 - 4x + \underline{\phantom{00}} + y^2 + 2y + \underline{\phantom{00}} = 4 + \underline{\phantom{0000}}$  Add $\left(\frac{-4}{2}\right)^2$ and $\left(\frac{2}{2}\right)^2$ to both sides.

$x^2 - 4x + \underline{\phantom{00}} + y^2 + 2y + \underline{\phantom{00}} = 4 + \underline{\phantom{00}}$  Simplify.

$(x - \underline{\phantom{00}})^2 + (y + \underline{\phantom{00}})^2 = \underline{\phantom{0000}}$  Factor.

**B**  Identify $h$, $k$, and $r$ to determine the center and radius.

$h = \underline{\phantom{0000}}$        $k = \underline{\phantom{0000}}$        $r = \underline{\phantom{0000}}$

So, the center is (\underline{\phantom{0000}}, \underline{\phantom{0000}}) and the radius is \underline{\phantom{0000}}.

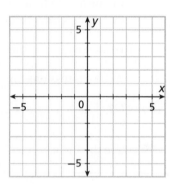

**C**  Graph the circle.

- Locate the center of the circle.
- Place the point of your compass at the center.
- Open the compass to the radius.
- Use the compass to draw the circle.

### REFLECT

**2a.** How can you check your graph by testing specific points from the graph in the
original equation? Give an example.

_____

_____

**2b.** Suppose you translate the circle by the translation $(x, y) \rightarrow (x + 4, y - 1)$.
What is the equation of the image of the circle? Explain.

_____

_____

## 3 EXAMPLE  Writing a Coordinate Proof

Prove or disprove that the point $(1, \sqrt{15})$ lies on the circle that is centered at the origin and contains the point $(0, 4)$.

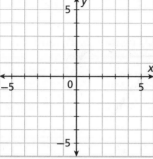

**A**  Plot a point at the origin and at $(0, 4)$. Use these to help you draw the circle centered at the origin that contains $(0, 4)$.

**B**  Determine the radius: $r =$ _____

**C**  Use the radius and the coordinates of the center to write the equation of the circle.

_____

**D**  Substitute the $x$- and $y$-coordinates of the point $(1, \sqrt{15})$ in the equation of the circle to check whether they satisfy the equation.

_____ $^2$ + _____ $^2$ $\overset{?}{=} 16$    Substitute.

_____ + _____ $= 16$    Simplify.

**E**  So, the point $(1, \sqrt{15})$ lies on the circle because

_____

**REFLECT**

**3a.**  Explain how to determine the radius of the circle.

_____

_____

**3b.**  Name another point with noninteger coordinates that lies on the circle. Explain.

_____

**3c.**  Explain how you can prove that the point $(2, \sqrt{5})$ does *not* lie on the circle.

_____

_____

Write the equation of the circle with the given center and radius.

**1.** center: $(0, 2)$; radius: 5

_____

**2.** center: $(-1, 3)$; radius 8

_____

**3.** center: $(-4, -5)$; radius: $\sqrt{2}$

_____

**4.** center: $(9, 0)$; radius $\sqrt{3}$

_____

**Find the center and radius of the circle with the given equation.
Then graph the circle.**

**5.** $x^2 - 2x + y^2 = 15$

_____

**6.** $x^2 + 4x + y^2 - 6y = -9$

_____

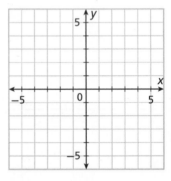

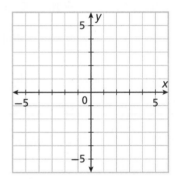

**7.** Prove or disprove that the point $(1, \sqrt{3})$ lies on the circle that is centered at the origin and contains the point $(0, 2)$.

_____

_____

_____

**8.** Prove or disprove that the point $(2, \sqrt{3})$ lies on the circle that is centered at the origin and contains the point $(-3, 0)$.

_____

_____

_____

**9.** Prove or disprove that the circle with equation $x^2 - 4x + y^2 = -3$ intersects the y-axis.

_____

_____

_____

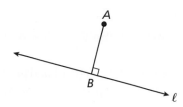

# The Equation of a Parabola

COMMON CORE

CC.9-12.G.GPE.2

**Essential question:** *How do you write the equation of a parabola given its focus and directrix?*

The distance from a point to a line is the length of the perpendicular segment from the point to the line. In the figure, the distance from point *A* to line ℓ is *AB*.

You will use the idea of the distance from a point to a line below.

## 1 EXPLORE   Creating a Parabola

Follow these instructions to plot a point. You will report the approximate coordinates of the point to your teacher, who will create a graph consisting of all points from everyone in the class. Be sure to work as accurately as possible.

**A**   Choose a point on line ℓ. Plot a point *Q* at this location.

**B**   Using a straightedge, draw a perpendicular to ℓ that passes through point *Q*. Label this line *m*.

**C**   Use the straightedge to draw $\overline{PQ}$. Then use a compass and straightedge to construct the perpendicular bisector of $\overline{PQ}$.

**D**   Plot a point *X* where the perpendicular bisector intersects line *m*.

**E**   Write the approximate coordinates of point *X* and report the coordinates to your teacher.

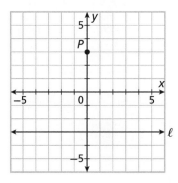

_____

### REFLECT

**1a.**  Use the figure to help you explain why the point *X* that you plotted is equidistant from point *P* and line ℓ.

_____

_____

**1b.**  What do you notice about the set of points your teacher plotted?

_____

_____

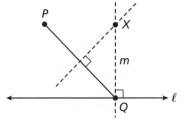

A **parabola** is the set of all points $P$ in a plane that are equidistant from a given point, called the **focus**, and a given line, called the **directrix**.

To derive the general equation of a parabola, you can use the above definition, the distance formula, and the idea that the distance from a point to a line is the length of the perpendicular segment from the point to the line.

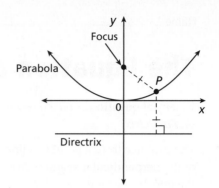

## 2 EXPLORE   Deriving the Equation of a Parabola

**A**  Let the focus of the parabola be $F(0, p)$ and let the directrix be the line $y = -p$. Let $P$ be a point on the parabola with coordinates $(x, y)$.

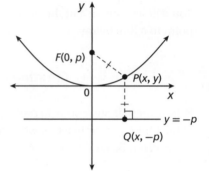

**B**  Let $Q$ be the point of intersection of the perpendicular from $P$ and the directrix. Then the coordinates of $Q$ are $(x, -p)$.

**C**  By the definition of a parabola, $FP = QP$.

By the distance formula,
$$FP = \sqrt{(x - 0)^2 + (y - p)^2} = \sqrt{x^2 + (y - p)^2}$$
and $QP = \sqrt{(x - x)^2 + (y - (-p))^2} = \sqrt{0 + (y + p)^2} = |y + p|.$

_____ = _____     Set $FP$ equal to $QP$.

_____ = _____     Square both sides.

_____ = _____     Expand the squared terms.

_____ = _____     Subtract $y^2$ and $p^2$ from both sides.

_____ = _____     Add $2py$ to both sides.

_____ = _____     Solve for $y$.

### REFLECT

**2a.** Explain how the value of $p$ determines whether the parabola opens up or down.

_____

_____

_____

_____

**2b.** Explain why the origin $(0, 0)$ is always a point on a parabola with focus $F(0, p)$ and directrix $y = -p$.

_____

_____

Write the equation of the parabola with focus $(0, -4)$ and directrix $y = 4$. Then graph the parabola.

**A**   The focus of the parabola is $(0, p)$, so $p =$ _____.

The general equation of a parabola is $y = \frac{1}{4p} x^2$.

So, the equation of this parabola is _____.

**B**   To graph the parabola, complete the table of values. Then plot points and draw the curve.

| x | y |
|---|---|
| −8 | |
| −4 | |
| 0 | |
| 4 | |
| 8 | |

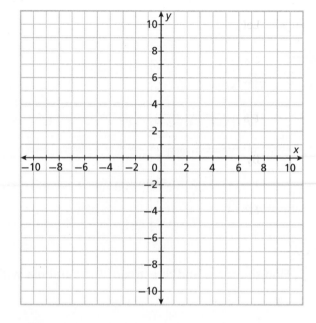

**REFLECT**

**3a.**   The *vertex* of a parabola is the midpoint of the perpendicular segment from the focus to the directrix. What is the vertex of the parabola you graphed?

_____

**3b.**   Does your graph lie above or below the *x*-axis? Why does this make sense based on the parabola's equation?

_____

_____

**3c.**   Describe any symmetry your graph has. Why does this make sense based on the parabola's equation?

_____

_____

_____

**Write the equation of the parabola with the given focus and directrix. Then graph the parabola.**

**1.** focus: $(0, 2)$; directrix: $y = -2$

**2.** focus: $(0, -5)$; directrix: $y = 5$

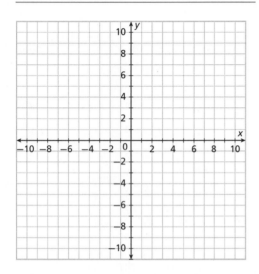

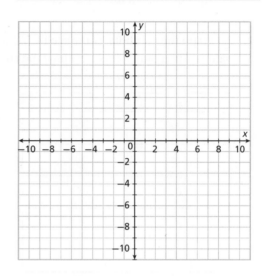

**Find the focus and directrix of the parabola with the given equation.**

**3.** $y = -\frac{1}{24}x^2$

**4.** $y = 2x^2$

**5.** Complete the table by writing the equation of each parabola. Then use a calculator to graph the equations in the same window to help you make a conjecture: What happens to the graph of a parabola as the focus and directrix move apart?

| Focus | (0, 1) | (0, 2) | (0, 3) | (0, 4) |
|---|---|---|---|---|
| Directrix | $y = -1$ | $y = -2$ | $y = -3$ | $y = -4$ |
| Equation | | | | |

**6.** Find the length of the line segment that is parallel to the directrix of a parabola, that passes through the focus, and that has endpoints on the parabola.

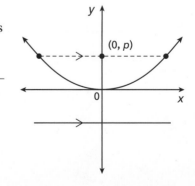

# Partitioning a Segment

COMMON
CORE

CC.9-12.G.GPE.6

**Essential question:** *How do you find the point on a directed line segment that partitions the segment in a given ratio?*

Recall that the *slope* of a straight line in a coordinate plane is the ratio of the *rise* to the *run*.

In the figure, the slope of $\overline{AB}$ is $\frac{\text{rise}}{\text{run}} = \frac{4}{8} = \frac{1}{2}$.

In the next several lessons, you will see how to use slope to solve geometry problems and to prove geometry theorems.

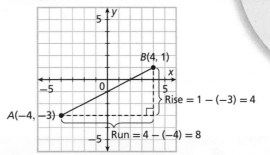

*B*(4, 1)

Rise = 1 − (−3) = 4

*A*(−4, −3)

Run = 4 − (−4) = 8

The following example also uses the idea of a *directed line segment.* This means the line segment has a direction associated with it, usually specified by moving from one endpoint to the other.

## 1 EXAMPLE  Partitioning a Segment

Find the coordinates of the point *P* that lies along the directed line segment from *A*(3, 4) to *B*(6, 10) and partitions the segment in the ratio 3 to 2.

**A**  Convert the ratio to a percent.

Point *P* is $\frac{3}{3+2} = \frac{3}{5}$ of the distance from *A* to *B*.

This is _____% of the distance from *A* to *B*.

*B*(6, 10)

*P*

*A*(3, 4)

**B**  Find the rise and run for $\overline{AB}$.

Rise = 10 − 4 = 6           Run = _____

**C**  The slope of $\overline{AP}$ must be the same as the slope of $\overline{AB}$.

So, to find the coordinates of *P*, add _____% of the run to the *x*-coordinate of

*A* and add _____% of the rise to the *y*-coordinate of *A*.

*x*-coordinate of *P* = 3 + ▢ · 3 = _____

*y*-coordinate of *P* = 4 + ▢ · ▢ = _____

So, the coordinates of *P* are _____.

**1a.** Explain how you can check that the slope of $\overline{AP}$ equals the slope of $\overline{AB}$.

_____

_____

**1b.** Explain how you can use the distance formula to check that $P$ partitions $\overline{AB}$ in the ratio 3 to 2.

_____

_____

# PRACTICE

**1.** Find the coordinates of the point $P$ that lies along the directed segment from $C(-3, -2)$ to $D(6, 1)$ and partitions the segment in the ratio 2 to 1.

_____

**2.** Find the coordinates of the point $P$ that lies along the directed segment from $R(-3, -4)$ to $S(5, 0)$ and partitions the segment in the ratio 2 to 3.

_____

**3.** Find the coordinates of the point $P$ that lies along the directed segment from $J(-2, 5)$ to $K(2, -3)$ and partitions the segment in the ratio 4 to 1.

_____

**4.** Find the coordinates of the point $P$ that lies along the directed segment from $M(5, -2)$ to $N(-5, 3)$ and partitions the segment in the ratio 1 to 3.

_____

**5.** The map shows a straight highway between two towns. Highway planners want to build two new rest stops between the towns so that the two rest stops divide the highway into three equal parts. Find the coordinates of the points at which the rest stops should be built.

_____

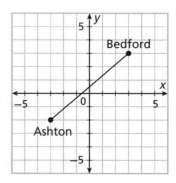

**6.** $\overleftrightarrow{RS}$ passes through $R(-3, 1)$ and $S(4, 3)$. Find a point $P$ on $\overleftrightarrow{RS}$ such that the ratio of $RP$ to $SP$ is 5 to 4. Is there more than one possibility? Explain.

_____

_____

_____

# Slope and Parallel Lines

**Essential question:** *What is the connection between slope and parallel lines?*

Slope is useful for determining whether two lines are parallel.

COMMON CORE

CC.9-12.G.GPE.5

> ### Slope Criterion for Parallel Lines
>
> Two non-vertical lines are parallel if and only if they have the same slope.

Because the theorem is stated as a biconditional (*if and only if*), the proof has two parts, one for each "direction" of the theorem.

## 1 PROOF     Parallel Lines Have the Same Slope

**Given:** Non-vertical lines $m$ and $n$, $m \parallel n$

**Proof:** Line $m$ and line $n$ have the same slope.

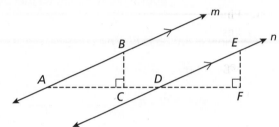

**A** Let $A$ and $B$ be two points on line $m$. Draw a horizontal line through $A$ and a vertical line through $B$ to create the "slope triangle," $\triangle ABC$.

Extend $\overline{AC}$ to intersect line $n$ at point $D$ and then extend it to point $F$ so that $AC = DF$. Draw a vertical line through $F$ intersecting line $n$ at point $E$.

**B** Since $m \parallel n$, $\angle BAC \cong \angle EDF$ by _____.

$\triangle BAC \cong \triangle EDF$ by _____.

So, $\overline{BC} \cong \overline{EF}$ by _____.

This means $BC = EF$, so $\frac{BC}{AC} = \frac{EF}{DF}$ by _____.

This shows that the slope of $m$ equals the slope of $n$ by the definition of slope.

### REFLECT

**1a.** Does the above proof work if the lines are horizontal? If not, does the theorem still hold? Explain.

_____

_____

**1b.** How can you estimate the slope of lines $m$ and $n$ in the above figure?

_____

**Given:** Line $m$ and line $n$ have the same slope.

**Proof:** $m \parallel n$

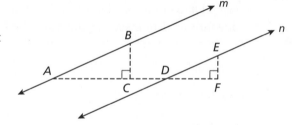

**A** Let $A$ and $B$ be two points on line $m$. Draw a horizontal line through $A$ and a vertical line through $B$ to create the "slope triangle," $\triangle ABC$.

Extend $\overline{AC}$ to intersect line $n$ at point $D$ and then extend it to point $F$ so that $DF = AC$. Draw a vertical line through $F$ intersecting line $n$ at point $E$.

**B** Since line $m$ and line $n$ have the same slope, $\dfrac{BC}{AC} = \dfrac{\phantom{xx}}{\phantom{xx}}$.

But $DF = AC$, so by substitution, $\dfrac{BC}{AC} = \dfrac{\phantom{xx}}{\phantom{xx}}$.

Multiplying both sides by $AC$ shows that $BC = $ _____.

**C** Now $\triangle BAC \cong \triangle EDF$ by _____.

So, $\angle BAC \cong \angle EDF$ by _____.

This shows $m \parallel n$ by _____.

**REFLECT**

**2a.** Suppose you extend $\overline{AC}$ to intersect line $n$ at point $D$ and then extend it to form the "slope triangle" $\triangle EDF$ for line $n$, but you do not do this in such a way that $DF = AC$. Explain how you can use similarity to complete the proof in this case.

_____

_____

_____

_____

Recall that a linear function can be expressed as a linear equation. You can write a linear equation in different forms depending upon the information you are given and the problem you are trying to solve.

**Slope-Intercept Form**

The equation of a line with slope $m$ and $y$-intercept $b$ is $y = mx + b$.

## Point-Slope Form

The equation of a line with slope $m$ that passes that passes through the point $(x_1, y_1)$ is $y - y_1 = m(x - x_1)$.

**3** **E X A M P L E**   **Writing Equations of Parallel Lines**

Write the equation of each line in slope-intercept form.

**A**   The line parallel to $y = -2x + 3$ that passes through $(1, -4)$

The given line is in slope-intercept form and its slope is _____.

The required line has slope _____ because parallel lines have the same slope.

$$y - y_1 = m(x - x_1)$$   Use point-slope form.

$y -$ _____ $=$ _____ $(x -$ _____$)$   Substitute for $m$, $x_1$, and $y_1$.

$y +$ _____ $=$ _____   Simplify each side of the equation.

$y =$ _____   Write the equation in slope-intercept form.

**B**   The line that passes through $(2, 3)$ and is parallel to the line through $(1, -2)$ and $(7, 1)$

The slope of the line through $(1, -2)$ and $(7, 1)$ is

$$m = \frac{y_2 - y_1}{x_2 - x_1} = \frac{\boxed{\phantom{xx}} - \boxed{\phantom{xx}}}{\boxed{\phantom{xx}} - \boxed{\phantom{xx}}} = \frac{\boxed{\phantom{xx}}}{\boxed{\phantom{xx}}} = \boxed{\phantom{xx}}.$$

So, the required line has slope _____ .

$$y - y_1 = m(x - x_1)$$   Use point-slope form.

$y -$ _____ $=$ _____ $(x -$ _____$)$   Substitute for $m$, $x_1$, and $y_1$.

$y =$ _____   Simplify and write slope-intercept form.

**REFLECT**

**3a.**  In Part A, how can you check that you wrote the correct equation?

_____

_____

**3b.**  In Part A, once you know the slope of the required line, how can you finish solving the problem using the slope-intercept form of a linear equation?

_____

_____

_____

**Write the equation of each line in slope-intercept form.**

**1.** The line with slope 3 that passes through $(0, 6)$

_____

**2.** The line with slope $-4$ that passes through $(0, -5)$

_____

**3.** The line with slope $-1$ that passes through $(3, 5)$

_____

**4.** The line with slope 5 that passes through $(2, -5)$

_____

**5.** The line parallel to $y = 5x + 1$ that passes through $(3, 8)$

_____

**6.** The line parallel to $y = -3x - 2$ that passes through $(-2, 7)$

_____

**7.** The line that passes through $(-1, 0)$ and is parallel to the line through $(0, 1)$ and $(2, -3)$

_____

**8.** The line that passes through $(3, 5)$ and is parallel to the line through $(3, 3)$ and $(-3, -1)$

_____

**9.** The line parallel to $x - 3y = -12$ that passes through $(-3, 4)$

_____

**10.** The line parallel to $3x + y = 8$ that passes through $(0, -4)$

_____

**11.** Use the slope-intercept form of a linear equation to prove that if two lines are parallel then they have the same slope. (*Hint:* Use an indirect proof. Assume the lines have different slopes, $m_1$ and $m_2$. Write the equations of the lines and show that there must be a point of intersection.)

_____

_____

_____

_____

# Slope and Perpendicular Lines

**Essential question:** *What is the connection between slope and perpendicular lines?*

COMMON CORE

CC.9-12.G.GPE.5

Slope is useful for determining whether two lines are perpendicular.

### Slope Criterion for Perpendicular Lines

Two non-vertical lines are perpendicular if and only if the product of their slopes is $-1$.

Like the Slope Criterion for Parallel Lines, the theorem is stated as a biconditional. Therefore, the proof has two parts, one for each "direction" of the theorem.

## 1 PROOF    Perpendicular Lines Have Slopes Whose Product Is $-1$

**Given:** Non-vertical lines $m$ and $n$, $m \perp n$

**Proof:** The product of the slope of line $m$ and the slope of line $n$ is $-1$.

**A**  Assume the lines intersect at point $P$, and assume the slope of line $m$ is positive. (You can write a similar proof in the case that the slope of line $m$ is negative.)

Let $Q$ be a point on line $m$, and draw the "slope triangle," $\triangle PQR$, as shown.

The slope of line $m$ is _____, where $a$ and $b$ are both positive.

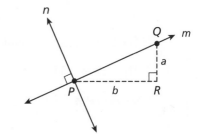

**B**  Rotate $\triangle PQR$ 90° around point $P$. This gives $\triangle PQ'R'$, as shown.

$\triangle PQ'R'$ is a slope triangle for line $n$.

Let the coordinates of $P$ be $(x_1, y_1)$ and let the coordinates of $Q'$ be $(x_2, y_2)$.

Then the slope of line $n$ is $\dfrac{y_2 - y_1}{x_2 - x_1} = \dfrac{b}{\rule{1cm}{0.4pt}} = -\dfrac{}{\rule{1cm}{0.4pt}}$.

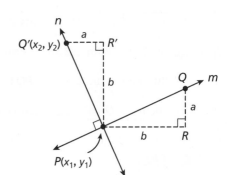

**C**  Find the product of the slope of line $m$ and the slope of line $n$.

The product of the slopes is _____ • _____ = _____.

So, the product of the slope of line $m$ and the slope of line $n$ is _____ .

### REFLECT

**1a.**  When you calculate the slope of line $n$, why is $x_2 - x_1$ negative?

_____

**1b.**  Does the theorem apply when one of the lines is horizontal? Explain.

_____

**Given:** The product of the slope of line $m$ and the slope of line $n$ is −1.

**Proof:** $m \perp n$

**A**   Let line $m$ have positive slope $\frac{a}{b}$, where $a$ and $b$ are both positive.

Let line $n$ have slope $z$. It is given that $z \cdot \frac{a}{b} = -1$.

Solving for $z$ shows that the slope of line $n$ is _____.

**B**   Assume the lines intersect at point $P$. Set up slope triangles for lines $m$ and $n$ as shown.

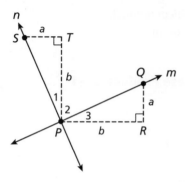

Then $\overline{ST} \cong$ _____ and $\overline{PT} \cong$ _____.

Also, $\angle T \cong \angle R$ because _____.

So, $\triangle STP \cong \triangle QRP$ by _____.

**C**   Now $\angle 1 \cong \angle 3$ by _____.

$\overline{PT}$ is a vertical line segment and $\overline{PR}$ is a horizontal line segment, so $\angle TPR$

is a right angle. This means $\angle 2$ and $\angle 3$ are _____.

By substitution, $\angle 2$ and $\angle 1$ are _____.

But $m\angle 1 + m\angle 2 = m\angle SPQ$ by the Angle Addition Postulate.

So, $m\angle SPQ =$ _____ and line $m$ is perpendicular to line $n$.

**REFLECT**

**2a.** The proof begins by assuming that line $m$ has a positive slope. If the product of the slopes of two lines is −1, how do you know that one of the lines must have a positive slope?

_____

_____

© Houghton Mifflin Harcourt Publishing Company

Write the equation of the line perpendicular to $y = 3x - 8$ that passes through $(3, 1)$.
Write the equation in slope-intercept form.

**A**   First find the slope of the required line.

The given line is in slope-intercept form and its slope is _____.

Let the required line have slope $m$. Since the lines are perpendicular, the product of their slopes is $-1$.

So, _____ $\cdot m = -1$, and therefore, $m =$ _____.

**B**   Now use point-slope form to find the equation of the required line.

$y - y_1 = m(x - x_1)$          Use point-slope form.

$y -$ _____ $=$ _____ $(x -$ _____ $)$          Substitute for $m$, $x_1$, and $y_1$.

$y -$ _____ $=$ _____          Distributive Property

$y =$ _____          Write the equation in slope-intercept form.

**REFLECT**

**3a.** How do you find the slope of the given line?

_____

_____

**3b.** How can you use graphing to check your answer?

_____

_____

**3c.** Confirm your answer by graphing on the grid below.

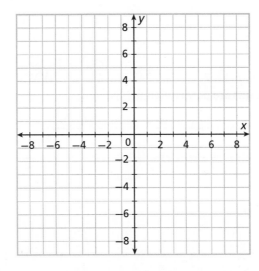

**Write the equation of each line in slope-intercept form.**

1. The line perpendicular to $y = \frac{1}{2}x + 1$ that passes through $(1, 4)$

   _____

2. The line perpendicular to $y = -x + 2$ that passes through $(-1, -7)$

   _____

3. The line that passes through $(1, 2)$ and is perpendicular to the line through $(3, -2)$ and $(-3, 0)$

   _____

4. The line that passes through $(-2, 3)$ and is perpendicular to the line through $(0, 1)$ and $(-3, -1)$

   _____

5. The line perpendicular to $2y = x + 5$ that passes through $(2, 1)$

   _____

6. The line perpendicular to $3x + y = 8$ that passes through $(0, -2)$

   _____

7. **Error Analysis** A student was asked to find the equation of the line perpendicular to $y - 2x = 1$ that passes through the point $(4, 3)$. The student's work is shown at right. Explain the error and give the correct equation.

   _____

   _____

   _____

   _____

   _____

   | | |
   |---|---|
   | The given line has slope $-2$, so the required line has slope $\frac{1}{2}$. | |
   | $y - y_1 = m(x - x_1)$ | *Use point-slope form.* |
   | $y - 3 = \frac{1}{2}(x - 4)$ | *Substitute for $m$, $x_1$, $y_1$.* |
   | $y - 3 = \frac{1}{2}x - 2$ | *Distributive Property* |
   | $y = \frac{1}{2}x + 1$ | *Add 3 to both sides.* |

8. Are the lines given by the equations $-4x + y = 5$ and $-x + 4y = 12$ parallel, perpendicular, or neither? Why?

   _____

   _____

9. Consider the points $A(-7, 10)$, $B(12, 7)$, $C(10, -24)$, and $D(-8, -3)$. Which two lines determined by these points are perpendicular? Explain.

   _____

   _____

# Coordinate Proofs Using Slope

**8-6**

COMMON
CORE

CC.9-12.G.GPE.4

**Essential question:** *How can you use slope in coordinate proofs?*

You have already used the distance formula and the midpoint formula in coordinate proofs. As you will see, slope is useful in coordinate proofs whenever you need to show that lines are parallel or perpendicular.

**1 EXAMPLE**  **Proving a Quadrilateral Is a Parallelogram**

Prove or disprove that the quadrilateral determined by the points $A(4, 4)$, $B(3, 1)$, $C(-2, -1)$, and $D(-1, 2)$ is a parallelogram.

**A**  Plot the points on the coordinate plane at right.

Then draw quadrilateral *ABCD*.

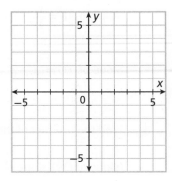

**B**  To determine whether *ABCD* is a parallelogram, find the slope of each side of the quadrilateral.

Slope of $\overline{AB} = \dfrac{y_2 - y_1}{x_2 - x_1} = \dfrac{1 - 4}{3 - 4} = \dfrac{-3}{-1} = 3$

Slope of $\overline{BC} = \dfrac{y_2 - y_1}{x_2 - x_1} = \dfrac{\boxed{\phantom{-}} - \boxed{\phantom{-}}}{\boxed{\phantom{-}} - \boxed{\phantom{-}}} = \dfrac{\boxed{\phantom{-}}}{\boxed{\phantom{-}}} = \boxed{\phantom{-}}$

Slope of $\overline{CD} = \dfrac{y_2 - y_1}{x_2 - x_1} = \dfrac{\boxed{\phantom{-}} - \boxed{\phantom{-}}}{\boxed{\phantom{-}} - \boxed{\phantom{-}}} = \dfrac{\boxed{\phantom{-}}}{\boxed{\phantom{-}}} = \boxed{\phantom{-}}$

Slope of $\overline{DA} = \dfrac{y_2 - y_1}{x_2 - x_1} = \dfrac{\boxed{\phantom{-}} - \boxed{\phantom{-}}}{\boxed{\phantom{-}} - \boxed{\phantom{-}}} = \dfrac{\boxed{\phantom{-}}}{\boxed{\phantom{-}}} = \boxed{\phantom{-}}$

**C**  Compare slopes. The slopes of opposite sides are _____.

This means opposite sides are _____.

So, _____.

**REFLECT**

**1a.**  Is there a way to write a proof that does not use slope? Explain.

_____

_____

Prove or disprove that the quadrilateral determined by the points $Q(2, -3)$, $R(-4, 0)$, $S(-2, 4)$, and $T(4, 1)$ is a rectangle.

**A** Plot the points on the coordinate plane at right.

Then draw quadrilateral $QRST$.

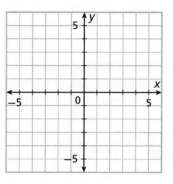

**B** To determine whether $QRST$ is a rectangle, find the slope of each side of the quadrilateral.

Slope of $\overline{QR} = \dfrac{y_2 - y_1}{x_2 - x_1} = \dfrac{0 - (-3)}{-4 - 2} = \dfrac{3}{-6} = -\dfrac{1}{2}$

Slope of $\overline{RS} = \dfrac{y_2 - y_1}{x_2 - x_1} = \dfrac{\boxed{\phantom{x}} - \boxed{\phantom{x}}}{\boxed{\phantom{x}} - \boxed{\phantom{x}}} = \dfrac{\boxed{\phantom{x}}}{\boxed{\phantom{x}}} = \boxed{\phantom{x}}$

Slope of $\overline{ST} = \dfrac{y_2 - y_1}{x_2 - x_1} = \dfrac{\boxed{\phantom{x}} - \boxed{\phantom{x}}}{\boxed{\phantom{x}} - \boxed{\phantom{x}}} = \dfrac{\boxed{\phantom{x}}}{\boxed{\phantom{x}}} = \boxed{\phantom{x}}$

Slope of $\overline{TQ} = \dfrac{y_2 - y_1}{x_2 - x_1} = \dfrac{\boxed{\phantom{x}} - \boxed{\phantom{x}}}{\boxed{\phantom{x}} - \boxed{\phantom{x}}} = \dfrac{\boxed{\phantom{x}}}{\boxed{\phantom{x}}} = \boxed{\phantom{x}}$

**C** Find the product of the slopes of adjacent sides.

(slope of $\overline{QR}$)(slope of $\overline{RS}$)  = _____ · _____ = _____

(slope of $\overline{RS}$)(slope of $\overline{ST}$)  = _____ · _____ = _____

(slope of $\overline{ST}$)(slope of $\overline{TQ}$)  = _____ · _____ = _____

(slope of $\overline{TQ}$)(slope of $\overline{QR}$)  = _____ · _____ = _____

You can conclude that adjacent sides are _____.

So, _____.

**REFLECT**

**2a.** What would you expect to find if you used the distance formula to calculate $SQ$ and $RT$? Explain.

_____

_____

**2b.** Explain how to prove that $QRST$ is not a square.

_____

_____

© Houghton Mifflin Harcourt Publishing Company

1. Prove or disprove that the quadrilateral determined by the points $J(-3, 1)$, $K(3, 3)$, $L(2, -1)$, and $M(-4, -3)$ is a parallelogram.

_____

_____

_____

2. Prove or disprove that the quadrilateral determined by the points $A(-2, 3)$, $B(5, 3)$, $C(3, -1)$, and $D(-3, -1)$ is a parallelogram.

_____

_____

_____

3. Prove or disprove that the quadrilateral determined by the points $Q(-3, 4)$, $R(5, 2)$, $S(4, -1)$, and $T(-4, 1)$ is a rectangle.

_____

_____

_____

4. Prove or disprove that the quadrilateral determined by the points $W(1, 5)$, $X(4, 4)$, $Y(2, -2)$, and $Z(-1, -1)$ is a rectangle.

_____

_____

_____

5. Prove or disprove that the quadrilateral determined by the points $D(-2, 3)$, $E(3, 4)$, $F(0, -2)$, and $G(-4, -1)$ is a trapezoid.

_____

_____

_____

**6.** Consider points $L(3, -4)$, $M(1, -2)$, and $N(5, 2)$.

    **a.** Find the coordinates of point $P$ so that the quadrilateral determined by points $L$, $M$, $N$, and $P$ is a parallelogram. Is there more than one possibility? Explain.

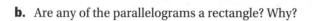

    **b.** Are any of the parallelograms a rectangle? Why?

**7.** You are using a coordinate plane to create a quadrilateral. You start by drawing $\overline{MN}$, as shown.

    **a.** You decide to translate $\overline{MN}$ by the translation $(x, y) \rightarrow (x + 3, y + 2)$. What type of quadrilateral is $MM'N'N$? Why?

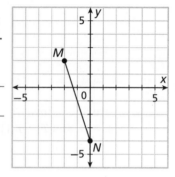

    **b.** Do you get the same type of quadrilateral for any translation of $\overline{MN}$ that results in a quadrilateral $MM'N'N$? Explain. (*Hint:* Find the coordinates of $M'$ and $N'$ under a general translation, $(x, y) \rightarrow (x + a, y + b)$. Then consider the slopes of the sides of quadrilateral $MM'N'N$.)

    **c.** You decide you want $MM'N'N$ to be a rectangle. What translations can you use? (*Hint:* What must be true about $a$ and $b$?)

**8.** Rhombus $OPQR$ has vertices $O(0, 0)$, $P(a, b)$, $Q(a + b, a + b)$, and $R(b, a)$.

Prove the diagonals of the rhombus are perpendicular.

# Systems of Equations

COMMON
CORE

CC.9-12.A.REI.7

**Essential question:** *How do you solve a system consisting of a linear equation in two variables and a quadratic equation in two variables?*

Recall that you can solve a system of two equations in two unknowns by graphing both equations and finding the point(s) of intersection of the graphs. You can also solve a system using the algebraic methods of substitution or elimination. In this lesson, you will see how these techniques may be used with systems that include a quadratic equation.

## 1 EXAMPLE  Solving a System by Graphing

Solve the system of equations. $\begin{cases} (x-1)^2 + (y-1)^2 = 16 \\ y = x + 4 \end{cases}$

**A**  Graph the equations.

The equation $(x-1)^2 + (y-1)^2 = 16$ represents a circle with center _____ and radius _____ .

The equation $y = x + 4$ represents a line with slope _____ and $y$-intercept _____ .

Use a compass and straightedge, and the above information, to help you graph the circle and the line.

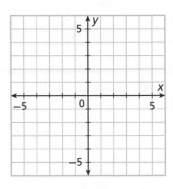

**B**  The solutions of $(x-1)^2 + (y-1)^2 = 16$ are exactly the points on the circle. The solutions of $y = x + 4$ are exactly the points on the line. The solutions of the system are points that lie on both the circle and the line. These are the points of intersection of the circle and the line.

So, the solutions of the system are _____ .

### REFLECT

**1a.** How can you check your solution?

_____

**1b.** How many solutions are possible when a system of equations involves a circle and a line? Explain.

_____

_____

**2 EXAMPLE** Solving a System Algebraically

Solve the system of equations. $\begin{cases} x^2 + y^2 = 13 \\ y = -5x \end{cases}$

**A** Use substitution to write an equation in one variable. The second equation is already solved for $y$, so substitute this expression for $y$ into the first equation.

| | |
|---|---|
| $x^2 + y^2 = 13$ | Write the first equation. |
| $x^2 + (\underline{\hspace{1cm}})^2 = 13$ | Substitute $-5x$ for $y$ in the equation. |
| $x^2 + \underline{\hspace{1cm}} = 13$ | Square the expression in parentheses. |
| $\underline{\hspace{1cm}} = 13$ | Combine like terms. |
| $x^2 = \underline{\hspace{1cm}}$ | Use the Division Property of Equality. |
| $x = \underline{\hspace{1cm}}$ | Take the square root of both sides. |
| $x = \underline{\hspace{1cm}}$ | Rationalize the denominator. |

**B** Substitute each $x$-value into one of the original equations to find the corresponding $y$-values.

Substitute into the simpler equation, $y = -5x$.

When $x = \underline{\hspace{1cm}}$, $y = \underline{\hspace{1cm}}$.

When $x = \underline{\hspace{1cm}}$, $y = \underline{\hspace{1cm}}$.

So, the solutions of the system are $\underline{\hspace{5cm}}$.

**REFLECT**

**2a.** Is it possible to solve this system of equations by graphing? Explain.

_____

_____

**2b.** Based on what you know about the graphs of the equations in this system, why does it make sense that there are two solutions?

_____

_____

© Houghton Mifflin Harcourt Publishing Company

## 3 EXAMPLE Solving a System Involving a Parabola

Solve the system of equations. $\begin{cases} y = x^2 - 3 \\ y = 8x - 19 \end{cases}$

**A** Use substitution to write an equation in one variable. Substitute the expression for $y$ from the second equation into the first equation.

| | |
|---|---|
| $y = x^2 - 3$ | Write the first equation. |
| _____ $= x^2 - 3$ | Substitute $8x - 19$ for $y$ in the equation. |
| $0 = $ _____ | Get 0 on one side of the equation. |
| $0 = $ _____ | Combine like terms. |
| $0 = $ _____ | Factor. |
| $0 = $ _____ | Take the square root of both sides. |
| $x = $ _____ | Solve for $x$. |

**B** Substitute the $x$-value into one of the original equations to find the corresponding $y$-value.

Substitute into the equation $y = x^2 - 3$.

When $x = $ _____, $y = $ _____.

So, the solution of the system is _____.

### REFLECT

**3a.** In Step B, what would happen if you substituted the value of $x$ in the other equation?

_____

**3b.** Verify that the slope of the line that contains $(0, -19)$ and $(4, 13)$ is 8.

_____

**3c.** Since there is only one solution of the system, what does this tell you about the line and the parabola that are represented by the equations?

_____

**3d.** How many solutions are possible when a system of equations involves a parabola and a line? Explain.

_____

_____

# PRACTICE

Solve each system of equations by graphing.

1. $\begin{cases} (x-2)^2 + y^2 = 4 \\ y = -x \end{cases}$

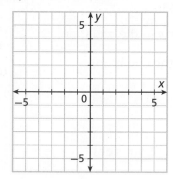

_____

2. $\begin{cases} (x+1)^2 + (y-1)^2 = 9 \\ y = x - 1 \end{cases}$

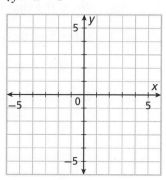

_____

3. $\begin{cases} y = x^2 - 1 \\ y = -x + 1 \end{cases}$

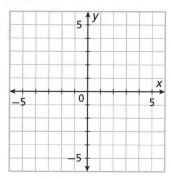

_____

Solve each system of equations algebraically.

4. $\begin{cases} x^2 + y^2 = 10 \\ y = -3x \end{cases}$

_____

5. $\begin{cases} x^2 + y^2 = 25 \\ y = 7x \end{cases}$

_____

6. $\begin{cases} x^2 + y^2 = 13 \\ y = -8x \end{cases}$

_____

7. $\begin{cases} y = x^2 \\ y = -x + 2 \end{cases}$

_____

8. $\begin{cases} y = x^2 + 2 \\ y = 4 \end{cases}$

_____

9. $\begin{cases} y = -x^2 + 2 \\ y = x - 4 \end{cases}$

_____

10. **Error Analysis** A student was asked to solve the system $\begin{cases} x^2 + y^2 = 9 \\ y = x \end{cases}$.

The student's solution is shown below. Critique the student's work.
If there is an error, give the correct solution.

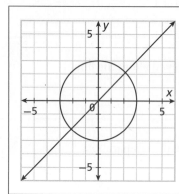

The graph of $x^2 + y^2 = 9$ is a circle centered at the origin with radius 3. The graph of $y = x$ is a straight line through the origin. The graphs intersect at $(2, 2)$ and $(-2, -2)$, so these are the solutions.

_____

_____

_____

Name _____ Class _____ Date _____

## MULTIPLE CHOICE

**1.** What is the center of the circle whose equation is $x^2 - 6x + y^2 + 6y = -9$?

   **A.** $(3, -3)$     **C.** $(-3, 3)$

   **B.** $(3, 3)$      **D.** $(-3, -3)$

**2.** What is the equation of the circle with center $(4, -5)$ and radius 4?

   **F.** $(x + 4)^2 + (y - 5)^2 = 4$

   **G.** $(x - 4)^2 + (y + 5)^2 = 4$

   **H.** $(x + 4)^2 + (y - 5)^2 = 16$

   **J.** $(x - 4)^2 + (y + 5)^2 = 16$

**3.** What is the equation of the parabola with focus $(0, -2)$ and directrix $y = 2$?

   **A.** $y = \frac{1}{8}x^2$     **C.** $y = \frac{1}{16}x^2$

   **B.** $y = -\frac{1}{8}x^2$    **D.** $y = -\frac{1}{16}x^2$

**4.** What is the equation of the line parallel to line $m$ that passes through point $P$?

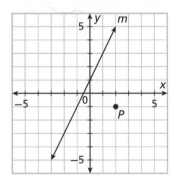

   **F.** $y = -2x + 3$    **H.** $y = -\frac{1}{2}x$

   **G.** $y = 2x - 5$     **J.** $y = \frac{1}{2}x - 2$

**5.** The ordered pair $(x, y)$ is a solution of this system of equations.

$$\begin{cases} x^2 + y^2 = 10 \\ y = 7x \end{cases}$$

Which of the following could be the value of $x$?

   **A.** $\frac{\sqrt{2}}{2}$     **C.** $\frac{\sqrt{5}}{2}$

   **B.** $\frac{\sqrt{5}}{5}$     **D.** $\frac{\sqrt{10}}{7}$

**6.** Which of the following points along the directed segment from $M$ to $N$ partitions the segment in the ratio 3 to 1?

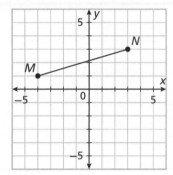

   **F.** $(-2.5, 6.25)$    **H.** $(-2.25, 1.5)$

   **G.** $(1.25, 2.5)$     **J.** $(5.25, 1.5)$

**7.** What is the equation of the line through the point $(3, 3)$ that is perpendicular to the line $y = -\frac{1}{2}x + 2$?

   **A.** $y = 2x - 3$    **C.** $y = -\frac{1}{2}x + \frac{9}{2}$

   **B.** $y = -2x - 9$   **D.** $y = 2x + 3$

## FREE RESPONSE

**8.** Find the equation of the line through the point $(1, 5)$ that is parallel to the line that passes through $(2, 1)$ and $(0, -5)$.

_____

**9.** Prove or disprove that the point $(2, \sqrt{5})$ lies on the circle that is centered at the origin and contains the point $(0, -3)$.

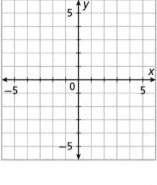

_____
_____
_____
_____
_____
_____
_____
_____

**10.** Prove or disprove that the quadrilateral determined by the points $A(-3, 1)$, $B(3, 3)$, $C(4, -1)$, and $D(-2, -3)$ is a rectangle.

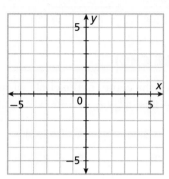

_____
_____
_____
_____
_____
_____
_____
_____
_____
_____

# Linear and Area Measurement

## Unit Focus

In this unit, you will explore linear measurement, such as length and perimeter, as well as area. First you will learn how to use significant digits to report the results of calculations based on measurements. Then you will learn how to calculate perimeters and areas of figures on the coordinate plane. The remainder of the unit focuses on measuring circles and parts of circles, including arcs and sectors.

## Unit at a Glance

COMMON CORE

| Lesson | Standards for Mathematical Content |
|---|---|
| 9-1  Precision and Significant Digits | CC.9-12.N.Q.3* |
| 9-2  Perimeter and Area on the Coordinate Plane | CC.9-12.G.GPE.7*, CC.9-12.G.MG.1*, CC.9-12.G.MG.2* |
| 9-3  Circumference | CC.9-12.G.GMD.1, CC.9-12.G.MG.1* |
| 9-4  Arc Length and Radian Measure | CC.9-12.G.CO.1, CC.9-12.G.C.5 |
| 9-5  Area of Circles and Sectors | CC.9-12.G.C.5, CC.9-12.G.GMD.1 |
| Test Prep | |

UNIT 9

# Unpacking the Common Core State Standards

Use the table to help you understand the Standards for Mathematical Content that are taught in this unit. Refer to the lessons listed after each standard for exploration and practice.

| COMMON CORE Standards for Mathematical Content | What It Means For You |
|---|---|
| **CC.9-12.N.Q.3 Choose a level of accuracy appropriate to limitations on measurement when reporting quantities.*** Lesson 9-1 | You will learn about precision and learn how to use significant digits to report the results of calculations based on measurements. |
| **CC.9-12.G.CO.1 Know** precise definitions of angle, circle, perpendicular line, parallel line, and line segment, based on the undefined notions of point, line, distance along a line, and **distance around a circular arc.** Lesson 9-4 | You have already used many undefined terms in this course. In this unit, you will be introduced to the undefined notion of arc length. |
| **CC.9-12.G.C.5 Derive using similarity the fact that the length of the arc intercepted by an angle is proportional to the radius, and define the radian measure of the angle as the constant of proportionality; derive the formula for the area of a sector.** Lessons 9-4, 9-5 | Proportional reasoning plays a big role in this unit. You will see how to use proportional reasoning to find the area of a wedge-shaped part of a circle. You will also use proportional reasoning to learn about radians, which are another way to measure angles. |
| **CC.9-12.G.GPE.7 Use coordinates to compute perimeters of polygons and areas of triangles and rectangles, e.g., using the distance formula.*** Lesson 9-2 | You have already worked with polygons on the coordinate plane. Now you will find perimeters and areas of such polygons. |
| **CC.9-12.G.GMD.1 Give an informal argument for the formulas for the circumference of a circle, area of a circle,** volume of a cylinder, pyramid, and cone. Lessons 9-3, 9-5 | In this unit, you will develop formulas for the circumference of a circle and the area of a circle, using informal limit arguments that involve trigonometry and dissection. |
| **CC.9-12.G.MG.1 Use geometric shapes, their measures, and their properties to describe objects (e.g., modeling a tree trunk or a human torso as a cylinder).*** Lessons 9-2, 9-3 | You will see how you can use mathematical concepts from this unit to model real-world objects and situations. |
| **CC.9-12.G.MG.2 Apply concepts of density based on area and volume in modeling situations (e.g., persons per square mile, BTUs per cubic foot).*** Lesson 9-2 | You will learn about density and learn how to calculate population density. |

# Precision and Significant Digits

**COMMON CORE**

CC.9-12.N.Q.3*

9-1

**Essential question:** *How do you use significant digits to report the results of calculations based on measurements?*

**Precision** is the level of detail an instrument can measure. For example, a ruler marked in millimeters is more precise than a ruler that is marked only in centimeters.

You can use precision to compare measurements. For example, a measurement of 25 inches is more precise than a measurement of 2 feet because an inch is a smaller unit than a foot. Similarly, 9.2 kg is more precise than 9 kg because a tenth of a kilogram is a smaller unit than a kilogram.

In the following activity, you will investigate how precision affects calculated measurements, such as area.

## 1 EXPLORE  Making Measurements to Calculate an Area

**A**  Work with a partner. One of you should measure the width of a book cover to the nearest centimeter. Record the width below.

Width of book cover: _____

The other person should measure the length of the book cover to the nearest tenth of a centimeter. Record the length below.

Length of book cover: _____

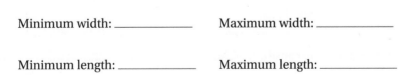

When measuring to the nearest centimeter, lengths in this range are rounded to 3 cm.

**B**  Determine the minimum and maximum possible values for the actual width and length of the book cover.

*Example:* When you measure an object to the nearest centimeter and get a measurement of 3 cm, the actual measurement is between 2.5 cm and 3.5 cm.

Minimum width: _____     Maximum width: _____

Minimum length: _____     Maximum length: _____

**C**  Use the minimum width and minimum length to calculate the minimum possible area of the book cover. Then use the maximum width and maximum length to calculate the maximum possible area of the book cover.

Minimum area: _____     Maximum area: _____

**1a.** How does the precision of the linear measurements (width and length) affect the calculated measurement (area)?

_____

_____

In the preceding Explore, you may have discovered that there was a wide range of possible values for the actual area of the book cover. This raises the question of how a calculated measurement, like an area, should be reported. Significant digits offer one way to resolve this dilemma.

**Significant digits** are the digits in a measurement that carry meaning contributing to the precision of the measurement. The table gives rules for determining the number of significant digits in a measurement.

| Rules for Determining Significant Digits | | | |
|---|---|---|---|
| Rule | Example | Significant Digits (Bold) | Number of Significant Digits |
| All nonzero digits | 37.85 | **37.85** | 4 |
| Zeros after the last nonzero digit and to the right of the decimal point | 0.0070 | 0.00**70** | 2 |
| Zeros between significant digits | 6500.0 | **6500.0** | 5 |

Note that zeros at the end of a whole number are usually not considered to be significant digits. For example, 4550 ft has 3 significant digits.

**2 EXAMPLE**   **Determining the Number of Significant Digits**

Determine the number of significant digits in each measurement.

  **A** 840.09 m         **B** 36,000 mi         **C** 0.010 kg

**A** The digits 8, 4, and 9 are significant digits because _____.

The zeros are significant digits because _____.

So, 840.09 m has _____ significant digits.

**B** The digits 3 and 6 are significant digits because _____.

The zeros are not significant because _____.

So, 36,000 mi has _____ significant digits.

© Houghton Mifflin Harcourt Publishing Company

**C** The digit 1 is a significant digit because _____.

The zero after the 1 is a significant digit because _____

_____

So, 0.010 kg has _____ significant digits.

**REFLECT**

**2a.** A student claimed that 0.045 m and 0.0045 m have the same number of significant digits. Do you agree or disagree? Why?

_____

_____

When you perform operations on measurements, use these rules for determining the number of significant digits you should report.

| Rules for Significant Digits in Calculations | |
|---|---|
| **Operations** | **Rule** |
| Addition Subtraction | Round the sum or difference to the same place as the last significant digit of the least precise measurement. |
| Multiplication Division | The product or quotient must have the same number of significant digits as the least precise measurement. |

## 3 EXAMPLE  Calculating with Significant Digits

A student measures the width of a book cover to the nearest centimeter and finds that the width is 16 cm. Another student measures the length of the cover to the nearest tenth of a centimeter and finds that the length is 23.6 cm. Use the correct number of significant digits to write the perimeter and area of the cover.

**A** Find the perimeter: 16 cm + 23.6 cm + 16 cm + 23.6 cm = 79.2 cm

The least precise measurement is 16 cm. Its last significant digit is in the units place. Round the sum to the nearest whole number.

So, the perimeter is _____.

**B** Find the area: 16 cm × 23.6 cm = 377.6 cm$^2$

The least precise measurement is 16 cm. It has 2 significant digits. Round the product to 2 significant digits.

So, the area is _____.

**3a.** Suppose the first student had measured the book cover to the nearest tenth of a centimeter and found that the width was 16.0 cm. Does this change how you would you report the perimeter and area? Explain.

_____

_____

# PRACTICE

**Choose the more precise measurement in each pair.**

**1.** 18 cm; 177 mm

**2.** 3 yd; 10 ft

**3.** 40.23 kg; 40.3 kg

_____     _____     _____

**4.** One student measures the length of a rectangular wall to the nearest meter and finds that the length is 5 m. Another student measures the height of the wall to the nearest tenth of a meter and finds that the height is 3.2 m. What are the minimum and maximum possible values for the area of the wall?

_____

**Determine the number of significant digits in each measurement.**

**5.** 12,080 ft

**6.** 0.8 mL

**7.** 1.0065 km

_____     _____     _____

**8.** You measure a rectangular window to the nearest tenth of a centimeter and find that the length is 81.4 cm. A friend measures the width to the nearest centimeter and finds that the width is 38 cm. Use the correct number of significant digits to write the perimeter and area of the window.

_____

**9. Error Analysis** A student measured the length and width of a square rug to the nearest hundreth of a meter. He found that the length and width were 1.30 m. The student was asked to report the area using the correct number of significant digits and he wrote the area as 1.7 m². Explain the student's error.

_____

**10.** Measure the length and width of the rectangle to the nearest tenth of a centimeter. Then use the correct number of significant digits to write the perimeter and area of the rectangle.

_____

# Perimeter and Area on the Coordinate Plane

COMMON
CORE

CC.9-12.G.GPE.7*,
CC.9-12.G.MG.1*,
CC.9-12.G.MG.2*

**Essential question:** *How do you find the perimeter and area of polygons on the coordinate plane?*

Recall that the perimeter of a polygon is the sum of the lengths of the polygon's sides. You can use the distance formula to help you find perimeters of polygons in a coordinate plane.

## 1 E X A M P L E    Finding a Perimeter

Find the perimeter of the pentagon with vertices $A(-4, 2)$, $B(-4, -2)$, $C(0, -3)$, $D(4, -2)$, and $E(2, 3)$. Round to the nearest tenth.

**A**  Plot the points. Then use a straightedge to draw the pentagon that is determined by the points.

**B**  Find the length of each side of the pentagon.

$\overline{AB}$ is vertical. You can find its length by counting units.

$AB = $ _____ units

Use the distance formula to find the remaining side lengths.

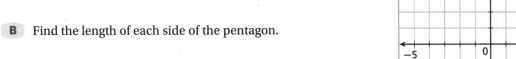

$$BC = \sqrt{(0 - (-4))^2 + (-3 - (-2))^2} = \sqrt{\boxed{\phantom{xx}} + \boxed{\phantom{xx}}} = \sqrt{\boxed{\phantom{xx}}}$$

$\overline{BC}$ and $\overline{CD}$ have the same length because

_____

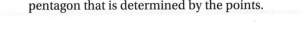

$$DE = \sqrt{\left(\boxed{\phantom{xx}} - \boxed{\phantom{xx}}\right)^2 + \left(\boxed{\phantom{xx}} - \boxed{\phantom{xx}}\right)^2} = \sqrt{\boxed{\phantom{xx}} + \boxed{\phantom{xx}}} = \sqrt{\boxed{\phantom{xx}}}$$

$$EA = \sqrt{\left(\boxed{\phantom{xx}} - \boxed{\phantom{xx}}\right)^2 + \left(\boxed{\phantom{xx}} - \boxed{\phantom{xx}}\right)^2} = \sqrt{\boxed{\phantom{xx}} + \boxed{\phantom{xx}}} = \sqrt{\boxed{\phantom{xx}}}$$

**C**  Find the sum of the side lengths.

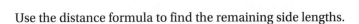

$AB + BC + CD + DE + EA = $ _____ + _____ + _____ + _____ + _____

Use a calculator to evaluate the expression. Then round to the nearest tenth.

So, the perimeter of $ABCDE$ is _____ units.

**1a.** Explain how you can find the perimeter of a rectangle to check that your answer is reasonable.

_____

_____

_____

The *density* of an object is its mass per unit volume. For example, the density of gold is 19.3 g/cm$^3$. This means each cubic centimeter of gold has a mass of 19.3 grams. You can also define density in other situations that involve area or volume. For example, the **population density** of a region is the population per unit area.

## 2 EXAMPLE  Approximating a Population Density

Vermont has a population of 621,760. Its border can be modeled by the trapezoid with vertices $A(0, 0)$, $B(0, 160)$, $C(80, 160)$, and $D(40, 0)$, where each unit of the coordinate plane represents one mile. Find the approximate population density of Vermont. Round to the nearest tenth.

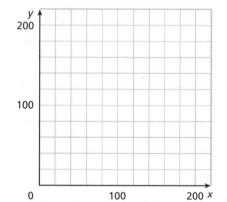

**A**  Plot the points. Then use a straightedge to draw the trapezoid that is determined by the points.

**B**  Find the area of the trapezoid. To do so, draw a perpendicular from $D$ to $\overline{BC}$. This forms a rectangle and a triangle. The area of the trapezoid is the sum of the area of the rectangle and the area of the triangle.

Area of rectangle $= \ell \cdot w =$ _____ $\cdot$ _____ $=$ _____

Area of triangle $= \frac{1}{2}bh = \frac{1}{2} \cdot$ _____ $\cdot$ _____ $=$ _____

Area of trapezoid $=$ _____ $+$ _____ $=$ _____ mi$^2$

**C**  Find the population density.

Population density $= \dfrac{\text{population}}{\text{area}} =$ _____ $\approx$ _____

Round to the nearest tenth.

So, the approximate population density of Vermont is _____ persons/mi$^2$.

**2a.** The actual area of Vermont is 9620 mi$^2$. Is your approximation of the population density an overestimate or underestimate? Why?

_____

_____

**2b.** Suppose the population of Vermont doubles in the next century. Would the population density change? If so, how?

_____

# PRACTICE

**1.** Find the perimeter of the pentagon with vertices $A(-5, 1)$, $B(0, 3)$, $C(5, 1)$, $D(4, -2)$, $E(0, -4)$, and $F(-2, -4)$. Round to the nearest tenth.

_____

**2.** Find the perimeter of the hexagon with vertices $J(0, 5)$, $K(4, 3)$, $L(4, -1)$, $M(0, -4)$, $N(-4, -1)$, and $P(-4, 3)$. Round to the nearest tenth.

_____

**3.** A plot of land is a pentagon with vertices $Q(-4, 4)$, $R(2, 4)$, $S(4, 1)$, $T(2, -4)$, and $U(-4, -4)$. Each unit of the coordinate grid represents one meter.

  **a.** Fencing costs \$24.75 per meter. What is the cost of placing a fence around the plot of land?  _____

  **b.** Sod costs \$1.85 per square meter. What is the cost of covering the plot of land with sod?  _____

**4.** Colorado has a population of 5,024,748. Its border can be modeled by the rectangle with vertices $A(-190, 0)$, $B(-190, 280)$, $C(190, 280)$, and $D(190, 0)$, where each unit of the coordinate plane represents one mile. Find the approximate population density of Colorado. Round to the nearest tenth.

_____

**5.** For the maximum grain yield, corn should be planted at a density of 38,000 plants per acre. A farmer has a field in the shape of a quadrilateral with vertices $J(0, 0)$, $K(0, 400)$, $L(500, 600)$, and $M(500, 0)$, where each unit of the coordinate plane represents one foot.

  **a.** What is the area of the field to the nearest hundredth of an acre? (*Hint:* 1 acre equals 43,560 ft$^2$.)  _____

  **b.** Approximately how many corn plants should be planted on the field for maximum grain yield? Round to the nearest ten thousand.  _____

# Circumference

**Essential question:** *How do you justify and use the formula for the circumference of a circle?*

COMMON
CORE

CC.9-12.G.GMD.1,
CC.9-12.G.MG.1*

> ### Circumference of a Circle Formula
> The circumference $C$ of a circle with radius $r$ is given by $C = 2\pi r$.

**1** **EXPLORE**    **Justifying the Circumference Formula**

**Plan:** To find the circumference of a given circle, consider regular polygons that are inscribed in the circle. As the number of sides of the polygons increases, the perimeter of the polygons gets closer to the circumference of the circle. The first steps of the argument consist of writing an expression for the perimeter of an inscribed $n$-gon.

Inscribed     Inscribed     Inscribed
pentagon     hexagon     octagon

**A**   Let circle $O$ be a circle with center $O$ and radius $r$. Inscribe a regular $n$-gon in circle $O$ and draw radii from $O$ to the vertices of the $n$-gon.

**B**   Let $\overline{AB}$ be one side of the $n$-gon. Draw $\overline{OM}$, the segment from $O$ to the midpoint of $\overline{AB}$.

Then $\triangle AOM \cong \triangle BOM$ by _____.

So, $\angle 1 \cong \angle 2$ by _____.

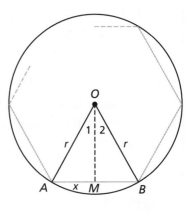

**C**   There are _____ triangles, all congruent to $\triangle AOB$, that surround point $O$ and fill the $n$-gon.

Therefore, m$\angle AOB =$ _____ and m$\angle 1 =$ _____.

**D**   Since $\angle OMA \cong \angle OMB$ by CPCTC, and $\angle OMA$ and $\angle OMB$ form a linear pair, these angles are supplementary and must have measures of 90°. So, $\triangle AOM$ and $\triangle BOM$ are right triangles.

In $\triangle AOM$, $\sin \angle 1 = \dfrac{\text{length of opposite leg}}{\text{length of hypotenuse}} = \dfrac{x}{r}$.

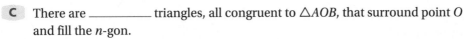

So, $x = r \sin \angle 1$ and substituting the expression for m$\angle 1$ from above gives

$x = r \sin ($ _____ $)$

**E**  Now express the perimeter of the *n*-gon in terms of *x*.

The length of $\overline{AB}$ is 2*x*, since _____.

This means the perimeter of the *n*-gon is _____.

Substitute the expression for *x* from Step D.

Then the perimeter is given by the expression _____.

**F**  Your expression for the perimeter of the *n*-gon should include $n \sin\left(\frac{180°}{n}\right)$ as a factor. Use a calculator, as follows, to find out what happens to the value of this expression as *n* gets larger.

- Enter the expression $x \sin\left(\frac{180}{x}\right)$ as $Y_1$.

- Go to the Table Setup menu and enter the values shown at right.

- View a table for the function.

- Use the arrow keys to scroll down.

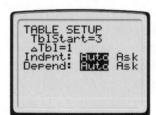

What happens to the value of $n \sin\left(\frac{180°}{n}\right)$ as *n* gets larger?

_____

**G**  Consider the expression you wrote for the perimeter of the *n*-gon at the end of Step E. What happens to the value of this expression as *n* gets larger?

_____

**REFLECT**

**1a.** When *n* is very large, does the perimeter of the *n*-gon ever equal the circumference of the circle? Why or why not?

_____

_____

**1b.** How does the above argument justify the formula $C = 2\pi r$?

_____

_____

_____

## 2 EXAMPLE  Finding the Circumference of a Circle

Find the circumference of circle $O$. Round to the nearest tenth.

**A** Find the radius. The diameter is twice the radius, so $r =$ _____.

**B** Use the formula $C = 2\pi r$.

$C = 2\pi($_____$)$    Substitute the value for $r$.

$C \approx$ _____    Use the $\pi$ key to evaluate the expression on a calculator. Then round.

### REFLECT

**2a.** Suppose you multiply the diameter of the circle by a factor $k$, for some $k > 0$. How does the circumference change? Explain.

_____

_____


## 3 EXAMPLE  Solving a Circumference Problem

The General Sherman tree in Sequoia National Park, California, is considered the world's largest tree. The tree is approximately circular at its base, with a circumference of 102.6 feet. What is the approximate diameter of the tree? Round to the nearest foot.

**A** Substitute 102.6 for $C$ in the formula for the circumference of a circle.

_____ $= 2\pi r$    Substitute 102.6 for $C$ in the formula.

_____ $= r$    Solve for $r$.

$r \approx$ _____    Use a calculator to evaluate the expression.

**B** The diameter of a circle is twice the radius.

So, the diameter of the tree is approximately _____.

### REFLECT

**3a.** The maximum distance across the base of the General Sherman tree is 36.5 feet. What explains the difference between this distance and the diameter you calculated above?

_____

_____

# PRACTICE

**Find the circumference of each circle. Round to the nearest tenth.**

**1.**

**2.**

**3.**

_____     _____     _____

**4.** The Parthenon is a Greek temple dating to approximately 445 BCE. The temple features 46 Doric columns, which are approximately cylindrical. The circumference of each column at the base is approximately 5.65 meters. What is the approximate diameter of each column? Round to the nearest tenth.

_____

**5.** A circular track for a model train has a diameter of 8.5 feet. The train moves around the track at a constant speed of 0.7 ft/s.

   **a.** To the nearest foot, how far does the train travel when it goes completely around the track 10 times?

                                                     _____

   **b.** To the nearest minute, how long does it take the train to go completely around the track 10 times?

                                                     _____

**6.** A standard bicycle wheel has a diameter of 26 inches. A student claims that during a one-mile bike ride the wheel makes more than 1000 complete revolutions. Do you agree or disagree? Explain. (*Hint:* 1 mile = 5280 feet)

_____

_____

_____

**7.** In the figure, $\overline{AB}$ is a diameter of circle $C$, $D$ is the midpoint of $\overline{AC}$, and $E$ is the midpoint of $\overline{AD}$. How does the circumference of circle $E$ compare to the circumference of circle $C$? Explain.

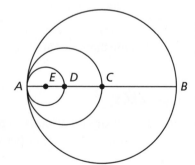

_____

_____

_____

© Houghton Mifflin Harcourt Publishing Company

# Arc Length and Radian Measure

COMMON
CORE

CC.9-12.G.CO.1,
CC.9-12.G.C.5

**Essential question:** *How do you find the length of an arc?*

**Arc length** is understood to be the distance along a circular arc measured in linear units (such as feet or centimeters). You can use proportional reasoning to find arc lengths.

**1  EXAMPLE**  Finding Arc Length

Find the arc length of $\overarc{AB}$. Express your answer in terms of $\pi$ and rounded to the nearest tenth.

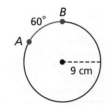

**A**  First find the circumference of the circle.

$C = 2\pi r =$ _____  Substitute 9 for *r*.

**B**  The entire circle is 360°, but $\overarc{AB}$ measures 60°. Therefore, the arc's length is $\frac{60}{360}$ or $\frac{1}{6}$ of the circumference.

Arc length of $\overarc{AB} = \frac{1}{6} \cdot$ _____  Arc length is $\frac{1}{6}$ of the circumference.

$=$ _____  Multiply.

$=$ _____  Use a calculator to evaluate. Then round.

So, the arc length of $\overarc{AB}$ is _____ or _____.

**REFLECT**

**1a.**  How could you use the above process to find the length of an arc of the circle that measures $m°$?

_____

_____

The proportional reasoning process you used above can be generalized. Given a circle with radius $r$, its circumference is $2\pi r$ and the arc length $s$ of an arc with measure $m°$ is $\frac{m}{360}$ times the circumference. This gives the following formula.

**Arc Length**

The arc length $s$ of an arc with measure $m°$ and radius $r$ is given by the formula $s = \frac{m}{360} \cdot 2\pi r$.

## 2 EXPLORE   Investigating Arc Lengths in Concentric Circles

Consider a set of concentric circles with center $O$ and radius 1, 2, 3, and so on. The central angle shown in the figure is a right angle and it cuts off arcs that measure 90°.

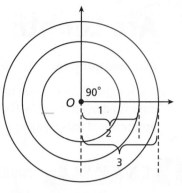

**A**  For each value of the radius $r$ listed in the table below, find the corresponding arc length. Write the length in terms of $\pi$ and rounded to the nearest hundredth.

For example, when $r = 1$, the arc length is $\frac{90}{360} \cdot 2\pi(1) = \frac{1}{2}\pi \approx 1.57$.

| Radius $r$ | 1 | 2 | 3 | 4 | 5 |
|---|---|---|---|---|---|
| Arc length $s$ in terms of $\pi$ | $\frac{1}{2}\pi$ | | | | |
| Arc length $s$ to nearest hundredth | 1.57 | | | | |

**B**  Plot the ordered pairs from your table on the coordinate plane at right.

What do you notice about the points?

_____

_____

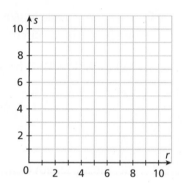

What type of relationship is the relationship between arc length and radius?

_____

What is the constant of proportionality for this relationship?

_____

## REFLECT

**2a.** What happens to the arc length when you double the radius? How is this connected to the idea that all circles are similar?

_____

_____

© Houghton Mifflin Harcourt Publishing Company

As you discovered in the Explore, when the central angle is fixed at $m°$, the length of the arc cut off by the central angle is proportional to (or varies directly with) the radius. In fact, you can see that the formula for arc length is a proportional relationship when $m$ is fixed.

$$s = \underbrace{\frac{m}{360} \cdot 2\pi}r$$
constant of proportionality

The constant of proportionality for the proportional relationship is $\frac{m}{360} \cdot 2\pi$. This constant of proportionality is defined to be the **radian measure** of the angle.

## 3 EXAMPLE  Converting to Radian Measure

Convert each angle measure to radian measure.

**A**  180°          **B**  60°

**A**  To convert 180° to radian measure, let $m = 180$ in the expression $\frac{m}{360} \cdot 2\pi$.

$$180° = \frac{\phantom{180}}{360} \cdot 2\pi \text{ radians} \qquad \text{Substitute 180 for } m.$$

$$= \underline{\hspace{2cm}} \text{ radians} \qquad \text{Simplify.}$$

**B**  To convert 60° to radian measure, let $m = 60$ in the expression $\frac{m}{360} \cdot 2\pi$.

$$180° = \frac{\phantom{180}}{360} \cdot 2\pi \text{ radians} \qquad \text{Substitute 180 for } m.$$

$$= \underline{\hspace{2cm}} \text{ radians} \qquad \text{Simplify.}$$

## REFLECT

**3a.** Explain why the radian measure for an angle of $m°$ is sometimes defined as the length of the arc cut off on a circle of radius 1 by a central angle of $m°$.

_____

_____

_____

**3b.** Explain how to find the degree measure of an angle whose radian measure is $\frac{\pi}{4}$.

_____

_____

_____

# PRACTICE

**Find the arc length of $\overset{\frown}{AB}$. Express your answer in terms of $\pi$ and rounded to the nearest tenth.**

**1.**

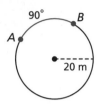

90° B
A
20 m

_____

**2.**

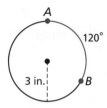

A
120°
3 in.
B

_____

**3.**

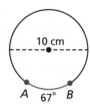

10 cm
A 67° B

_____

**4.**

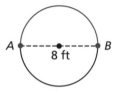

A · · · B
8 ft

_____

**5.**

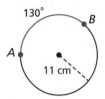

130° B
A
11 cm

_____

**6.**

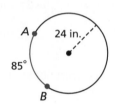

A 24 in.
85°
B

_____

**7.** It is convenient to know the radian measure for benchmark angles such as 0°, 30°, 45°, and so on. Complete the table by finding the radian measure for each of the given benchmark angles.

| Benchmark Angles | | | | | | | | | |
|---|---|---|---|---|---|---|---|---|---|
| **Degree Measure** | 0° | 30° | 45° | 60° | 90° | 120° | 135° | 150° | 180° |
| **Radian Measure** | | | | | | | | | |

**8.** The minute hand of a clock is 4 inches long. To the nearest tenth of an inch, how far does the tip of the minute hand travel as the time progresses from 12:00 to 12:25?

_____

**9. Error Analysis** A student was asked to find the arc length of $\overset{\frown}{PQ}$. The student's work is shown at right. Explain the student's error and give the correct arc length.

_____

_____

_____

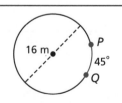

16 m
P
45°
Q

The entire circumference is $2\pi \cdot 16 = 32\pi$ and 45° is $\frac{1}{8}$ of the circle, so the arc length is $\frac{1}{8} \cdot 32\pi = 4\pi$ m.

# Area of Circles and Sectors

**Essential question:** *How do you find the area of a circle and the area of a sector?*

COMMON
CORE

CC.9-12.G.C.5,
CC.9-12.G.GMD.1

**1  EXPLORE**  **Developing a Formula for the Area of a Circle**

**A**  Use a compass to draw a large circle on a sheet of paper. Cut out the circle.

**B**  Fold the circle in half. Then fold the resulting semicircle in half.
Then fold the resulting quarter-circle in half.

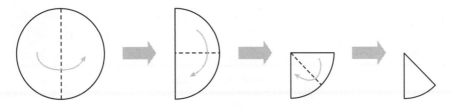

**C**  Unfold the paper and cut along the folds to make 8 wedges.

**D**  Rearrange the wedges as shown to make a
shape that resembles a parallelogram.

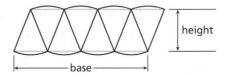

Assume the original circle has
radius *r*. What is the approximate
height of the parallelogram?  _____

The base of the parallelogram can be approximated by half the
circumference of the circle. Express the base in terms of *r*.  _____

Recall that the area of a parallelogram is the base times the height.
What is the approximate area of the parallelogram?  _____

**REFLECT**

**1a.**  What happens as you repeat the process, cutting the circle into more and more
wedges each time?

_____

_____

**1b.**  Make a conjecture: What do you think is the formula for the area *A* of a circle with
radius *r*? Why?

_____

_____

_____

## Area of a Circle

The area $A$ of a circle with radius $r$ is given by $A = \pi r^2$.

A **sector** of a circle is a region bounded by two radii and their intercepted arc. A sector is named by the endpoints of the arc and the center of the circle. For example, the figure shows sector $POQ$.

In the same way that you used proportional reasoning to find the length of an arc, you can use proportional reasoning to find the area of a sector.

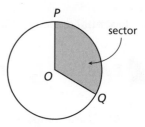

**2** **EXAMPLE**    **Finding the Area of a Sector**

Find the area of sector $AOB$. Express your answer in terms of $\pi$ and rounded to the nearest tenth.

**A**  First find the area of the circle.

$A = \pi r^2 = \pi\,(\underline{\hspace{1.5cm}})^2$        Substitute 15 for $r$.

$= \underline{\hspace{1.5cm}}$        Simplify.

**B**  The entire circle is 360°, but $\angle AOB$ measures 120°. Therefore, the sector's area is $\frac{120}{360}$ or $\frac{1}{3}$ of the circle's area.

Area of sector $AOB = \frac{1}{3} \cdot \underline{\hspace{1.5cm}}$        The area is $\frac{1}{3}$ of the circle's area.

$= \underline{\hspace{1.5cm}}$        Simplify.

$= \underline{\hspace{1.5cm}}$        Use a calculator to evaluate. Then round.

So, the area of sector $AOB$ is $\underline{\hspace{1.5cm}}$ or $\underline{\hspace{1.5cm}}$.

**REFLECT**

**2a.** How could you use the above process to find the area of a sector of the circle whose central angle measures $m°$?

_____

_____

**2b.** Make a conjecture: What do you think is the formula for the area of a sector with a central angle of $m°$ and radius $r$?

_____

© Houghton Mifflin Harcourt Publishing Company

The proportional reasoning process you used in the example can be generalized. Given a sector with a central angle of $m°$ and radius $r$, the area of the entire circle is $\pi r^2$ and the area of the sector is $\frac{m}{360}$ times the circle's area. This gives the following formula.

### Area of a Sector

The area $A$ of a sector of a circle with a central angle of $m°$ and radius $r$ is given by $A = \frac{m}{360} \cdot \pi r^2$.

# PRACTICE

**Find the area of sector *AOB*. Express your answer in terms of $\pi$ and rounded to the nearest tenth.**

**1.**

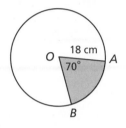

**2.**

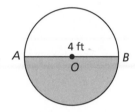

**3.**

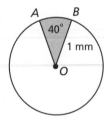

_____  _____  _____

**4.**

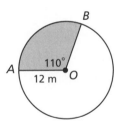

**5.**

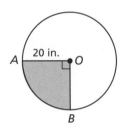

**6.**

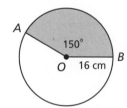

_____  _____  _____

**7.** The area of sector *AOB* is $\frac{9}{2}\pi\,\text{m}^2$. Explain how to find m∠*AOB*.

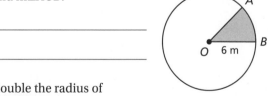

_____

_____

**8. Error Analysis** A student claims that when you double the radius of a sector while keeping the measure of the central angle constant, you double the area of the sector. Do you agree or disagree? Explain.

_____

_____

_____

Name _____ Class _____ Date _____

## MULTIPLE CHOICE

**1.** A student measures the length of a rectangular poster to the nearest centimeter and finds that the length is 44 cm. Another student measures the poster's width to the nearest tenth of a centimeter and finds that the width is 21.3 cm. How should the students report the area of the poster using the correct number of significant digits?

**A.** 940 cm$^2$          **C.** 937 cm$^2$

**B.** 937.2 cm$^2$        **D.** 930 cm$^2$

**2.** The figure shows a polygonal fence for part of a garden. Each unit of the coordinate plane represents one meter. What is the length of the fence to the nearest tenth of a meter?

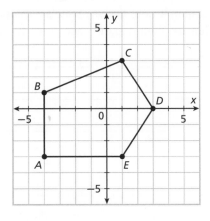

**F.** 16.1 m          **H.** 21.6 m

**G.** 18.0 m          **J.** 31.0 m

**3.** A geologist reports the mass of a rock to 3 significant digits. Which of the following could be the mass of the rock?

**A.** 42.00 kg          **C.** 0.42 kg

**B.** 4.20 kg           **D.** 0.042 kg

**4.** Using the figure below, Andrea discovers that the length of the arc intercepted by the 60° angle is proportional to the radius. What is the constant of proportionality for the relationship?

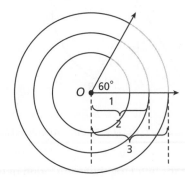

**F.** $\frac{\pi}{6}$          **H.** $\frac{1}{6}$

**G.** $\frac{\pi}{3}$          **J.** $\frac{1}{3}$

**5.** Meteor Crater, near Flagstaff, Arizona, is an approximately circular crater, with a circumference of 2.32 miles. What is the diameter of the crater to the nearest hundredth of a mile?

**A.** 0.37 mi          **C.** 1.48 mi

**B.** 0.74 mi          **D.** 7.29 mi

**6.** What is the radian measure of the angle whose degree measure is 20°?

**F.** $\frac{\pi}{20}$          **H.** $\frac{\pi}{9}$

**G.** $\frac{\pi}{18}$          **J.** $\frac{2\pi}{9}$

## FREE RESPONSE

**7.** In order to justify the formula for the circumference of a circle, you inscribe a regular *n*-gon in a circle of radius *r*, as shown in the figure.

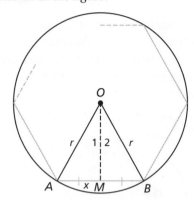

You show that $\triangle AOM \cong \triangle BOM$ and conclude that $\angle 1 \cong \angle 2$ by CPCTC. Then you state that $m\angle AOB = \frac{360°}{n}$ and $m\angle 1 = \frac{180°}{n}$. Describe the main steps for finishing the justification of the circumference formula.

_____

_____

_____

_____

_____

_____

**8.** Write an expression in terms of *m* that you can use to find the area of sector *AOB*.

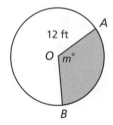

_____

**9.** The border of Utah can be modeled by the polygon with vertices $A(0, 0)$, $B(0, 350)$, $C(160, 350)$, $D(160, 280)$, $E(270, 280)$, and $F(270, 0)$. Each unit on the coordinate plane represents 1 mile.

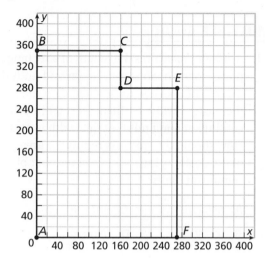

**a.** What is the approximate area of the state?

_____

**b.** The population of Utah is 2,784,572. Explain how to find the state's population density. Round to the nearest tenth.

_____

_____

_____

_____

_____

_____

_____

_____

# Three-Dimensional Figures and Volume

## Unit Focus

In this unit, you will turn your attention to three-dimensional figures. You will begin by exploring cross sections of three-dimensional figures and learn how to generate three-dimensional figures by rotating two-dimensional figures around a line. Then you will develop and justify volume formulas for a variety of solids. Finally, you will apply what you have learned to solve problems in which you must design a three-dimensional figure given one or more constraints.

## Unit at a Glance

COMMON CORE

© Houghton Mifflin Harcourt Publishing Company

# Unpacking the Common Core State Standards

Use the table to help you understand the Standards for Mathematical Content that are taught in this unit. Refer to the lessons listed after each standard for exploration and practice.

| COMMON CORE Standards for Mathematical Content | What It Means For You |
|---|---|
| **CC.9-12.G.GMD.1 Give an informal argument for the formulas for the circumference of a circle, area of a circle, volume of a cylinder, pyramid, and cone.** Lessons 10-2, 10-3, 10-4 | You may already be familiar with some of the formulas for volumes of three-dimensional figures, but now you will give logical arguments to justify the formulas. |
| **CC.9-12.G.GMD.2(+) Give an informal argument using Cavalieri's principle for the formulas for the volume of a sphere and other solid figures.** Lessons 10-2, 10-5 | You will learn how to use Cavalieri's principle, which is a powerful tool for developing and justifying volume formulas. |
| **CC.9-12.G.GMD.3 Use volume formulas for cylinders, pyramids, cones, and spheres to solve problems.\*** Lessons 10-2, 10-3, 10-4, 10-5, 10-6 | Cylinders, pyramids, cones, and spheres occur in a wide range of real-world applications. You will learn how to use volume formulas to solve problems that involve these figures. |
| **CC.9-12.G.GMD.4 Identify the shapes of two-dimensional cross-sections of three-dimensional objects, and identify three-dimensional objects generated by rotations of two-dimensional objects.** Lesson 10-1 | Visualization is an important element of working with three-dimensional figures. You will learn to visualize cross sections and rotations around a line in space. |
| **CC.9-12.G.G.MG.1 Use geometric shapes, their measures, and their properties to describe objects (e.g., modeling a tree trunk or a human torso as a cylinder).\*** Lesson 10-2 | You will see how you can model real-world objects with three-dimensional figures in order to solve problems. |
| **CC.9-12.G.MG.2 Apply concepts of density based on area and volume in modeling situations (e.g., persons per square mile, BTUs per cubic foot).\*** Lessons 10-2, 10-5 | You will do further work with density and learn how to measure the energy content of a fuel in terms of BTUs per unit of volume. |
| **CC.9-12.G.MG.3 Apply geometric methods to solve design problems (e.g., designing an object or structure to satisfy physical constraints or minimize cost; working with typographic grid systems based on ratios).\*** Lesson 10-6 | You will solve problems in which you are asked to design a three-dimensional figure that meets given conditions. |

UNIT 10

10-1

# Visualizing Three-Dimensional Figures

COMMON
CORE

CC.9-12.G.GMD.4

**Essential question:** *How do you identify cross sections of three-dimensional figures and how do you use rotations to generate three-dimensional figures?*

Recall that an *intersection* is the set of all points that two or more figures have in common. A **cross section** is the intersection of a three-dimensional figure and a plane.

## 1 EXAMPLE   Identifying Cross Sections of a Cylinder

Describe each cross section of a cylinder.

**A**
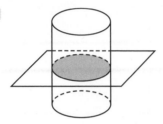

**B**
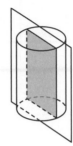

**A**   Each base of the cylinder is a _____.

The cross section is formed by a plane that is parallel to the bases of the cylinder. Any cross section of a cylinder made by a plane parallel to the bases will have the same shape as the bases.

So, the cross section is a _____.

**B**   The bases of the cylinder are parallel, so the cross section is a quadrilateral with at least one pair of opposite sides that are parallel.

The bases of the cylinder meet the lateral (curved) surface at right angles, so the cross section must contain four right angles.

So, the cross section is a _____.

### REFLECT

**1a.** In Part A, why does the cross section appear to be an oval or ellipse?

_____

_____

**1b.** Is it possible for a cross section of a cylinder to have a shape other than those you identified above? Explain.

_____

_____

You have learned how to perform transformations in a plane. Transformations may also be carried out in three-dimensional space. In particular, you can rotate a two-dimensional figure around a line to generate a three-dimensional figure.

## 2 EXAMPLE   Generating Three-Dimensional Figures

Sketch and describe the figure that is generated by each rotation in three-dimensional space.

**A**   Rotate a right triangle around a line that contains one of its legs.

- Draw a right triangle and draw a line that contains one of its legs, as shown at right.

- To model the rotation of the triangle around the line, trace and cut out the triangle. Then tape the triangle to a piece of string so that one leg of the triangle is attached to the string. Hold both ends of the string and twirl it between your fingers to see the three-dimensional figure generated by the rotation. Sketch the figure at right.

| Sketch of Two-Dimensional Figure and Line of Rotation | Sketch of Three-Dimensional Figure Generated by the Rotation |
|---|---|
| 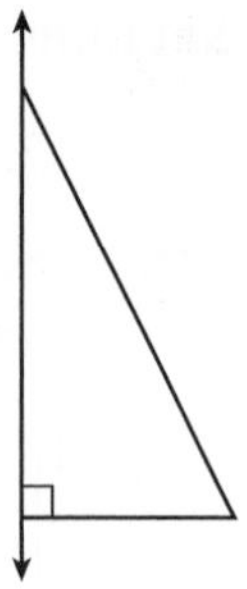 | |

So, the figure that is generated by the rotation is a _____.

**B**   Rotate a rectangle around a line that contains one of its sides.

- Draw a rectangle and draw a line that contains one of its sides, as shown at right.

- To model the rotation of the rectangle around the line, trace and cut out the rectangle. Then tape the rectangle to a piece of string so that one side of the rectangle is attached to the string. Hold both ends of the string and twirl it between your fingers to see the three-dimensional figure generated by the rotation. Sketch the figure at right.

| Sketch of Two-Dimensional Figure and Line of Rotation | Sketch of Three-Dimensional Figure Generated by the Rotation |
|---|---|
| 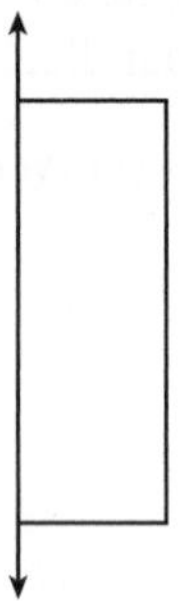 | |

So, the figure that is generated by the rotation is a _____.

**2a.** In Part A, suppose you rotate the triangle around the line that contains the other leg of the triangle. Do you get the same result? Explain.

_____

_____

**2b.** In Part B, how are the length and width of the rectangle related to the dimensions of the three-dimensional figure that is generated by the rotation?

_____

_____

# PRACTICE

**Describe each cross section.**

**1.**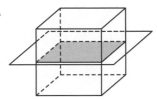

**2.**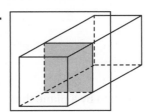

**3.**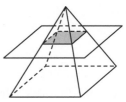

_____     _____     _____

**4.**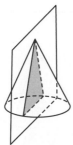

**5.**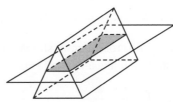

**6.**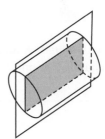

_____     _____     _____

**7.** Describe the cross section formed by the intersection of a cone and a plane parallel to the base of the cone.

_____

**8.** Describe the cross section formed by the intersection of a sphere and a plane that passes through the center of the sphere.

_____

**Sketch and describe the figure that is generated by each rotation in three-dimensional space.**

**9.** Rotate a semicircle around a line through the endpoints of the semicircle.

**10.** Rotate an isosceles triangle around the triangle's line of symmetry.

_____

_____

**11.** Rotate an isosceles right triangle around a line that contains the triangle's hypotenuse.

**12.** Rotate a line segment around a line that is perpendicular to the segment and that passes through an endpoint of the segment.

_____

_____

**13.** A cube with sides of length _s_ is intersected by a plane that passes through three of the cube's vertices, forming the cross section shown at right. What type of triangle is the cross section? Explain.

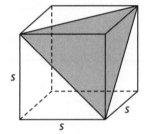

_____

_____

**14. Error Analysis** A student drew the cross section shown at right as a parallelogram. Did the student make an error? Explain.

_____

_____

_____

_____

**15.** Is it possible for a cross section of a cube to be an octagon? Why or why not?

_____

_____

_____

_____

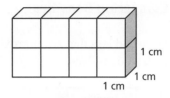

# Volume of Prisms and Cylinders

**Essential question:** *How do you calculate the volume of a prism or cylinder?*

Recall that the *volume* of a three-dimensional figure is the number of nonoverlapping cubic units contained in the interior of the figure. For example, the prism at right has a volume of 8 cubic centimeters. You can use this idea to develop volume formulas.

COMMON CORE

CC.9-12.G.GMD.1,
CC.9-12.G.GMD.2(+),
CC.9-12.G.GMD.3*,
CC.9-12.G.MG.1*,
CC.9-12.G.MG.2*

---

**1 EXPLORE**   **Developing a Basic Volume Formula**

**A** Consider a figure that is the base of a prism or cylinder. Assume the figure has an area of *B* square units.

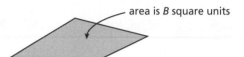
area is *B* square units

**B** Use the base to build a prism or cylinder with height 1 unit.

This means the prism or cylinder contains _____ cubic units.

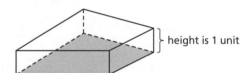
height is 1 unit

**C** Now use the base to build a prism or cylinder with a height of *h* units.

The volume of this prism or cylinder must be _____ times the volume of the prism or cylinder whose height is 1 unit.

So, the volume of the prism or cylinder is _____ cubic units.

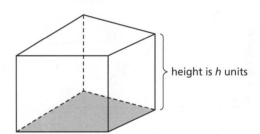
height is *h* units

**REFLECT**

**1a.** Suppose the figure that is the base of the prism is a rectangle with length $\ell$ and width *w*. Explain how you can use your work in the Explore to write a formula for the volume of the prism.

_____

_____

**1b.** Explain how you can use your work in the Explore to write a formula for the volume of a cylinder whose base is a circle with radius *r*.

_____

## Volume of a Cylinder

The volume $V$ of a cylinder with base area $B$ and height $h$ is given by $V = Bh$ (or $V = \pi r^2 h$, where $r$ is the radius of the base).

## 2 EXAMPLE   Comparing Densities

You gather data about two wood logs that are approximately cylindrical. Based on the data in the table, which wood is denser, Douglas fir or American redwood?

| Type of Wood | Diameter (ft) | Height (ft) | Weight (lb) |
|---|---|---|---|
| Douglas fir | 1 | 6 | 155.5 |
| American redwood | 3 | 4 | 791.7 |

**A**   Find the volume of the Douglas fir log.

$V = \pi r^2 h$

$V = \pi (\underline{\quad\quad})^2 \cdot \underline{\quad\quad}$      Substitute 0.5 for $r$ and 6 for $h$.

$V \approx \underline{\quad\quad}$ ft$^3$      Use a calculator. Round to the nearest tenth.

**B**   Find the volume of the American redwood log.

$V = \pi r^2 h$

$V = \pi (\underline{\quad\quad})^2 \cdot \underline{\quad\quad}$      Substitute 1.5 for $r$ and 4 for $h$.

$V \approx \underline{\quad\quad}$ ft$^3$      Use a calculator. Round to the nearest tenth.

**C**   Calculate and compare densities.

The density of the wood is the _____ per _____.

Density of Douglas fir =  $\approx$ _____ lb/ft$^3$      Round to the nearest unit.

Density of American redwood =  $\approx$ ____ lb/ft$^3$      Round to the nearest unit.

So, _____ is denser than _____.

## REFLECT

**2a.**  Explain in your own words what your results tell you about the two types of wood.

_____

_____

The axis of a cylinder is the segment whose endpoints are the centers of the bases. A right cylinder is a cylinder whose axis is perpendicular to the bases. An **oblique cylinder** is a cylinder whose axis is not perpendicular to the bases. Cavalieri's principle makes it possible to extend the formula for the volume of a cylinder to oblique cylinders.

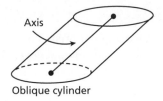

Axis

Oblique cylinder

**Cavalieri's Principle**

If two solids have the same height and the same cross-sectional area at every level, then the two solids have the same volume.

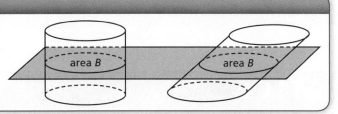

area *B*        area *B*

You can think of any oblique cylinder as a right cylinder that has been "pushed over" so that the cross sections at every level have equal areas. By Cavalieri's principle, the volume of an oblique cylinder is equal to the volume of the associated right cylinder. This means the formula $V = Bh = \pi r^2 h$ works for any cylinder.

**3** **EXAMPLE**    **Finding the Volume of an Oblique Cylinder**

The height of the cylinder shown here is twice the radius. What is the volume of the cylinder? Round to the nearest tenth.

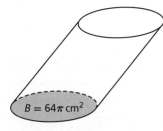

$B = 64\pi\ cm^2$

**A** Find the height of the cylinder. To do so, first find the radius of the cylinder.

Use the fact that the area of the base *B* is $64\pi$ cm².

| | |
|---|---|
| $\pi r^2 = 64\pi$ | The base is a circle, so $B = \pi r^2$. |
| $r^2 = $ _____ | Divide both sides by $\pi$. |
| $r = $ _____ cm | Take the square root of both sides. |

Since the height is twice the radius, the height is _____ cm.

**B** Find the volume of the cylinder.

| | |
|---|---|
| $V = Bh$ | The volume *V* of any cylinder is $V = Bh$. |
| $V = $ _____ · _____ | Substitute. |
| $V \approx$ _____ cm³ | Use a calulator. Round to the nearest tenth. |

© Houghton Mifflin Harcourt Publishing Company

**3a.** A rectangular prism has the same height as the oblique cylinder in the example. The cross-sectional area at every level of the prism is $64\pi$ cm$^2$. Can you use Cavalieri's principle to make a conclusion about the volume of the prism? Why or why not?

_____

_____

# PRACTICE

**Find the volume of each prism or cylinder. Round to the nearest tenth.**

**1.**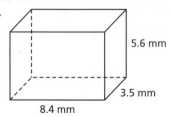
5.6 mm
3.5 mm
8.4 mm

**2.**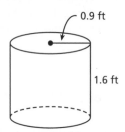
0.9 ft
1.6 ft

**3.**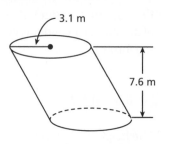
3.1 m
7.6 m

_____  _____  _____

**4.** You gather data about two wood logs that are approximately cylindrical. The data are shown in the table. Based on your data, which wood is denser, aspen or juniper? Explain.

| Type of Wood | Diameter (ft) | Height (ft) | Weight (lb) |
|---|---|---|---|
| Aspen | 1.5 | 3 | 137.8 |
| Juniper | 2 | 5 | 549.8 |

_____

_____

**5.** A vase in the shape of an oblique cylinder has the dimensions shown at right. How many liters of water does the vase hold? Round to the nearest tenth. (*Hint:* 1 liter $= 1000$ cm$^3$)

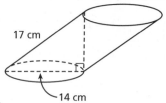
17 cm
14 cm

_____

**6. Error Analysis** A student claims that the cylinder and cone at right have the same volume by Cavalieri's principle. Explain the student's error.

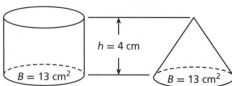
$h = 4$ cm
$B = 13$ cm$^2$
$B = 13$ cm$^2$

_____

_____

© Houghton Mifflin Harcourt Publishing Company

# Volume of Pyramids

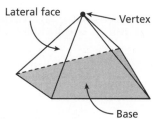

**Essential question:** *How do you calculate the volume of a pyramid?*

Recall that a *pyramid* is a polyhedron formed by a polygonal base and triangular lateral faces that meet at a common point, called the vertex of the pyramid. The goal of this lesson is to develop a formula for volume of a pyramid.

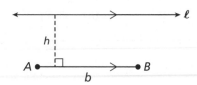

Lateral face — Vertex

Base

**COMMON CORE**

CC.9-12.G.GMD.1, CC.9-12.G.GMD.3*

## 1 EXPLORE   Developing a Volume Postulate

**A**   Consider a segment, $\overline{AB}$, with length $b$ and a line $\ell$ that is parallel to $\overline{AB}$. Let $h$ be the distance between $\overline{AB}$ and line $\ell$.

Choose a point $C$ on line $\ell$ and draw $\triangle ABC$. What is the area of $\triangle ABC$ in terms of $b$ and $h$?

_____

**B**   Choose a different point C on line $\ell$ and draw $\triangle ABC$. What is the area of $\triangle ABC$ in terms of $b$ and $h$?

_____

**C**   What do you think is true about all triangles that share the same base and have the same height?

_____

### REFLECT

**1a.**   Consider a three-dimensional figure that is analogous to the situation you explored above. Suppose you are given a polygon and a plane $R$ that is parallel to the plane containing the polygon. You can form a pyramid by choosing a point in plane $R$ and connecting it to each vertex of the polygon. What do you think is true of all pyramids formed in this way?

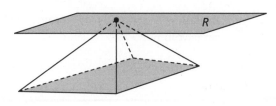

_____

Based on your work in the Explore, the following postulate should seem reasonable.

### Postulate

Pyramids that have equal base areas and equal heights have equal volumes.

In order to find a formula for the volume of any pyramid, you will first find a formula for the volume of a "wedge pyramid." A wedge pyramid is one in which the base is a triangle and a perpendicular segment from the pyramid's vertex to the base intersects the base at a vertex of the triangle. Pyramid *A-BCD* is a wedge pyramid.

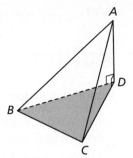

## 2 EXPLORE   Finding the Volume of a Wedge Pyramid

To find the volume of pyramid *A-BCD*, first let the area of △*BCD* be *B* and let the height of the pyramid, *AD*, be *h*.

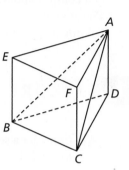

**A** Form a triangular prism as shown. The edges $\overline{EB}$ and $\overline{FC}$ are congruent to $\overline{AD}$ and parallel to $\overline{AD}$. The bases of the prism, △*EFA* and △*BCD* are congruent.

**B** What is the volume of the triangular prism in terms of *B* and *h*? Explain.

_____

_____

**C** You will now compare the volume of pyramid *A-BCD* and the volume of the triangular prism.

Draw $\overline{EC}$. This is the diagonal of a rectangle so, △ _____ ≅ △ _____.

Explain why pyramids *A-EBC* and *A-CFE* have the same volume.

_____

_____

_____

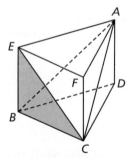

Explain why pyramids *C-EFA* and *A-BCD* have the same volume.

_____

_____

_____

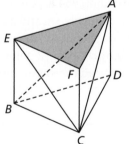

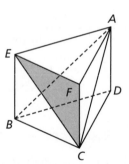

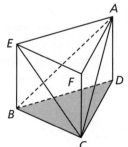

**D** You have shown that the three pyramids that form the triangular prism all have the same volume. Compare the volume of pyramid *A-BCD* and the volume of the triangular prism.

_____

_____

**E** Write the volume of pyramid *A-BCD* in terms of *B* and *h*.

_____

**REFLECT**

**2a.** Explain how you know that the three pyramids that form that triangular prism all have the same volume.

_____

_____

_____

_____

In the Explore, you showed that the volume of any "wedge pyramid" is one-third the product of the base area and the height. Now consider a general pyramid. As shown in the figure, the pyramid can be partitioned into nonoverlapping wedge pyramids by drawing a perpendicular from the vertex to the base.

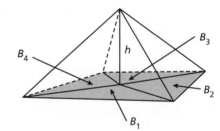

The volume *V* of the given pyramid is the sum of the volumes of the wedge pyramids.

That is, $V = \frac{1}{3}B_1h + \frac{1}{3}B_2h + \frac{1}{3}B_3h + \frac{1}{3}B_4h$.

Using the distributive property, this may be rewritten as $V = \frac{1}{3}h(B_1 + B_2 + B_3 + B_4)$.

Notice that $B_1 + B_2 + B_3 + B_4 = B$, where *B* is the base area of the given pyramid.

So, $V = \frac{1}{3}Bh$.

The above argument provides an informal justification for the following result.

> ### Volume of a Pyramid
>
> The volume *V* of a pyramid with base area *B* and height *h* is given by
>
> $V = \frac{1}{3}Bh$.

© Houghton Mifflin Harcourt Publishing Company

**3** **E X A M P L E**   **Solving a Volume Problem**

The Great Pyramid in Giza, Egypt, is approximately a
square pyramid with the dimensions shown. The pyramid
is composed of stone blocks that are rectangular prisms.
An average block has dimensions 1.3 m by 1.3 m by 0.7 m.
Approximately how many stone blocks were used to build the
pyramid? Round to the nearest hundred thousand.

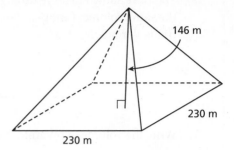

146 m

230 m

230 m

**A**   Find the volume of the pyramid.

The area of the base *B* is the area of a square with sides of length 230 m.

So, $B =$ _____

The volume *V* of the pyramid is $\frac{1}{3}Bh = \frac{1}{3} \cdot$ _____ $\cdot$ _____

So, $V =$ _____

**B**   Find the volume of an average block.

The volume of a rectangular prism is given by the formula _____.

So, the volume *W* of an average block is _____.

**C**   Find the approximate number of stone blocks in the pyramid.

To estimate the number of blocks in the pyramid, divide _____ by _____.

So, the approximate number of blocks is _____.

**REFLECT**

**3a.** What aspects of the model in this problem may lead to inaccuracies in your
estimate?

_____

_____

_____

**3b.** Suppose you are told that the average height of a stone block is 0.69 m rather than
0.7 m. Would this increase or decrease your estimate of the total number of blocks
in the pyramid? Explain.

_____

© Houghton Mifflin Harcourt Publishing Company

# PRACTICE

**Find the volume of each pyramid. Round to the nearest tenth.**

**1.**

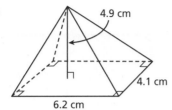

4.9 cm

4.1 cm

6.2 cm

_____

**2.**

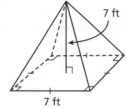

7 ft

7 ft

_____

**3.**

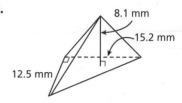

8.1 mm

15.2 mm

12.5 mm

_____

**4.** As shown in the figure, polyhedron *ABCDEFGH* is a cube and *P* is any point on face *EFGH*. Compare the volume of pyramid *P-ABCD* and the volume of the cube.

_____

_____

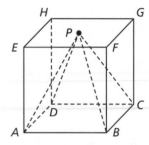

**5.** A storage container for grain is in the shape of a square pyramid with the dimensions shown.

   **a.** What is the volume of the container in cubic centimeters?

_____

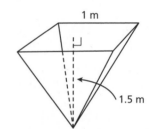

1 m

1.5 m

   **b.** Grain leaks from the container at a rate of 4 cm³ per second. Assuming the container starts completely full, about how many hours does it take until the container is empty?

_____

**6.** A piece of pure silver in the shape of a rectangular pyramid with the dimensions shown at right has a mass of 19.7 grams. What is the density of silver? Round to the nearest tenth.

_____

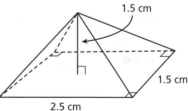

1.5 cm

1.5 cm

2.5 cm

**7.** A pyramid has a square base and a height of 5 ft. The volume of the pyramid is 60 ft³. Explain how to find the length of a side of the pyramid's base.

_____

_____

_____

**10-4**

# Volume of Cones

**Essential question:** *How do you calculate the volume of a cone?*

COMMON CORE

CC.9-12.G.GMD.1,
CC.9-12.G.GMD.3*

Recall that a *cone* is a three-dimensional figure with a circular base and a curved lateral surface that connects the base to a point called the vertex. You can use the formula for the volume of a pyramid to develop a formula for the volume of a cone.

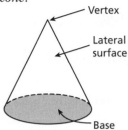

Vertex

Lateral surface

Base

---

**1  EXPLORE  Developing a Volume Formula**

**Plan:** To find the volume of a given cone, consider pyramids with regular polygonal bases that are inscribed in the cone. As the number of sides of the polygonal bases increases, the volume of the pyramid gets closer to the volume of the cone. The first steps of the argument consist of writing an expression for the volume of an inscribed pyramid.

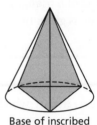
Base of inscribed pyramid has 3 sides.

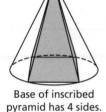
Base of inscribed pyramid has 4 sides.

Base of inscribed pyramid has 5 sides.

**A**  Let *O* be the center of the cone's base and let *r* be the radius of the cone. Let *h* be the height of the cone. Inscribe a pyramid whose base is a regular *n*-gon in the cone. Draw radii from *O* to the vertices of the *n*-gon.

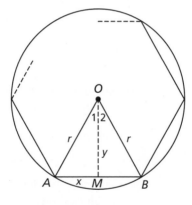

**B**  Let $\overline{AB}$ be one side of the *n*-gon. Draw $\overline{OM}$, the segment from *O* to the midpoint of $\overline{AB}$.

Then $\triangle AOM \cong \triangle BOM$ by _____.

So, $\angle 1 \cong \angle 2$ by _____.

**C**  There are _____ triangles, all congruent to $\triangle AOB$, that surround point *O* and fill the *n*-gon.

Therefore, m$\angle AOB$ = _____ and m$\angle 1$ = _____.

**D**  Since $\angle OMA \cong \angle OMB$ by CPCTC, and $\angle OMA$ and $\angle OMB$ form a linear pair, these angles are supplementary and must have measures of 90°. So, $\triangle AOM$ and $\triangle BOM$ are right triangles.

In $\triangle AOM$, $\sin \angle 1 = \frac{x}{r}$, so $x = r \sin \angle 1$.

Substituting the expression for m$\angle 1$ from above gives $x = r \sin$ (_____).

**E** In △AOM, cos ∠1 = $\frac{y}{r}$, so $y = r \cos ∠1$.

Substituting the expression for m∠1 from above gives $y = r \cos ($ _____ $)$.

**F** To write an expression for the area of the base of the pyramid, first write an expression for the area of △AOB.

Area(△AOB) = $\frac{1}{2}$ · base · height = $\frac{1}{2}$ · 2x · y = xy

Substituting the expressions for x and y from above gives the following.

Area (△AOB) = _____

The base of the pyramid is composed of n triangles that are congruent to △AOB, so the area of the base of the pyramid is given by the following.

Area (base of pyramid) = _____

The volume of the pyramid is $\frac{1}{3}$ · base · height, which may be written as

Volume (pyramid) = _____

**G** Your expression for the pyramid's volume should include the expression

$$n \sin \left(\frac{180°}{n}\right) \cos \left(\frac{180°}{n}\right)$$

as a factor. Use a calculator, as follows, to find out what happens to the value of this expression as n gets larger and larger.

- Enter the expression
  $x \sin \left(\frac{180}{x}\right) \cos \left(\frac{180}{x}\right)$ as $Y_1$.
- Go to the Table Setup menu and enter the values shown at right.
- View a table for the function.
- Use the arrow keys to scroll down.

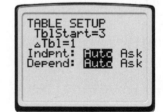
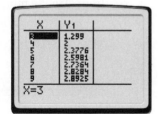

What happens to the value of $n \sin \left(\frac{180°}{n}\right) \cos \left(\frac{180°}{n}\right)$ as n gets larger?

_____

**H** Consider the expression you wrote for the volume of the inscribed pyramid at the end of Step F. What happens to the value of this expression as n gets larger?

_____

**1a.** How is the formula for the volume of a cone, which you derived above, similar to the formula for the volume of a pyramid?

_____

_____

The argument in the Explore provides a justification for the following result.

### Volume of a Cone

The volume $V$ of a cone with base area $B$ and height $h$ is given by $V = \frac{1}{3}Bh$ (or $V = \frac{1}{3}\pi r^2 h$, where $r$ is the radius of the base).

## 2 EXAMPLE   Solving a Volume Problem

A conical paper cup has the dimensions shown. How many fluid ounces of liquid does the cup hold? Round to the nearest tenth. (*Hint:* 1 in.$^3 \approx 0.554$ fl oz.)

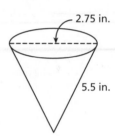

2.75 in.

5.5 in.

**A** Find the radius and height of the cone.

The radius $r$ is half the diameter, so $r =$ _____.

To find the height $h$ of the cone, use the Pythagorean Theorem.

$$h^2 + r^2 = 5.5^2$$    Pythagorean Theorem

$$h^2 + (\text{\_\_\_\_\_})^2 = 5.5^2$$    Substitute the value of $r$.

$$h^2 = \text{_____}$$    Solve for $h^2$.

$$h \approx \text{_____}$$    Solve for $h$. Round to the nearest thousandth.

$r$

$h$    5.5 in.

**B** Find the volume of the cone to the nearest hundredth.

$$V = \frac{1}{3}\pi r^2 h = \frac{1}{3}\pi \cdot (\text{_____})^2 \cdot (\text{_____}) \approx \text{_____}$$

**C** Convert the volume to fluid ounces.

_____ in.$^3 \approx$ _____ $\cdot$ 0.554 fl oz $\approx$ _____ fl oz

So, the cup holds approximately _____ fluid ounces.

**2a.** A cylindrical cup has the same diameter and height as the conical cup. How can you find the number of fluid ounces that the cylindrical cup holds?

_____

_____

# PRACTICE

**Find the volume of each cone. Round to the nearest tenth.**

**1.**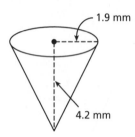
1.9 mm

4.2 mm

**2.**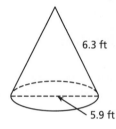
6.3 ft

5.9 ft

**3.**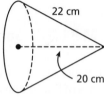
22 cm

20 cm

_____ _____ _____

**4.** The figure shows a water tank that consists of a cylinder and cone. How many gallons of water does the tank hold? Round to the nearest gallon. (*Hint:* 1 ft$^3$ ≈ 7.48 gal)

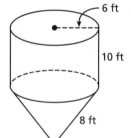
6 ft

10 ft

8 ft

_____

**5.** Popcorn is available in two cups: a square pyramid or a cone, as shown. The price of each cup of popcorn is the same. Which cup is the better deal? Explain.

_____

_____

_____

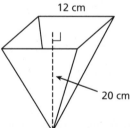
12 cm

12 cm

20 cm

**6.** A sculptor removes a cone from a cylindrical block of wood so that the vertex of the cone is the center of the cylinder's base, as shown. Explain how the volume of the remaining solid compares with the volume of the original cylindrical block of wood.

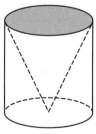

_____

_____

_____

# Volume of Spheres

**Essential question:** *How do you calculate the volume of a sphere?*

Recall that a *sphere* is the set of points in space that are a fixed distance from a point called the *center* of the sphere. The intersection of a sphere and a plane that contains the center of the sphere is a *great circle*. A great circle divides a sphere into two congruent halves that are called *hemispheres*.

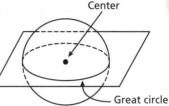

COMMON
CORE

CC.9-12.G.GMD.2(+),
CC.9-12.G.GMD.3*,
CC.9-12.G.MG.2*

## 1 EXPLORE  Developing a Volume Formula

**Plan:** To find the volume of a given sphere, consider a hemisphere of the sphere and a cylinder with the same radius and height as the hemisphere from which a cone has been removed. Show that the two solids have the same cross-sectional area at every level and apply Cavalieri's principle to conclude that the figures have the same volume.

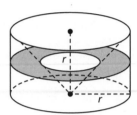

**A**  To show that cross sections have the same area at every level, consider cross sections at a distance of $x$ above the base, as shown.

The cross section of the hemisphere is a disc. Use the Pythagorean Theorem to write a relationship among $r$, $x$, and $R$.

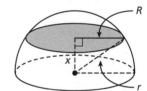

_____

Solving for $R$ gives $R =$ _____.

So, the area of the cross-sectional disc is $\pi R^2$ or _____.

The cross section of the cylinder with the cone removed is a ring. To find the area of the ring, find the area of the outer circle and subtract the area of the inner circle.

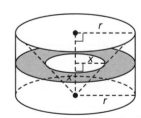

The outer circle has radius _____, so its area is _____ .

The figure includes a pair isosceles right triangles that are similar. This makes it possible to find the radius of the inner circle.

The inner circle has radius _____, so its area is _____.

So, the area of the cross-sectional ring is _____.

By the distributive property, the areas of the cross sections are equal.

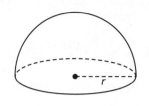
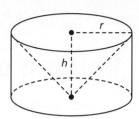

**B** By Cavalieri's principle, the hemisphere has the same volume as the cylinder with the cone removed.

$V(\text{hemisphere}) = V(\text{cylinder}) - V(\text{cone})$

$= \pi r^2 h - \frac{1}{3}\pi r^2 h$          Use volume formulas.

$=$ _____          Subtract.

$=$ _____          The height $h$ is equal to the radius $r$.

The volume of the sphere is twice the volume of the hemisphere.

So, the volume of the sphere is _____.

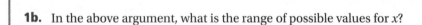

### REFLECT

**1a.** How do you know that the height $h$ of the cylinder with the cone removed is equal to the radius $r$?

_____

_____

_____

**1b.** In the above argument, what is the range of possible values for $x$?

_____

**1c.** What happens to the cross-sectional areas when $x = 0$? when $x = r$?

_____

_____

_____

_____

The argument in the Explore provides a justification for the following formula.

**Volume of a Sphere**

The volume $V$ of a sphere with radius $r$ is given by $V = \frac{4}{3}\pi r^3$.

© Houghton Mifflin Harcourt Publishing Company

A British thermal unit (BTU) is a unit of energy. It is approximately the amount of energy needed to increase the temperature of one pound of water by one degree Fahrenheit. As you will see in the following example, the energy content of a fuel may be measured in BTUs per unit of volume.

## 2 EXAMPLE  Solving a Volume Problem

A spherical gas tank has the dimensions shown. When filled with natural gas, it provides 275,321 BTU. How many BTUs does one cubic foot of natural gas yield? Round to the nearest BTU.

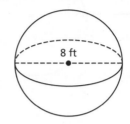

**A**  Find the volume of the sphere.

The diameter is 8 feet, so the radius $r$ is _____.

$V = \frac{4}{3}\pi r^3$          Use the volume formula for a sphere.

$V =$ _____          Substitute for $r$.

$V =$ _____          Simplify. Leave the answer in terms of $\pi$.

**B**  Find the number of BTUs contained in one cubic foot of natural gas.

Since there are 275,321 BTU in _____ ft$^3$ of natural gas, divide

_____ by _____ to find the number of BTUs in 1 ft$^3$.

Use a calculator to divide. Round to the nearest whole number.

So, one cubic foot of natural gas yields about _____ BTU.

## REFLECT

**2a.**  How many gallons of water can be heated from 59°F to 60°F by one cubic foot of natural gas? Explain.

_____

_____

**2b.**  How many gallons of water can be heated from 70°F to 83°F by one cubic foot of natural gas? Explain.

_____

_____

# PRACTICE

**Find the volume of each sphere. Round to the nearest tenth.**

**1.**

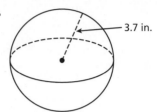

3.7 in.

_____

**2.**

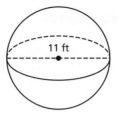

11 ft

_____

**3.**

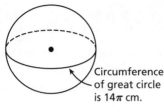

Circumference of great circle is 14π cm.

_____

**4.** One gallon of propane yields approximately 91,500 BTU. About how many BTUs does the spherical storage tank at right provide? Round to the nearest million BTUs. (*Hint:* 1 ft$^3$ ≈ 7.48 gal)

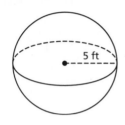

5 ft

_____

**5. Error Analysis** A student solved the following problem as shown below. Explain the student's error and give the correct answer to the problem.

A spherical gasoline tank has a radius of 0.5 ft. When filled, the tank provides 446,483 BTU. How many BTUs does one gallon of gasoline yield? Round to the nearest thousand BTUs and use the fact that 1 ft$^3$ ≈ 7.48 gal.

> The volume of the tank is $\frac{4}{3}\pi r^3 = \frac{4}{3}\pi(0.5)^3$ ft$^3$. Multiplying by 7.48 shows that this is approximately 3.92 gal. So the number of BTUs in one gallon of gasoline is approximately 446,483 × 3.92 ≈ 1,750,000 BTU.

_____

_____

**6.** The aquarium shown at right is a rectangular prism that is filled with water. You drop a spherical ball with a diameter of 6 inches into the aquarium. The ball sinks, causing water to spill from the tank. How much water is left in the tank? Express your answer to the nearest cubic inch and nearest gallon. (*Hint:* 1 in.$^3$ ≈ 0.00433 gal)

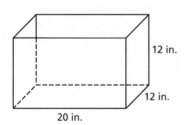

12 in.

12 in.

20 in.

_____

**7.** How does the volume of a sphere change when you multiply its radius by a factor $k$, where $k > 0$? Explain.

_____

_____

_____

# Solving Design Problems

**COMMON CORE**

CC.9-12.G.GMD.3*,
CC.9-12.G.MG.3*

**Essential question:** *How do you use geometry to solve design problems?*

A design problem is one is which you must design an object that satisfies given conditions or minimizes cost. Volume formulas from this unit are often helpful in solving such problems.

**1 EXAMPLE** Determining Dimensions Given a Volume

You want to make a cylindrical candle using exactly 100 cm$^3$ of wax. You want the candle's height to be equal to its diameter. What radius and height should the candle have?

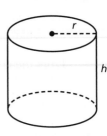

**A** Let the radius of the candle be $r$ and let the height of the candle be $h$.

The diameter of the candle is _____.

The height is equal to the diameter, so $h =$ _____.

The volume $V$ of the candle is $V = \pi r^2 h$.

Substituting the expression for $h$ and simplifying gives $V =$ _____.

**B** Use the fact that the volume $V$ of the candle is 100 cm$^3$ to write an equation that has $r$ as its only variable.

_____

**C** To solve the equation, use your calculator.

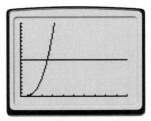

- Enter the left side of the equation as $Y_1$.
- Enter the right side of the equation as $Y_2$.
- Graph the equations. Be sure to choose a viewing window in which you can see the intersection of the two graphs.
- The $x$-coordinate of the point of intersection is the solution of the equation. Go to the Calc menu and choose **5:intersect** to find the coordinates of the point of intersection.

So, the radius of the candle should be approximately _____.

The height of the candle should be approximately _____.

**REFLECT**

**1a.** How can you check that your answer is reasonable?

_____

_____

**E X A M P L E**    **Designing a Box with Maximum Volume**

You want to build a storage box from a piece of plywood that is 4 feet by 8 feet. You must use 6 pieces (for the top, bottom, and sides of the box) and you must make cuts that are parallel and perpendicular to the edges of the plywood. Describe three possible designs. What do you think is the maximum possible volume for the box?

**A**   Consider Design 1 at right. The top, bottom, front, and back of the box are congruent rectangles. The ends are squares. The gray piece is waste.

From the figure, $4x =$ _____, so $x =$ _____ ft

and $8 - x =$ _____ ft.

$V =$ _____ • _____ • _____ = _____ ft$^3$

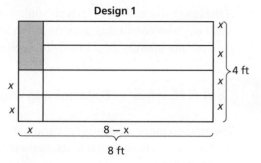

Design 1

**B**   Consider Design 2 at right. The top, bottom, front, and back of the box are congruent rectangles. The ends are squares. The gray piece is waste.

From the figure, $5x =$ _____, so $x =$ _____ ft.

$V =$ _____ • _____ • _____ = _____ ft$^3$

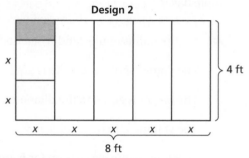

Design 2

**C**   Consider Design 3 at right. The top, bottom, front, and back of the box are congruent rectangles. The ends are squares. There is no waste.

From the figure, $2x =$ _____, so $x =$ _____ ft

and $\frac{8-x}{2} =$ _____ ft.

$V =$ _____ • _____ • _____ = _____ ft$^3$

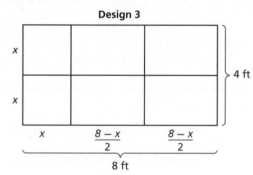

Design 3

**D**   Based on these designs, the maximum possible volume appears to be _____.

**REFLECT**

**2a.**   Is it possible to make a box all of whose sides are not squares? If so, give the dimensions of the box and find its volume.

_____

_____

**2b.**   Is it possible to say what the maximum volume of the box is based on your work above? Why or why not?

_____

_____

1. You have 500 cm$^3$ of clay and want to make a sculpture in the shape of a cone. You want the height of the cone to be 3 times the cone's radius and you want to use all the clay. What radius and height should the sculpture have?

_____

2. You want to build a box in the shape of a rectangular prism. The box must have a volume of 420 in.$^3$ As shown in the figure, the ends of the box must be squares. In order to minimize the cost, you want to use the least possible amount of material. Follow these steps to determine the dimensions you should use for the box.

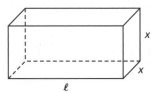

   a. Let the ends of the box be $x$ in. by $x$ in. and let the length of the box be $\ell$ in. The amount of material $M$ needed to make the box is its surface area. Write an expression for $M$ by adding the areas of the six faces.

   _____

   b. Write an equation for the volume of the box and then solve it for $\ell$.

   _____

   c. Substitute the expression for $\ell$ in the expression for $M$ from part (a).

   _____

   d. To find the value of $x$ that minimizes $M$, enter the expression for $M$ as $Y_1$ in your calculator. Graph the function in a suitable viewing window. Go to the Calc menu and choose **3: minimum** to find the value of $x$ that minimizes $M$. Use your equation from part (b) to find the corresponding value of $\ell$. What dimensions should you use for the box?

   _____

3. You have a flexible piece of sheet metal that measures 4 feet by 8 feet. You want to build a cylinder by cutting out two circles for the bases and a rectangular piece that can be bent to form the lateral surface.

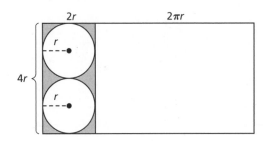

   a. Let $r$ be the radius of the cylinder. From the figure, there are two constraints on $r$: $r \leq 4$ (based on the width of the metal) and $2r + 2\pi r \leq 8$ (based on the length of the metal). What is the greatest value of $r$ that satisfies both constraints?

   _____

   b. What is the approximate volume of the cylinder with this radius?

   _____

**Name** _____ **Class** _____ **Date** _____

## MULTIPLE CHOICE

**1.** The figure shows a rectangular prism that is intersected by a plane parallel to a face of the prism. Which is the most precise description of the cross section?

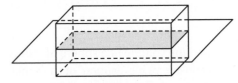

**A.** parallelogram    **C.** trapezoid

**B.** rectangle    **D.** triangle

**2.** In the figure, $\overline{BA} \cong \overline{BC}$. You rotate $\angle ABC$ around a line that bisects the angle. What figure is generated by this rotation in three-dimensional space?

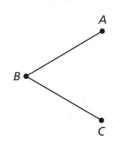

**F.** cone    **H.** pyramid

**G.** cylinder    **J.** sphere

**3.** A wood log is approximately cylindrical with the dimensions shown below. The log weighs 206.8 pounds. What is the density of the wood, to the nearest whole number?

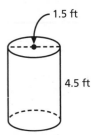

**A.** $7 \text{ lb/ft}^3$    **C.** $20 \text{ lb/ft}^3$

**B.** $8 \text{ lb/ft}^3$    **D.** $26 \text{ lb/ft}^3$

**4.** A wire frame in the shape of the cube is used to support a pyramid-shaped basket, as shown. The vertex of the pyramid lies in the same plane as a face of the cube. To the nearest tenth, what is the volume of the pyramid-shaped basket?

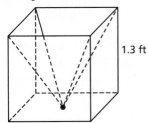

1.3 ft

**F.** $0.7 \text{ ft}^3$    **H.** $2.2 \text{ ft}^3$

**G.** $1.7 \text{ ft}^3$    **J.** $2.3 \text{ ft}^3$

**5.** A food manufacturer sells yogurt in cone-shaped cups with the dimensions shown. To the nearest tenth, how many fluid ounces of yogurt does the cup hold? (*Hint:* $1 \text{ cm}^3 \approx 0.034 \text{ fl oz}$)

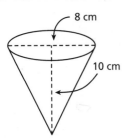

8 cm

10 cm

**A.** 0.6 fl oz    **C.** 17.1 fl oz

**B.** 5.7 fl oz    **D.** 22.8 fl oz

**6.** You want to design a cylindrical container for oatmeal that has a volume of 90 in.$^3$ You also want the height of the container to be 3.5 times the radius. To the nearest tenth, what should the radius of the container be?

**F.** 2.0 in.    **H.** 3.0 in.

**G.** 2.9 in.    **J.** 3.1 in.

# FREE RESPONSE

**7.** In order to develop and justify the formula for the volume of a cone, you begin with a given cone that has radius $r$ and height $h$. You consider pyramids with regular polygonal bases that are inscribed in the cone.

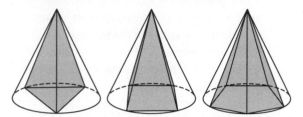

You show that when the inscribed pyramid has a base that is a regular $n$-gon, the volume of the pyramid is given by the following expression.

$$\frac{1}{3}r^2 hn \sin\left(\frac{180°}{n}\right)\cos\left(\frac{180°}{n}\right)$$

Describe the remaining steps of the argument.

_____

_____

_____

_____

_____

_____

_____

_____

**8.** A spherical gas tank has the dimensions shown. When filled with butane, it provides 468,766 BTU. How many BTUs does one cubic foot of butane yield? Round to the nearest BTU.

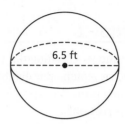

6.5 ft

_____

**9.** To find the volume of a sphere of radius $r$, you consider a hemisphere of the sphere and a cylinder with the same radius and height as the hemisphere from which a cone has been removed. You show that the solids have the same cross-sectional area at every level. Explain how to use the solids to derive the formula for the volume of a sphere.

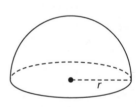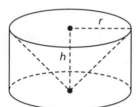

_____

_____

_____

_____

_____

_____

_____

# Probability

## Unit Focus

Probability theory is the branch of mathematics concerned with situations involving chance. You will learn how to use set theory to help you calculate basic probabilities and will investigate the role of permutations and combinations in probability. You will also learn how to determine the probability of mutually exclusive events, overlapping events, independent events, and dependent events. Along the way, you will perform simulations and learn how to use probability to make and analyze decisions.

## Unit at a Glance

COMMON CORE

| Lesson | Standards for Mathematical Content |
|---|---|
| 11-1 Probability and Set Theory | CC.9-12.S.CP.1* |
| 11-2 Random Sampling and Probability | CC.9-12.S.MD.6(+)* |
| 11-3 Permutations and Probability | CC.9-12.S.CP.9(+)* |
| 11-4 Combinations and Probability | CC.9-12.S.CP.9(+)* |
| 11-5 Mutually Exclusive and Overlapping Events | CC.9-12.S.CP.7* |
| 11-6 Conditional Probability | CC.9-12.S.CP.3*, CC.9-12.S.CP.4*, CC.9-12.S.CP.5*, CC.9-12.S.CP.6* |
| 11-7 Independent Events | CC.9-12.S.CP.2*, CC.9-12.S.CP.3*, CC.9-12.S.CP.4*, CC.9-12.S.CP.5* |
| 11-8 Dependent Events | CC.9-12.S.CP.8(+)* |
| 11-9 Making Fair Decisions | CC.9-12.S.MD.6(+)* |
| 11-10 Analyzing Decisions | CC.9-12.S.CP.4*, CC.9-12.S.MD.7(+)* |
| Test Prep | |

UNIT 11

# Unpacking the Common Core State Standards

Use the table to help you understand the Standards for Mathematical Content that are taught in this unit. Refer to the lessons listed after each standard for exploration and practice.

| COMMON CORE Standards for Mathematical Content | What It Means For You |
|---|---|
| **CC.9-12.S.CP.1** Describe events as subsets of a sample space (the set of outcomes) using characteristics (or categories) of the outcomes, or as unions, intersections, or complements of other events ("or," "and," "not").* Lesson 11-1 | You will see that set notation and vocabulary is useful for calculating simple probabilities. |
| **CC.9-12.S.CP.2** Understand that two events *A* and *B* are independent if the probability of *A* and *B* occurring together is the product of their probabilities, and use this characterization to determine if they are independent.* Lesson 11-7 | Two events are independent if the occurrence of one event does not affect the occurrence of the other. You will learn how to determine whether two events are independent. |
| **CC.9-12.S.CP.3** Understand the conditional probability of *A* given *B* as *P(A* and *B)/P(B)*, and interpret independence of *A* and *B* as saying that the conditional probability of *A* given *B* is the same as the probability of *A*, and the conditional probability of *B* given *A* is the same as the probability of *B*.* Lessons 11-6, 11-7 | You will find the probability of an event given that another event has already occurred. |
| **CC.9-12.S.CP.4** Construct and interpret two-way frequency tables of data when two categories are associated with each object being classified. Use the two-way table as a sample space to decide if events are independent and to approximate conditional probabilities.* Lessons 11-6, 11-7, 11-10 | A two-way table is a useful tool for working with probabilities. You will make and interpret two-way tables. |
| **CC.9-12.S.CP.5** Recognize and explain the concepts of conditional probability and independence in everyday language and everyday situations.* Lessons 11-6, 11-7 | You will see how to use ideas from probability to help you understand a variety of real-world situations. |
| **CC.9-12.S.CP.6** Find the conditional probability of *A* given *B* as the fraction of *B*'s outcomes that also belong to *A*, and interpret the answer in terms of the model.* Lesson 11-6 | You will find the probability of an event given that another event has already occurred and you will explain the meaning of your answer. |
| **CC.9-12.S.CP.7** Apply the Addition Rule, *P(A* or *B) = P(A) + P(B) − P(A* and *B)*, and interpret the answer in terms of the model.* Lesson 11-5 | You will learn to use a rule to find the probability of events consisting of more than one outcome. |

**UNIT 11**

| COMMON CORE Standards for Mathematical Content | What It Means For You |
|---|---|
| **CC.9-12.S.CP.8(+)  Apply the general Multiplication Rule in a uniform probability model,** $P(A \text{ and } B) = P(A)\, P(B \mid A) = P(B)\, P(A \mid B)$**, and interpret the answer in terms of the model.*** Lesson 11-8 | You will learn to use a rule to find the probability of events when the outcome of one event affects the probability of the other event. |
| **CC.9-12.S.CP.9(+)  Use permutations and combinations to compute probabilities of compound events and solve problems.*** Lessons 11-3, 11-4 | Permutations and combinations will be helpful when you count the number of outcomes in a probability experiment. |
| **CC.9-12.S.MD.6(+)  Use probabilities to make fair decisions (e.g., drawing by lots, using a random number generator).*** Lessons 11-2, 11-9 | You will explore the connection between probability and decision making. |
| **CC.9-12.S.MD.7(+)  Analyze decisions and strategies using probability concepts (e.g., product testing, medical testing, pulling a hockey goalie at the end of a game).*** Lesson 11-10 | As you will see, ideas from probability can help you decide if a decision is good or bad. |

# Probability and Set Theory

**Essential question:** *How can you use set theory to help you calculate theoretical probabilities?*

COMMON CORE

CC.9-12.S.CP.1*

**11-1**

## 1 ENGAGE    Introducing the Vocabulary of Sets

You will see that set theory is useful in calculating probabilities. A **set** is a well-defined collection of distinct objects. Each object in a set is called an **element** of the set. A set may be specified by writing its elements in braces. For example, the set $S$ of prime numbers less than 10 may be written as $S = \{2, 3, 5, 7\}$.

The number of elements in a set $S$ may be written as $n(S)$. For the set $S$ of prime numbers less than 10, $n(S) = 4$.

The set with no elements is the **empty set** and is denoted by $\varnothing$ or $\{\ \}$. The set of all elements under consideration is the **universal set** and is denoted by $U$. The following terms describe how sets are related to each other.

| Term | Notation | Venn Diagram |
|---|---|---|
| Set $A$ is a **subset** of set $B$ if every element of $A$ is also an element of $B$. | $A \subset B$ | |
| The **intersection** of sets $A$ and $B$ is the set of all elements that are in both $A$ and $B$. | $A \cap B$ | |
| The **union** of sets $A$ and $B$ is the set of all elements that are in $A$ or $B$. | $A \cup B$ | |
| The **complement** of set $A$ is the set of all elements in the universal set $U$ that are not in $A$. | $A^c$ | |

### REFLECT

**1a.** For any set $A$, what is $A \cap \varnothing$? Explain.

_____

_____

Recall that a *probability experiment* is an activity involving chance. Each repetition of the experiment is a *trial* and each possible result is an *outcome*. The *sample space* of an experiment is the set of all possible outcomes. An *event* is a set of outcomes.

When all outcomes of an experiment are equally likely, the **theoretical probability** that an event $A$ will occur is given by $P(A) = \frac{n(A)}{n(S)}$, where $S$ is the sample space.

**2 EXAMPLE** **Calculating Theoretical Probabilities**

**You roll a number cube. Event *A* is rolling an even number. Event *B* is rolling a prime number. Calculate each of the following probabilities.**

**A** $P(A)$     **B** $P(A \cup B)$     **C** $P(A \cap B)$     **D** $P(A^c)$

**A** $P(A)$ is the probability of rolling an even number. To calculate $P(A)$, first identify the sample space $S$.

$S = $ _____ , so $n(S) = $ _____ .

$A = $ _____ , so $n(A) = $ _____ .

So, $P(A) = \frac{n(A)}{n(S)} = \frac{\phantom{xx}}{\phantom{xx}} = \frac{\phantom{xx}}{\phantom{xx}}$ .

**B** $P(A \cup B)$ is the probability of rolling an even number *or* a prime number.

$A \cup B = $ _____ , so $n(A \cup B) = $ _____ .

So, $P(A \cup B) = \frac{n(A \cup B)}{n(S)} = \frac{\phantom{xx}}{\phantom{xx}}$ .

**C** $P(A \cap B)$ is the probability of rolling an even number *and* a prime number.

$A \cap B = $ _____ , so $n(A \cap B) = $ _____ .

So, $P(A \cap B) = \frac{n(A \cap B)}{n(S)} = \frac{\phantom{xx}}{\phantom{xx}}$ .

**D** $P(A^c)$ is the probability of rolling a number that is *not* even.

$A^c = $ _____ , so $n(A^c) = $ _____ .

So, $P(A^c) = \frac{n(A^c)}{n(S)} = \frac{\phantom{xx}}{\phantom{xx}} = \frac{\phantom{xx}}{\phantom{xx}}$ .

**REFLECT**

**2a.** Explain what $P(S)$ represents and then calculate this probability. Do you think this result is true in general? Explain.

_____

_____

You may have noticed in the example that $P(A) + P(A^c) = 1$. To see why this is true in general, note that an event and its complement represent all outcomes in the sample space, so $n(A) + n(A^c) = n(S)$.

$$P(A) + P(A^c) = \frac{n(A)}{n(S)} + \frac{n(A^c)}{n(S)}$$   Definition of theoretical probability

$$= \frac{n(A) + n(A^c)}{n(S)}$$   Add.

$$= \frac{n(S)}{n(S)} = 1$$   $n(A) + n(A^c) = n(S)$

You can write this relationship as $P(A) = 1 - P(A^c)$ and use it to help you find probabilities when it is more convenient to calculate the probability of the complement of an event.

### Probabilities of an Event and Its Complement

The probability of an event and the probability of its complement have a sum of 1. So, the probability of an event is one minus the probability of its complement. Also, the probability of the complement of an event is one minus the probability of the event.

$$P(A) + P(A^c) = 1$$

$$P(A) = 1 - P(A^c)$$

$$P(A^c) = 1 - P(A)$$

### 3 EXAMPLE   Using the Complement of an Event

**You roll a blue number cube and white number cube at the same time. What is the probability that you do not roll doubles?**

**A** Let $A$ be the event that you do not roll doubles. Then $A^c$ is the event that you do roll doubles.

Complete the table at right to show all outcomes in the sample space.

Circle the outcomes in $A^c$ (rolling doubles).

**White Number Cube**

| | 1 | 2 | 3 | 4 | 5 | 6 |
|---|---|---|---|---|---|---|
| 1 | 1-1 | 1-2 | 1-3 | 1-4 | 1-5 | 1-6 |
| 2 | 2-1 | | | | | |
| 3 | 3-1 | | | | | |
| 4 | 4-1 | | | | | |
| 5 | 5-1 | | | | | |
| 6 | 6-1 | | | | | |

Blue Number Cube

**B** Find the probability of rolling doubles.

$$P(A^c) = \frac{n(A^c)}{n(S)} = \frac{\phantom{x}}{\phantom{x}} = \frac{\phantom{x}}{\phantom{x}}$$

**C** Find the probability that you do not roll doubles.

$$P(A) = 1 - P(A^c) = 1 - \frac{\phantom{x}}{\phantom{x}} = \frac{\phantom{x}}{\phantom{x}}$$

**3a.** Describe a different way you could have calculated the probability that you do not roll doubles.

_____

_____

# PRACTICE

You have a set of 10 cards numbered 1 to 10. You choose a card at random. Event *A* is choosing a number less than 7. Event *B* is choosing an odd number. Calculate each of the following probabilities.

**1.** $P(A)$

_____

**2.** $P(B)$

_____

**3.** $P(A \cup B)$

_____

**4.** $P(A \cap B)$

_____

**5.** $P(A^c)$

_____

**6.** $P(B^c)$

_____

**7.** A bag contains 5 red marbles and 10 blue marbles. You choose a marble without looking. Event *A* is choosing a red marble. Event *B* is choosing a blue marble. What is $P(A \cap B)$? Explain.

_____

**8.** A standard deck of cards has 13 cards (2, 3, 4, 5, 6, 7, 8, 9, 10, jack, queen, king, ace) in each of 4 suits (hearts, clubs, diamonds, spades). You choose a card from a deck at random. What is the probability that you do not choose an ace? Explain.

_____

_____

**9.** You choose a card from a standard deck of cards at random. What is the probability that you do not choose a club? Explain.

_____

_____

**10. Error Analysis** A bag contains white tiles, black tiles, and gray tiles. $P(W)$, the probability of choosing a tile at random and choosing a white tile, is $\frac{1}{4}$. A student claims that the probability of choosing a black tile, $P(B)$, is $\frac{3}{4}$ since $P(B) = 1 - P(W) = 1 - \frac{1}{4} = \frac{3}{4}$. Do you agree? Explain.

_____

_____

# Random Sampling and Probability

**Essential question:** *How can you use probabilites to help you make fair decisions?*

## 1 ENGAGE    Introducing a Decision-Making Problem

A small town has 25 residents. The state has given the town money that must be used for something that benefits the community. The town's mayor has decided that the money will be used to build a teen center or a senior center.

In order to make a decision about the type of community center to build, the mayor plans to survey a subset of town residents. There are two survey methods: a random sample and a convenience sample. The convenience sample will be conducted by surveying town residents at a local movie theater.

In the table below, each resident of the town is identified by a number from 1 to 25. The table shows each resident's preference: T for the teen center, S for the senior center. The table also gives the probability that each resident is at the movie theater when the convenience-sample survey is conducted.

| 1 | 2 | 3 | 4 | 5 |
|---|---|---|---|---|
| S | S | T | S | T |
| 0.2 | 0.3 | 0.8 | 0.1 | 0.8 |
| **6** | **7** | **8** | **9** | **10** |
| T | S | T | S | S |
| 0.7 | 0.2 | 0.8 | 0.1 | 0.3 |
| **11** | **12** | **13** | **14** | **15** |
| S | T | S | S | S |
| 0.1 | 0.7 | 0.2 | 0.2 | 0.4 |
| **16** | **17** | **18** | **19** | **20** |
| T | S | S | S | T |
| 0.6 | 0.7 | 0.1 | 0.1 | 0.6 |
| **21** | **22** | **23** | **24** | **25** |
| S | S | S | S | T |
| 0.3 | 0.2 | 0.3 | 0.1 | 0.9 |

### REFLECT

**1a.** Based on the data in the table, what percent of all residents favor the teen center? the senior center?

_____

**1b.** If it were possible for the mayor to survey every resident, what decision do you think the mayor would make? Why?

_____

Suppose the mayor of the town is not able to survey every resident, so the mayor decides to survey a random sample of 10 residents.

**A**  You can use your calculator to simulate the process of choosing and surveying a random sample of residents.

- Go to the MATH menu.

- Use the right arrow key to access the PRB menu.

- Use the down arrow key to select **5:randInt(** .

- Use "randInt(1,25)" as shown at the right.

- Each time you press Enter, the calculator will return a random integer from 1 to 25.

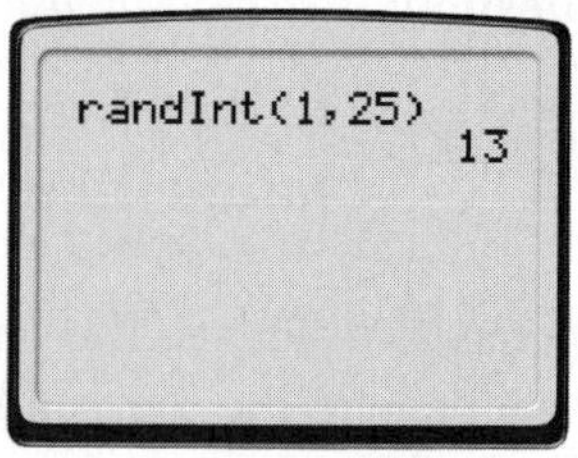

```
randInt(1,25)
              13
```

Generate 10 random integers in this way. For each integer, note the corresponding preference (T or S) of that resident of the town. (If a number is selected more than once, ignore the duplicates and choose a new number. This ensures that no resident is surveyed more than once.) Record your results in the table.

| Resident Number | | | | | | | | | | |
|---|---|---|---|---|---|---|---|---|---|---|
| Preference (T or S) | | | | | | | | | | |

**B**  Based on the random sample, what percent of residents favor the teen center? the senior center?

_____

**REFLECT**

**2a.** What is the probability that any resident is chosen to be part of the random sample? Explain.

_____

_____

**2b.** What decision do you think the mayor would make based on the random sample? Why?

_____

**2c.** Compare your results with those of other students. In general, how well do the results of the random sample predict the preferences of the town as a whole?

_____

## 3 EXPLORE  Using a Convenience Sample

The mayor of the town decides to use a convenience sample by surveying the first 10 residents of the town to leave a local movie theater.

**A**  You can use slips of paper to simulate the process of choosing and surveying this convenience sample.

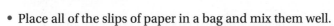

- For each resident, prepare 1 to 10 small slips of paper with the resident's number on them. The number of slips of paper is determined by the probability that the resident is at the movie theater when the survey is conducted. For example, Resident 1 has a 0.2 probability of being at the theater, so prepare 2 slips of paper with the number 1; Resident 2 has a 0.3 probability of being at the theater, so prepare 3 slips of paper with the number 2; and so on.

- Place all of the slips of paper in a bag and mix them well.

- Choose slips of paper one at a time without looking.

Choose 10 residents in this way. For each resident, note the corresponding preference (T or S) using the table on the first page of the lesson. (If a resident is selected more than once, ignore the duplicates and choose a new number from the bag. This ensures that no resident is surveyed more than once.) Record your results in the table.

| Resident Number | | | | | | | | | | |
|---|---|---|---|---|---|---|---|---|---|---|
| Preference (T or S) | | | | | | | | | | |

**B**  Based on the convenience sample, what percent of residents favor the teen center? the senior center?

_____

### REFLECT

**3a.**  Why do some residents of the town have more slips of paper representing them than other residents? How does this connect to the way the convenience sample is conducted?

_____

_____

_____

_____

© Houghton Mifflin Harcourt Publishing Company

**3b.** What decision do you think the mayor would make based on the convenience sample? Why?

_____

**3c.** Compare your results with those of other students. In general, how well do the results of the convenience sample predict the preferences of the town as a whole?

_____

_____

**3d.** Which sampling method is more likely to lead to fair decision-making? Explain.

_____

_____

**3e.** What factors might explain why the results of the convenience sample are different from the results of the random sample?

_____

_____

_____

**3f.** When you conduct the random-sample simulation is it possible that you might choose 10 residents who all favor the senior center? Is this result possible when you conduct the convenience-sample simulation? In which simulation do you think this result is more likely?

_____

_____

_____

**3g.** What are some limitations or drawbacks of the simulations?

_____

_____

_____

**3h.** In a town of 25 residents, it is likely that the mayor could actually survey all the residents, instead of using a random sample or convenience sample. What are some reasons that sampling might be used in situations involving populations that are much larger than 25?

_____

_____

# Permutations and Probability

COMMON CORE

CC.9-12.S.CP.9(+)*

11-3

**Essential question:** *What are permutations and how can you use them to calculate probabilities?*

A **permutation** is a selection of a group of objects in which order is important. For example, there are 6 permutations of the letters A, B, and C.

| | |
|---|---|
| ABC | ACB |
| BAC | BCA |
| CAB | CBA |

## 1 EXAMPLE    Finding Permutations

**The members of a club want to choose a president, a vice-president, and a treasurer. Seven members of the club are eligible to fill these positions. In how many different ways can the positions be filled?**

**A**  Consider the number of ways each position can be filled.

There are _____ different ways the position of president can be filled.

Once the president has been chosen, there are _____ different ways the position of vice-president can be filled.

Once the president and vice-president have been chosen, there are _____ different ways the position of treasurer can be filled.

**B**  Multiply to find the total number of different ways the positions can be filled.

| President | Vice-President | Treasurer |
|---|---|---|

_____ × _____ × _____ = _____ permutations

So, there are _____ different ways that the positions can be filled.

### REFLECT

**1a.** Suppose the club members also want to choose a secretary from the group of 7 eligible members. In how many different ways can the four positions (president, vice-president, treasurer, secretary) be filled? Explain.

_____

**1b.** Suppose 8 members of the club are eligible to fill the original three positions (president, vice-president, treasurer). In how many different ways can the positions be filled? Explain.

_____

The process you used in the example can be generalized to give a formula for permutations. To do so, it is helpful to use factorials. For a positive integer $n$, **n factorial**, written $n!$, is defined as follows.

$$n! = n \cdot (n - 1) \cdot (n - 2) \cdot \ldots \cdot 3 \cdot 2 \cdot 1$$

That is, $n!$ is the product of $n$ and all the positive integers less than $n$. Note that $0!$ is defined to be 1.

In the example, the number of permutations of 7 objects taken 3 at a time is

$$7 \cdot 6 \cdot 5 = \frac{7 \cdot 6 \cdot 5 \cdot \cancel{4} \cdot \cancel{3} \cdot \cancel{2} \cdot \cancel{1}}{\cancel{4} \cdot \cancel{3} \cdot \cancel{2} \cdot \cancel{1}} = \frac{7!}{4!} = \frac{7!}{(7 - 3)!}.$$

This can be generalized as follows.

> ### Permutations
>
> The number of permutations of $n$ objects taken $r$ at a time is given by
>
> $$_nP_r = \frac{n!}{(n - r)!}.$$

## 2 EXAMPLE  Using Permutations to Calculate a Probability

**Every student at your school is assigned a four-digit code, such as 6953, to access the computer system. In each code, no digit is repeated. What is the probability that you are assigned a code with the digits 1, 2, 3, and 4 in any order?**

**A**   Let $S$ be the sample space. Find $n(S)$.

The sample space consists of all permutations of 4 digits taken from the 10 digits 0 through 9.

$$n(S) = {}_{10}P_4 = \frac{10!}{(10 - 4)!} = \frac{10!}{6!} = \frac{10 \cdot 9 \cdot 8 \cdot 7 \cdot \cancel{6} \cdot \cancel{5} \cdot \cancel{4} \cdot \cancel{3} \cdot \cancel{2} \cdot \cancel{1}}{\cancel{6} \cdot \cancel{5} \cdot \cancel{4} \cdot \cancel{3} \cdot \cancel{2} \cdot \cancel{1}} = \underline{\qquad}$$

**B**   Let $A$ be the event that your code has the digits 1, 2, 3, and 4. Find $n(A)$.

The event consists of all permutations of 4 digits chosen from the 4 digits 1 through 4.

$$n(A) = {}_4P_4 = \frac{4!}{(4 - 4)!} = \frac{4!}{0!} = \underline{\qquad} = \underline{\qquad}$$

**C**   Find $P(A)$.

$$P(A) = \frac{n(A)}{n(S)} = \underline{\qquad} = \underline{\qquad}$$

So, the probability that your code has the digits 1, 2, 3, and 4 is $\underline{\qquad\qquad}$.

© Houghton Mifflin Harcourt Publishing Company

**2a.** What is the probability that you are assigned the code 1234? Explain.

_____

_____

# PRACTICE

**1.** An MP3 player has a playlist with 12 songs. You select the shuffle option for the playlist. In how many different orders can the songs be played?

_____

**2.** There are 10 runners in a race. Medals are awarded for 1st, 2nd, and 3rd place. In how many different ways can the medals be awarded?

_____

**3.** There are 9 players on a baseball team. In how many different ways can the coach choose players for first base, second base, third base, and shortstop?

_____

**4.** You have 15 photographs of your school. In how many different ways can you arrange 6 of them in a line for the cover of the school yearbook?

_____

**5.** A bag contains 9 tiles, each with a different number from 1 to 9. You choose a tile, put it aside, choose a second tile, put it aside, and then choose a third tile. What is the probability that you choose tiles with the numbers 1, 2, and 3 in that order?

_____

**6.** There are 11 students on a committee. To decide which 3 of these students will attend a conference, 3 names are chosen at random by pulling names one at a time from a hat. What is the probability that Sarah, Jamal, and Mai are chosen in any order?

_____

**7.** **Error Analysis** A student solved the problem at right. The student's work is shown. Did the student make an error? If so, explain the error and provide the correct answer.

_____

_____

_____

_____

_____

A bag contains 6 tiles with the letters A, B, C, D, E, and F. You choose 4 tiles one at a time without looking and line up the tiles as you choose them. What is the probability that your tiles spell BEAD?

Let $S$ be the sample space and let $A$ be the event that the tiles spell BEAD.

$$n(S) = {}_6P_4 = \frac{6!}{(6-4)!} = \frac{6!}{2!} = 360$$

$$n(A) = {}_4P_4 = \frac{4!}{(4-4)!} = \frac{4!}{0!} = 4! = 24$$

So, $P(A) = \frac{n(A)}{n(S)} = \frac{24}{360} = \frac{1}{15}$.

# Combinations and Probability

COMMON
CORE

CC.9-12.S.CP.9(+)*

**11-4**

**Essential question:** *What are combinations and how can you use them to calculate probabilities?*

A **combination** is a grouping of objects in which order does not matter. For example, when you choose 3 letters from the letters A, B, C, and D, there are 4 different combinations.

**ABC     ABD     ACD     BCD**

## 1 EXAMPLE   Finding Combinations

**A restaurant offers 8 side dishes. When you order an entree, you can choose 3 of the side dishes. In how many ways can you choose 3 side dishes?**

| Side Dishes | |
|---|---|
| Beets | Rice |
| Potatoes | Broccoli |
| Carrots | Cole slaw |
| Salad | Apple sauce |

**A**  First find the number of ways to choose 3 sides dishes when order does matter. This is the number of permutations of 8 objects taken 3 at a time.

$$_8P_3 = \frac{8!}{(8-3)!} = \frac{8!}{5!} = \underline{\hspace{4cm}} = \underline{\hspace{2cm}}$$

**B**  In this problem, order does not matter, since choosing beets, carrots, and rice is the same as choosing rice, beets, and carrots.

Divide the result from Step A by $_3P_3$, which is the number of ways the 3 side dishes can be ordered.

$$_3P_3 = \underline{\hspace{3cm}} = \underline{\hspace{3cm}} = \underline{\hspace{2cm}}$$

So, the number of ways you can choose 3 side dishes is $\dfrac{\phantom{xxx}}{\phantom{xxx}} = \underline{\hspace{2cm}}$.

### REFLECT

**1a.** Suppose the restaurant offers a special on Mondays that allows you to choose 4 side dishes. In how many ways can you choose the side dishes?

_____

**1b.** In general, are there more ways or fewer ways to select objects when order does not matter? Why?

_____

_____

The process you used in the example can be generalized to give a formula for combinations. In order to find $_8C_3$, the number of combinations of 8 objects taken 3 at a time, you first found the number of permutations of 8 objects taken 3 at a time, then you divided by 3! That is,

$$_8C_3 = \frac{8!}{(8-3)!} \div 3! \text{ or } \frac{8!}{3!(8-3)!}.$$

This can be generalized as follows.

### Combinations

The number of combinations of $n$ objects taken $r$ at a time is given by

$$_nC_r = \frac{n!}{r!(n-r)!}.$$

## 2 EXAMPLE   Using Combinations to Calculate a Probability

**There are 5 boys and 6 girls in a school play. The director randomly chooses 3 of the students to meet with a costume designer. What is the probability that the director chooses all boys?**

**A**   Let $S$ be the sample space. Find $n(S)$.

The sample space consists of all combinations of 3 students taken from the group of 11 students.

$$n(S) = {}_{11}C_3 = \frac{11!}{3!(11-3)!} = \frac{11!}{3! \cdot 8!} = \frac{11 \cdot 10 \cdot 9 \cdot \cancel{8} \cdot \cancel{7} \cdot \cancel{6} \cdot \cancel{5} \cdot \cancel{4} \cdot \cancel{3} \cdot \cancel{2} \cdot \cancel{1}}{3 \cdot 2 \cdot 1 \cdot \cancel{8} \cdot \cancel{7} \cdot \cancel{6} \cdot \cancel{5} \cdot \cancel{4} \cdot \cancel{3} \cdot \cancel{2} \cdot \cancel{1}} = \underline{\hspace{2cm}}$$

**B**   Let $A$ be the event that the director chooses all boys. Find $n(A)$.

Suppose the 11 students are $B_1, B_2, B_3, B_4, B_5, G_1, G_2, G_3, G_4, G_5, G_6$, where the $B$s represent boys and the $G$s represent girls.

The combinations in event $A$ are combinations like $B_2B_4B_5$ and $B_1B_3B_4$. That is, event $A$ consists of all combinations of 3 boys taken from the set of 5 boys.

So, $n(A) = {}_5C_3 = \underline{\hspace{2cm}} = \underline{\hspace{2cm}} = \underline{\hspace{2cm}} = \underline{\hspace{2cm}}.$

**C**   Find $P(A)$.

$$P(A) = \frac{n(A)}{n(S)} = \underline{\hspace{2cm}} = \underline{\hspace{2cm}}$$

So, the probability that the director chooses all boys is $\underline{\hspace{2cm}}$.

© Houghton Mifflin Harcourt Publishing Company

**2a.** Is the director more likely to choose all boys or all girls? Why?

_____

_____

# PRACTICE

**1.** A cat has a litter of 6 kittens. You plan to adopt 2 of the kittens. In how many ways can you choose 2 of the kittens from the litter?

_____

**2.** An amusement park has 11 roller coasters. In how many ways can you choose 4 of the roller coasters to ride during your visit to the park?

_____

**3.** A school has 5 Spanish teachers and 4 French teachers. The school's principal randomly chooses 2 of the teachers to attend a conference. What is the probability that the principal chooses 2 Spanish teachers?

_____

**4.** There are 6 fiction books and 8 nonfiction books on a reading list. Your teacher randomly assigns you 4 books to read over the summer. What is the probability that you are assigned all nonfiction books?

_____

**5.** A bag contains 26 tiles, each with a different letter of the alphabet written on it. You choose 3 tiles from the bag without looking. What is the probability that you choose the tiles containing the letters A, B, and C?

_____

**6.** You are randomly assigned a password consisting of 6 different characters chosen from the digits 0 to 9 and the letters A to Z. As a percent, what is the probability that you are assigned a password consisting of only letters?

_____

**7.** Calculate $_{10}C_6$ and $_{10}C_4$.

**a.** What do you notice about these values? Explain why this makes sense.

_____

_____

_____

**b.** Use your observations to help you state a generalization about combinations.

_____

_____

**8.** Use the formula for combinations to make a generalization about $_nC_n$. Explain why this makes sense.

_____

_____

# Mutually Exclusive and Overlapping Events

COMMON CORE

CC.9-12.S.CP.7*

**Essential question:** *How do you find the probability of mutually exclusive events and overlapping events?*

Two events are **mutually exclusive events** if the events cannot both occur in the same trial of an experiment. For example, when you toss a coin, the coin landing heads up and the coin landing tails up are mutually exclusive events.

## 1 EXAMPLE   Finding the Probability of Mutually Exclusive Events

**A dodecahedral number cube has 12 sides numbered 1 through 12. What is the probability that you roll the cube and the result is an even number or a 7?**

**A** Let event $A$ be the event that you roll an even number. Let event $B$ be the event that you roll a 7. Let $S$ be the sample space.

Complete the Venn diagram by writing all outcomes in the sample space in the appropriate region.

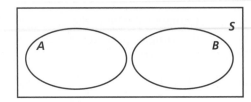

**B** You must find the probability of $A$ or $B$.

$n(S) =$ _____

$n(A \text{ or } B) = n(A) + n(B)$          $A$ and $B$ are mutually exclusive events.

$\phantom{n(A \text{ or } B)} =$ _____ + _____          Use the Venn diagram to find $n(A)$ and $n(B)$.

$\phantom{n(A \text{ or } B)} =$ _____          Add.

So, $P(A \text{ or } B) = \dfrac{n(A \text{ or } B)}{n(S)} = \dfrac{\phantom{xxx}}{\phantom{xxx}}$.

### REFLECT

**1a.** Does the probability you calculated seem reasonable? Why?

_____

_____

**1b.** Is it always true that $n(A \text{ or } B) = n(A) + n(B)$? Explain.

_____

**1c.** How is $P(A \text{ or } B)$ related to $P(A)$ and $P(B)$? Do you think this is always true?

_____

_____

The process you used in the example can be generalized to give a formula for the probability of mutually exclusive events.

**Mutually Exclusive Events**

If $A$ and $B$ are mutually exclusive events, then $P(A \text{ or } B) = P(A) + P(B)$.

Two events are **overlapping events** (or *inclusive events*) if they have one or more outcomes in common.

**2 EXAMPLE** Finding the Probability of Overlapping Events

**What is the probability that you roll a dodecahedral number cube and the result is an even number or a number greater than 7?**

**A** Let event $A$ be the event that you roll an even number. Let event $B$ be the event that you roll a number greater than 7. Let $S$ be the sample space.

Complete the Venn diagram by writing all outcomes in the sample space in the appropriate region.

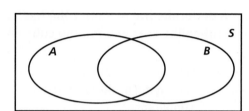

**B** You must find the probability of $A$ or $B$.

$n(S) = \underline{\hspace{2cm}}$

$n(A \text{ or } B) = n(A) + n(B) - n(A \text{ and } B)$        $A$ and $B$ are overlapping events.

$= \underline{\hspace{1.5cm}} + \underline{\hspace{1.5cm}} - \underline{\hspace{1.5cm}}$        Use the Venn diagram.

$= \underline{\hspace{1.5cm}}$        Simplify.

So, $P(A \text{ or } B) = \dfrac{n(A \text{ or } B)}{n(S)} = \dfrac{\phantom{xx}}{\phantom{xx}} = \dfrac{\phantom{xx}}{\phantom{xx}}$.

**REFLECT**

**2a.** Why is $n(A \text{ or } B)$ equal to $n(A) + n(B) - n(A \text{ and } B)$?

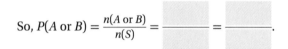

_____

_____

_____

**2b.** Is $P(A \text{ or } B)$ equal to $P(A) + P(B)$ in this case? Explain.

_____

In the previous example you saw that for overlapping events $A$ and $B$, $n(A \cup B) = n(A) + n(B) - n(A \cap B)$. You can convert these counts to probabilities by dividing each term by $n(S)$ as shown below.

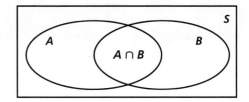

$$\frac{n(A \cup B)}{n(S)} = \frac{n(A)}{n(S)} + \frac{n(B)}{n(S)} - \frac{n(A \cap B)}{n(S)}$$

Rewriting each term as a probability results in the following rule.

### Addition Rule

$P(A \text{ or } B) = P(A) + P(B) - P(A \text{ and } B)$

Notice that when $A$ and $B$ are mutually exclusive events, $P(A \text{ and } B) = 0$, and the rule becomes the simpler rule for mutually exclusive events on the previous page.

**3 EXAMPLE**   Using the Addition Rule

**You shuffle a standard deck of playing cards and choose a card at random. What is the probability that you choose a king or a heart?**

**A**   Let event $A$ be the event that you choose a king. Let event $B$ be the event that you choose a heart. Let $S$ be the sample space.

There are 52 cards in the deck, so $n(S) =$ _____.

There are 4 kings in the deck, so $n(A) =$ _____ and $P(A) =$ _____.

There are 13 hearts in the deck, so $n(B) =$ _____ and $P(B) =$ _____.

There is one king of hearts in the deck, so $P(A \text{ and } B) =$ _____.

**B**   Use the Addition Rule.

$P(A \text{ or } B) = P(A) + P(B) - P(A \text{ and } B)$

$= $ _____ $+$ _____ $-$ _____     Substitute.

$= $ _____ or _____     Simplify.

So, the probability of choosing a king or a heart is _____.

**REFLECT**

**3a.**   What does the answer tell you about the likelihood of choosing a king or a heart from the deck?

_____

_____

# PRACTICE

1. A bag contains 3 blue marbles, 5 red marbles, and 4 green marbles. You choose a marble without looking. What is the probability that you choose a red marble or a green marble?

_____

2. An icosahedral number cube has 20 sides numbered 1 through 20. What is the probability that you roll the cube and the result is a number that is less than 4 or greater than 11?

_____

3. A bag contains 26 tiles, each with a different letter of the alphabet written on it. You choose a tile without looking. What is the probability that you choose a vowel or a letter in the word GEOMETRY?

_____

4. You roll two number cubes at the same time. Each cube has sides numbered 1 through 6. What is the probability that the sum of the numbers rolled is even or greater than 9?

_____

5. You shuffle a standard deck of playing cards and choose a card at random. What is the probability that you choose a face card (jack, queen, or king) or a club?

_____

6. You have a set of 25 cards numbered 1 through 25. You shuffle the cards and choose a card at random. What is the probability that you choose a multiple of 3 or a multiple of 4?

_____

7. The two-way table provides data on the students at a high school. You randomly choose a student at the school. Find each probability.

|  | Freshman | Sophomore | Junior | Senior | TOTAL |
|---|---|---|---|---|---|
| Boy | 98 | 104 | 100 | 94 | 396 |
| Girl | 102 | 106 | 96 | 108 | 412 |
| TOTAL | 200 | 210 | 196 | 202 | 808 |

a. The student is a senior. _____

b. The student is a girl. _____

c. The student is a senior and a girl. _____

d. The student is a senior or a girl. _____

8. A survey of the 1108 employees at a software company finds that 621 employees take a bus to work and 445 employees take a train to work. Some employees take both a bus and a train, and 312 employees take only a train. To the nearest percent, what is the probability that a randomly-chosen employee takes a bus or a train to work? (*Hint:* Make a Venn diagram.)

_____

9. Suppose *A* and *B* are complementary events. Explain how you can rewrite the Addition Rule in a simpler form for this case.

_____

# Conditional Probability

**Essential question:** *How do you calculate a conditional probability?*

The probability that event $B$ occurs given that event $A$ has already occurred is called the **conditional probability** of $B$ given $A$ and is written $P(B \mid A)$.

11-6

COMMON
CORE

CC.9-12.S.CP.3*,
CC.9-12.S.CP.4*,
CC.9-12.S.CP.5*,
CC.9-12.S.CP.6*

## 1 EXAMPLE   Finding Conditional Probabilities

One hundred people who frequently get migraine headaches were chosen to participate in a study of a new anti-headache medicine. Some of the particpants were given the medicine; others were not. After one week, the participants were asked if they got a headache during the week. The two-way table summarizes the results.

| | Took Medicine | No Medicine | TOTAL |
|---|---|---|---|
| **Headache** | 12 | 15 | 27 |
| **No Headache** | 48 | 25 | 73 |
| **TOTAL** | 60 | 40 | 100 |

**A** **To the nearest percent, what is the probability that a participant who took the medicine did not get a headache?**

Let event $A$ be the event that a participant took the medicine. Let event $B$ be the event that a participant did not get a headache.

To find the probability that a participant who took the medicine did not get a headache, you must find $P(B \mid A)$. You are only concerned with participants who took the medicine, so look at the data in the "Took Medicine" column.

There were _____ participants who took the medicine.

Of these participants, _____ participants did not get a headache.

So, $P(B \mid A) = \dfrac{\phantom{XXX}}{\phantom{XXX}} = $ _____.

**B** **To the nearest percent, what is the probability that a participant who did not get a headache took the medicine?**

To find the probability that a participant who did not get a headache took the medicine, you must find $P(A \mid B)$. You are only concerned with participants who did not get a headache, so look at the data in the "No headache" row.

There were _____ participants who did not get a headache.

Of these participants, _____ participants took the medicine.

So, $P(A \mid B) = \dfrac{\phantom{XXX}}{\phantom{XXX}} \approx $ _____.

**1a.** In general, do you think $P(B \mid A) = P(A \mid B)$? Why or why not?

_____

**1b.** How can you use set notation to represent the event that a participant took the medicine and did not get a headache? Is the probability that a participant took the medicine and did not get a headache equal to either of the conditional probabilities you calculated in the example?

_____

_____

## 2 EXPLORE   Developing a Formula for Conditional Probability

You can generalize your work from the previous example to develop a formula for finding conditional probabilities.

**A** Recall how you calculated $P(B \mid A)$, the probability that a participant who took the medicine did not get a headache.

You found that $P(B \mid A) = \frac{48}{60}$.

Use the table shown here to help you write this quotient in terms of events $A$ and $B$.

|  |  | Event A | | |
|---|---|---|---|---|
|  |  | **Took Medicine** | **No Medicine** | **TOTAL** |
| | **Headache** | 12 | 15 | 27 |
| **Event B** | **No Headache** | $48 = n(A \cap B)$ | 25 | $73 = n(B)$ |
| | **TOTAL** | $60 = n(A)$ | 40 | 100 |

$P(B \mid A) = \underline{\hspace{3cm}}$

**B** Now divide the numerator and denominator of the quotient by $n(S)$, the number of outcomes in the sample space. This converts the counts to probabilities.

$$P(B \mid A) = \frac{\phantom{xxx}\Big/ n(S)}{\phantom{xxx}\Big/ n(S)} = \underline{\hspace{2cm}}$$

**2a.** Write a formula for $P(A \mid B)$ in terms of $n(A \cap B)$ and $n(B)$.

_____

**2b.** Write a formula for $P(A \mid B)$ in terms of $P(A \cap B)$ and $P(B)$.

_____

You may have discovered the following formula for conditional probability.

**Conditional Probability**

The conditional probability of $B$ given $A$ (the probability that event $B$ occurs given that event $A$ occurs) is given by the following formula:

$$P(B \mid A) = \frac{P(A \cap B)}{P(A)}$$

**3 EXAMPLE**  Using the Conditional Probability Formula

**In a standard deck of playing cards, find the probability that a red card is a queen.**

**A**  Let event $Q$ be the event that a card is a queen. Let event $R$ be the event that a card is red. You are asked to find $P(Q \mid R)$. First find $P(R \cap Q)$ and $P(R)$.

$R \cap Q$ represents cards that are both red and a queen; that is, red queens.

There are _____ red queens in the deck of 52 cards, so $P(R \cap Q) = $ _____.

There are _____ red cards in the deck, so $P(R) = $ _____.

**B**  Use the formula for conditional probability.

$P(Q \mid R) = \frac{P(Q \cap R)}{P(R)} = $ _____    Substitute probabilities from above.

$= $ _____    Multiply numerator and denominator by 52.

$= $ _____    Simplify.

So, the probability that a red card is a queen is _____.

**REFLECT**

**3a.**  How can you interpret the probability you calculated above?

_____

_____

**3b.**  Is the probability that a red card is a queen equal to the probability that a queen is red? Explain.

_____

1. In order to study the connection between the amount of sleep a student gets and his or her school performance, data was collected about 120 students. The two-way table shows the number of students who passed and failed an exam and the number of students who got more or less than 6 hours of sleep the night before.

| | Passed Exam | Failed Exam | TOTAL |
|---|---|---|---|
| **Less than 6 hours of sleep** | 12 | 10 | 22 |
| **More than 6 hours of sleep** | 90 | 8 | 98 |
| **TOTAL** | 102 | 18 | 120 |

   a. To the nearest percent, what is the probability that a student who failed the exam got less than 6 hours of sleep? _____

   b. To the nearest percent, what is the probability that a student who got less than 6 hours of sleep failed the exam? _____

   c. To the nearest percent, what is the probability that a student got less than 6 hours of sleep and failed the exam? _____

2. A botanist studied the effect of a new fertilizer by choosing 100 orchids and giving 70% of these plants the fertilizer. Of the plants that got the fertilizer, 40% produced flowers within a month. Of the plants that did not get the fertilizer, 10% produced flowers within a month. Find each probability to the nearest percent. (*Hint:* Construct a two-way table.)

   a. Find the probability that a plant that produced flowers got the fertilizer. _____

   b. Find the probability that a plant that got the fertilizer produced flowers. _____

3. At a school fair, a box contains 24 yellow balls and 76 red balls. One-fourth of the balls of each color are labeled "Win a prize." Find each probability as a percent.

   a. Find the probability that a ball labeled "Win a prize" is yellow. _____

   b. Find the probability that a ball labeled "Win a prize" is red. _____

   c. Find the probability that a ball is labeled "Win a prize" and is red. _____

   d. Find the probability that a yellow ball is labeled "Win a prize." _____

**In Exercises 4–9, consider a standard deck of playing cards and the following events: *A*: the card is an ace; *B*: the card is black; *C*: the card is a club. Find each probability as a fraction.**

4. $P(A \mid B)$

_____

5. $P(B \mid A)$

_____

6. $P(A \mid C)$

_____

7. $P(C \mid A)$

_____

8. $P(B \mid C)$

_____

9. $P(C \mid B)$

_____

# Independent Events

COMMON
CORE

CC.9-12.S.CP.2*,
CC.9-12.S.CP.3*,
CC.9-12.S.CP.4*,
CC.9-12.S.CP.5*

**Essential question:** *How do you determine if two events are independent events?*

Two events are **independent events** if the occurrence of one event does not affect the occurrence of the other event. For example, rolling a 1 on a number cube and choosing an ace at random from a deck of cards are independent events.

If two events $A$ and $B$ are independent events, then the fact that event $B$ has occurred does not affect the probability of event $A$. In other words, for independent events $A$ and $B$, $P(A) = P(A \mid B)$. You can use this as a criterion to determine whether two events are independent.

## 1 EXAMPLE   Determining If Events are Independent

**An airport employee collects data on 180 random flights that arrive at the airport. The data is shown in the two-way table. Is a late arrival independent of the flight being an international flight? Why or why not?**

| | Late Arrival | On Time | TOTAL |
|---|---|---|---|
| **Domestic Flight** | 12 | 108 | · 120 |
| **International Flight** | 6 | 54 | 60 |
| **TOTAL** | 18 | 162 | 180 |

**A** Let event $A$ be the event that a flight arrives late. Let event $B$ be the event that a flight is an international flight.

To find $P(A)$, first note that there is a total of _____ flights.

Of these flights, there is a total of _____ late flights.

So, $P(A) = \dfrac{\phantom{xx}}{\phantom{xx}} = $ _____.

To find $P(A \mid B)$, first note that there is a total of _____ international flights.

Of these flights, there is a total of _____ late flights.

So, $P(A \mid B) = \dfrac{\phantom{xx}}{\phantom{xx}} = $ _____.

**B** Compare $P(A)$ and $P(A \mid B)$.

So, a late arrival is independent of the flight being an international flight because

_____

_____

## REFLECT

**1a.** In the example, you compared $P(A)$ and $P(A \mid B)$. Suppose you compare $P(B)$ and $P(B \mid A)$. What do you find? What does this tell you?

_____

You can use a tree diagram to help you understand the formula for the probability of independent events. For example, consider tossing a coin two times. The outcome of one toss does not affect the outcome of the other toss, so the events are independent.

The tree diagram shows that the probability of the coin landing heads up on both tosses is $\frac{1}{4}$ because this is 1 of 4 equally-likely outcomes at the end of Toss 2. This probability is simply the product of the probabilities of the coin landing heads up on each individual toss: $\frac{1}{2} \cdot \frac{1}{2} = \frac{1}{4}$.

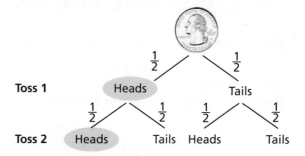

Toss 1     $\frac{1}{2}$   Heads   $\frac{1}{2}$   Tails

$\frac{1}{2}$   $\frac{1}{2}$    $\frac{1}{2}$   $\frac{1}{2}$

Toss 2   Heads    Tails   Heads    Tails

---

### Probability of Independent Events

*A* and *B* are independent events if and only if $P(A \text{ and } B) = P(A) \cdot P(B)$.

---

## 2 EXAMPLE   Using the Formula

**You spin the spinner at right two times. What is the probability that you spin an even number on the first spin followed by an odd number on the second spin?**

**A**   Let event *A* be the event that you spin an even number on the first spin. Let event *B* be the event that you spin an odd number on the second spin.

$$P(A) = \underline{\phantom{xxx}}\qquad\qquad P(B) = \underline{\phantom{xxx}}$$

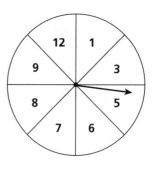

**B**   The outcome of the first spin does not affect the outcome of the second spin, so the events are independent events.

$P(A \text{ and } B) = P(A) \cdot P(B)$      Use the formula for independent events.

$= (\underline{\phantom{xxx}}) \cdot (\underline{\phantom{xxx}})$   Substitute.

$= \underline{\phantom{xxxxxx}}$      Simplify.

So, the probability that you spin an even number on the first spin followed by an odd number on the second spin is $\underline{\phantom{xxxxx}}$.

---

### REFLECT

**2a.** What is the probability that you spin an odd number on the first spin followed by an even number on the second spin? What do you notice?

_____

_____

_____

The formula for the probability of independent events gives you another way to determine whether two events are independent. That is, two events $A$ and $B$ are independent events if $P(A \text{ and } B) = P(A) \cdot P(B)$.

## 3 EXAMPLE  Showing that Events are Independent

The two-way table shows the data from the first example. Show that a flight arriving on time and a flight being a domestic flight are independent events.

|  | Late Arrival | On Time | TOTAL |
|---|---|---|---|
| **Domestic Flight** | 12 | 108 | 120 |
| **International Flight** | 6 | 54 | 60 |
| **TOTAL** | 18 | 162 | 180 |

**A**  Let event $A$ be the event that a flight arrives on time. Let event $B$ be the event that a flight is a domestic flight.

To find $P(A)$, $P(B)$, and $P(A \text{ and } B)$ note that there is a total of _____ flights.

There is a total of _____ on-time flights.

So, $P(A) = \dfrac{\quad}{\quad} = \dfrac{\quad}{\quad}$ .

There is a total of _____ domestic flights.

So, $P(B) = \dfrac{\quad}{\quad} = \dfrac{\quad}{\quad}$ .

There is a total of _____ on-time domestic flights.

So, $P(A \text{ and } B) = \dfrac{\quad}{\quad} = \dfrac{\quad}{\quad}$ .

**B**  Compare $P(A \text{ and } B)$ and $P(A) \cdot P(B)$.

$P(A) \cdot P(B) = (\underline{\quad}) \cdot (\underline{\quad}) = \underline{\quad}$

So, the events are independent events because

_____

_____

### REFLECT

**3a.** Describe a different way you can show that a flight arriving on time and a flight being a domestic flight are independent events.

_____

_____

1. A farmer wants to know if an insecticide is effective in preventing small insects called aphids from living on tomato plants. The farmer checks 80 plants. The data is shown in the two-way table. Is having aphids independent of being sprayed with the insecticide? Why or why not?

| | Has Aphids | No Aphids | TOTAL |
|---|---|---|---|
| Was sprayed with insecticide | 12 | 40 | 52 |
| Was not sprayed with insecticide | 14 | 14 | 28 |
| TOTAL | 26 | 54 | 80 |

_____

_____

**You spin a spinner with 8 equal sections numbered 1 through 8 and you roll a number cube with sides numbered 1 through 6. Find the probability of each of the following. Write the probabilities as fractions.**

2. The spinner lands on 1 and you roll a 5. _____

3. The spinner lands on an even number and you roll an even number. _____

4. The spinner lands on a prime number and you roll a number greater than 4. _____

5. The sum of the number on which the spinner lands and the number you roll is 14. _____

6. A student wants to know if right-handed people are more or less likely to play a musical instrument than left-handed people. The student collects data from 250 people, as shown in the two-way table. Show that being right handed and playing a musical instrument are independent events.

| | Right Handed | Left Handed | TOTAL |
|---|---|---|---|
| Plays a musical instrument | 44 | 6 | 50 |
| Does not play a musical instrument | 176 | 24 | 200 |
| TOTAL | 220 | 30 | 250 |

_____

_____

# Dependent Events

*Essential question: How do you find the probability of dependent events?*

COMMON
CORE

CC.9-12.S.CP.8(+)*

## 1 ENGAGE    Introducing Dependent Events

Two events are **dependent events** if the occurrence of one event affects the occurrence of the other event.

Suppose you have a bag containing 2 blue marbles and 2 black marbles. You choose a marble without looking, put it aside, and then choose a second marble. Consider the following events.

Event $A$: The first marble you choose is blue.

Event $B$: The second marble you choose is black.

Events $A$ and $B$ are dependent events, because the marble you choose for your first pick changes the sample space for your second pick. That is, the occurrence of event $A$ affects the probability of event $B$.

Recall that in Lesson 11-6 you developed the following formula for conditional probability.

$$P(B \mid A) = \frac{P(A \text{ and } B)}{P(A)}$$

Multiplying both sides by $P(A)$ results in $P(A) \cdot P(B \mid A) = P(A \text{ and } B)$. This is known as the Multiplication Rule.

### Multiplication Rule

$P(A \text{ and } B) = P(A) \cdot P(B \mid A)$, where $P(B \mid A)$ is the conditional probability of event $B$, given that event $A$ has occurred.

You can use the Multiplication Rule to find the probability of dependent or independent events. Note that when $A$ and $B$ are independent events, $P(B \mid A) = P(B)$ and the rule may be rewritten as $P(A \text{ and } B) = P(A) \cdot P(B)$, which is the rule for independent events that you used in Lesson 11-7.

### REFLECT

**1a.** How can you write the Multiplication Rule in a different way by starting with the formula for the conditional probability $P(A \mid B)$ and multiplying both sides of that equation by $P(B)$?

_____

_____

There are 5 tiles with the letters A, B, C, D, and E in a bag. You choose a
tile without looking, put it aside, and then choose another tile. Find the
probability that you choose a consonant followed by a vowel.

**A**  Let event $A$ be the event that the first tile is a consonant.
Let event $B$ be the event that the second tile is a vowel.
Find $P(A)$ and $P(B \mid A)$.

$P(A) = \dfrac{\phantom{x}}{\phantom{x}}$          Of the 5 tiles, 3 are consonants.

$P(B \mid A) = \dfrac{\phantom{x}}{\phantom{x}} = \dfrac{\phantom{x}}{\phantom{x}}$          Of the 4 remaining tiles, 2 are vowels.

**B**  Use the Multiplication Rule.

$P(A \text{ and } B) = P(A) \cdot P(B \mid A)$          Use the Multiplication Rule.

$= (\underline{\phantom{xxx}}) \cdot (\underline{\phantom{xxx}})$          Substitute.

$= \underline{\phantom{xxxxx}}$          Multiply.

So, the probability that you choose a consonant followed by a vowel is _____.

**REFLECT**

**2a.**  Complete the tree diagram below. Then explain how you can use it to check
your answer.

1st tile     A            B            C

2nd tile   B   C   D   E   A   C   D   E

_____

_____

_____

**2b.**  What does your answer tell you about the likelihood of choosing a consonant
followed by a vowel?

_____

1. A basket contains 6 bottles of apple juice and 8 bottles of grape juice. You choose a bottle without looking, put it aside, and then choose another bottle. What is the probability that you choose a bottle of apple juice followed by a bottle of grape juice?

_____

2. You have a set of ten cards that are numbered 1 through 10. You shuffle the cards and choose a card at random. You put the card aside and choose another card. What is the probability that you choose an even number followed by an odd number?

_____

3. A bag contains 3 red marbles and 5 green marbles. You choose a marble without looking, put it aside, and then choose another marble.

   a. What is the probability that you choose two red marbles? _____

   b. Is the probability different if you replace the first marble before choosing the second marble? Explain.

   _____

   _____

4. There are 12 boys and 14 girls in Ms. Garcia's class. She chooses a student at random to solve a geometry problem at the board. Then she chooses another student at random to check the first student's work. Is she more likely to choose a boy followed by a girl, a girl followed by a boy, or are these both equally likely? Explain.

   _____

   _____

5. You roll a blue number cube and a red number cube at the same time. You are interested in the probability that you roll a 2 on the blue cube and that the sum of the numbers shown on the cubes is 7.

   a. Are these dependent events or independent events? Explain.

   _____

   _____

   b. What is the probability? _____

6. A bag contains 4 blue marbles and 4 red marbles. You choose a marble without looking, put it aside, and then choose another marble. Is there a greater than or less than 50% chance that you choose two marbles with different colors? Explain.

   _____

   _____

   _____

# Making Fair Decisions

**COMMON CORE**

CC.9-12.S.MD.6(+)*

**Essential question:** *How can you use probability to help you make fair decisions?*

Probability theory arose from a need to make decisions fairly. In fact, the decision-making situation that you will investigate in this lesson is based on a famous problem that was studied by the French mathematicians Blaise Pascal and Pierre de Fermat in the 17th century. Their work on the problem launched the branch of mathematics now known as probability.

## 1 ENGAGE   Introducing the Problem of Points

Two students, Lee and Rory, find a box containing 100 baseball cards. To determine who should get the cards, they decide to play a game with the rules shown at right.

As Lee and Rory are playing the game they get interrupted and are unable to continue. When they are interrupted, Lee has 18 points and Rory has 17 points.

> **Game Rules**
> - One of the students repeatedly tosses a coin.
> - When the coin lands heads up, Lee gets a point.
> - When the coin lands tails up, Rory gets a point.
> - The first student to reach 20 points wins the game and gets the baseball cards.

How should the 100 baseball cards be divided between the students given that the game was interrupted at this moment? This is known as the "Problem of Points."

### REFLECT

**1a.** Which student has a greater probability of winning the game if it were to continue until someone reaches 20 points? Why?

_____

_____

_____

**1b.** If the students divide the baseball cards between themselves, which student do you think should get a greater number of cards? Why?

_____

_____

_____

**1c.** Describe one way you might divide the baseball cards between Lee and Rory.

_____

_____

_____

You may have decided that it would be fair to divide the baseball cards in proportion to the number of points each student scored, as summarized at right.

However, this solution doesn't work well if the game is interrupted very early. If Rory won the first point and ended the game, it would not be fair to give Rory all the cards just because Rory had 1 point and Lee had 0 points.

The following solution is the one proposed by Blaise Pascal and Pierre de Fermat.

## 2 EXPLORE    Solving the Problem of Points

Consider the different ways the game might have continued if it had not been interrupted.

**A**  What is the maximum number of coin tosses that would have been needed for someone to win the game? _____

**B**  Make an organized list to show all possible results of these coin tosses. The list has been started below. Look for patterns to help you complete the list.
(H = heads; T = Tails)

| 0T, 4H | 1T, 3H | 2T, 2H | 3T, 1H | 4T, 0H |
|--------|--------|--------|--------|--------|
| H H H H | T H H H | T T H H | _____ | _____ |
|        | H T H H | T H T H | _____ |        |
|        | H H T H | T H H T | _____ |        |
|        | H H H T | H T T H | _____ |        |
|        |        | _____ |        |        |
|        |        | _____ |        |        |

**C**  Circle the above outcomes in which Lee wins the game.

In how many outcomes would Lee win? _____

In how many outcomes would Rory win? _____

**D**  What is the probability that Lee would have won had the game continued? _____

What is the probability that Rory would have won had the game continued? _____

### REFLECT

**2a.**  Based on your work in the Explore, what do you think is a fair way to divide the baseball cards?

_____

_____

# Analyzing Decisions

COMMON CORE

CC.9-12.S.CP.4*,
CC.9-12.S.MD.7(+)*

**Essential question:** *How can you use probability to help you analyze decisions?*

You can use a two-way table and what you know about probability to help you evaluate decisions.

## 1 EXAMPLE   Analyzing a Decision

**A test for a virus correctly identifies someone who has the virus (by returning a positive result) 99% of the time. The test correctly identifies someone who does not have the virus (by returning a negative result) 99% of the time. It is known that 0.5% of the population has the virus. A doctor decides to treat anyone who tests positive for the virus. Is this a good decision?**

**A**  In order to analyze the decision, you need to know the probability that someone who tests positive actually has the virus.

Make a two-way table. Begin by assuming a large overall population of 1,000,000. This value appears in the cell at the lower right, as shown.

- Use the fact that 0.5% of the population has the virus to complete the rightmost column.
- Use the fact that the test correctly identifies someone who has the virus 99% of the time to complete the "Has the virus" row.
- Use the fact that the test correctly identifies someone who does not have the virus 99% of the time to complete the "Does not have the virus" row.
- Finally, complete the bottom row of the table by finding totals.
- Check your work by verifying that the numbers in the bottom row have a sum of 1,000,000.

|  | Tests Positive | Tests Negative | TOTAL |
|---|---|---|---|
| **Has the virus** |  |  |  |
| **Does not have the virus** |  |  |  |
| **TOTAL** |  |  | 1,000,000 |

**B**  Use the table to find the the probability that someone who tests positive actually has the virus.

There is a total of _____ people who test positive.

Of these people, _____ people actually have the virus.

So, the probability that some who tests positive has the virus is _____.

**1a.** Do you think the doctor made a good decision in treating everyone who tests positive for the virus? Why or why not?

_____

_____

The method that you used in the example can be generalized. The generalization is known as Bayes's Theorem.

## Bayes's Theorem

Given two events $A$ and $B$ with $P(B) \neq 0$, $P(A|B) = \dfrac{P(B|A) \cdot P(A)}{P(B)}$.

The following example shows how you can use Bayes's Theorem to help you analyze a decision.

## 2 EXAMPLE — Using Bayes's Theorem

**The principal of a school plans a school picnic for June 2. A few days before the event, the weather forecast predicts rain for June 2, so the principal decides to cancel the picnic. Consider the following information.**

- **In the school's town, the probability that it rains on any day in June is 3%.**
- **When it rains, the forecast correctly predicts rain 90% of the time.**
- **When it does not rain, the forecast incorrectly predicts rain 5% of the time.**

**Do you think the principal made a good decision? Why or why not?**

**A** Let event $A$ be the event that it rains on a day in June. Let event $B$ be the event that the forecast predicts rain. To evaluate the decision to cancel the picnic, you want to know $P(A|B)$, the probability that it rains given that the forecast predicts rain.

In order use Bayes's Theorem to calculate $P(A|B)$, you must find $P(B|A)$, $P(A)$, and $P(B)$. For convenience, find these probabilities as decimals.

$P(B|A)$ is the probability of a prediction of rain given that it actually rains. This value is provided in the given information.

$P(B|A) = $ _____

$P(A)$ is the probability of rain on any day in June.
This value is also provided in the given information.

$P(A) = $ _____

$P(B)$ is the probability of a prediction of rain. This value is not provided in the given information. In order to calculate $P(B)$, make a tree diagram, as shown on the following page.

**B** Make a tree diagram to find $P(B)$. The values on the "branches" show the probability of the associated event. Complete the right side of the tree diagram by writing the correct probabilities. Remember that the probabilities of events that are complements must add up to 1.

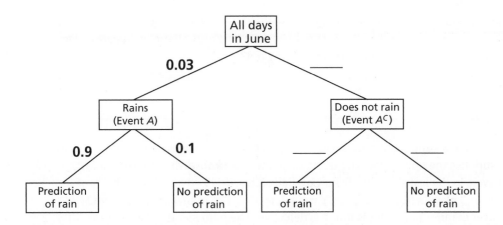

$P(B)$ is the probability that there is a prediction of rain when it actually rains plus the probability that there is a prediction of rain when it does not rain.

$P(B) = P(A) \cdot P(B|A) + P(A^c) \cdot P(B|A^c)$

$= 0.03 \cdot 0.9 + \underline{\hspace{1.5cm}} \cdot \underline{\hspace{1cm}}$    Substitute values from the tree diagram.

$= \underline{\hspace{1.5cm}}$    Simplify.

**C** Use Bayes's Theorem to find $P(A \mid B)$.

$P(A \mid B) = \dfrac{P(B|A) \cdot P(A)}{P(B)}$    Use Bayes's Theorem.

$= \dfrac{\phantom{xxxx} \cdot \phantom{xxxx}}{\phantom{xxxxxxx}}$    Substitute.

$\approx \underline{\hspace{1.5cm}}$    Simplify. Round to the nearest thousandth.

So, as a percent, the probability that it rains given
that the forecast predicts rain is approximately \underline{\hspace{1.5cm}}.

**REFLECT**

**2a.** Do you think the principal made a good decision when canceling the picnic?
Why or why not?

_____

_____

**2b.** What would $P(A)$, the probability that it rains on any day in June, have to be for the
value of $P(A \mid B)$ to be greater than 50%? Explain.

_____

_____

1. It is known that 2% of the population has a certain allergy. A test correctly identifies people who have the allergy 98% of the time. The test correctly identifies people who do not have the allergy 94% of the time. A doctor decides that anyone who tests positive for the allergy should begin taking anti-allergy medication. Do you think this a good decision? Why or why not?

_____

_____

2. Company X supplies 20% of the MP3 players to an electronics store and Company Y supplies the remainder. The manager of the store knows that 80% of the MP3 players in the last shipment from Company X were defective, while only 5% of the MP3 players from Company Y were defective. The manager chooses an MP3 player at random and finds that it is defective. The manager decides that the MP3 player must have come from Company X. Do you think this is a good decision? Why or why not?

_____

_____

3. You can solve Example 2 using a two-way table. Consider a population of 10,000 randomly chosen June days. Complete the table. Then explain how to find the probability that it rains given that the forecast predicts rain.

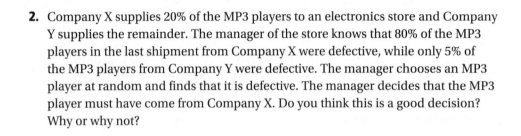

|  | Rains | Does not rain | TOTAL |
|---|---|---|---|
| **Prediction of rain** |  |  |  |
| **No prediction of rain** |  |  |  |
| **TOTAL** |  |  | 10,000 |

_____

_____

4. Explain how to derive Bayes's Theorem using the Multiplication Rule.
   (*Hint:* The Multiplication Rule can be written as $P(A \text{ and } B) = P(B) \cdot P(A \mid B)$ or as $P(A \text{ and } B) = P(A) \cdot P(B \mid A)$.)

_____

_____

_____

Name _____ Class _____ Date _____

## MULTIPLE CHOICE

**1.** You spin a spinner with 10 equal sections that are numbered 1 through 10. Event $A$ is rolling an odd number. Event $B$ is rolling a number greater than 5. What is $P(A \cap B)$?

   **A.** $\frac{1}{8}$        **C.** $\frac{1}{2}$

   **B.** $\frac{1}{5}$        **D.** $\frac{4}{5}$

**2.** There are 9 players on a basketball team. For a team photo, 4 of the players are seated on a row of chairs and 5 players stand behind them. In how many different ways can 4 players be arranged on the row of chairs?

   **F.** 24        **H.** 180

   **G.** 126       **J.** 3024

**3.** There are 5 peaches and 4 nectarines in a bowl. You randomly choose 2 pieces of fruit to pack in your lunch. What is the probability that you choose 2 peaches?

   **A.** $\frac{5}{36}$       **C.** $\frac{2}{5}$

   **B.** $\frac{5}{18}$       **D.** $\frac{5}{9}$

**4.** You shuffle the cards shown below and choose one at random. What is the probability that you choose a gray card or an even number?

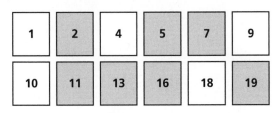

   **F.** $\frac{1}{10}$       **H.** $\frac{5}{6}$

   **G.** $\frac{35}{144}$      **J.** 1

The two-way table provides data about 240 randomly chosen people who visit a movie theater. Use the table for Items 5 and 6.

| | Discount Admission | Regular Admission | TOTAL |
|---|---|---|---|
| **Purchases a snack** | 24 | 72 | 96 |
| **Purchases no snack** | 36 | 108 | 144 |
| **TOTAL** | 60 | 180 | 240 |

**5.** Consider the following events.

   Event $A$: Pays for a regular admission.
   Event $B$: Purchases a snack.

   Which is the best description of the two events?

   **A.** complementary events

   **B.** dependent events

   **C.** independent events

   **D.** mutually exclusive events

**6.** What is the probability that a visitor to the movie theater purchases a snack given that the visitor pays for a discount admission?

   **F.** 0.1       **H.** 0.4

   **G.** 0.25     **J.** 0.75

**7.** A bag contains 8 yellow marbles and 4 blue marbles. You choose a marble, put it aside, and then choose another marble. What is the probability that you choose two yellow marbles?

   **A.** $\frac{7}{18}$       **C.** $\frac{4}{9}$

   **B.** $\frac{14}{33}$      **D.** $\frac{2}{3}$

**8.** Events $A$ and $B$ are independent events. Which of the following must be true?

**F.** $P(A \text{ and } B) = P(A) \cdot P(B)$

**G.** $P(A \text{ and } B) = P(A) + P(B)$

**H.** $P(A) = P(B)$

**J.** $P(B|A) = P(A|B)$

**9.** Which expression can you use to calculate the conditional probability of event $A$ given that event $B$ has occurred?

**A.** $P(A) + P(B) - P(A \text{ and } B)$

**B.** $P(B) \cdot P(A|B)$

**C.** $\dfrac{P(A \text{ and } B)}{P(B)}$

**D.** $\dfrac{P(A)}{P(B)}$

## FREE RESPONSE

**10.** It is known that 1% of all mice in a laboratory have a genetic mutation. A test for the mutation correctly identifies mice that have the mutation 98% of the time. The test correctly identifies mice that do not have the mutation 96% of the time. A lab assistant tests a mouse and finds that the mouse tests positive for the mutation. The lab assistant decides that the mouse must have the mutation. Is this a good decision? Explain.

_____

_____

_____

_____

**11.** Two students, Naomi and Kayla, play a game using the rules shown below. The winner of the game gets a box of 80 fruit chews.

| **Game Rules** |
| --- |
| • One student repeatedly tosses a coin. |
| • When the coin lands heads up, Naomi gets a point. |
| • When the coin lands tails up, Kayla gets a point. |
| • The first student to reach 8 points wins the game and gets the fruit chews. |

The game gets interrupted when Naomi has 7 points and Kayla has 5 points. How should the 80 fruit chews be divided between the students given that the game was interrupted at this moment? Explain why your answer provides a fair way to divide the fruit chews.

_____

_____

_____

_____

_____

_____

_____

_____

# Postulates, Theorems, and Formulas

| Lesson | Postulates, Theorems, and Formulas |
|---|---|
| 1-2 | **The Distance Formula**<br>The <u>distance between two</u> points $(x_1, y_1)$ and $(x_2, y_2)$ in the coordinate plane is $\sqrt{(x_2 - x_1)^2 + (y_2 - y_1)^2}$ . |
| 1-3 | **The Midpoint Formula**<br>The midpoint $M$ of $\overline{AB}$ with endpoints $A(x_1, y_1)$ and $B(x_2, y_2)$ is given by $M\left(\frac{x_1 + x_2}{2}, \frac{y_1 + y_2}{2}\right)$. |
| 1-6 | **Properties of Equality**<br>Addition Property of Equality:        If $a = b$, then $a + c = b + c$.<br>Subtraction Property of Equality:    If $a = b$, then $a - c = b - c$.<br>Multiplication Property of Equality:  If $a = b$, then $ac = bc$.<br>Division Property of Equality:        If $a = b$ and $c \neq 0$, then $\frac{a}{c} = \frac{b}{c}$.<br>Reflexive Property of Equality:       $a = a$<br>Symmetric Property of Equality:    If $a = b$, then $b = a$.<br>Transitive Property of Equality:     If $a = b$ and $b = c$, then $a = c$.<br>Substitution Property of Equality:  If $a = b$, then $b$ can be substituted for $a$ in any expression. |
| 1-6 | **Segment Addition Postulate**<br>If $B$ is between $A$ and $C$, then $AB + BC = AC$. |
| 1-6 | **Common Segments Theorem**<br>If $A$, $B$, $C$, and $D$ are collinear, as shown in the figure, with $AB = CD$, then $AC = BD$.  |
| 1-6 | **Angle Addition Postulate**<br>If $D$ is in the interior of $\angle ABC$, then $m\angle ABD + m\angle DBC = m\angle ABC$. |
| 1-6 | **Linear Pair Theorem**<br>If two angles form a linear pair, then they are supplementary. |
| 1-6 | **Vertical Angles Theorem**<br>If two angles are vertical angles, then they have equal measures. |
| 1-7 | **Same-Side Interior Angles Postulate**<br>If two parallel lines are cut by a transversal, then the pairs of same-side interior angles are supplementary. |
| 1-7 | **Alternate Interior Angles Theorem**<br>If two parallel lines are cut by a transversal, then the pairs of alternate interior angles have the same measure. |
| 1-7 | **Corresponding Angles Theorem**<br>If two parallel lines are cut by a transversal, then the pairs of corresponding angles have the same measure. |
| 1-7 | **Converse of the Same-Side Interior Angles Postulate**<br>If two lines are cut by a transversal so that a pair of same-side interior angles are supplementary, then the lines are parallel. |
| 1-7 | **Converse of the Alternate Interior Angles Theorem**<br>If two lines are cut by a transversal so that a pair of alternate interior angles have the same measure, then the lines are parallel. |
| 1-7 | **Converse of the Corresponding Angles Theorem**<br>If two lines are cut by a transversal so that a pair of corresponding angles have the same measure, then the lines are parallel. |

© Houghton Mifflin Harcourt Publishing Company

| Lesson | Postulates, Theorems, and Formulas |
|--------|-----------------------------------|
| 1-7 | **Equal-Measure Linear Pair Theorem**<br>If two intersecting lines form a linear pair of angles with equal measures, then the lines are perpendicular. |
| 2-1 | **Properties of Rigid Motions (Isometries)**<br>Rigid motions preserve distance, angle measure, betweenness, and collinearity. If a figure is determined by certain points, then its image under a rigid motion is determined by the images of those points. |
| 2-3 | **Angle Bisection Theorem**<br>If a line bisects an angle, then each side of the angle is the image of the other under a reflection across the line. |
| 2-3 | **Converse of the Angle Bisection Theorem**<br>If each side of an angle is the image of the other under a reflection across a line, then the line bisects the angle. |
| 2-3 | **Reflected Points on an Angle Theorem**<br>If two points of an angle are located the same distance from the vertex but on different sides of the angle, then the points are images of each other under a reflection across the line that bisects the angle. |
| 2-4 | **Perpendicular Bisector Theorem**<br>If a point is on the perpendicular bisector of a segment, then it is equidistant from the endpoints of the segment. |
| 2-4 | **Converse of the Perpendicular Bisector Theorem**<br>If a point is equidistant from the endpoints of a segment, then it lies on the perpendicular bisector of the segment. |
| 3-1 | **Properties of Congruence**<br>Reflexive Property of Congruence: $\overline{AB} \cong \overline{AB}$<br>Symmetric Property of Congruence: If $\overline{AB} \cong \overline{CD}$, then $\overline{CD} \cong \overline{AB}$.<br>Transitive Property of Congruence: If $\overline{AB} \cong \overline{CD}$ and $\overline{CD} \cong \overline{EF}$, then $\overline{AB} \cong \overline{EF}$. |
| 3-2 | **Corresponding Parts of Congruent Triangles are Congruent Theorem (CPCTC)**<br>If two triangles are congruent, then corresponding sides are congruent and corresponding angles are congruent. |
| 3-3 | **SSS Congruence Criterion**<br>If three sides of one triangle are congruent to three sides of another triangle, then the triangles are congruent. |
| 3-3 | **SAS Congruence Criterion**<br>If two sides and the included angle of one triangle are congruent to two sides and the included angle of another triangle, then the triangles are congruent. |
| 3-3 | **ASA Congruence Criterion**<br>If two angles and the included side of one triangle are congruent to two angles and the included side of another triangle, then the triangles are congruent. |
| 3-5 | **Triangle Sum Theorem**<br>The sum of the angle measures in a triangle is 180°. |
| 3-5 | **Parallel Postulate**<br>Through a point $P$ not on a line $\ell$, there is exactly one line parallel to $\ell$. |
| 3-5 | **Exterior Angle Theorem**<br>The measure of an exterior angle of a triangle is equal to the sum of the measures of its remote interior angles. |
| 3-5 | **Quadrilateral Sum Theorem**<br>The sum of the angle measures in a quadrilateral is 360°. |
| 3-6 | **Isosceles Triangle Theorem**<br>The base angles of an isosceles triangle are congruent. |

© Houghton Mifflin Harcourt Publishing Company

| Lesson | Postulates, Theorems, and Formulas |
|--------|-----------------------------------|
| 3-6 | **AAS Congruence Criterion**<br>If two angles and a non-included side of one triangle are congruent to two angles and the corresponding non-included side of another triangle, then the triangles are congruent. |
| 3-6 | **Converse of the Isosceles Triangle Theorem**<br>If two angles of a triangle are congruent, then the sides opposite them are congruent. |
| 3-8 | **Midsegment Theorem**<br>A midsegment of a triangle is parallel to the third side of the triangle and is half as long as the third side. |
| 3-9 | **Concurrency of Medians Theorem**<br>The medians of a triangle are concurrent. |
| 4-2 | **Theorem**<br>If a quadrilateral is a parallelogram, then opposite sides are congruent. |
| 4-2 | **Theorem**<br>If a quadrilateral is a parallelogram, then opposite angles are congruent. |
| 4-3 | **Theorem**<br>If a quadrilateral is a parallelogram, then the diagonals bisect each other. |
| 4-4 | **Opposite Sides Criterion for a Parallelogram**<br>If both pairs of opposite sides of a quadrilateral are congruent, then the quadrilateral is a parallelogram. |
| 4-4 | **Opposite Angles Criterion for a Parallelogram**<br>If both pairs of opposite angles of a quadrilateral are congruent, then the quadrilateral is a parallelogram. |
| 4-4 | **Bisecting Diagonals Criterion for a Parallelogram**<br>If the diagonals of a quadrilateral bisect each other, then the quadrilateral is a parallelogram. |
| 4-5 | **Rectangle Theorem**<br>A rectangle is a parallelogram with congruent diagonals. |
| 4-5 | **Properties of Rhombuses**<br>If a quadrilateral is a rhombus, then the quadrilateral is a parallelogram, the diagonals are perpendicular, and each diagonal bisects a pair of opposite angles. |
| 5-1 | **Properties of Dilations**<br>• Dilations preserve angle measure.<br>• Dilations preserve betweenness.<br>• Dilations preserve collinearity.<br>• A dilation maps a line not passing through the center of dilation to a parallel line and leaves a line passing through the center unchanged.<br>• The dilation of a line segment is longer or shorter in the ratio given by the scale factor. |
| 5-3 | **Theorem**<br>All circles are similar. |
| 5-4 | **AA Similarity Criterion**<br>If two angles of one triangle are congruent to two angles of another triangle, then the triangles are similar. |
| 5-4 | **SAS Similarity Criterion**<br>If two sides of one triangle are proportional to two sides of another triangle and their included angles are congruent, then the triangles are similar. |
| 5-6 | **Triangle Proportionality Theorem**<br>If a line parallel to one side of a triangle intersects the other two sides, then it divides those sides proportionally. |
| 5-6 | **Converse of the Triangle Proportionality Theorem**<br>If a line divides two sides of a triangle proportionally, then it is parallel to the third side. |

© Houghton Mifflin Harcourt Publishing Company

| Lesson | Postulates, Theorems, and Formulas |
|--------|-------------------------------------|
| 5-7 | **Pythagorean Theorem**<br>In a right triangle, the sum of the squares of the lengths of the legs is equal to the square of the length of the hypotenuse. |
| 6-5 | **Area of a Triangle**<br>The area $A$ of $\triangle ABC$ is given by $A = \frac{1}{2} ab \sin C$. |
| 6-6 | **Law of Sines**<br>For $\triangle ABC$, $\frac{\sin A}{a} = \frac{\sin B}{b} = \frac{\sin C}{c}$. |
| 6-7 | **Law of Cosines**<br>For $\triangle ABC$, $a^2 = b^2 + c^2 - 2bc \cos A$, $b^2 = a^2 + c^2 - 2ac \cos B$, and $c^2 = a^2 + b^2 - 2ab \cos C$. |
| 7-1 | **Arc Addition Postulate**<br>The measure of an arc formed by two adjacent arcs is the sum of the measures of the two arcs. |
| 7-1 | **Inscribed Angle Theorem**<br>The measure of an inscribed angle is half the measure of its intercepted arc. |
| 7-1 | **Theorem**<br>The endpoints of a diameter lie on an inscribed angle if and only if the inscribed angle is a right angle. |
| 7-4 | **Inscribed Quadrilateral Theorem**<br>If a quadrilateral is inscribed in a circle, then its opposite angles are supplementary. |
| 7-4 | **Converse of the Inscribed Quadrilateral Theorem**<br>If the opposite angles of a quadrilateral are supplementary, then the quadrilateral can be inscribed in a circle. |
| 7-5 | **Tangent-Radius Theorem**<br>If a line is tangent to a circle, then it is perpendicular to the radius drawn to the point of tangency. |
| 7-5 | **Converse of the Tangent-Radius Theorem**<br>If a line is perpendicular to a radius of a circle at a point on the circle, then the line is a tangent to the circle. |
| 7-5 | **Circumscribed Angle Theorem**<br>A circumscribed angle of a circle and its associated central angle are supplementary. |
| 8-1 | **Equation of a Circle**<br>The equation of a circle with center $(h, k)$ and radius $r$ is $(x - h)^2 + (y - k)^2 = r^2$. |
| 8-2 | **Equation of a Parabola**<br>The equation of the parabola with focus $(0, p)$ and directrix $y = -p$ is $y = \frac{1}{4p} x^2$. |
| 8-4 | **Slope Criterion for Parallel Lines**<br>Two non-vertical lines are parallel if and only if they have the same slope. |
| 8-5 | **Slope Criterion for Perpendicular Lines**<br>Two non-vertical lines are perpendicular if and only if the product of their slopes is $-1$. |
| 9-3 | **Circumference of a Circle**<br>The circumference $C$ of a circle with radius $r$ is given by $C = 2\pi r$. |
| 9-4 | **Arc Length**<br>The arc length $s$ of an arc with measure $m°$ and radius $r$ is given by the formula $s = \frac{m}{360} \cdot 2\pi r$. |
| 9-5 | **Area of a Circle**<br>The area $A$ of a circle with radius $r$ is given by $A = \pi r^2$. |

© Houghton Mifflin Harcourt Publishing Company

| Lesson | Postulates, Theorems, and Formulas |
|--------|-----------------------------------|
| 9-5 | **Area of a Sector**<br>The area $A$ of a sector of a circle with a central angle of $m°$ and radius r is given by $A = \frac{m}{360} \cdot \pi r^2$. |
| 10-2 | **Volume of a Cylinder**<br>The volume $V$ of a cylinder with base area $B$ and height $h$ is given by $V = Bh$ (or $V = \pi r^2 h$, where $r$ is the radius of a base). |
| 10-2 | **Cavalieri's Principle**<br>If two solids have the same height and the same cross-sectional area at every level, then the two solids have the same volume. |
| 10-3 | **Postulate**<br>Pyramids that have equal base areas and equal heights have equal volumes. |
| 10-3 | **Volume of a Pyramid**<br>The volume $V$ of a pyramid with base area $B$ and height $h$ is given by $V = \frac{1}{3} Bh$. |
| 10-4 | **Volume of a Cone**<br>The volume $V$ of a cone with base area $B$ and height $h$ is given by $V = \frac{1}{3} Bh$ (or $V = \frac{1}{3} \pi r^2 h$, where $r$ is the radius of the base). |
| 10-5 | **Volume of a Sphere**<br>The volume $V$ of a sphere with radius $r$ is given by $V = \frac{4}{3} \pi r^3$. |
| 11-1 | **Probabilities of an Event and Its Complement**<br>The probability of an event and the probability of its complement have a sum of 1. So, the probability of an event is one minus the probability of its complement. Also, the probability of the complement of an event is one minus the probability of the event. |
| 11-3 | **Permutations**<br>The number of permutations of $n$ objects taken $r$ at a time is given by $_nP_r = \frac{n!}{(n-r)!}$. |
| 11-4 | **Combinations**<br>The number of combinations of $n$ objects taken $r$ at a time is given by $_nC_r = \frac{n!}{r!(n-r)!}$. |
| 11-5 | **Mutually Exclusive Events**<br>If $A$ and $B$ are mutually exclusive events, then $P(A \text{ or } B) = P(A) + P(B)$. |
| 11-5 | **Addition Rule**<br>$P(A \text{ or } B) = P(A) + P(B) - P(A \text{ and } B)$. |
| 11-6 | **Conditional Probability**<br>The conditional probability of $B$ given $A$ (the probability that event $B$ occurs given that event A occurs) is given by the formula $P(B|A) = \frac{P(A \text{ and } B)}{P(A)}$. |
| 11-7 | **Probability of Independent Events**<br>$A$ and $B$ are independent events if and only if $P(A \text{ and } B) = P(A) \cdot P(B)$. |
| 11-8 | **Multiplication Rule**<br>$P(A \text{ and } B) = P(A) \cdot P(B|A)$, where $P(B|A)$ is the conditional probability of event $B$, given that event $A$ has occurred. |
| 11-10 | **Bayes's Theorem**<br>Given two events $A$ and $B$ with $P(B) \neq 0$, $P(A|B) = \frac{P(B|A) \cdot P(A)}{P(B)}$. |

© Houghton Mifflin Harcourt Publishing Company

COMMON CORE **Correlations**

# Correlation of *On Core Mathematics* to the Common Core State Standards

| Standards | Algebra 1 | Geometry | Algebra 2 |
|---|---|---|---|
| **Number and Quantity** | | | |
| **The Real Number System** | | | |
| **CC.9-12.N.RN.1** Explain how the definition of the meaning of rational exponents follows from extending the properties of integer exponents to those values, allowing for a notation for radicals in terms of rational exponents. | | | Lesson 1-2 |
| **CC.9-12.N.RN.2** Rewrite expressions involving radicals and rational exponents using the properties of exponents. | | | Lesson 1-2 |
| **CC.9-12.N.RN.3** Explain why the sum or product of two rational numbers is rational; that the sum of a rational number and an irrational number is irrational; and that the product of a nonzero rational number and an irrational number is irrational. | | | Lesson 1-1 |
| **Quantities** | | | |
| **CC.9-12.N.Q.1** Use units as a way to understand problems and to guide the solution of multi-step problems; choose and interpret units consistently in formulas; choose and interpret the scale and the origin in graphs and data displays.* | Lessons 1-1, 1-2, 1-3, 1-5, 1-6, 2-3, 2-8, 3-6, 4-2, 4-3, 7-6 | | Lesson 2-6 |
| **CC.9-12.N.Q.2** Define appropriate quantities for the purpose of descriptive modeling.* | Lessons 1-3, 1-4, 2-3, 2-8, 3-6, 7-6 | | |
| **CC.9-12.N.Q.3** Choose a level of accuracy appropriate to limitations on measurement when reporting quantities.* | | **Lesson 9-1** | |
| **The Complex Number System** | | | |
| **CC.9-12.N.CN.1** Know there is a complex number $i$ such that $i^2 = -1$, and every complex number has the form $a + bi$ with $a$ and $b$ real. | | | Lesson 1-3 |
| **CC.9-12.N.CN.2** Use the relation $i^2 = -1$ and the commutative, associative, and distributive properties to add, subtract, and multiply complex numbers. | | | Lesson 1-3 |
| **CC.9-12.N.CN.3(+)** Find the conjugate of a complex number; use conjugates to find moduli and quotients of complex numbers. | | | Lesson 1-4 |

(+) Advanced      * = Also a Modeling Standard

© Houghton Mifflin Harcourt Publishing Company

| Standards | Algebra 1 | Geometry | Algebra 2 |
|---|---|---|---|
| **CC.9-12.N.CN.7** Solve quadratic equations with real coefficients that have complex solutions. | | | Lesson 1-5 |
| **CC.9-12.N.CN.9(+)** Know the Fundamental Theorem of Algebra; show that it is true for quadratic polynomials. | | | Lesson 3-10 |
| **Algebra** | | | |
| **Seeing Structure in Expressions** | | | |
| **CC.9-12.A.SSE.1** Interpret expressions that represent a quantity in terms of its context.*<br>**a.** Interpret parts of an expression, such as terms, factors, and coefficients.<br>**b.** Interpret complicated expressions by viewing one or more of their parts as a single entity. | Lessons 1-1, 1-2, 1-3, 2-8 | | Lessons 2-6, 3-5, 3-11, 4-4, 4-5, 9-4, 9-5 |
| **CC.9-12.A.SSE.2** Use the structure of an expression to identify ways to rewrite it. | Lessons 1-2, 1-3, 2-1, 2-2, 8-1 | | Lessons 3-9, 3-10 |
| **CC.9-12.A.SSE.3** Choose and produce an equivalent form of an expression to reveal and explain properties of the quantity represented by the expression.<br>**a.** Factor a quadratic expression to reveal the zeros of the function it defines.<br>**b.** Complete the square in a quadratic expression to reveal the maximum or minimum value of the function it defines.<br>**c.** Use the properties of exponents to transform expressions for exponential functions. | Lessons 8-2, 8-3, 8-10 | | Lessons 2-4, 2-5, 6-4, 6-6 |
| **CC.9-12.A.SSE.4** Derive the formula for the sum of a finite geometric series (when the common ratio is not 1), and use the formula to solve problems. | | | Lessons 9-4, 9-5 |
| **Arithmetic with Polynomials and Rational Expressions** | | | |
| **CC.9-12.A.APR.1** Understand that polynomials form a system analogous to the integers, namely, they are closed under the operations of addition, subtraction, and multiplication; add, subtract, and multiply polynomials. | Lessons 4-6, 8-1 | | Lessons 3-5, 3-6, 3-7, 3-8 |
| **CC.9-12.A.APR.2** Know and apply the Remainder Theorem: For a polynomial $p(x)$ and a number $a$, the remainder on division by $x - a$ is $p(a)$, so $p(a) = 0$ if and only if $(x - a)$ is a factor of $p(x)$. | | | Lesson 3-8 |
| **CC.9-12.A.APR.3** Identify zeros of polynomials when suitable factorizations are available, and use the zeros to construct a rough graph of the function defined by the polynomial. | | | Lesson 3-9 |
| **CC.9-12.A.APR.4** Prove polynomial identities and use them to describe numerical relationships. | | | Lesson 3-6 |

(+) Advanced     * = Also a Modeling Standard

© Houghton Mifflin Harcourt Publishing Company

| Standards | Algebra 1 | Geometry | Algebra 2 |
|-----------|-----------|----------|-----------|
| **CC.9-12.A.APR.5(+)** Know and apply the Binomial Theorem for the expansion of $(x + y)^n$ in powers of $x$ and $y$ for a positive integer $n$, where $x$ and $y$ are any numbers, with coefficients determined for example by Pascal's Triangle. (The Binomial Theorem can be proved by mathematical induction or by a combinatorial argument.) | | | Lesson 3-7 |
| **CC.9-12.A.APR.6** Rewrite simple rational expressions in different forms; write $a(x)/b(x)$ in the form $q(x) + r(x)/b(x)$, where $a(x)$, $r(x)$, $q(x)$, and $r(x)$ are polynomials with the degree of $r(x)$ less than the degree of $b(x)$, using inspection, long division, or, for the more complicated examples, a computer algebra system. | | | Lesson 4-3 |
| **CC.9-12.A.APR.7(+)** Understand that rational expressions form a system analogous to the rational numbers, closed under addition, subtraction, multiplication, and division by a nonzero rational expression; add, subtract, multiply, and divide rational expressions. | | | Lessons 4-4, 4-5 |
| **Creating Equations** | | | |
| **CC.9-12.A.CED.1** Create equations and inequalities in one variable and use them to solve problems.* | Lessons 1-4, 2-3, 5-5, 6-5, 7-4, 7-5, 8-3, 8-7 | | Lessons 3-11, 4-6, 6-7, 7-4 |
| **CC.9-12.A.CED.2** Create equations in two or more variables to represent relationships between quantities; graph equations on coordinate axes with labels and scales.* | Lessons 2-3, 2-5, 2-8, 3-6, 4-2, 4-3, 4-5, 4-6, 5-1, 5-5, 5-6, 5-8, 6-1, 6-2, 6-3, 6-4, 6-5, 6-6, 7-1, 7-2, 7-3, 7-4, 7-6, 8-9, 8-10 | | Lessons 2-3, 2-4, 2-5, 2-6, 3-9, 3-11, 4-1, 4-2, 4-3, 4-7, 5-1, 5-2, 5-3, 5-5, 5-6, 6-2, 6-3, 6-4, 6-5, 6-6, 7-5, 8-9 |
| **CC.9-12.A.CED.3** Represent constraints by equations or inequalities, and by systems of equations and/or inequalities, and interpret solutions as viable or nonviable options in a modeling context.* | Lessons 1-4, 2-3, 2-8, 3-6 | | Lessons 2-6, 3-11, 9-5 |
| **CC.9-12.A.CED.4** Rearrange formulas to highlight a quantity of interest, using the same reasoning as in solving equations.* | Lesson 2-5 | | Lesson 7-5 |
| **Reasoning with Equations and Inequalities** | | | |
| **CC.9-12.A.REI.1.** Explain each step in solving a simple equation as following from the equality of numbers asserted at the previous step, starting from the assumption that the original equation has a solution. Construct a viable argument to justify a solution method. | Lessons 2-1, 2-2, 2-4 | | |
| **CC.9-12.A.REI.2** Solve simple rational and radical equations in one variable, and give examples showing how extraneous solutions may arise. | | | Lessons 4-6, 5-7 |
| **CC.9-12.A.REI.3** Solve linear equations and inequalities in one variable, including equations with coefficients represented by letters. | Lessons 2-1, 2-2, 2-3, 2-4 | | |

(+) Advanced    * = Also a Modeling Standard

| Standards | Algebra 1 | Geometry | Algebra 2 |
|---|---|---|---|
| **CC.9-12.A.REI.4** Solve quadratic equations in one variable.<br>**a.** Use the method of completing the square to transform any quadratic equation in $x$ into an equation of the form $(x - p)^2 = q$ that has the same solutions. Derive the quadratic formula from this form.<br>**b.** Solve quadratic equations by inspection (e.g., for $x^2 = 49$), taking square roots, completing the square, the quadratic formula and factoring, as appropriate to the initial form of the equation. Recognize when the quadratic formula gives complex solutions and write them as $a \pm bi$ for real numbers $a$ and $b$. | Lessons 7-5, 8-2, 8-3, 8-4, 8-5, 8-6, 8-7, 8-9, 8-10 | | Lesson 1-5 |
| **CC.9-12.A.REI.5** Prove that, given a system of two equations in two variables, replacing one equation by the sum of that equation and a multiple of the other produces a system with the same solutions. | Lesson 3-4 | | |
| **CC.9-12.A.REI.6** Solve systems of linear equations exactly and approximately (e.g., with graphs), focusing on pairs of linear equations in two variables. | Lessons 3-1, 3-2, 3-3, 3-4, 3-6 | | |
| **CC.9-12.A.REI.7** Solve a simple system consisting of a linear equation and a quadratic equation in two variables algebraically and graphically. | Lesson 8-9 | **Lesson 8-7** | |
| **CC.9-12.A.REI.10** Understand that the graph of an equation in two variables is the set of all its solutions plotted in the coordinate plane, often forming a curve (which could be a line). | Lessons 2-6, 2-7 | | |
| **CC.9-12.A.REI.11** Explain why the $x$-coordinates of the points where the graphs of the equations $y = f(x)$ and $y = g(x)$ intersect are the solutions of the equation $f(x) = g(x)$; find the solutions approximately, e.g., using technology to graph the functions, make tables of values, or find successive approximations. Include cases where $f(x)$ and/or $g(x)$ are linear, polynomial, rational, absolute value, exponential, and logarithmic functions.* | Lessons 4-5, 5-5, 5-8, 6-5, 7-4 | | Lessons 4-6, 5-7, 6-7, 7-4 |
| **CC.9-12.A.REI.12** Graph the solutions to a linear inequality in two variables as a half-plane (excluding the boundary in the case of a strict inequality), and graph the solution set to a system of linear inequalities in two variables as the intersection of the corresponding half-planes. | Lessons 2-6, 2-7, 3-5, 3-6 | | |
| **Functions** | | | |
| **Interpreting Functions** | | | |
| **CC.9-12.F.IF.1** Understand that a function from one set (called the domain) to another set (called the range) assigns to each element of the domain exactly one element of the range. If $f$ is a function and $x$ is an element of its domain, then $f(x)$ denotes the output of $f$ corresponding to the input $x$. The graph of $f$ is the graph of the equation $y = f(x)$. | Lessons 1-5, 1-6, 4-2, 4-7, 5-2 | | Lesson 8-3 |

(+) Advanced      * = Also a Modeling Standard

© Houghton Mifflin Harcourt Publishing Company

| Standards | Algebra 1 | Geometry | Algebra 2 |
|---|---|---|---|
| **CC.9-12.F.IF.2** Use function notation, evaluate functions for inputs in their domains, and interpret statements that use function notation in terms of a context. | Lessons 1-5, 1-6, 4-1, 4-2, 4-7, 5-1, 6-1, 6-2, 6-3, 6-4, 6-6, 7-1, 7-2, 7-3, 7-6, 8-10 | | Lessons 2-1, 2-2, 2-3, 2-4, 2-5, 2-6, 3-4, 4-1, 4-2, 4-3, 4-7, 5-1, 5-2, 5-3, 5-5, 5-6, 6-1, 6-2, 6-3, 6-4, 6-5, 7-1, 7-5, 8-9, 9-1 |
| **CC.9-12.F.IF.3** Recognize that sequences are functions, sometimes defined recursively, whose domain is a subset of the integers. | Lessons 4-1, 5-1 | | Lesson 9-1 |
| **CC.9-12.F.IF.4** For a function that models a relationship between two quantities, interpret key features of graphs and tables in terms of the quantities, and sketch graphs showing key features given a verbal description of the relationship.* | Lessons 4-3, 4-4, 4-5, 5-3, 5-4, 6-1, 6-6, 7-1, 7-2, 7-3, 7-6, 8-8, 8-9, 8-10 | | Lessons 2-6, 3-11, 4-1, 4-2, 4-3, 4-7, 5-5, 5-6, 6-2, 6-3, 6-6, 7-5, 8-9 |
| **CC.9-12.F.IF.5** Relate the domain of a function to its graph and, where applicable, to the quantitative relationship it describes.* | Lessons 1-5, 1-6, 4-1, 4-2, 5-1, 5-2, 5-8, 6-1, 6-6, 7-1, 8-8 | | Lessons 2-6, 3-11 |
| **CC.9-12.F.IF.6** Calculate and interpret the average rate of change of a function (presented symbolically or as a table) over a specified interval. Estimate the rate of change from a graph.* | Lessons 4-3, 4-5, 8-10 | | Lessons 2-6 |
| **CC.9-12.F.IF.7** Graph functions expressed symbolically and show key features of the graph, by hand in simple cases and using technology for more complicated cases.* <br> **a.** Graph linear and quadratic functions and show intercepts, maxima, and minima. <br> **b.** Graph square root, cube root, and piecewise-defined functions, including step functions and absolute value functions. <br> **c.** Graph polynomial functions, identifying zeros when suitable factorizations are available, and showing end behavior. <br> **d.** (+) Graph rational functions, identifying zeros and asymptotes when suitable factorizations are available, and showing end behavior. <br> **e.** Graph exponential and logarithmic functions, showing intercepts and end behavior, and trigonometric functions, showing period, midline, and amplitude. | Lessons 4-1, 4-3, 4-5, 5-1, 5-2, 5-3, 5-8, 6-1, 6-2, 6-3, 6-4, 6-6, 7-1, 7-2, 7-3, 8-8 | | Lessons 2-1, 2-2, 2-3, 2-4, 2-5, 2-6, 3-1, 3-2, 3-3, 3-4, 3-9, 3-11, 4-1, 4-2, 4-3, 4-7, 5-1, 5-2, 5-3, 5-4, 5-5, 5-6, 6-1, 6-2, 6-3, 6-4, 6-5, 6-6, 6-7, 7-1, 7-2, 8-5, 8-6, 8-7, 8-8, 8-9 |
| **CC.9-12.F.IF.8** Write a function defined by an expression in different but equivalent forms to reveal and explain different properties of the function. <br> **a.** Use the process of factoring and completing the square in a quadratic function to show zeros, extreme values, and symmetry of the graph, and interpret these in terms of a context. <br> **b.** Use the properties of exponents to interpret expressions for exponential functions. | Lessons 8-2, 8-3, 8-8, 8-10 | | Lessons 2-4, 2-5, 6-4, 6-6 |
| **CC.9-12.F.IF.9** Compare properties of two functions each represented in a different way (algebraically, graphically, numerically in tables, or by verbal descriptions). | Lessons 4-2, 8-10 | | Lesson 4-7 |

(+) Advanced     * = Also a Modeling Standard

| Standards | Algebra 1 | Geometry | Algebra 2 |
|---|---|---|---|
| **Building Functions** | | | |
| **CC.9-12.F.BF.1** Write a function that describes a relationship between two quantities.*<br>**a.** Determine an explicit expression, a recursive process, or steps for calculation from a context.<br>**b.** Combine standard function types using arithmetic operations.<br>**c.** (+) Compose functions. | Lessons 1-6, 2-3, 2-8, 4-5, 4-6, 4-9, 5-5, 5-6, 5-8, 6-1, 6-2, 6-3, 6-4, 6-6, 7-1, 7-2, 7-3, 7-6, 8-3, 8-8, 8-10 | | Lessons 2-6, 3-5, 3-11, 4-1, 4-2, 4-3, 4-4, 4-5, 4-7, 5-5, 5-6, 6-2, 6-3, 6-4, 6-6, 7-5, 8-9, 9-1, 9-2, 9-3 |
| **CC.9-12.F.BF.2** Write arithmetic and geometric sequences both recursively and with an explicit formula, use them to model situations, and translate between the two forms.* | Lesson 4-1 | | Lessons 9-2, 9-3 |
| **CC.9-12.F.BF.3** Identify the effect on the graph of replacing $f(x)$ by $f(x) + k$, $kf(x)$, $f(kx)$, and $f(x + k)$ for specific values of $k$ (both positive and negative); find the value of $k$ given the graphs. Experiment with cases and illustrate an explanation of the effects on the graph using technology. | Lessons 4-4, 5-4, 6-2, 6-3, 6-4, 7-1, 7-2, 7-3 | | Lessons 2-1, 2-2, 2-3, 3-1, 3-2, 3-3, 4-1, 4-2, 5-4, 6-2, 6-3, 6-4, 6-5, 7-2, 8-7, 8-8, 8-9 |
| **CC.9-12.F.BF.4** Find inverse functions.<br>**a.** Solve an equation of the form $f(x) = c$ for a simple function $f$ that has an inverse and write an expression for the inverse.<br>**b.** (+) Verify by composition that one function is the inverse of another.<br>**c.** (+) Read values of an inverse function from a graph or a table, given that the function has an inverse.<br>**d.** (+) Produce an invertible function from a non-invertible function by restricting the domain. | Lesson 4-7 | | Lessons 5-1, 5-2, 5-3, 5-5, 5-6 |
| **CC.9-12.F.BF.5(+)** Understand the inverse relationship between exponents and logarithms and use this relationship to solve problems involving logarithms and exponents. | | | Lessons 7-1, 7-3 |
| **Linear, Quadratic, and Exponential Models** | | | |
| **CC.9-12.F.LE.1** Distinguish between situations that can be modeled with linear functions and with exponential functions.*<br>**a.** Prove that linear functions grow by equal differences over equal intervals, and that exponential functions grow by equal factors over equal intervals.<br>**b.** Recognize situations in which one quantity changes at a constant rate per unit interval relative to another.<br>**c.** Recognize situations in which a quantity grows or decays by a constant percent rate per unit interval relative to another. | Lessons 5-2, 5-3, 5-6, 5-7, 5-8 | | |
| **CC.9-12.F.LE.2** Construct linear and exponential functions, including arithmetic and geometric sequences, given a graph, a description of a relationship, or two input-output pairs (include reading these from a table).* | Lessons 4-5, 4-6, 5-1, 5-2, 5-3, 5-5, 5-8 | | Lessons 6-2, 6-3, 6-4, 6-5, 9-2, 9-3 |

(+) Advanced     * = Also a Modeling Standard

© Houghton Mifflin Harcourt Publishing Company

| Standards | Algebra 1 | Geometry | Algebra 2 |
|---|---|---|---|
| **CC.9-12.F.LE.3** Observe using graphs and tables that a quantity increasing exponentially eventually exceeds a quantity increasing linearly, quadratically, or (more generally) as a polynomial function.* | Lesson 5-7 | | Lessons 6-1, 6-6 |
| **CC.9-12.F.LE.4** For exponential models, express as a logarithm the solution to $ab^{ct} = d$ where $a$, $c$, and $d$ are numbers and the base $b$ is 2, 10, or $e$; evaluate the logarithm using technology.* | | | Lesson 7-4 |
| **CC.9-12.F.LE.5** Interpret the parameters in a linear or exponential function in terms of a context.* | Lessons 4-4, 4-5, 4-6, 4-9, 4-10, 5-2, 5-3, 5-6, 5-8 | | Lessons 6-4, 6-5 |
| **Trigonometric Functions** | | | |
| **CC.9-12.F.TF.1** Understand radian measure of an angle as the length of the arc on the unit circle subtended by the angle. | | | Lesson 8-2 |
| **CC.9-12.F.TF.2** Explain how the unit circle in the coordinate plane enables the extension of trigonometric functions to all real numbers, interpreted as radian measures of angles traversed counterclockwise around the unit circle. | | | Lesson 8-3 |
| **CC.9-12.F.TF.3(+)** Use special triangles to determine geometrically the values of sine, cosine, tangent for $\pi/3$, $\pi/4$ and $\pi/6$, and use the unit circle to express the values of sine, cosines, and tangent for $x$, $\pi + x$, and $2\pi - x$ in terms of their values for $x$, where $x$ is any real number. | | | Lesson 8-3 |
| **CC.9-12.F.TF.4(+)** Use the unit circle to explain symmetry (odd and even) and periodicity of trigonometric functions. | | | Lessons 8-5, 8-6 |
| **CC.9-12.F.TF.5** Choose trigonometric functions to model periodic phenomena with specified amplitude, frequency, and midline.* | | | Lesson 8-9 |
| **CC.9-12.F.TF.8** Prove the Pythagorean identity $\sin^2(\theta) + \cos^2(\theta) = 1$ and use it to calculate trigonometric ratios. | | | Lesson 8-4 |
| **Geometry** | | | |
| **Congruence** | | | |
| **CC.9-12.G.CO.1** Know precise definitions of angle, circle, perpendicular line, parallel line, and line segment, based on the undefined notions of point, line, distance along a line, and distance around a circular arc. | | **Lessons 1-1, 1-4, 1-5, 9-4** | |
| **CC.9-12.G.CO.2** Represent transformations in the plane using, e.g., transparencies and geometry software; describe transformations as functions that take points in the plane as inputs and give other points as outputs. Compare transformations that preserve distance and angle to those that do not (e.g., translation versus horizontal stretch). | | **Lessons 2-1, 2-2, 2-3, 2-4, 2-5, 2-6, 5-1, 5-2** | |

(+) Advanced     * = Also a Modeling Standard

© Houghton Mifflin Harcourt Publishing Company

| Standards | Algebra 1 | Geometry | Algebra 2 |
|---|---|---|---|
| **CC.9-12.G.CO.3** Given a rectangle, parallelogram, trapezoid, or regular polygon, describe the rotations and reflections that carry it onto itself. | | Lesson 4-1 | |
| **CC.9-12.G.CO.4** Develop definitions of rotations, reflections, and translations in terms of angles, circles, perpendicular lines, parallel lines, and line segments. | | Lessons 2-2, 2-5, 2-6 | |
| **CC.9-12.G.CO.5** Given a geometric figure and a rotation, reflection, or translation, draw the transformed figure using, e.g., graph paper, tracing paper, or geometry software. Specify a sequence of transformations that will carry a given figure onto another. | | Lessons 2-2, 2-5, 2-6, 3-1 | |
| **CC.9-12.G.CO.6** Use geometric descriptions of rigid motions to transform figures and to predict the effect of a given rigid motion on a given figure; given two figures, use the definition of congruence in terms of rigid motions to decide if they are congruent. | | Lessons 2-2, 2-5, 2-6, 3-1 | |
| **CC.9-12.G.CO.7** Use the definition of congruence in terms of rigid motions to show that two triangles are congruent if and only if corresponding pairs of sides and corresponding pairs of angles are congruent. | | Lessons 3-2, 3-3 | |
| **CC.9-12.G.CO.8** Explain how the criteria for triangle congruence (ASA, SAS, and SSS) follow from the definition of congruence in terms of rigid motions. | | Lesson 3-3 | |
| **CC.9-12.G.CO.9** Prove geometric theorems about lines and angles. | | Lessons 1-6, 1-7, 2-3, 2-4 | |
| **CC.9-12.G.CO.10** Prove theorems about triangles. | | Lessons 3-5, 3-6, 3-7, 3-8, 3-9 | |
| **CC.9-12.G.CO.11** Prove theorems about parallelograms. | | Lessons 4-2, 4-3, 4-4, 4-5 | |
| **CC.9-12.G.CO.12** Make formal geometric constructions with a variety of tools and methods (compass and straightedge, string, reflective devices, paper folding, dynamic geometry software, etc.). | | Lessons 1-1, 1-4, 1-5 | |
| **CC.9-12.G.CO.13** Construct an equilateral triangle, a square, and a regular hexagon inscribed in a circle. | | Lesson 7-3 | |
| **Similarity, Right Triangles, and Trigonometry** | | | |
| **CC.9-12.G.SRT.1** Verify experimentally the properties of dilations given by a center and a scale factor:<br>**a.** A dilation takes a line not passing through the center of the dilation to a parallel line, and leaves a line passing through the center unchanged.<br>**b.** The dilation of a line segment is longer or shorter in the ratio given by the scale factor. | | Lesson 5-1 | |

(+) Advanced      * = Also a Modeling Standard

© Houghton Mifflin Harcourt Publishing Company

| Standards | Algebra 1 | Geometry | Algebra 2 |
|---|---|---|---|
| **CC.9-12.G.SRT.2** Given two figures, use the definition of similarity in terms of similarity transformations to decide if they are similar; explain using similarity transformations the meaning of similarity for triangles as the equality of all corresponding angles and the proportionality of all corresponding pairs of sides. | | Lessons 5-3, 5-4 | |
| **CC.9-12.G.SRT.3** Use the properties of similarity transformations to establish the AA criterion for two triangles to be similar. | | Lesson 5-4 | |
| **CC.9-12.G.SRT.4** Prove theorems about triangles. | | Lessons 5-6, 5-7 | |
| **CC.9-12.G.SRT.5** Use congruence and similarity criteria for triangles to solve problems and prove relationships in geometric figures. | | Lessons 3-4, 4-2, 4-3, 4-4, 4-5, 5-5, 5-6, 5-7 | |
| **CC.9-12.G.SRT.6** Understand that by similarity, side ratios in right triangles are properties of the angles in the triangle, leading to definitions of trigonometric ratios for acute angles. | | Lessons 6-1, 6-2, 6-3 | |
| **CC.9-12.G.SRT.7** Explain and use the relationship between the sine and cosine of complementary angles. | | Lessons 6-2, 6-3 | |
| **CC.9-12.G.SRT.8** Use trigonometric ratios and the Pythagorean Theorem to solve right triangles in applied problems. | | Lesson 6-4 | |
| **CC.9-12.G.SRT.9(+)** Derive the formula $A = 1/2\ ab\ \sin(C)$ for the area of a triangle by drawing an auxiliary line from a vertex perpendicular to the opposite side. | | Lesson 6-5 | |
| **CC.9-12.G.SRT.10(+)** Prove the Laws of Sines and Cosines and use them to solve problems. | | Lessons 6-6, 6-7 | |
| **CC.9-12.G.SRT.11(+)** Understand and apply the Law of Sines and the Law of Cosines to find unknown measurements in right and non-right triangles (e.g., surveying problems, resultant forces). | | Lessons 6-6, 6-7 | |
| **Circles** | | | |
| **CC.9-12.G.C.1** Prove that all circles are similar. | | Lesson 5-3 | |
| **CC.9-12.G.C.2** Identify and describe relationships among inscribed angles, radii, and chords. | | Lessons 7-1, 7-5 | |
| **CC.9-12.G.C.3** Construct the inscribed and circumscribed circles of a triangle, and prove properties of angles for a quadrilateral inscribed in a circle. | | Lessons 7-2, 7-4, 7-6 | |
| **CC.9-12.G.C.4(+)** Construct a tangent line from a point outside a given circle to the circle. | | Lesson 7-5 | |

(+) Advanced      * = Also a Modeling Standard

| Standards | Algebra 1 | Geometry | Algebra 2 |
|---|---|---|---|
| **CC.9-12.G.C.5** Derive using similarity the fact that the length of the arc intercepted by an angle is proportional to the radius, and define the radian measure of the angle as the constant of proportionality; derive the formula for the area of a sector. | | Lessons 9-4, 9-5 | Lesson 8-1 |
| **Expressing Geometric Properties with Equations** | | | |
| **CC.9-12.G.GPE.1** Derive the equation of a circle of given center and radius using the Pythagorean Theorem; complete the square to find the center and radius of a circle given by an equation. | | Lesson 8-1 | |
| **CC.9-12.G.GPE.2** Derive the equation of a parabola given a focus and directrix. | | Lesson 8-2 | |
| **CC.9-12.G.GPE.4** Use coordinates to prove simple geometric theorems algebraically. | | Lessons 1-2, 1-3, 3-7, 3-8, 3-9, 8-1, 8-6 | |
| **CC.9-12.G.GPE.5** Prove the slope criteria for parallel and perpendicular lines and use them to solve geometric problems (e.g., find the equation of line parallel or perpendicular to a given line that passes through a given point). | | Lessons 8-4, 8-5 | |
| **CC.9-12.G.GPE.6** Find the point on a directed line segment between two given points that partitions the segment in a given ratio. | | Lesson 8-3 | |
| **CC.9-12.G.GPE.7** Use coordinates to compute perimeters of polygons and areas of triangles and rectangles, e.g., using the distance formula.* | | Lesson 9-2 | |
| **Geometric Measurement and Dimension** | | | |
| **CC.9-12.G.GMD.1** Give an informal argument for the formulas for the circumference of a circle, area of a circle, volume of a cylinder, pyramid, and cone. | | Lessons 9-3, 9-5, 10-2, 10-3, 10-4 | |
| **CC.9-12.G.GMD.2(+)** Give an informal argument using Cavalieri's principle for the formulas for the volume of a sphere and other solid figures. | | Lessons 10-2, 10-5 | |
| **CC.9-12.G.GMD.3** Use volume formulas for cylinders, pyramids, cones, and spheres to solve problems.* | | Lessons 10-2, 10-3, 10-4, 10-5, 10-6 | |
| **CC.9-12.G.GMD.4** Identify the shapes of two-dimensional cross-sections of three-dimensional objects, and identify three-dimensional objects generated by rotations of two-dimensional objects. | | Lesson 10-1 | |

(+) Advanced      * = Also a Modeling Standard

© Houghton Mifflin Harcourt Publishing Company

| Standards | Algebra 1 | Geometry | Algebra 2 |
|---|---|---|---|
| **Modeling with Geometry** | | | |
| **CC.9-12.G.MG.1** Use geometric shapes, their measures, and their properties to describe objects (e.g., modeling a tree trunk or a human torso as a cylinder).* | | **Lessons 9-2, 9-3, 10-2** | |
| **CC.9-12.G.MG.2** Apply concepts of density based on area and volume in modeling situations (e.g., persons per square mile, BTUs per cubic foot).* | | **Lessons 9-2, 10-2, 10-5** | |
| **CC.9-12.G.MG.3** Apply geometric methods to solve design problems (e.g., designing an object or structure to satisfy physical constraints or minimize cost; working with typographic grid systems based on ratios).* | | **Lessons 5-5, 10-6** | |
| **Statistics and Probability** | | | |
| **Interpreting Categorical and Quantitative Data** | | | |
| **CC.9-12.S.ID.1** Represent data with plots on the real number line (dot plots, histograms, and box plots).* | Lessons 9-2, 9-3, 9-4 | | Lessons 10-2, 10-3 |
| **CC.9-12.S.ID.2** Use statistics appropriate to the shape of the data distribution to compare center (median, mean) and spread (interquartile range, standard deviation) of two or more different data sets.* | Lessons 9-1, 9-2, 9-3, 9-4 | | |
| **CC.9-12.S.ID.3** Interpret differences in shape, center, and spread in the context of the data sets, accounting for possible effects of extreme data points (outliers).* | Lesson 9-2 | | Lesson 10-2 |
| **CC.9-12.S.ID.4** Use the mean and standard deviation of a data set to fit it to a normal distribution and to estimate population percentages. Recognize that there are data sets for which such a procedure is not appropriate. Use calculators, spreadsheets, and tables to estimate areas under the normal curve.* | | | Lesson 10-4 |
| **CC.9-12.S.ID.5** Summarize categorical data for two categories in two-way frequency tables. Interpret relative frequencies in the context of the data (including joint, marginal, and conditional relative frequencies). Recognize possible associations and trends in the data.* | Lesson 9-5 | | |
| **CC.9-12.S.ID.6** Represent data on two quantitative variables on a scatter plot, and describe how the variables are related.* <br> **a.** Fit a function to the data; use functions fitted to data to solve problems in the context of the data. <br> **b.** Informally assess the fit of a function by plotting and analyzing residuals. <br> **c.** Fit a linear function for a scatter plot that suggests a linear association. | Lessons 4-9, 4-10, 5-6, 5-8 | | Lessons 5-5, 5-6, 6-6 |

(+) Advanced     * = Also a Modeling Standard

© Houghton Mifflin Harcourt Publishing Company

| Standards | Algebra 1 | Geometry | Algebra 2 |
|---|---|---|---|
| **CC.9-12.S.ID.7** Interpret the slope (rate of change) and the intercept (constant term) of a linear model in the context of the data.* | Lessons 4-9, 4-10 | | |
| **CC.9-12.S.ID.8** Compute (using technology) and interpret the correlation coefficient of a linear fit.* | Lessons 4-8, 4-10 | | |
| **CC.9-12.S.ID.9** Distinguish between correlation and causation.* | Lesson 4-8 | | |
| **Making Inferences and Justifying Conclusions** | | | |
| **CC.9-12.S.IC.1** Understand statistics as a process for making inferences about population parameters based on a random sample from that population.* | | | Lesson 10-1 |
| **CC.9-12.S.IC.2** Decide if a specified model is consistent with results from a given data-generating process, e.g., using simulation.* | | | Lesson 10-3 |
| **CC.9-12.S.IC.3** Recognize the purposes of and differences among sample surveys, experiments, and observational studies; explain how randomization relates to each.* | | | Lesson 10-7 |
| **CC.9-12.S.IC.4** Use data from a sample survey to estimate a population mean or proportion; develop a margin of error through the use of simulation models for random sampling.* | | | Lessons 10-5, 10-6 |
| **CC.9-12.S.IC.5** Use data from a randomized experiment to compare two treatments; use simulations to decide if differences between parameters are significant.* | | | Lesson 10-8 |
| **CC.9-12.S.IC.6** Evaluate reports based on data.* | Lesson 4-8 | | Lesson 10-7 |
| **Conditional Probability and the Rules of Probability** | | | |
| **CC.9-12.S.CP.1** Describe events as subsets of a sample space (the set of outcomes) using characteristics (or categories) of the outcomes, or as unions, intersections, or complements of other events ("or," "and," "not").* | | Lesson 11-1 | |
| **CC.9-12.S.CP.2** Understand that two events $A$ and $B$ are independent if the probability of $A$ and $B$ occurring together is the product of their probabilities, and use this characterization to determine if they are independent.* | | Lesson 11-7 | |
| **CC.9-12.S.CP.3** Understand the conditional probability of $A$ given $B$ as $P(A \text{ and } B)/P(B)$, and interpret independence of $A$ and $B$ as saying that the conditional probability of $A$ given $B$ is the same as the probability of $A$, and the conditional probability of $B$ given $A$ is the same as the probability of $B$.* | | Lessons 11-6, 11-7 | |

(+) Advanced     * = Also a Modeling Standard

© Houghton Mifflin Harcourt Publishing Company

| Standards | Algebra 1 | Geometry | Algebra 2 |
|-----------|-----------|----------|-----------|
| **CC.9-12.S.CP.4** Construct and interpret two-way frequency tables of data when two categories are associated with each object being classified. Use the two-way table as a sample space to decide if events are independent and to approximate conditional probabilities.* | | Lessons 11-6, 11-7, 11-10 | |
| **CC.9-12.S.CP.5** Recognize and explain the concepts of conditional probability and independence in everyday language and everyday situations.* | | Lessons 11-6, 11-7 | |
| **CC.9-12.S.CP.6** Find the conditional probability of $A$ given $B$ as the fraction of $B$'s outcomes that also belong to $A$, and interpret the answer in terms of the model.* | | Lesson 11-6 | |
| **CC.9-12.S.CP.7** Apply the Addition Rule, $P(A \text{ or } B) = P(A) + P(B) - P(A \text{ and } B)$, and interpret the answer in terms of the model.* | | Lesson 11-5 | |
| **CC.9-12.S.CP.8(+)** Apply the general Multiplication Rule in a uniform probability model, $P(A \text{ and } B) = P(A)P(B|A) = P(B)P(A|B)$, and interpret the answer in terms of the model.* | | Lesson 11-8 | |
| **CC.9-12.S.CP.9(+)** Use permutations and combinations to compute probabilities of compound events and solve problems.* | | Lessons 11-3, 11-4 | |
| **Using Probability to Make Decisions** | | | |
| **CC.9-12.S.MD.6(+)** Use probabilities to make fair decisions (e.g., drawing by lots, using a random number generator).* | | Lessons 11-2, 11-9 | |
| **CC.9-12.S.MD.7(+)** Analyze decisions and strategies using probability concepts (e.g., product testing, medical testing, pulling a hockey goalie at the end of a game).* | | Lesson 11-10 | |

**(+) Advanced**    * = Also a Modeling Standard